# KNOWLEDGE
# AND
# CONTROL

*New Directions for the Sociology of Education*

Edited by

MICHAEL F. D. YOUNG

COLLIER MACMILLAN
LONDON

A Collier Macmillan book published by
CASSELL & COLLIER MACMILLAN PUBLISHERS LIMITED,
35 Red Lion Square, London WC1R 4SG
Sydney, Auckland, Toronto, Johannesburg

An affiliate of Macmillan Publishing Co. Inc.
New York

© Cassell & Collier Macmillan Publishers Ltd, 1971
ISBN 0 02 978360 7

Library of Congress Catalog Card Number: 70-170875

First printing 1971
Second printing 1972
Third printing 1975
Fourth printing 1976

Printed and bound in Great Britain by
BUTLER & TANNER LTD
Frome and London

# TABLE OF CONTENTS

# PREFACE AND ACKNOWLEDGEMENTS

The idea of this book was first conceived in a discussion between Pierre Bourdieu, Basil Bernstein and myself after the Durham Conference of the British Sociological Association, of April 1970. It would certainly never have got off the ground without the constant support, encouragement and advice from Basil Bernstein. I should also like to thank Pat Dyehouse, Marion and Freda of the administrative staff of the department of Sociology of Education, University of London Institute of Education, for the calmness, competence and good humour with which they completed the secretarial work involved.

My thanks are due to Basil Bernstein, Geoffrey Esland and Nell Keddie for allowing me to use their unpublished manuscripts, and to Alan Blum, Pierre Bourdieu, Ioan Davies and Robin Horton for allowing me to reprint their papers. I should also like to thank Roger Brown, editor of the British Sociological Association Conference papers (1970), for allowing me to use ideas first developed in a paper given at that conference to prepare the paper for this volume.

I should also like to acknowledge my debt to the Editor of *Sociology* and the British Sociological Association (for permission to reprint Ioan Davies's paper), the editors of *Social Science Information* and the *International Social Science Journal*, UNESCO and the International Social Science Council (for permission to reprint Pierre Bourdieu's papers), the editors and publishers (Appleton-Century-Crofts) of *Theoretical Sociology* (for permission to reprint Alan Blum's paper), the editor of *Africa* and the International African Institute (for permission to reprint Robin Horton's paper).

*Michael F. D. Young*

London, July 1971

One day young captain Jonathan,
he was eighteen at the time,
Captured a Pelican
On an island in the Far East.
In the morning,
This Pelican
of Jonathan's,
Laid a white egg
and out of it came
A Pelican
Astonishingly like the first.
And this second Pelican
laid in its turn
A white egg,
From which came inevitably
Another
who did the same again.
This sort of thing can go on
A very long time,
if you don't make an omelette.

ROBERT DESNOS: *Chantefleurs, Chantefables*

By permission of Librairie Gründ, Paris. Translated from the French by Elizabeth McGovern.

# KNOWLEDGE
# AND
# CONTROL

# INTRODUCTION

## MICHAEL F. D. YOUNG

### *Knowledge and Control**

One characteristic of the way sociological ideas are made available is that what is called 'theory' tends to be treated separately from the special concerns of sociologists which are usually identified as a 'sociology of . . .'. Most writers agree that the predominant concern of 'theorists' has been what is commonly referred to as 'the problem of order' (Cohen, 1968; Dawe, 1970), which may account for the fact that those special fields substantively concerned with aspects of social order are the ones in which one finds any serious theoretical debates—the obvious examples are stratification, deviance, politics and organizations. It is suggested that it is partly for this reason and partly on account of the institutional contexts of its development,[1] that the sociology of education is one of the major examples of an area of enquiry in which both explicit 'theory' and theoretical debates have been noticeably absent. Durkheim, Weber and to an even greater extent Marx, whose writings have dominated the intellectual context in which sociological 'theorizing' has developed, get little more than ritual reference in contemporary texts.[2] Similarly the major contemporary debates among sociologists about 'functionalist' and 'conflict' models, and 'structural' and 'interactional' levels of explanation, hardly make their appearance.

Seeley (1966) makes the valuable distinction between the 'taking' and 'making' of problems. On the whole, sociologists have 'taken' educators' problems, and, by not making their assumptions explicit, have necessarily taken them for granted. These implicit assumptions, of most sociologists of education and of educators, might be adequately characterized by what Dawe (1970) has called an 'order' doctrine, which, as he suggests, leads to explanations in terms of a system perspective. This, starting from a loosely defined consensus on goals or values (in this case values about 'what a good education is'), conceives of change (or innovation), in terms of a structural differentiation towards such goals, and defines 'order' problems as failures of socialization (a concept

* I am very grateful to Basil Bernstein, Geoffrey Esland and Nell Keddie for commenting on various parts of this introductory paper.

which as Bernstein[3] says, is trivialized in the process). This 'failure' may be of working-class children not achieving academically, of parents not giving encouragement, or of schools and universities not producing enough scientists. These then represent only some of the educators' problems that sociologists have 'taken' and, as Seeley suggests in his paper, they have often attempted to 'remake' the problems so that the result is not merely 'the expected outcome of naive acceptance'. An important example of this is the early work on the class determinants of educational opportunity, well summarized by Westergaard and Little (1964). This research, by treating as problematic the grouping and selection procedures taken for granted by educational administrators, and the relations between home and school not questioned by teachers, raised important questions about 'streaming', 'selection' and the unintended consequences of educational arrangements (Lacey, 1970). However, by treating as unproblematic 'what it is to be educated', such enquiries do little more than provide what is often a somewhat questionable legitimacy to the various pressures for administrative and curricular 'reform'. To begin to move to explanations of how pupils, teachers and knowledge are organized (and it is only through such explanations that we shall be able to develop alternatives), existing categories that for parents, teachers, children and many researchers distinguish home from school, learning from play, academic from non-academic, and 'able' or 'bright' from 'dull' or 'stupid', must be conceived of as socially constructed, with some in a position to impose their constructions or meanings on others.

In the end, to return to Seeley's paper, there is no alternative but for the sociologist to 'make' his own problems, among which may be to treat educators' problems as phenomena to be explained; this is not just to criticize earlier sociological research, but to ask what implicit assumptions led some questions (about selection) to be asked and others (about academic education) to be treated as given. It is suggested that in this way, certain fundamental features of educators' worlds which are taken for granted, such as what counts as educational knowledge, and how it is made available, become objects of enquiry.

The primary aim of this book is to open up some alternative and, it is hoped, fruitful directions for sociological enquiry in education. It in no sense intends to provide a definition of the field for the sociology of education, but to define a set of problems, which up to now appear to have been largely neglected. Two limitations in relation to these aims are important; first, the papers raise predominantly conceptual issues and their methodological implications for research are not made explicit. Secondly, most of the papers have a relatively narrow focus on the organization of knowledge in the formal educational institutions of industrialized societies; they may, therefore, unwittingly, take certain categories for granted that are a characteristic of this institutional framework. Horton's paper (p. 208), which will be considered later in this essay, is of particular importance in this respect.

Though it will be obvious to the reader that all the contributors do not share either a common doctrine or perspectives, it would be true to say that what they hold in common is that they do not take for granted existing definitions of educational reality, and therefore do 'make' rather than 'take' problems for the sociology of education. They are inevitably led to consider, often from widely different perspectives, 'what counts as educational knowledge' as problematic. The implication of this is that one major focus of the sociology of education becomes an enquiry into the social organization of knowledge in educational institutions. Thus, and this has important implications for the organization of sociological knowledge, sociology of education is no longer conceived as the area of enquiry distinct from the sociology of knowledge.

In this introductory paper, I shall first attempt to suggest what might be involved in a sociology of education which makes the problems of control[4] and the organization of knowledge and their interrelations its core concern. Secondly, as the papers collected here represent a radical and widely differing set of departures from what might be included under a 'textbook definition' of the sociology of education, I will attempt to pick out some of the common themes of each section and to indicate their possible relevance for students of education, whether they be involved in teaching, research, or actually taking courses.

In order to explore these suggestions for defining problems for the sociology of education, it is necessary to examine first in more general terms the implications of a meta-theory or doctrine of control, and secondly what is involved in treating the knowledge ('transmitted' in education) as neither absolute, nor arbitrary, but as 'available sets of meanings', which in any context do not merely 'emerge', but are collectively 'given'. As Dawe (1970) suggests, the alternative to the 'problem of order', what he refers to as the doctrine of control, has been one of the main strands underlying sociological enquiry since the eighteenth century; at any time it has involved the critical questioning of whatever is taken as inviolable, whether 'God-given' or through 'natural law'. This questioning has been paralleled by attempts to assert man's control over his institutions and to participate in changing them. In the eighteenth century it was predominantly the feudal and clerical orders that social criticism and enquiry focused on, whereas nineteenth-century control doctrines, dominated increasingly by Marxism, were primarily concerned with the assumed absolutism of the market and its laws, and with attempts, as Blum points out in his paper (p. 123), to expose the social meanings of the market economy in terms of its underlying exploitative character. Much of this social criticism, and the alternatives implicit in it, has been based on a new absolutism, that of science and reason. Today it is the commonsense conceptions of 'the scientific' and 'the rational', together with the various social, political and educational beliefs, that are assumed to follow from them that represent the dominant legitimizing categories. It therefore becomes the task of sociological enquiry to treat these categories not as absolutes but as constructed realities realized in particular institutional contexts. Thus, like the feudal, clerical and market dogmas of earlier centuries, the dogmas of rationality and science become open to enquiry; the necessary preliminary to conceiving of alternatives. It is evident that such a conception of sociology, for which no special originality is claimed, is bounded historically, both in terms of its explanations and the content of the dominant categories, to be treated as

3

problematic; likewise, by its focus on actions rather than systems, it will be situationally specific. If we take the notion of situational specificity as referring to the nature of sociological explanations, then these will be in terms of 'available meanings'. However, as this 'availability' will be a variable which is socially distributed, it needs to be conceived of historically as a structural contingency on action not accessible within an interactional framework alone.

If we take, with Dawe, the notion of control to involve the 'imposition of meaning', when members construct definitions of situations in which the constraints are in part the definitions of others, then enquiries will be concerned with discrepancies between ideals and actualities, between 'doctrine and commitment' as Selznick puts it.[5] For the sociology of education, this suggests a primary concern for the shared and imposed meanings of school personnel, whether teachers or pupils, and their possible congruences and discrepancies with non-school meanings and activities. Some major conceptual problems can be hinted at rather than resolved; they are in no way specific to sociological research in education. For example, a question raised by the doctrine of control concerns the differential access or distribution of resources, whether those of conceptual legitimacy (such as ideas of 'the rational' and 'the worthwhile'), or of economic facilities. Such questions involve spelling out links between institutions, and of trying to formulate empirically ideas such as structural contingencies of action and interaction. It is part of the conventional wisdom of the sociology of education that the universities and the economy 'control' the content and distribution of educational opportunities; in other words, it is assumed that they provide the structural constraints (or contingencies) within which school activities take place. But how? These kinds of statement which tend to be treated as explanations rather than as 'to be explained', are in practice accepting uncritically some kind of mechanistic relationship between *the* universities, *the* economy and *the* educational system, which seem more likely to lead to mystification than to pose research questions. For these questions of control to be treated empirically, we must return to a study of the sets of activities and assumptions that are involved in such processes.[6]

One criticism of control doctrines (or forms of action theory as they are sometimes referred to), has been that they are 'rationalistic'. The point is made about the work of Max Weber by Marcuse and Parsons from two totally different standpoints.[7] However, as Dawe again very usefully points out, such criticisms start from prior assumptions about what is 'rational', to which a very narrow definition is given. The weaknesses of this definition of rationality, which corresponds closely to nineteenth-century 'economic man' always choosing the most effective means to achieve one of his many collectively defined 'ends', have been excellently discussed by both Schutz (1943) and Garfinkel (1967). A much more open version of sociological explanation being 'rational' in the sense that this means 'understandable to the participants',[8] allows the kind of understanding, which may in particular situations be close to economic rationality, to be treated as an empirical question.

As suggested earlier, the research implications of the meta-theoretical position being proposed is that the sociology of education (or any sociology for that matter) must take into account the historical and situationally specific character of both its phenomena and its explanations. Thus, in order to explore situationally defined meanings in taken for granted institutional contexts such as schools, very detailed case studies are necessary which treat as problematic the curricular, pedagogic and assessment categories held by school personnel. However, such studies on their own, which give accounts of the realities which emerge from the interactions of members, cannot help avoiding the socio-historical contexts in which such realities become available. This point is nowhere better demonstrated than in Gouldner's (1968) critique of the labelling theories of deviance. These studies, he suggests, end up by doing little more than describing how badly mental patients, pupils, prisoners and delinquents are treated by nurses, teachers, warders and police. We are thus left without an explanation of why such occupational groups which Everett Hughes has acutely described as 'the dirty workers'[9] act in this way. The methodological lesson from this perhaps rather savage criticism is that these interactional studies must be complemented by attempts to conceptualize the links between interactions and changing social structures in such a way as to point to new kinds of research which at present seem almost wholly lacking. A rare example of an attempt to do this is reported by Breton (1970), who starts from Cicourel and Kitsuse's (1963) well-known case study of Lakeshore High School, and examines the structural determinants of academic stratification and its consequences in the Canadian school system.

Before extending further these suggestions for a sociology of education, let us explore the implications of treating knowledge or 'what counts as knowledge', as socially constituted or constructed. Mills (1939) makes the significant point that what we call 'reasoning', 'being logical', or validating the truth of an assertion, all involve a self-reflection or criticism of one's own thoughts in terms of various standardized models. These models will necessarily be sets of shared meanings of 'what a good argument is, what is logical, valid etc. . . .' For ordinary discourse, in philosophy or science or everyday communication, or the interactions in a lesson between teacher and pupils, these shared meanings are taken for granted as sets of unquestioned assumptions; however, like all shared meanings, they can be treated as problematic and become the objects of enquiry. One can immediately see important new research possibilities stemming from this proposal which might examine how 'subjects' or disciplines are socially constructed as sets of shared meanings, and the process of negotiation between examiners and students about what counts as 'a sound exam answer'. Mills goes on to suggest that the rules of logic, whether practical or academic, are conventional, and will be shaped and selected in accordance with the purpose of the discourse or the intentions of the enquiries. If logic, 'good' reasoning, asking questions, and all the various sets of activities prescribed for the learner, are conceived of from one perspective as sets of social conventions which have meanings common to the prescribers, then the failure to comply with the prescriptions can be conceived, not as in the everyday world of the teacher as 'wrong', 'bad spelling or grammar', or 'poorly argued and expressed', but as forms of deviance. This does not imply anything about the absolute 'rightness' or 'wrongness' of the teachers' or pupils' statements, but does suggest that the interaction involved is in part a product of the dominant defining categories which are taken for granted by the teacher. Thus the direction of research for a sociology of educational knowledge becomes to explore how and why certain dominant categories persist and the nature of their possible links to sets of interests or activities such as occupational groupings. Much of Pierre Bourdieu's work, of which two papers appear in this volume, has been directed to this kind of enquiry. Both Bernstein and Mary Douglas (1970) refer to the classification of knowledge in society; if our 'educational problems' are dependent on our educators' classifications, then an exploration of the relation of what Bernstein refers to as the 'deep structure' of such classifications, to characteristics of the socio-economic order, should be a central concern for sociological enquiry into education. The difficulty of such an endeavour is apparent when one starts to treat such distinctions as educational success and failure, subject and object, 'natural and social' and 'teacher and taught' as problematic. They are no less embedded in our educational institutions than the honour and esteem granted to the aged in ancient China.[10]

What Jack Douglas (1970) refers to as the subversion of absolutism by sociology is of crucial importance for the sociology of education; he is using the idea to refer to the way sociologists have conceived of societies as products of competing definitions and claims to cognitive and moral legitimacy rather than as integrated around a core set of absolute values. It is worth exploring this idea more generally by drawing on Mills's work before turning to its implications for education. In his examination of the epistemological consequences of the sociology of knowledge, Mills (1940a) suggests that an absolutist model of validity has its intellectual origins in pre-relativity physics in which the process of enquiry was conceived of as quite separate from the results.[11] Historically, Mills shows that one can trace the absolutist model to the traditions of a centralized intellectual elite with close links to those holding economic and political power. For sociological research, the obvious empirical possibility of different sets of criteria of validity, which themselves only emerge and can be said to exist in the practice of actual enquiries and interactions, is of considerable importance; it opens up the whole question of the relations between theory (educational and other) and practice. It thus becomes possible to study how 'educational theory acts selectively as a set of assumptions, which, while having in one context originated in practice, in others becomes institutionalized and so either legitimates practice or selectively determines its assessment (Eastman, 1967).

In considering the importance of this notion of 'subverting absolutism', we find a curious parallel in the social science literature. On the one hand there is the anthropologist's reluctance to take his respondent's ideas at their face value as the explanations they claim to be,[12] and on the other is the sociologist's reluctance to treat as problematic the same hierarchical definitions of ability that are held by most teachers and pupils, and institutionalized in our curricula and examinations.[13] Both the anthropologists' 'rejection' and the sociologists' 'acceptance' are a product of starting from assumptions about what it is 'to explain, be scientific, or be able', that treat Western academic standards as absolutes. The control doctrine referred to earlier in this paper, and the 'intellectualist stance' of Horton (1968), seem to be pointing in the same direction. They are both suggesting that we should treat members' explanations (whether they be African tribesmen, teachers or pupils) as ways which to them make sense and order of their world. Without any preconceptions about 'good explanations' or a 'higher order rationality', we should then explore the possible origins of the particular explanations provided. If the control doctrine we have been referring to directs our enquiry into how people impose meaning or give consistency to their experience, this not only leads us to treat African animism, and American college students' grade point perspectives,[14] as attempts to 'impose meaning', but also to ask questions about the wider institutional context within which this experience is made available. Similar research questions might be posed about how young secondary school children with widely different junior school and home backgrounds 'make sense of' a ten-subject, forty-period school week. Horton (1968) compares the 'mistakes' of African traditional theories with the 'revolutions' of scientists;[15] if we took the comparison further to children's 'wrong' answers, we might be able to explore more systematically the institutional context of schools in which children became frightened of giving anything but the 'right' answer (Holt, 1967). If the sociologist is able to suspend, in his enquiry, the taken for granted moral and intellectual absolutism of the teacher, who in his everyday situation has no such alternative, then the phenomena of the classroom and the school can be studied for what they might mean to the participants; such distinctions, then, as right or wrong, strict or slack, interesting or dull, which may be used by either teacher or taught, become phenomena to be explained.

The previous paragraphs are in no sense exhaustive of the possible problems raised for the sociological enquiry in education by treating knowledge and control as problematic. They do attempt a loose framework which may suggest questions to others, many of which are explored in the papers that follow. In different ways each contribution moves outside and beyond the framework I have outlined, and it is the aim of the final section of this introduction to pick out some of these. The discussion will be intentionally selective. Not only will readers find other points of significance, but the emphasis will be to treat very briefly the papers specifically focusing on the sociology of education (Young, Bernstein, Esland, Keddie, Davies), and to say rather more about the importance for the sociology of education of the two papers by Blum and Horton, and those by Bourdieu, which though specifically concerned with the sociology of education, are likely to be least familiar to English readers.

## PART 1: CURRICULA, TEACHING AND LEARNING AS THE ORGANIZATION OF KNOWLEDGE

The three papers in this section are substantively concerned with curricula (and, with regard to those of Bernstein and Esland, with teaching and learning as well); however, each in very different ways goes beyond the substantive problems and attempts to raise more general questions about sociological knowledge.

In the first paper, after examining the possible explanations of the failure of sociologists to raise questions and develop research into the social organization of educational knowledge, I attempt to explore a crucial structural dimension of this 'organization', the 'stratification of knowledge', and the ways in which variations in the stratification of knowledge may be expressed by educators. The paper tries to tackle one of the central issues raised earlier in the introduction; this is the dialectical relationship between access to power and the opportunity to legitimize certain dominant categories, and the processes by which the availability of such categories to some groups enables them to assert power and control over others.

Bernstein's paper is an extension and development of his work in the sociology of language; here his concerns are with the social class effects on the distribution of knowledge, and the varying consequences of the institutionalization of elaborated codes (Bernstein, 1965). More specifically he develops the concepts of framing and classification to suggest explanations of possible changes in the organization of educational knowledge and their consequences. In the paper these concepts are used to examine relations between teachers and taught, the distinctions between lesson contents (curricula), and changes in what counts as valid presentation of knowledge (evaluation). However, it raises a point of more general sociological significance; the ideas of framing and classification suggest ways of reconceptualizing the process of socialization, or the process of creation and maintenance of identities, which are potentially applicable to any context where this process takes place, work and home as well as school.

In the third paper of this section, Esland develops a theoretical framework which draws together a symbolic interactionist perspective with a phenomenological sociology of knowledge to suggest how teaching and learning might be studied as interrelated processes of organizing knowledge. He starts from an assumption that the objectified realities which define the activities of teaching must be understood in terms of their subjective meanings for teachers and taught. These realities Esland conceptualizes as the pedagogic, 'subject' and career perspectives of teachers, and the major part of the paper examines the range of cognitive structures that underlie them, in particular their possible epistemologies and psychological paradigms.

## PART 2: SOCIAL DEFINITIONS OF KNOWLEDGE

The three papers in this section raise the question 'what counts as knowledge?'; in Blum's paper at the very general level of considering the normative basis of any body of knowledge being possible at all; in Keddie's paper the focus is specifically on what counts as knowledge in the classroom, and in Bourdieu's paper the question is posed in relation to social definitions of intellectual cultures.

Treating 'what we know' as problematic, in order that it becomes the object of enquiry rather than a given, is difficult, and perhaps nowhere more so than in education. The 'out-thereness' of the content of what is taught, whether it be as subjects, forms of enquiry, topics, or ways of knowing, is very much part of the educator's taken for granted world, and, as is suggested by Keddie (p. 151), the acceptance of this 'world' is a prerequisite for being academically successful. It is in suggesting a way of conceiving of 'bodies of knowledge' as 'normative orders' or sets of defining rules which members, in the process of constructing the bodies of knowledge come to share, that Blum's paper is important. It leads him to pose as an empirical question 'how is sociology possible?', but equally we could ask, what tacit understandings are involved in the construction of history, mathematics, or 'science for the less able'.

Blum elaborates the notion of a corpus of knowledge by looking at Hobbes, Descartes and Marx, by showing how each of them conceived of knowledge as 'a product of the informal understandings negotiated among members of an organized intellectual collectivity'. Furthermore he shows that this conception led them not only to treat different bodies of knowledge in this way (non-mathematical knowledge for Descartes, and political philosophy for Hobbes), but that their specific grounds for treating knowledge as problematic varied. Blum sees Hobbes' criterion for criticizing the traditional political philosophy as 'applicability'—whether members (in Hobbes' case the aristocratic ruling class) 'are able to use such knowledge as normative orders in formulating routine courses of action'. A study of forms of 'professional knowledge', from management science to educational theory and social work training, which make assumptions about their 'applicability' is suggested by this critique. Descartes, Blum suggests, used a model of one body of knowledge (mathematics) to criticize others on the assumption of the 'certainty' of mathematical truth; this points to the general process of redefining 'what counts as knowledge' as members draw on alternative models, like mathematics, often in efforts to increase 'credibility'.

In his depiction of Marx's critique of knowledge, Blum makes the point that for Marx 'the construction of a corpus of knowledge is inextricably linked to the interests of those who produce it', who generate 'their own self-justifying standards of evaluation'. For Marx the interests referred to property, though clearly the idea is important if one extends it to occupational groups or administrative hierarchies.

Drawing on the three thinkers Blum suggests we look at the way organizational practices become features of the knowledge produced. In seeing sociological investigation as a topic for enquiry, he argues that in order to proceed at all sociologists (and by implication other knowledge practitioners) accept a 'common culture' which is never described or analysed by them. Keddie in her paper on classroom knowledge draws on the idea of a common culture when referring to what has to be accepted in 'mastering a subject' in school. An illustration of mathematicians' 'common culture' is given by a recent comment: 'It is a statistical truism that ... half of a population of kidney beans will be of shorter than average length ... despite efforts of breeders ... to produce

9

longer beans. In the educational scene the below average pupil will always be with us . . .' (Floyd, 1970). It also indicates the significance of Blum's point that the methodical character of marriages, divorces and suicides is seen and made possible by the organized practices of sociologists; likewise the inevitable normal distribution of kidney beans, the patterns of marks in examinations, and the regular 50–60% of passes in the General Certificate are seen and made possible by the organized activities of breeders and examiners. It is to the organizational practices of which these phenomena, like the bodies of knowledge we call 'subjects', are products that Blum directs our enquiry in the sociology of education.

Keddie's paper in this section can be seen in part as an example of how Blum's ideas might be used in the sociology of education. She conceives of 'ability' and 'subjects' as bodies of knowledge, and examines the features of teachers' everyday practice which produce them. Drawing on field study data, she shows how teachers construct their knowledge about pupils and how this relates not only to what knowledge they make available to pupils, but also to the way they scan pupil classroom activity for appropriate and expected meanings. The data illustrates the distinctions teachers make between school knowledge, which is ordered by 'subjects', and commonsense or non-school knowledge of both pupils and teachers. It is, Keddie suggests, the hierarchical conception of 'what counts as knowledge, and ability' held by teachers, and that are implicit in this ordering, that play a crucial part in the differentiating processes within the school.

Sociologists, in this country and in the U.S.A., have hardly considered the *content* of education, either in terms of how the education system might influence publicly available meanings (the expressive and literary arts, the sciences, fashions, etc.) or with how contemporary definitions of culture have consequences for the organization of knowledge in the school system. These questions have been considered by non-sociologists, but usually from a rather narrow perspective which either treats academic 'high culture' as an unquestioned 'good' sanctioned by tradition (particularly the Arnold–Leavis school in this country) or applies the Marxist terminology of bourgeois culture in an equally uncritical way. Even Raymond Williams, who comes nearest to finding a sociological alternative (1957, 1961), has not been able to develop a framework for analysing how styles, media, and forms of presentation in the 'arts' are socially constructed, and are the historical products of the shared activities of those involved.

It is to these problems that Bourdieu's paper is directed. He conceives of the 'intellectual field' as the mediating set of agencies in which various groups of producers compete for cultural legitimacy. In elaborating on the idea of 'intellectual field' Bourdieu suggests the social and economic context for three aspects of the literary and art 'worlds' that are normally taken for granted. 1) The belief in 'art for art's sake'. 2) The assumption of the 'public's' incompetence and the consequent refusal of artists to respond to public demands. 3) The growth of groups of critics who interpret artistic work for the public and give it its legitimacy. Bourdieu refers to 'creative project' as the activity in which the intrinsic demands of the 'intellectual field' and the external context of the social and economic order of the time are joined in the work of art itself. Thus he suggests works of art and literature are formed in a context of public categories or definitions like 'nouvelle vague' or 'new novel' in terms of which the artist is defined and defines himself.

Bourdieu sees the 'intellectual field' as characterized by the differential distribution of power (to confer legitimacy) among groups. In any society, he argues, one will find a hierarchy of 'cultural legitimacy' institutionalized in the academic system, in terms of which claims for recognition are made and cultural values defined. It is through the process of conferral of cultural legitimacy that the schools are crucial, for there is a close relation between those forms of artistic expression which are systematically taught, and form regular parts of school curricula, and their recognition or social definition as legitimate in terms of aesthetic criteria accepted at the time. As illustrative of his thesis Bourdieu compares classical music and literature which have unquestioned cultural legitimacy and which are systematically 'taught' in academic curricula, with interior decoration, cookery and cosmetics which are only 'taught' in specialist 'vocational' curricula and for which no 'cultural legitimacy' in terms of aesthetic criteria is claimed.

Bourdieu's third concept, the 'cultural unconscious', refers to the axioms and postulates of artistic activity which are unarticulated, but are the preconditions for cultural production to occur at all (I suggest they are akin to the tacit understandings referred to by Blum). These postulates are the ways of thought and stylistic expression that are taken for granted in any national culture but have an 'elective affinity' (presumably Bourdieu is using the phrase in the sense Max Weber did in *The Protestant Ethic and the Spirit of Capitalism*) with the dominant social interests of the time. Bourdieu is suggesting that it is through the schools that these unconscious intellectual choices characteristic of a society are made, and that we should investigate the relation between educational practices and works of art in terms, as he puts it, of what they may say or betray about the society of their time.

## PART 3: COGNITIVE STYLES IN COMPARATIVE PERSPECTIVE

It was suggested earlier in this introduction that much research in education, like the educators that are often the objects of the research, starts from an absolutist view of cognitive categories such as 'rational' and 'abstract'. This view in effect prevents these categories from being treated as themselves socially constructed and therefore open to sociological enquiry. Many of the assumptions of our academic culture are deeply embedded in the institutional framework of 'what everyone knows is education'. It may therefore only be through comparative study in which this culture is treated as 'strange' and therefore 'to be explained', in the way anthropologists treat belief-systems of non-industrialized societies, that such assumptions can be made explicit. It is to aspects of these general problems that the three papers of this section address themselves. However, before considering them it may be useful to illustrate the point I want to make by a specific example drawn from a study by Gay and Cole (1967).

A group of illiterate Kpelle adults and a group of 60 U.S. Peace Corps volunteers were given two problems. First they were asked to estimate the number of cups of rice that could be obtained from a large bowl, and secondly they were asked to sort in three different ways sets of eight cards, with two or five, red or green squares or triangles on them. In the first experiment the Peace Corps error was on average 35%, four times the average error of the Kpelle. In the second experiment, the Peace Corps volunteers completed the task without hesitation, but the Kpelle found great difficulties, and two-thirds failed to complete three sortings. The point the investigators make is that to describe the Kpelle performance in the second test as evidence of limited mathematical ability is no more justified than to describe the American volunteers' errors in the first test as inept, unless we already start with preconceptions of mathematical competence.

The general point, therefore, is that if we do not begin by assuming what mathematical (or other) knowledge is, we can compare the way, under different social and economic conditions, men have constructed different styles of thought and kinds of explanation, and how in industrialized societies these have been institutionalized in formal educational systems.

In the first paper, Bourdieu draws most of his material from French society, in exploring the way, through the school system, particular classes maintain their dominance by being able to confer cultural legitimacy on certain styles of thought and therefore on certain aspects of reality. If we recognize, as Davies points out at the end of his paper, that comparative studies are a means to offering explanations of the particular characteristics of cultures and institutions, then Bourdieu, by spelling out the relationships between pedagogic styles and systems of thought, gives us an important lead for the direction which comparative studies might take.

Bourdieu's paper, like the one in the previous section, is essentially a structural analysis, focusing in this case on the interrelations of the pedagogic and curricular practices of the French school system and how they maintain the styles of thought characteristic of French academic culture. He conceives of educational practices as providing models of the 'right' kind of intellectual activity which not only influence the styles of thought within the school system but of the various activities that those who have been through the school system enter (among the examples he cites are the styles of government reports and journalism). There are two general points of importance raised by Bourdieu's paper which relate to a common theme among many of the contributors to this volume. Firstly, Bourdieu treats educational practices such as essay topics, lecture techniques and forms of assessment as problematic in the sense that they are indices of the way educational knowledge is institutionalized. They thus become a central concern of comparative enquiries. Secondly, in his discussion of class cultures in an education system where educational opportunity is even more unequally distributed than in this country, he locates the mechanisms of this process of distribution not in the characteristics of the classes, but in the scholarly culture itself—'a whole uniform of distinctions' as Pearce (1967) calls it. In another paper referred to by Pearce, Bourdieu (1966) reports on a study of a technical training centre which demonstrates this. He finds that trades are ranked according to the criteria of the learned culture, so that the pupils of the highest prestige do not produce objects, or manipulate utensils, but read instruments.

... because it prevents one taking anything for granted an unfamiliar idiom can help to show up all sorts of puzzles and problems inherent in an intellectual process which normally seems trouble-free (Horton, p. 211 this vol.).

This quotation from Horton's paper is a good indication of its potential importance for a sociology of education. Intellectual processes, whether or not they are characteristics of educational activities, are often misinterpreted and rarely understood because they are so often taken for granted and therefore in the educator's world (and often the sociologist's) are non-problematic and not seen in need of being explained. One of the difficulties encountered by sociologists, and referred to before, is the need to move outside of the conceptual framework common to their society so that they can view their own and alter native thought systems other than through their own dominant categories Through the hierarchy implicit in these categories they are led to define alternatives as not just different but inferior. This then directs research enquiries to the assumed deficiences of the alternatives, rather than to the way the unequal distribution of resources is linked to particular hierarchies and provides the context for the development of different cognitive systems. This kind of sequence has been demonstrated in large-scale research on developing countries (Geertz, 1969), intervention programmes for Indians and Negroes in the U.S.A. (Wax and Wax, 1964; Baratz and Baratz, 1970), compensatory education for working-class children (Bernstein, 1970), and much anthropological field study (Horton, 1968). One of the many merits of Horton's paper is that he offers us a 'cultural-diversity model', with which different thought systems (in this case Western science and African religion) are shown to have marked similarities in the way they are organized to provide explanations. Formal education is based on the assumption that thought systems organized in curricula are in some sense 'superior' to the thought systems of those who are to be (or have not been) educated. It is just this implicit 'superiority' that Horton is questioning when he compares Western and African 'theoretical' thought in his paper.

Horton is therefore suggesting that if we suspend such assumptions of superiority then we can look at any set of cognitive categories as offering potential explanations. The research problems then become to discover how some categories and not others gain institutional legitimacy, and how in examining the experience and environment of those with different thought categories we can account for their differences in content.

The second implication of Horton's cultural-diversity model is that it opens up a whole range of questions about the relations between commonsense and theoretical categories, the forms they take and the situations in which members (in Horton's case chemists or Kalabari, but equally teachers and pupils) move in and out of them; in the school situation it is more likely that the pupils will be expected to move from one theoretical world to another. The process of abstraction, often considered a unique characteristic of scientific thinking and a key stage in certain developmental psychologies, is shown to be not peculiar to science but a characteristic of all attempts to provide explanations, the differences being not in the process but in what is abstracted. For research in education, this suggests investigations of how teachers impose 'subject' defined abstractions on pupils, and into the less formal abstractions of commonsense theorizing of both teachers and taught. Horton's example of the chemist's theorizing about salt can be extended to suggest questions about the structuring of curricula. Commonsense experience of salt might be that it melts ice on roads, that it produces dehydration of the body if absent from the diet, or that it colours flames yellow; the extension of these commonsense realities into theory takes us into what in the school curricula are quite arbitrarily distinguished and institutionalized as the 'subjects', physics, biology and chemistry.* We can summarize the argument in the first part of Horton's paper by turning to page 228; in taking belief systems at their face value, Horton is casting doubts on many common dichotomies (intellectual/emotional, rational/mystical, abstract/concrete . . .), each of which presuppose just those assumptions about intellectual processes that it should be the task of the sociologist to study.

In the second part of the paper, Horton characterizes the core difference between the thought systems he compares in terms of their 'open' and 'closed' predicaments, which refer to whether or not members are aware of alternatives to their own systems of thought. He points out that except in the case of the scientist 'doing science' (and then only to a partial extent [Barnes, 1969; Kuhn, 1970]), the similarities between the 'closed' predicaments of African tribesmen and members of urban industrial societies may be more significant than the differences. The intellectual processes that follow from the 'closed' predicament (taboo, secondary elaboration, etc.) he discusses in turn, and by looking at the varying examples he gives, we may be able to suggest parallel processes in our own society and possible explanations of their differences in content.

I would contend that this paper is one of the classic examples of comparative research into thought systems, which might form a paradigm for a comparative sociology of educational knowledge. Starting from the relatively familiar theoretical scheme of Western science, Horton moves by analogy and model to explanations of the unfamiliar, African religions, and implicitly suggests research into the ecological and economic conditions in which they were generated. These explanations can then be used to examine the shared understandings of our own society, that are familiar, to return to Blum, only 'because they are never described or analysed'.

* One might compare science curricula constructed on quite other abstraction criteria (see for example the Schools Council project for 'Science for the average and below average pupil; 13–16 yrs old').

In the final paper of this section, Davies discusses some of the problems of comparative studies in the sociology of education. Drawing on a wide range of sources from different societies, he points to the limitations of a typology such as Hopper's (1968) which focuses on selection processes. In two important ways Davies makes suggestions that parallel those raised by other contributors. Firstly, legitimating ideologies (which justify who gets schooling) or value-systems, like other aspects of educational reality, are constructed, and so research cannot start by presupposing them. Thus a comparative study of selection must investigate not just the inputs to the schools (pupils) or their outputs (where in the occupational structure they distribute their 'leavers'), but the organizational practices involved. Secondly, education is about the selection of knowledge, as well as of people, so comparative research which neglects the cultural content of education as a variable may end up, as Davies says, in not being about education at all.

## NOTES AND REFERENCES

[1] This point is explored in more detail in the second section of the first paper (Young p. 24).

[2] I am thinking of texts and readers such as Banks (1968), Swift (1969), Musgrove (1966) in this country, and Havinghurst and Neugarten (1967) and Corwin (1964) in the U.S.A., though this list is in no sense exhaustive.

[3] The point is taken from Bernstein's paper (p. 47). I shall elaborate on this later in the introduction, but it is perhaps worth mentioning here that though substantively the paper is concerned with curricula, pedagogy and evaluation, the framework of analysis can be seen to represent a major attempt to conceptualize an alternative to the trivialized approaches to socialization that Bernstein refers to here.

[4] The usage of the term control is drawn from the paper by Dawe (1970).* In this sense it is not a concept but a doctrine or set of ideas which give substantive meaning to concepts, and point to a focus on action and interaction as the 'imposition of meaning' rather than properties of systems, as the focus of sociological enquiry. Dawe's paper is, I suggest, a model of clarity, precision and originality in the presentation of the major theoretical problems for any sociology. The more specific suggestions for a sociology of education outlined in this introduction draw extensively on it. My other major intellectual debt is to Wright Mills (1939; 1940), whose highly original contributions to the sociology of knowledge seem to have been too long neglected, as much by his admirers as his critics.

[5] The distinction is from *T.V.A. and the Grassroots* and is quoted in full in the paper by Keddie (p. 35).

[6] The organization of university examining boards, and the kind of participation in them of grammar school VIth-form masters would seem important to consider in this context.

[7] The criticisms referred to are in Marcuse's (1965) paper in which he argues that Weber uses a historical economic rationality of a particular epoch to formulate an ahistorical notion of 'rational man' as a model for sociological explanation. Parsons is more specifically concerned with Weber's apparent neglect of the non-rational, which he elaborates in his introduction to Weber (1964).

[8] The point is again taken from Dawe's (1970) paper.

[9] The term is first used by Hughes (1958), and the idea has recently been extended to occupational groups such as teachers, by Rainwater (1967).

---

* Dawe makes very clear (*op. cit.*, note 16) the distinction between this use of the term control and the functionalist concept 'social control'; the former is more akin to the notion of power.

[10] The relation between social structure and linguistic categories in ancient China is discussed in Mills (1940).

[11] This 'objectivistic' view of science has probably been accepted with less criticism in this country and in the U.S.A. than on the continent. The issues are fruitfully discussed by Habermas (1970).

[12] This discussion draws heavily on Horton's (1968) excellent discussion.

[13] The 'achievement motivation' literature is a classic example of this. An excellent critical summary of the field will be found in the early chapters of Colquhoun (1970).

[14] See Becker, et al. (1969).

[15] The term 'revolution' is used here in the Kuhnian sense (1961) of a change of world view, which does in one sense make the findings of previous research 'mistakes'.

# BIBLIOGRAPHY

BANKS, O. (1968). *The Sociology of Education.* London: B. T. Batsford.

BARATZ, J., and BARATZ, S. (1970). 'Early Childhood Intervention; the Social Science Basis of Institutionalized Racism'. *Harvard Educational Review,* 40, February.

BARNES, S. B. (1969). 'Paradigms, Social and Scientific', *Man,* (n.s.) Vol. 4(1).

BECKER, H. S., GEER, B., HUGHES, E., and STRAUSS, A. (1969). *Making the Grade.* New York: John Wiley & Sons.

BOURDIEU, P. (1966). 'L'École Conservatrice. Les Inegalités devant l'École et devant la Culture'. *Revue Française de Sociologie,* VII(3).

BERNSTEIN, B. B. (1965). 'A Sociolinguistic Approach to Social Learning' in GOULD, J. S. (ed.), *Penguin Survey of Social Sciences.* Harmondsworth: Penguin.

—— (1970). 'A Critique of the Concept of Compensatory Education' in RUBENSTEIN, D., and STONEMAN, C., *Education for Democracy.* Harmondsworth: Penguin.

BRETON, R. (1970). 'Academic Stratification in Secondary Schools'. *Canadian Review of Sociology and Social Anthropology,* 7(1).

CICOUREL, A. V., and KITSUSE, J. I. (1963). *The Educational Decision Makers.* Indianapolis: Bobbs-Merrill.

COHEN, P. (1968). *Modern Social Theory.* London: Heinemann.

COLQUHOUN, R. (1970). *Some Sociological Approaches to Pupil Motivation.* M.A. (Ed.) thesis, University of London.

CORWIN, R. (1953). *A Sociology of Education.* New York: Appleton-Century-Crofts.

DAWE, A. (1970). 'The Two Sociologies'. *British Journal of Sociology,* XXI(2).

DOUGLAS, J. (1970). *The Relevance of Sociology.* New York: Appleton-Century-Crofts.

DOUGLAS, M. (1970). 'Environments at Risk'. *Times Literary Supplement,* October 31, 1970.

EASTMAN, G. (1967). 'The Ideologizing of Theories; John Dewey, a Case in Point'. *Educational Theory,* I(1).

FLOYD, P. (1970). 'Not good enough for heaven nor bad enough for hell'. *Times Educational Supplement,* October 30, 1970.

GARFINKEL, H. (1967). *Studies in Ethnomethodology.* Englewood Cliffs, N.J.: Prentice-Hall.

GAY, J., and COLE, M. (1967). *The New Mathematics and an Old Culture.* New York: Holt, Rinehart & Winston.

GEERTZ, C. (1969). 'Myrdal's Mythology'. *Encounter,* July.

GOULDNER, A. (1968). 'The Sociologist as Partisan'. *American Sociologist,* (3).

HABERMAS, J. (1970). 'Knowledge and Interest' in EMMETT, A., and MCINTYRE, A. (eds.), *Philosophical Analysis and Sociological Theory.* London: Macmillan.

HAVINGHURST, R., and NEUGARTEN, B. (1967). *Society and Education*. Rockleigh, N.J.: Allyn & Bacon.

HOLT, J. (1967). *How Children Fail*. New York; Pitman.

HOPPER, E. (1968). 'A Typology for the Classification of Educational Systems'. *Sociology*, 2(1).

HORTON, R. (1968) 'Neo-Tylorianism; Sound Sense or Sinister Prejudice'. *Man*, (n.s.) Vol. 3.

HUGHES, E. (1958). *Men and Their Work*. Glencoe, Illinois: The Free Press.

KUHN, T. S. (1970). *The Structure of Scientific Revolutions*, Chicago: Chicago University Press.

LACEY, C. (1970). *Hightown Grammar*. Manchester: Manchester University Press.

MARCUSE, H. (1965). 'Capitalism and Industrialization'. *New Left Review*, 32.

MILLS, C. W. (1939). 'Language, Logic and Culture'. *American Sociological Review*, IV(5).

——(1940a). 'The Methodological Consequences of the Sociology of Knowledge'. *American Journal of Sociology*, XLVI(3).

——(1940b). *The Language and Ideas of Ancient China*. (Mimeographed.) (All reprinted in HOROWITZ, I. (ed.), *Power, Politics and People; The Collected Papers of C. Wright Mills*. London: Oxford University Press.

MUSGRAVE, P. W. (1966). *The Sociology of Education*. London: Methuen.

PEARCE, A. (1967). 'Sociologists and Education'. *International Social Science Journal*, XIX(3).

RAINWATER, L. (1967). 'The Revolt of the Dirty Workers'. *Transaction*, November.

SCHUTZ, A. (1943). 'The Problem of Rationality in the Social World'. *Economica*, 10.

SEELEY, J. (1966). 'The "Making" and "Taking" of Problems'. *Social Problems*, 14.

SWIFT, D. F. (1968). *The Sociology of Education*. London: Routledge & Kegan Paul.

WAX, M., and WAX, R. (1964). 'Formal Education in an American Indian Community'. *Social Problems Monograph*, II(4).

WEBER, M. (1964). *Theory of Social and Economic Organization*. New York: The Free Press.

WESTERGAARD, J., and LITTLE, A. (1964). 'Trends in Social Class Differentials in Educational Opportunity'. *British Journal of Sociology*, XV.

WILLIAMS, R. (1957). *Culture and Society*. London: Chatto & Windus.

——(1961). *The Long Revolution*. London: Chatto & Windus.

# PART ONE

## CURRICULA, TEACHING AND LEARNING AS THE ORGANIZATION OF KNOWLEDGE

## I • MICHAEL F. D. YOUNG
### An Approach to the Study of Curricula as Socially Organized Knowledge*[1]

The almost total neglect by sociologists of how knowledge is selected, organized and assessed in educational institutions (or in any other institutions for that matter) hardly needs documenting. Some answers to the question why this happened, and an attempt to show that this neglect arises out of narrow definitions of the major schools of sociological thought (in particular, those stemming from Marx, Weber and Durkheim) rather than out of their inadequacies, may provide a useful perspective from which to suggest the directions in which such work might develop. This paper explicitly does not set out to offer a general theory of culture, or to be a direct contribution to the sociology of knowledge, except to the extent that it raises questions about what might be meant by the notion of knowledge being socially organized or constructed. It has the more limited aim of trying to suggest ways in which questions may be framed about how knowledge is organized and made available in curricula. However, it would be my contention that if such questions became the foci of research in the sociology of education, then we might well see significant advances in the sociology of knowledge in particular, and sociological theory in general. The paper then has four parts:

1. The changing focus of the public debates about education in the last twenty years.
2. A brief examination of the limitations and possibilities of existing approaches to the sociology of education and the sociology of knowledge in generating either fruitful theories or research in the field of curricula.

* First published in this volume. An earlier and shorter version of this paper was presented at the Annual Conference of the British Sociological Association, April 1970, and will be published under the title 'Curricula and the Social Organization of Knowledge' in the collection of the Conference papers—*Sociology of Education*, edited by Richard Brown (Tavistock).

3. An outline of some of the possibilities of the Marxist, Weberian and Durk-heimian traditions.
4. An elaboration of the implications of the previous sections to suggest a frame-work and some possible directions for future research.[2]

*1*

One can only speculate on the explanations, but it is clearly possible to trace three stages in the public debates on education in England in the last fifteen to twenty years; the foci have been *equality of opportunity* and the *wastage of talent*, *organization and selection of pupils*, and the *curriculum*. In each case one can distinguish the political, sociological and educational components, and though both of the sets of distinctions are over-simplified and schematic, they do pro-vide a useful context for considering the problems posed in this paper. The latter three distinctions do not refer to the content of issues, but to the groups involved and the way they defined the problems.[3] In the first stage, the facts of educational 'wastage' were documented by the Early Leaving and Crowther Reports (and later by Robbins) and the 'class' nature of the lack of opportunity was demonstrated by Floud and Halsey. Though the sociological research largely complemented the public reports and was tacitly accepted as a basis for an expansionist policy by successive ministers, it also threw up a new set of questions concerning the social nature of selection, and the organization of secondary education in particular. Thus, the second phase of public debate from the midsixties focused on the issues of *selection* and *comprehensive re-organization*. That the debate now became an issue of political conflict is an indication that the policies involved, such as the abolition of selective schools, threatened certain significant and powerful interests in society—particularly the career-grammar, direct-grant and public school staff and the parents of the children who expected to go to such schools. The manifest inefficiency and less well-documented injustice of the 11+[4] made its abolition a convenient political commitment for reformist politicians. This debate was paralleled by an in-creasing interest by sociologists in all kinds of organizations and the possibility of applying the more general models of 'organization theory' to schools and colleges.[5]

It is only in the last two or three years that the focus of the debate has moved again from *organization* to *curriculum*, and again one can only speculate on the reasons. Four might be worth exploring; the first three particularly, in relation to the kind of projects on curriculum reform sponsored by the Schools Council:

1.) *Government pressure for more and better technologists and scientists*

The origins and implications of this are highly complex and can only be briefly referred to here. Mcpherson (1969), Blaug and Gannicott (1969) and Gorbutt (1970) have all cast doubts on the widely held notions that pupils in secondary schools are 'swinging from science'. This swing has been an 'official' problem, with various 'official' sets of remedies since the publication of the Dainton Report (1968). Gorbutt (1970) draws on the earlier studies and suggests that what has been called the 'swing from' science may be less the product of an identifiable change in the pattern of 'subject' choice by school pupils, and more an indication of how particular interest groups 'use' official statistics.

The failure of sociologists to make explicit the theoretical assumptions underlying contemporary definitions of this problem and the research it has generated is worth considering here. The whole 'subject-choice' and 'swing from science' debate presupposes taking as 'given' the social definitions implicit in our commonsense distinction between 'arts' and 'sciences'. What 'does' and 'does not' count as 'science' depends on the social meaning given to science, which will vary not only historically and cross-culturally but within societies and situationally. The dominant English cultural definitions of science might be characterized as what Habermas (1970) calls 'objectivistic', by which he means that we accept the scientists' claim that they 'apply their method without thought for their guiding interests'. In other words an idea of science has developed in which what is thought of as scientific knowledge is abstracted from the institutional contexts in which it is generated and used. Goodman (1969b) is making a similar point in discussing the implications of alternative social definitions of technology. Once the meanings associated with 'science' and 'technology', and 'pure' and 'applied', are seen as socially determined, not only does it become possible to explore how these social meanings become part of the school context of pupil preference, but a sociological enquiry into the intellectual content of what counts as science becomes possible (King, 1971).

## 2.) *The commitment to raising the school leaving age*

The implications of this change stem from the obvious if neglected fact that length of educational career is probably the single most important determinant of pupils' curricular experience. Thus for the 50% of pupils who at present leave when school is no longer legally compulsory, by 1973 teachers will be forced to conceive of curricula for a further 'terminal year'.

One development, which can be seen as a possible 'solution' to the 'extra year', has been the extension, to at least one half of all school leavers, of publicly recognized school exams. The extension of 'mode 3' or 'teacher based' exams has introduced a potentially greater flexibility in approach and the possibility of a more critical questioning of existing syllabi. The 'guiding interests' of the examination boards have so far remained outside the field of sociological enquiry. It is possible that such 'interests' may become more 'public' if the various pressures to abolish G.C.E. 'O' level grow.

## 3.) *Comprehensive amalgamations*

Many of these involve grammar schools which are obliged to receive an unselective pupil intake. Thus teachers who for years have successfully produced good 'A' level results from highly selected groups of pupils are now faced with

many pupils who appear to neither know how to 'learn' the 'academic knowledge', nor appear to want to. This inevitably poses for teachers quite new
problems of finding alternatives.

4.) *Student participation*

It is undeniable that as the demands of students in colleges and universities
have moved from the arena of union and leisure activities to discipline and
administrative authority and finally to a concern to participate in the planning
of the structure and content of courses and their assessment, staff have themselves begun to re-examine the principles that underlay their curricula and
which have for so long been taken for granted. It is more rather than less likely
that this pressure from the students will increase and extend to the senior forms
of the schools. Perhaps the most dramatic demonstration of this trend is the
Negro students in the U.S.A. who are demanding courses in black studies.

Again the public debate has taken place on two levels, the 'political' and the
'educational'—though such a distinction is necessarily an over-simplification,
and it is not intended to suggest that educational ideas do not have a political
content. At the political level the main protagonists have been the Marxist
'left' (Anderson, 1969) and the conservative or Black Paper (Cox and Dyson,
1969a, 1969b) 'right'. The 'left' criticizes contemporary curricula for 'mystifying
the students' and 'fragmenting knowledge into compartments'. They also claim
that such curricula, by denying students the opportunity to understand society
as a 'totality', act as effective agents of social control.* The conservative 'right'
criticize progressive teaching methods, unstreaming and the various curricular
innovations in English, history, and maths, as well as the expansion of the 'soft'
social sciences. In the name of preserving 'our cultural heritage' and providing
opportunities for the most able to excel, they seek to conserve the institutional
support for the educational tradition they believe in—particularly the public
and direct-grant grammar schools. What is significant for the sociology of education is that in spite of attempts, the politics of the curriculum has remained
outside of Westminster. Apart from compulsory religious instruction, the
headmaster or principal's formal autonomy over the curriculum is not questioned.
That this autonomy is in practice extremely limited by the control of VIth-form
(and therefore lower form) curricula by the universities,† both through their
entrance requirements and their domination of all but one of the school examination boards, hardly needs emphasizing. Furthermore any likelihood of the new
'polytechnics' developing alternative sets of criteria is limited by the powerful
indirect control (of all degree-based courses) held by universities through their
membership of the C.N.A.A. Boards. It becomes apparent that it is the legitimacy of university control, rather than teacher autonomy, that is being upheld.

* Considerably more sophisticated versions of this thesis, which are not considered
here, have been put forward by French and German social scientists (for instance,
H. Lefebvre [1969]).

† No direct control is implied here, but rather a process by which teachers legitimate
their curricula through their shared assumptions about 'what we all know the universities
want'.

It is as if by what has been called in another context the 'politics of non-decision making' (Bachrach and Baratz, 1963) through which the range of issues for party political debate are limited, that consideration of the curriculum is avoided[6] except for broad discussions about the need for more scientists. There are sufficient parallels in other contexts to suggest that the avoidance of such discussion is an indication of the interrelationship between the existing organization of knowledge and the distribution of power, the consideration of which might not be comfortable in an era of consensus politics.[7]

The context of the 'educationalists'' debate about the curriculum has been different and inevitably less contentious. This lack of contentiousness is in stark contrast with the kind of direct confrontation that exists in America between the American academic establishment and its critics (Goodman, Friedenburg, Chomsky, Holt, *et al.*). It is possible that this contrast may in part be accounted for by the different contexts and historical antecedents of the prevailing 'liberal' orthodoxies in each country. The difference is also apparent when we consider some of the issues of the 'educationalists'' debate in this country; early tracking into the sciences or arts, over-specialization and neglect of applied science in the VIth form, as well as the possibility of introducing new knowledge areas such as the social sciences. On another level, what has been labelled the 'tyranny of subjects' typical of much secondary education has been opposed by suggestions for integrated curricula based on 'themes' and 'topics'.

Three features that have characterized the educationalists' part in this debate should also be mentioned: 1) *The emphasis on secondary curricula.* Virtually all the issues have focused on aspects of secondary school curricula, which have in practice undergone least change; the absence of debate over changes at the primary level would seem to point, paradoxically, to the much greater autonomy of that part of the educational system with the lowest status. 2) *The stream of working papers and proposals of the Schools Council.** 3) *The critiques of the philosophers of education.* Starting from certain *a priori* assumptions about the organization (or forms) of knowledge (Hirst, 1969), their criticisms focus either on new topic-based syllabi which neglect these 'forms of understanding', or on new curricula for the so-called 'less able' or 'Newsom child' which they argue are consciously restricting them from access to those forms of understanding which in the philosopher's sense are 'education'. The problem with this kind of critique is that it appears to be based on an absolutist conception of a set of distinct forms of knowledge which correspond closely to the traditional areas of the academic curriculum and thus justify, rather than examine, what are no more than the socio-historical constructs of a particular time. It is important to stress that it is not 'subjects', which Hirst recognizes as the socially constructed ways that teachers organize knowledge, but forms of understanding, that it is claimed are 'necessarily' distinct. The point I wish to make here is that unless such *necessary* distinctions or intrinsic logics are treated as problematic, philosophical criticism cannot examine the assumptions of academic curricula.

Unlike in the debates on *equality* and *organization*, sociologists, except as

* This point will be taken up later in the paper.

political protagonists, have remained silent. We have had virtually no theoretical perspectives or research to suggest explanations of how curricula, which are no less social inventions than political parties or new towns, arise, persist and change, and what the social interests and values involved might be.

2

## A. Sociology of Education and the Curriculum

Having mapped out the context of the debates on the curriculum, let us turn to the sociology of education and consider why its contribution has been so negligible.[8] Sociologists seem to have forgotten, to paraphrase Raymond Williams, that education is not a product like cars and bread, but a selection and organization from the available knowledge at a particular time which involves conscious or unconscious choices. It would seem that it is or should be the central task of the sociology of education to relate these principles of selection and organization that underly curricula to their institutional and interactional setting in schools and classrooms and to the wider social structure. I want to suggest that we can account for the failure of sociologists to do this by examining on the one hand the ideological and methodological assumptions of the sociologists, and on the other hand the institutional context within which the sociological study of education has developed. However, perhaps as significant a fact as any in accounting for the limited conception of the sociology of education in Britain has been that in spite of the interest in the field reported by respondents to Carter's recent survey (Carter, 1967), *very few* sociologists have been involved in research in education.

Much British sociology in the late fifties and the sociology of education in particular drew its ideological perspective from Fabian socialism and its methodology from the demographic tradition of Booth and Rowntree. They broadened the notion of poverty from lack of income to lack of education, which was seen as a significant part of working-class life chances. The stark facts of the persistence of inequalities over decades and in spite of an overall expansion do not need repeating, but what is important is that these studies and those such as Douglas and Plowden which followed, in their concern for increasing equality of opportunity, focused primarily on the characteristics of the failures, the early leavers and the drop-outs. By using a model of explanation of working-class school failure which justified reformist social policies, they were unable to examine the socially constructed character of the education that the working-class children failed at—for instance, the peculiar content of the grammar school curriculum for the sixteen-year-old in which pupils are obliged to do up to ten different subjects which bear little relation either to each other or to anything else. It would not be doing these studies an injustice to say that they developed primarily from a sociological interest in stratification in the narrow sense rather than education. They were concerned to show how the distribution of life

24

chances through education can be seen as an aspect of the class structure. Inevitably this led to an over-mechanistic conception of 'class' which isolated the 'class' characteristics of individuals from the 'class' content of their educational experience. It may clarify this point by looking at the implicit model more formally as follows:

| Assumptions | Independent variable | Dependent variable |
|---|---|---|
| Criteria of educational success—curricula, methods and evaluation. What counts as 'knowledge and knowing' in school | Social characteristics of the success and failure groups | Distribution of success and failure at various stages—stream, 11 +, 'O' level, etc. |

Though the table illustrates the point in a crude and over-simplified form, it does show that within that framework the content of education is taken as a 'given' and is not subject to sociological enquiry—the 'educational failures' become a sort of 'deviant'.[9] We can usefully reformulate the problem in a similar way to that suggested by Cicourel and Kitsuse (1963a) in their discussion of how 'official statistics' on crime are produced, and ask what are the processes by which rates of educational success and failure come to be produced. We are then led to ask questions about the context and definition of success and how they are legitimized. In other words, the methods of assessment, selection and organization of knowledge and the principles underlying them become our focus of study. The point is important because what is implied is that questions have to be raised about matters that have either not been considered important or have been tacitly accepted as 'given'. How does the education that poor working-class children fail at come to be provided? What are the social assumptions that are implicit in the criteria used in the Crowther Report to delineate a 'second group' who 'should be taught a sensible practicality—moral standards and a wise use of leisure time'? One could raise similar questions about the Newsom Report's 'below average child', and in fact about much educational research. One can see that this kind of reformulation would not have been consistent either with the methods or with the ideology of most British sociological research, particularly that concerned with social class and educational opportunity. A similar point can be made about studies of schools and colleges as 'organizations'. They have either begun with 'models' from 'organizational theory' or have compared schools with mental hospitals and prisons as 'people processing organizations'.[10] In neither case is it recognized that it is not only people but knowledge in the educational institutions that is 'processed', and that unless what is 'knowledge' is to be taken as 'given', it is the interrelation of the two processes of organization that must form the beginning of such studies.[11] An examination of the knowledge teachers have of children and how this influences the knowledge they make available to them would provide one way of tackling this empirically (Keddie, 1970).

Turning to the institutional context, it does seem clear that most of the teaching and published work in the sociology of education has taken place in colleges, institutes and departments of education. It is only very recently that university departments of sociology have offered main options at either B.Sc. or M.Sc. level in this field. Thus sociology of education has developed in institutions devoted to the 'academic' study of education where ten to fifteen years ago it hardly existed. We can pose the question as to how did the new specialists legitimate their contribution to educational studies and justify their particular field of expertise—particularly when the ex-school subject specialists and the philosophers had defined their area of competence as covering the curriculum and pedagogy. Not surprisingly, the sociologists mapped out new unexplored areas. They started from the social context of education, with an emphasis on social class, relationships to the economy, the occupational structure and the family, and moved to the consideration of schools as organizations and pupil subcultures. Through an arbitrary division of labour which had no theoretical basis, this allowed the expansion of sociology of education with the minimum of 'boundary disputes'. Inevitably this is speculation, but it does suggest an explanation of what appears to have been a consensus among sociologists and non-sociologists alike that the curriculum was not a field for sociological research.

Although this discussion has focused on British sociology, the points are equally applicable to the American situation. Functionalist theory, which has been the perspective of the majority of sociologists in the U.S.A., presupposes at a very general level an agreed set of societal values or goals which define both the selection and organization of knowledge in curricula. With one or two notable exceptions,[12] even the best American work in the sociology of education has been concerned with the 'organization' or 'processing' of people (whether pupils or students), and takes the organization of knowledge for granted.[13] It is important to stress that this limitation has also been characteristic of the work of those who have criticized the structural-functionalists.[14] This is of importance as it points to the limitations of the symbolic interactionist perspective. This perspective, derived largely from the ideas of G. H. Mead, has given rise to valuable studies of lawyers, medical students, nurses and others. These studies have raised questions that are not considered by functionalists about the processes of interaction and the situational significance of beliefs and values. However, they have not been able to consider as problematic the knowledge that is made available in such interactions. This would have led to considering the structural contingencies influencing what is defined as legal, medical, nursing or other knowledge, and would inevitably take the research out of the 'situated action' and therefore out of the symbolic interactionist framework.

## B. Sociology of Knowledge and the Curriculum

It would have seemed that a field which was concerned with the social conditions influencing the development of knowledge, and with attempts to place ideas in their socio-historical setting, would have seen educational institutions and how knowledge is selected and organized in them as an obvious area for research. However, the main tradition which stems from Marx has been largely restricted to philosophies, political theories and theologies. These comments do not refer to the sociology of knowledge that stems from the phenomenology of Alfred Schutz, until recently totally neglected by sociologists. Schutz treats the institutional definitions or typifications (whether of education, or families or politics) as the intersubjective reality which men have constructed to give meaning to their world; therefore though they are part of the accepted world of everyday life for teachers, mothers and politicians, they can become the objects of sociological enquiry. In other words, if 'knowledge' or 'what is taken for knowledge' is ideal-typical in construction, Schutz is pointing to a study of the 'construction' of subjects, disciplines and syllabi as sets or provinces of meaning which form the basis of the intersubjective understandings of educators. The school curriculum becomes just one of the mechanisms through which knowledge is 'socially distributed'. As Schaffer (1970) suggests, the question 'how do children learn mathematics' presupposes answers to the prior question as to what is the social basis of the 'set of meanings that come to be typified under the term mathematics'?

Three strands, which characterize the more familiar traditions in the sociology of knowledge, indicate not its lack of potential but why the direction it has taken has made its contribution to the sociology of education so insignificant. Firstly, except in the American work on mass media, most writings have either, like Child[15] and Mannheim, been on the border of sociology and epistemology and have been concerned primarily with the existential nature of knowledge, or more recently have been little more than overviews. In both cases, with the exception of Mannheim's essay on 'Conservative Thought' (Mannheim, 1936), substantive empirical research has been eschewed. Secondly, there has been, since Marx, a persistent neglect of the cognitive dimension of the categories of thought and how they are socially constrained—studies have been restricted to the values, standards and 'views of the world' of different groups.[16] Thirdly, and most importantly for the issues raised in this paper, the process of transmission, as *itself* a social condition, has not been studied. If it had, as we shall demonstrate in referring to Bourdieu's comments on Durkheim, the sociology of knowledge would have been inevitably concerned with the curricula through which knowledge is transmitted.


### 3


## A. The Marxist Tradition

Marx himself wrote very little about education, though a notion of 'polytechnical education' which underlies the educational policy of the 'communist' countries can be found in one of his early speeches.[17] Though Marx does have a theory which at a very general level can account for the changes in men's consciousness or categories of thought in terms of the changing means of production and the social relations they generate, he does not extend this to a systematic analysis of the educational system of his time comparable with his analysis of the economy. The limitations of Marxist theory also relate to its focus on how the knowledge is controlled and legitimized and its neglect of the equally important process of its acquisition. However, Marx's claim that education in a 'capitalist society' is a 'tool of ruling class interest', does direct one to examine the relation between the interests of economically dominant groups and the prevailing ideas of education as 'good' or 'worthwhile' in itself. It follows that the dominant emphasis of the education systems of capitalist societies, which might be described as the competitive concern with exams, grades and degrees, can be seen as one expression of the principles of a market economy (Hellerich, 1970). It is difficult to avoid the view that while these ideas may be true up to a point, they are on such a general level as to make them of limited value as starting points for the analysis of elite curricula. They do not point to explanations of the dynamics and particular configurations of different curricula.

However, the Italian Marxist Antonio Gramsci was more specifically concerned with education, and although only fragments of his work (Gramsci, 1957, 1967) are available in English, his primary concern with both the role of intellectuals (and by implication 'their kind of knowledge') and what he called the cultural hegemony which he saw as imposed on the working classes who are thus prevented from thinking for themselves, is important for any consideration of the content of education. Two aspects of Gramsci's thought that I refer to below are no more than illustrative and do not claim to be necessarily his most important ideas. His deep interest in the role of intellectuals in different kinds of society led him to consider many of the educational distinctions which we take for granted as historical products. They therefore become not 'given' but open to explanation and change. Examples such as 'theory' and 'practice', creation and propagation of knowledge (or in contemporary terms 'teaching' and 'research'), and what he calls the 'laws of scholarship' and the 'limits of scientific research' are all unexamined parts of the framework within which most formal education takes place. The second aspect relates to his distinction between 'common sense' and 'philosophy' in which he sees that some people's common sense becomes formally recognized as philosophy, and other people's does not, depending on their access to certain institutional contexts. This suggests that sociologists should raise the wider question of the relation between school knowledge and commonsense knowledge, of how, as Gramsci suggests, knowledge available to certain groups becomes 'school knowledge' or 'educational' and that available to others does not.

The most interesting recent attempt within a Marxist framework is that of Anderson (1969) in which he attempts to relate the content of the humanities in English academic curricula to the historical development of the class struggle. It is relatively easy and not very helpful to show that the examples of English culture that he takes are not representative and are selected to suit his thesis. However, a more important theoretical weakness is in his claim to a *structural analysis*, which seems unwittingly to exhibit the same flaws as most functional analyses of institutions. It emphasizes the interrelations of existing patterns of culture rather than seeing them as developing through the interaction of competing beliefs and ideas in the context of developing knowledge and a changing institutional setting. This 'structural' analysis allows Anderson to treat cases that do not fit as 'deviant' and not in need of explanation, another parallel with functional theories.

With a neo-Marxist framework, Williams (1961) provides perhaps the most promising and (by sociologists) most neglected approach to the study of the content of education. He distinguishes four distinct sets of educational philosophies or ideologies which rationalize different emphases in the selection of the content of curricula, and relates these to the social position of those who hold them. He then suggests that curricula changes have reflected the relative power of the different groups over the last hundred years. These can conveniently be summarized in the table below. He makes the significant point that the last of the foci was only recognized as legitimate outside the formal educational system. It is paradoxical when one considers the persisting subordinate position of the manual worker, that aspects of the populist educational ideology are now being 'resurrected' not by manual workers but in student demands for participation in the planning of curricula of universities,[18] institutions to which only about 3% of the sons of manual workers ever attain.

| Ideology | Social position | Educational policies |
|---|---|---|
| 1. Liberal/ conservative | Aristocracy/gentry | Non-vocational—the 'educated' man, an emphasis on character |
| 2. Bourgeois | Merchant and professional classes | Higher vocational and professional courses. Education as access to desired positions |
| 3. Democratic | Radical reformers | Expansionist—'education for all' |
| 4. Populist/ proletarian | Working classes/ subordinate groups | Student relevance, choice, participation |

In placing curricular developments in their historical context, Williams's chapter is original and insightful though inevitably lacking in substantive evidence. It is only regrettable that in the nine intervening years no sociologist has followed it up. Perhaps the greatest weaknesses of the approach are that little attention is given to the changing power relations between the groups which might account for curricular changes, and one is left in doubt as to how the 'democratic' and 'bourgeois' ideologies arise from what would appear to be the same social group. Other attempts have been made to develop more systematically the Marxist concept of ideology for empirical research, though not primarily in the field of education. However, one study which warrants note in the context of this paper is Mills's (1943) early account of the professional ideology of social problem-orientated sociologists in the twenties and thirties. He characterized their 'common thought style' from a content analysis of a wide range of popular texts, and showed the relation of this to their common social origins and professional experience. It is a model study of how to relate complex empirical data to a theoretical perspective in order to show how, in this case, university sociology syllabuses developed at a particular time. It would seem to have relevance as an approach, given the dominating influence of textbooks on secondary education, to a wide range of knowledge areas, particularly in the humanities.

## B. The Weberian Contribution

Max Weber's ideas (and not only his writings on bureaucracy) have not been neglected by sociologists of education, for the well-known analyses of the changing function of universities have been based on his ideal-types of the 'expert' and the 'cultivated man'.[19] However, with the exception of Musgrove,[20] the possibilities of his work for posing questions about the selection and organization of knowledge have not been examined. I shall not try here to redress the balance, but refer by way of illustration to his study of Confucian education.[21] Weber identified three characteristics of the education of the Chinese literati (or administrators):

1. An emphasis on propriety and 'bookishness', with a curriculum largely restricted to the learning and memorizing of classical texts.
2. This curriculum was a very narrow selection from the available knowledge in a society where mathematicians, astronomers, scientists, and geographers were not uncommon. However, all these fields of knowledge were classified by the literati as 'vulgar', or perhaps in more contemporary terms 'non-academic'.
3. Entry into the administrative elite was controlled by examinations on this narrow curriculum, so that the 'non-bookish' were for the purposes of the Chinese society of the time 'not educated'.

Weber explains this curriculum selection by relating it to the characteristics of what he called the patrimonial bureaucracy, in which administration was carried out by referring to the classical texts. Any change in curriculum would have undermined the legitimacy of the power of the administration whose skills therefore had to be defined as 'absolute'. As the whole question is secondary to Weber's main interest in comparative religion, we do not get suggestions as to the relationships of those with access to 'non-bookish' knowledge, and the possibility of their forming a competing power group with a radically different definition of education. Drawing on Weber, Wilkinson (1964) has a similar thesis about the classical curriculum of the nineteenth-century English public schools. Both writers are suggesting that curricula are defined in terms of the dominant group's idea of the 'educated man', which directs us back to the question raised implicitly earlier as to what model of the educated man is implicit in the 'worthwhile activities' or 'forms of understanding' of contemporary philosophies of education. Each of these studies, like Ben-David's (1963) interesting comparison of the relative influence of local pressure groups and elite values on American and English university curricula, are limited by the lack of an overall framework for linking the principles of selection of content to the social structure. However, both Weber and Ben-David, as well as a recent symposium on elite education (Wilkinson, 1969), point to the value of comparative studies in suggesting how different definitions of legitimate academic study arise and persist.

## C. Durkheim

His specific works on education, apart from the emphasis on the social nature of curricula and pedagogy, are not very helpful, though it is important to remember that these books are collections of his lectures to student teachers and not systematic studies in sociology. The familiar criticisms, which do not need elaborating, are however applicable—firstly, his undifferentiated view of society which blurs the culture/social structure distinction and assumes them to be either synonymous or congruent or functionally related; and secondly, an over-emphasis on the value-component of education which he envisages as having a primarily integrative rather than stratifying and differentiating function. However, recent writers such as Bourdieu (1967) and Bernstein (1967) have focused on Durkheim's work as a whole and suggested that it is his work on religion and primitive classification (Durkheim and Mauss, 1963) leading indirectly to a sociology of knowledge that are of most significance for the sociological study of education. Bourdieu suggests that there is an analogy between Durkheim's account of the social origins of the categories of thought in small-scale societies with the development of thought categories through the process of transmission of culture in the school. Implicit in this process of transmission are criteria of what is topical, and the legitimacy of a hierarchy of 'study objects' becomes built into categories of thought themselves. Bernstein's work will be referred to in more detail later in the paper, but it is worth pointing out that he has extended Durkheim's work in two ways that are important here. He has elaborated the link between social change (mechanical to organic solidarity) and cultural change (the move from collection to integrated-type curricula) and secondly, by emphasizing language and the curriculum he has moved the Durkheimian approach to education to the cognitive as well as the evaluative level.

To summarize this section, an attempt has been made to show that sociological research drawing on the Marxist, Weberian and Durkheimian traditions can contribute to a reorientation of the sociology of education that would no longer neglect curricula nor, as Talcott Parsons treats 'power', consider it as an epiphenomenon.

## 4

The previous section has, from different points of view, suggested that consideration of the assumptions underlying the selection and organization of knowledge by those in positions of power may be a fruitful perspective for raising sociological question about curricula. We can make this more explicit by starting with the assumptions that those in positions of power will attempt to define what is to be taken as knowledge, how accessible to different groups any knowledge is, and what are the accepted relationships between different knowledge areas and between those who have access to them and make them available. It is thus the exploration of how these processes happen, since they tend in other than pre-literate societies to take place in and through educational institutions, that should form the focus of a sociology of education. Our understanding of the processes is so rudimentary at present, that it is doubtful if we can postulate any clear links between the organization of knowledge at the level of social structure and the process as it involves teachers in classrooms. However, from these assumptions we can, drawing on Bernstein (1968), pose three interrelated questions about how knowledge is organized in curricula.

1.) The power of some to define what is 'valued' knowledge leads to problems of accounting for how 'stratified' knowledge is and by what criteria. Implicit in this idea of 'stratification of knowledge' is the distinction between the 'prestige' and the 'property' components of stratification. To the former are linked the different social evaluations placed on different knowledge areas,[22] and to the latter are the notions of 'ownership' and freedom (or restriction of access).[23] Thus the 'property' aspect of stratification points to 'knowledge' in use, and the reward structure associated with it. It suggests that in different societies the dominant conception of knowledge may be akin to 'private property', property shared by particular groups, or communally available on the analogy of 'common land'. The analysis which follows implicitly places greater emphasis on the prestige component of the stratification of knowledge. This is in part because the focus of the analysis is on curricula in one society rather than across societies, when it would become easier to conceptualize different definitions of 'knowledge as property'.

2.) The restriction of the accessibility of knowledge areas to different groups, poses the question in relation to curricula as to what is the *scope* of curricula available to different age groups, and more specifically to the social factors influencing the degree and kind of specialization at any age level.

3.) Earlier in the paper I raised the question as to what fields of enquiry were, at different times and in different cultures, embraced by a term like 'science'. More broadly this raises the question of the relation between knowledge areas and between those with access to them.

It may be useful to conceive of these three questions dichotomously and to represent the possible curricular alternative diagrammatically. (See table on opposite page.)

Bernstein's two ideal-type curricula, the 'integrated' and 'collection' types (1968) are shown to include different sub-types in which the stratification and specialization of knowledge is high or low. The conceptual structure implicit in the diagram was suggested by Bernstein (1968, 1971), though he concentrates his analysis primarily on types 4 and 5 and some of their 'variants' on account of their obvious historical significance. While it is not suggested, as some typologists do, that we should expect to find all of the types, it might be valuable to speculate on the conditions that we would expect to give rise to the various types.[24]

The expansion of knowledge, and the access to it, is paralleled by its increasing differentiation. *Empirically* we could no doubt also demonstrate that increasing differentiation is a necessary condition for some groups to be in a position to legitimize 'their knowledge' as superior or of high value. This high value is institutionalized by the creation of formal educational establishments to 'transmit' it to specially selected members of the society. Thus highly-valued knowledge becomes enshrined in the academy or school and provides a standard against which all else that is known is compared. That this description is analogous to the process described by Davis and Moore (1945) when discussing social

*Dimensions of the Social Organization*
*of Knowledge in Curricula*

How related are the knowledge areas ? (openness)

| What is the scope of knowledge areas ? (degree of specialization) | | OPEN | | CLOSED | |
|---|---|---|---|---|---|
| | | NARROW (specialized) | BROAD | NARROW | BROAD (unspecialized) |
| How stratified are the knowledge areas ? (degree of stratification) | HIGH | I | 2 | 5 | 6 |
| | LOW | 3 | 4 | 7 | 8 |

[alternatives 1–4 represent 'integrated' types and 5–8 represent 'collection' types in Bernstein's terminology]

stratification is not unintended; the limitations of the latter point also to those of the analysis presented above. The important point, made originally by Buckley (1958), is that, though empirically differential social evaluation often follows from increasing differentiation, there is no necessary relationship between the two processes. In other words the pattern of social evaluation must be explained, independently of the process of differentiation, in terms of the restricted access to certain kinds of knowledge and the opportunity for those who have access to them to legitimize their higher status and control their availability.

The framework presented focuses on the principles of organization and selection of knowledge and only implicitly suggests how these are related to the social structure. The sociological assumption is that the most explicit relation between the dominant institutional order and the organization of knowledge will be on the dimension of stratification; moves therefore to 'destratify' or give equal value to different kinds of knowledge, or 'restratify' (moves to legitimize other criteria of evaluation), by posing a threat to the power structure of that 'order', will be resisted. This proposition is made on a very general level to which two qualifications should be made. Firstly, the notion of a dominant institutional order implies that among various economic, political, bureaucratic, cultural and educational interest groups which make up such an order, there is a consensus on the definitions of knowledge which is only likely under certain specific conditions. One would imagine, for example, that business and academic elites would not, except if faced with a common threat, share assumptions in their definitions of knowledge (see for example Thompson, 1970). Secondly, although one can trace historically (Williams, 1961; Birnbaum, 1970), some of the mechanisms of resistance and change, and also explore them in case studies at the organizational and interactional level, we still lack, as was indicated earlier, a way of conceptualizing the relationship between these levels.

Similarly, movements to make the scope of knowledge in a curriculum less restricted (a decrease in specialization), and the relations between knowledge areas more 'open', will also pose threats to the patterns of social relations implicit in the more restricted and less open forms, and likewise will be resisted.[25] It should therefore be possible to account for the persistence of some characteristics, particularly of academic curricula, and the changes of others in terms of whether they involve changes in either the criteria of evaluation of knowledge, or its scope or relations.[26] I want to suggest, therefore, that it may be through this idea of the stratification of knowledge that we can suggest relations between the patterns of dominant values and the distribution of rewards and power, and the organization of knowledge. Such analysis would be necessary both historically and cross-culturally on the societal level[27] and also at different age levels and in different knowledge areas.[28]

Academic curricula in this country involve assumptions that some kinds and areas of knowledge are much more 'worthwhile' than others: that as soon as possible all knowledge should become specialized and with minimum explicit emphasis on the relations between the subjects specialized in and between the specialist teachers involved. It may be useful, therefore, to view curricular changes as involving changing definitions of knowledge along one or more of the dimensions towards a less or more stratified, specialized and open organization of knowledge. Further, that as we assume some patterns of social relations associated with any curriculum, these changes will be resisted in so far as they are perceived to undermine the values, relative power and privileges of the dominant groups involved.

Before looking in more detail at the stratification of knowledge, I should like to indicate by examples the kind of questions that the ideas of scope and openness suggest.[29] First, *scope*: by referring to the degree of specialization, we are by implication concerned with the distribution of resources (pupil and teacher time, resources and materials).[30] This suggests why, in spite of much publicity to the contrary, specialization is so firmly entrenched. Its institutional basis in the schools would seem an important area of sociological enquiry.[31] Let us take as an illustration recent changes in medical and engineering curricula, which bring out the ways in which the characteristics and content of curricula are influenced by the changing values and interests of the controlling groups involved.

One feature that medical and engineering curricula have in common is that those controlling them have recently appeared concerned to introduce a social science component into the courses. In the absence of research, one can only speculate about the changing definitions of socially relevant knowledge involved in this broadening of the curriculum. Conceivably, these changes reflect a change in the position of the engineer and doctor, who both find themselves working increasingly in large organizations isolated from the direct consequences of their work, but still subject to public criticisms of what they do. The significance of this example is to point out the way changes in the social or occupational structure may influence definitions of relevant knowledge and thus curricula.

Turning to the question of *openness*; there are critical research problems here, for the idea of curricula consisting of knowledge areas in 'open' or closed relation to each other presupposes that definitions of knowledge areas or 'subjects' are not problematic. It is important to recognize that 'subjects' or, even as was suggested earlier in this paper, broad fields like 'arts' and 'sciences', though they may be part of educators' taken for granted world, cannot be seen as such by sociologists. However, in order to conceptualize the changing relationships between teachers, some assumptions have to be made, and it may be valuable as an illustration of the utility of the framework to point to some of the differences that are likely to arise from 'integration' in the 'arts' and in the 'sciences'. The characteristic of all teaching of sciences at any level is that however strong subject loyalties and identification may be (and this is likely to be closely associated with the level of teaching), those teaching do tend to share implicitly or explicitly norms and values which define what science is about, and thus chemistry, physics and biology are at one level 'integrated'. It is not surprising, therefore, that in an area of the academic curriculum not striking for its innovations, the VIth form, both biological and physical sciences are increasingly taught as fully-integrated courses. An indication of the significance of the stratification dimension of knowledge is that the core base of the former is biochemistry and of the latter is mathematics: both high-status knowledge fields among scientists. Evidence of the different situation that arises when attempts to integrate appear to reduce the status of the knowledge is the failure of the general science movement after World War II. Whereas the physicist and biologist share a fairly explicit set of values through being scientists, it is doubtful if being in the 'humanities' has any common meaning for historians, geographers and those in English and foreign languages.* In this case, any movement to 'integration' involves the construction of new values to replace subject identities. It is not surprising that this side of the academic VIth-form curriculum has undergone very little change.

The third question that was raised about the organization of knowledge concerned how far and by what criteria were different knowledge areas *stratified*. I would argue that it is the most important, for it is through this idea that we

* Except in the situation where they all see themselves competing for resources with the scientists.

are led to consider the social basis of different kinds of knowledge and we can begin to raise questions about relations between the power structure and curricula, the access to knowledge and the opportunities to legitimize it as 'superior', and the relation between knowledge and its functions in different kinds of society.

If knowledge is highly stratified there will be a clear distinction between what is taken to count as knowledge, and what is not, on the basis of which processes of selection and exclusion for curricula will take place. It would follow that this type of curricular organization presupposes and serves to legitimate a rigid hierarchy between teacher and taught, for if not, some access to control by the pupils would be implied, and thus the processes of exclusion and selection would become open for modification and change. The degree to which this model characterizes the contemporary university and its implications for student movements would seem worth exploring. A further point is that access to control by pupils or students implies that alternative definitions of knowledge are available to them. It would be useful to examine the conditions under which such alternative definitions were available, and to compare different age groups, and different areas of study.

So taken for granted by most educators is the model referred to in the previous paragraph, that it is difficult to conceive of the possibility of a curriculum based on knowledge which is differentiated but not stratified. That it poses a revolutionary alternative is apparent, when one considers whether the terms teacher, pupil and examination in the sense normally used would have any meaning at all. It suggests that assumptions about the stratification of knowledge are implicit in our ideas of what education 'is' and what teachers 'are'.

As previously suggested, the contemporary British educational system is dominated by academic curricula with a rigid stratification of knowledge. It follows that if teachers and children are socialized within an institutionalized structure which legitimates such assumptions, then for teachers, high status (and rewards) will be associated with areas of the curriculum that are 1) formally assessed, 2) taught to the 'ablest' children, 3) taught in homogeneous ability groups of children who show themselves most successful within such curricula.

Two other implications follow which would seem to warrant exploration.

1.) If pupils do identify high-status knowledge as suggested, and assume that the characteristics of 'worthwhile knowledge' to be that it is taught in 'sets', formally examined, and not studied by the 'less able', they could well come to reject curricular and pedagogic innovations which necessarily involve changing definitions of relevant knowledge and teaching methods.

2.) If the criteria of high-status knowledge are associated with the value of the dominant interest groups, particularly the universities, one would expect maximum resistance to any change of the high status of knowledge associated with academic curricula. This, as I shall elaborate on later, is supported by evidence of the Schools Council proposals for curriculum reform. The Council has accepted the existing stratification of knowledge and produces most of its recommendations for reform in the low-status knowledge areas. These are associated with curricula which are for the young and less able and do not undermine the interests of those in positions of power in the social structure.

Let us explore a bit further the idea of knowledge being stratified. It does suggest two kinds of questions to be asked:

1.) In any society, by what criteria are different areas of, kinds of and approaches to knowledge given different social value? Those criteria will inevitably have developed in a particular social and historical context, but, if isolated, may be useful if related to social, political and economic factors in accounting for changes and resistances to changes in curricula.

2.) How can we relate the extent to which knowledge is stratified in different societies, and the kinds of criteria on which such stratification may be based,[32] to characteristics of the social structures?

The first question requires an attempt to postulate some of the common characteristics of academic curricula, and to show how, over a particular historical period, they have become legitimated as of high status by those in positions of power. As suggested earlier, these characteristics are not absolute, but sociohistorical constructs, so it is not inappropriate to draw on three strands of thinking which emphasize this. These are, first, the comparative perspective on pre- and post-literate societies (Mead, 1938); secondly, consideration of the consequences of literacy for contemporary culture (Goody and Watt, 1962); and thirdly the way a gradual 'bureaucratization' of the education systems of industrializing societies has led to an increasing emphasis on 'examinations' as the most 'objective' means of assessing (and therefore identifying) 'expert' knowledge (Weber, 1952). Weber discusses the process of what he calls the 'bureaucratic domination of the nature of education'. He implicitly suggests that the major constraint on what counts as knowledge in society will be whether it can be 'objectively assessed'.[33] There is an interesting and not entirely fortuitous parallel with Kelvin's sentiment that 'when you cannot express it in numbers, your knowledge is of a meagre and unsatisfactory kind'[34] in the idea implicit in contemporary education that 'if you cannot examine it, it's not worth knowing'.[35] The way formal examinations place an increasing emphasis on literacy rather than oral expression is raised by Davie (1961), and the implications of the 'literate' character of modern culture brought out by Goody and Watt (1962). They argue that so great is the discontinuity or even the contradictions between the private oral traditions of family and home and the public literate tradition of the school that 'literate skills form one of the major axes of differentiation in industrial societies'. They go on to suggest that reading and writing (which are the activities which occupy most of the timetable of most of those being educated) are inevitably solitary activities, and so a literate culture brings with it an increasing individualization. This individualization is symbolized in its most dramatic form in the various ways in which those being educated are assessed or examined.

In comparing literate and non-literate cultures Goody and Watt suggest that the peculiar characteristics of the former are 'an abstraction which disregards an individual's social experience . . . and a compartmentalization of knowledge which restricts the kind of connections which the individual can establish and ratify with the natural and social world'.[36] The final point they make is how most knowledge in a literate culture is fundamentally at odds with that of daily life and common experience. In discussing the way educational emphases have moved from 'learning' to 'teaching', Mead (1938) brings out a related point, when she links the idea of groups holding some kinds of knowledge as superior and the notion of 'a hierarchical arrangement of cultural views of experience', to the increasing emphasis on changing the beliefs, habits, knowledge, ideas and allegiances that children bring with them to school.

Over-simplifying, we can draw together the main ideas of the previous paragraphs to suggest the dominant characteristics of high-status knowledge, which we will hypothesize as the organizing principles underlying academic curricula. These are literacy, or an emphasis on written as opposed to oral presentation; individualism (or avoidance of group work or co-operativeness,[37] which focuses on how academic work is assessed and is a characteristic of both the 'process' of knowing and the way the 'product' is presented; abstractness of the knowledge and its structuring and compartmentalizing independently of the knowledge of the learner;[38] finally and linked to the former is what I have called the unrelatedness of academic curricula, which refers to the extent to which they are 'at odds' with daily life and common experience.[39]

If status of knowledge is accorded in terms of these criteria, academic curricula would be organized on such principles; in other words they will tend to be abstract, highly literate, individualistic and unrelated to non-school knowledge. It may also be useful as a preliminary way of posing questions to see curricula ranked on these characteristics which then become four dimensions in terms of which knowledge is stratified. Thus one can suggest conditions under which (non-academic) curricula will be organized in terms of oral presentation, group activity and assessment, concreteness of the knowledge involved and its relatedness to non-school knowledge.

One way is to view these characteristics as the specific historical consequences of an education system based on a model of bookish learning for medieval priests which was extended first to lawyers and doctors, and increasingly has come to dominate all education of older age groups in industrial societies (Goodman, 1969a). However, their use to sociologists may be to highlight the unquestioned dimensions of academic curricula—to elaborate—these characteristics can be seen as social definitions of educational value, and thus become problematic in the sense that if they persist it is not because knowledge is in any meaningful way best made available according to the criteria they represent, but because they are conscious or unconscious cultural choices which accord with the values and beliefs of dominant groups at a particular time.[40] It is thus in terms of these choices that educational success and failure are defined. One might speculate that it is not that particular skills and competences are associated with highly-valued occupations because some occupations 'need' recruits with knowledge defined and assessed in this way. Rather it is suggested that any very different cultural choices, or the granting of equal status to sets of cultural choices that reflect variations in terms of the suggested characteristics, would involve a massive redistribution of the labels 'educational' 'success' and 'failure', and thus also a parallel redistribution of rewards in terms of wealth, prestige and power.

Two important limitations of this approach must be mentioned; firstly, not only are the categories highly tentative but they are formal, and no operational rules are suggested with direct relevance to analysing questions of substantive content.[41] Their use in the analysis of texts, syllabi, reports, exam questions 'marking' criteria and the day-to-day activities of the classroom would lead either to narrower but more substantive categories, or their modification, depending on the nature of the research problem posed. Secondly, by its primary emphasis on the social organization and not the social functions of knowledge, this approach does not make explicit that access to certain kinds of knowledge is also potential access to the means of changing the criteria of social evaluation of knowledge itself and therefore to the possibility of creating new knowledge, as well as the means of preserving these criteria. However, changing criteria involve social actions which inevitably are concrete, corporate and related as well as involving oral as well as written communication. Perhaps it is through the disvaluing of social action and the elevation of the value placed on 'knowledge for its own sake' through the separation of knowledge from action, well symbolized by the values implicit in such distinctions as 'pure and applied' and 'theory and practice', that knowledge of social alternatives in our educational system is both restricted and, when available, is perceived as 'alternatives in theory'.[42] However, we can illustrate some more specific ways in which this approach might be useful for a sociology of educational knowledge:

1.) If the relations between the patterns of domination and the organization of knowledge are as have been suggested, one would only expect a reduction in specialization for any particular age group, an increase in inter-subject integration, or a widening of the criteria of social evaluation of knowledge, if they were to follow or be closely dependent on changes in these patterns of domination.[43]

If we assume the absence of such changes we would expect most so-called 'curricular innovations' to be of two kinds:

a.) Those in which existing academic curricula are modified but there is no change in the existing social evaluation of knowledge.[44]

Two examples are the new Nuffield 'O' level science syllabuses and the integrated science projects referred to earlier. A significant research problem would be to examine the influence of the Nuffield sponsors, the Science Masters' Association (now the Association for Science Education, and an organization which has close links with the universities and traditionally an active membership drawn largely from public, direct-grant and grammar schools with large science VIths) and the university advisors, which led to the Nuffield Project being directed, in the first place, to 'O' level, which is taken by a maximum of 30% of pupils, rather than to reforming secondary school science as a whole.

b.) 'Innovations' which disregard the social evaluations implicit in British academic curricula, but are restricted in their availability to less able pupils.

In becoming the major sponsor for such innovations, the Schools Council can be seen as legitimizing the existing organization of knowledge in two ways.

Firstly, by taking the assumptions of the academic curricula for granted, the social evaluations of knowledge implicit in such curricula are by implication being assumed to be in some sense 'absolute' and therefore not open to enquiry. Secondly, by creating new courses in 'low status' knowledge areas, and restricting their availability to those who have already 'failed' in terms of academic definitions of knowledge, these failures are seen as individual failures, either of motivation, ability or circumstances, and not failures of the academic system itself. These courses, which explicitly deny pupils access to the kinds of knowledge which are associated with rewards, prestige and power in our society are thus given a kind of legitimacy, which masks the fact that educational success in terms of them would still be defined as 'failure'. The link with teachers' definitions of the raising of the school leaving age as being a problem of social control rather than of intellectual development is not difficult to see.

2.) It should be fruitful to explore the syllabus construction of knowledge practitioners in terms of their efforts to enhance or maintain their academic legitimacy. Some examples worth investigation would be the various professional examining bodies, the attempts to obtain university entrance recognition for new knowledge areas, and the presentation of previously non-degree knowledge areas (particularly technical and administrative fields, art, dance and physical education) as suitable for degree status.[45]

Returning to the second question of this section, which was concerned with how we account for the criteria implicit in the different ways knowledge is stratified, we do not know how relations between the economy and the educational system produce different degrees and kinds of stratification of knowledge. It is possible to trace schematically a set of stages from non-literate societies where educational institutions are not differentiated from other institutions, to feudal type societies where formal education in separate schools is almost entirely restricted to a priestly caste, and, through the church ownership of land, such schools remained largely independent (at least in regard to the curricula) of the economic and political processes of the time. Gradually schools and colleges became increasingly differentiated and dependent on the economies of the societies they were in, when clearly the dominant economic and political orders became the major determinants of the stratification of knowledge. Comparative studies of educational arrangements in developing countries might shed light on these relationships in more detail. One way would be to compare the kinds of knowledge stratification in countries like North Korea where the schools are less separate from the economy and many activities of learning are also activities of production, with systems like our own where in school nothing is 'for real', even in the workshops.

To sum up, then, an attempt has been made to offer a sociological approach to the organization of knowledge in curricula. The inevitably limited and schematic nature of the outline presented together with the total lack of research by sociologists in the field turns us back to the question posed at the beginning of this paper. Why no sociology of the curriculum? Perhaps the organization of knowledge implicit in our own curricula is so much part of our taken for granted world that we are unable to conceive of alternatives. Are we then reluctant to accept that academic curricula and the forms of assessment associated with them are sociological inventions to be explained like men's other inventions, mechanical and sociological?

## ACKNOWLEDGEMENTS

I should like to thank my colleagues, Basil Bernstein and Brian Davies for their comments of earlier drafts, and to express my appreciation to them and the other members of the departmental seminar for the valuable discussion that arose out of some of the preliminary ideas in this paper. A similar debt is owed to those graduate students of the department with whom I have benefited from many discussions around the themes of this paper. This extended and revised version owes much to the many hours of discussion I had with Basil Bernstein, whose constructive criticisms I only came to appreciate fully when it came to re-writing. Also I have continued to learn much from my graduate students, in particular, Nell Keddie and Geoff Esland.

## NOTES AND REFERENCES

[1] The title would imply that we can make statements about curricula in general which when one considers the diversities within even one education system, would seem unwarranted. In effect, the paper focuses largely on what is commonly called the 'academic curriculum' of secondary and higher education in England. The relevance of any of the general ideas presented for infant and junior curricula or the various technical courses available must remain doubtful.

[2] These ideas represent a development from a preliminary attempt by the author (Young, 1967) to begin a 'sociology of the curriculum'. Here the analogy between explanations of 'educational failure' and 'deviance' in contemporary sociology is explored in more detail.

[3] A detailed historical study of the social composition of the groups involved and the social and political circumstances in which their educational ideas developed and influenced 'educational practice' would make an important contribution to our understanding of the origins, persistence and change of educational ideologies. Banks (1955) and Taylor (1963) are perhaps the only significant attempts to carry out such a study in this country. Each, however, is limited by an implicit conceptual framework which takes 'academic knowledge' as 'given' rather than 'to be explained'.

The unsatisfactory use of the concept 'educational ideology' in the literature stems in large part from a lack of substantive studies, but in part also from the failure to relate the sets of beliefs, their social contexts and their implications for practical action. Those using the concept have either, like Hoare (1967), Burnett and Palmer (1967) and D. I. Davies (1969), relied on broad 'political' categories without demonstrating that they have any necessary 'educational' implications, or like Brameld (1967) have developed typologies of educational ideas without linking them to either a theory of social change or to the social origins of those who are assumed to have held them. It seems likely that the more limited approach of exploring how 'beliefs' about children implicit in psychological theories become institutionalized and situationally significant in providing 'explanations' for various curricular and pedagogic practices, may be more fruitful (Friedman, 1967; Eastman, 1967; Esland, 1970).

[4] This 'inefficiency' refers to the evidence collected or summarized by writers such as Vernon (1957) and Westergaard and Little (1964) concerning the arbitrariness of the 11+ (in terms of predicting future attainment) and the discrepancy between the distribution of opportunity for selective education and the distribution of *measured* intelligence that has been produced by the 11+; in neither case does one find serious counter-claims in the literature. The 'injustice' presupposes that some other administrative technique which

would replace the 11+ (e.g. parental 'choice', teacher recommendation, 'flexible grouping in non-selective secondary schools'), would be both 'less arbitrary' and in some sense 'fairer'. The evidence, such as it is, points to the opposite being as likely an outcome of the change (Floud, 1957; Douglas, 1969; Ford, 1969).

5 The possible explanations of why such studies have focused on 'pupil subcultures' is discussed fully elsewhere (W. B. Davies, 1970; Seaman, 1970). In this context it is perhaps worth pointing out that as in the earlier phase of the educational debate which focused on 'equality' and 'wastage', the sociological definition of the problem complements those of teachers and research sponsors. In this case the problem is one of 'control' of pupils, which leads to a concern to isolate their common characteristics. These are conceptualized as the 'subculture', particularly of the least 'controllable' pupils. Though there is much more in each study, this is the primary emphasis of both Hargreaves (1968) and Lacey (1970).

6 The financing of a new statutory body, the Schools Council, with responsibility for sponsoring curriculum development 'projects', and having specific powers over how secondary school children are examined, is itself an indication of an increasing political concern over the control of educational knowledge. The Schools Council's much-publicized 'autonomy' from the D.E.S., together with the recruitment of 'practising teachers' on to its staff and committees, suggests an attempt to deny that the Schools Council marks anything other than an extension by teachers of their 'traditional' control over the curriculum.

7 This point needs exploring in specific circumstances, but might be illustrated by referring to examples from other kinds of institutions. With regard to the Church, we might consider the Vatican's resistance to allowing celibacy and 'natural law' to be on the agenda of the Bishops' Conference. A similar example was the persistent refusal of those controlling the Anglican Lambeth Conference to allow 'freemasonry" to be discussed. Other examples from political parties would also point to the way legitimate areas of discussion are defined by existing hierarchies.

8 It is ironical that the one outstanding study, which looks at the various social, cultural and institutional factors influencing the organization of knowledge, is by a philosopher, G. E. Davie. His study of curricular change in the nineteenth-century Scottish universities raises many of the issues about selection of content and relation between areas of knowledge that are considered later in the paper (Davie, 1961).

9 The analogy between explanations of 'deviancy' and 'educability' which take social class as their independent variable is explored in more detail (Young, 1967). The analogy points to how both explanations rely on similar functionalist presuppositions which, in each case, demonstrate the significance of *social class*, but are unable to account for the process through which this significance is active.

10 For example Swift (1969) and Shipman (1968).

11 One of the few empirical studies to attempt this is Burton Clark's *Open Door College* (1961).

12 See Burton Clark (1960).

13 See Gross, *et al.* (1957).

14 Cicourel and Kitsuse (1963b), Becker, *et al.* (1961, 1969).

15 Child (1943).

16 A useful outline of trends in the sociology of knowledge which implicitly makes this point is given by Bottomore (1956).

17 Blake (1968).

18 The most dramatic example has been the development of demands for black studies courses in the U.S.A.

19 Halsey (1960).

20 Musgrove (1968).

21 Weber (1952).

22 By the use of such terms as 'academic', 'pure', 'theoretical', etc.

23 I am referring here to the secret knowledge that 'professionals' protect as if it was their own.

24 A much more detailed analysis than those yet available, of the genesis of examples of any particular curricular-types, would be a necessary preliminary to such an exercise.

25 It may be possible to examine the whole history of the arguments about secondary school specialization from Crowther (1959) and Petersen (1960) to today in this perspective.

26 An illustration of this is to compare the resistance to the introduction of new know-

ledge areas for the curriculum for the same age group in different institutions (e.g. the grammar school VIth form and the College of Further Education).

[27] The work of Ben-David (1963), Davie (1961) and Rothblatt (1969) is a valuable beginning in this direction.

[28] Perhaps the only significant study here is that of Reisman, Gusfield and Gamson (1970 in press).

[29] The possible implications of this specialization and the degree of insulation between what is studied as well as of changes are explored in detail by Bernstein (1971).

[30] It is a paradox of the English educational system worth exploring, that while those most in need of education get least of it, those with the longest educational careers have curricula of the most limited scope.

[31] Studies relating the career structure of teachers in different knowledge areas and the strategies of the various subject-based associations would be one possible way of exploring this question empirically.

[32] Ben-David (1963) in comparing university curricula in the U.S.A., U.S.S.R. and U.K., among other countries, shows wide variations in the criteria on which the stratification of knowledge is based in different countries.

[33] There are two ways in which Weber's discussion is unsatisfactory, both of which raise important questions for any sociological research on examinations. First he took for granted that process by which some activities are selected as 'worth objective assessment', a prior question to his consideration of the 'effects' of examinations. Secondly the notion of what is meant by the 'objectivity' of examinations is left unexplored. The point touched on briefly elsewhere about the priority given to 'knowledge as product' as opposed to 'knowing as process' is only one aspect of this.

[34] Curiously but significantly on the façade of the University of Chicago Social Science Research Building!

[35] The fact that non-examined curricula are relegated to 'leisure' courses, liberal and general studies, and courses for the 'less able' is indicative of the implicit validity of this thesis.

[36] Goody and Watt, *op. cit.*

[37] The term *individualism* is far from satisfactory, as it is ambiguous and has a much wider meaning than is intended here.

[38] There are problems in the use of the term 'abstract' because it presupposes some kind of absolute notion of what is 'abstract', and neglects the way in which one can have different 'kinds of abstraction', some of which may be 'labelled' concrete by others using different 'abstraction' criteria. Horton (1967, 1968) explores this question indirectly, but it is an area that sociologists have too readily taken as not requiring research. While 'abstractness' seems to be a satisfactory category for describing academic curricula, the problems raised by Horton mean that as an analytic category it presupposes just those assumptions that one would want to treat as problematic. It may be possible to reconceptualize the problem by treating 'abstractness' as an 'educators' category' to be explained.

[39] See the section earlier on Gramsci for a more detailed consideration of this. The concept *'unrelatedness'* refers to a similar characteristic of formal educational systems that Henry (1960) calls 'disjunctiveness'. Again we are faced with conceptual problems, not surprisingly since the question of school and non-school knowledge has hardly been considered by sociologists. Similarly (and I am very grateful to Mr Derek Frampton of Garnett College for pointing this out to me), these categories are unable to deal with professional curricula where the knowledge is undoubtedly of high status, but not on the criteria that have been suggested in this paper.

[40] See note 31.

[41] For instance, the gradual disappearance of classics (particularly Greek) from most secondary school curricula is not accountable in these terms. Nor specifically is the changing content of school history, geography or English literature.

[42] An interesting example of the 'philosophical sleight of hand' required to reach this position appears in an otherwise excellent paper by Rytina and Loomis (1970). After criticizing Marx and Dewey for using *metaphysical* justifications of the truth of what men 'know' in terms of what men 'do', they do likewise in drawing on a *metaphysical* 'out there' in terms of which, they claim, we must check out our theories against our practice.

[43] Specific reservations were made earlier about such an all-embracing phrase.

Clearly the crucial 'dominating' factor is the limited access to higher education, which enables universities to control secondary school curricula. Limited changes, such as the breakdown of the near monopoly, by university boards, of school examinations, would be important but secondary to this.

44 Most of the discussion of curriculum reform is of this kind. In general the question is asked, given that we know our objectives, how can we more efficiently achieve them? There is an enormous literature in this field which demonstrates the concern of those who have been aptly labelled 'the curriculum mongers'* to create and institutionalize an autonomous discipline 'curriculum studies' with its own so-called 'theory', house journals and professors. Most of the writing, with the exception of parts of Miles (1964), is more informative about the writer's perspectives and beliefs than about school curricula.

45 The activities of the Council for National Academic Awards Boards of Studies would be particularly important to study in terms of the assumptions polytechnic staff have of what these boards will recognize as 'honours degree standard'.

# BIBLIOGRAPHY

ANDERSON, P. (1969). 'Patterns of National Culture' in COCKBURN, A., and ANDERSON, P. (eds.), *Student Power*. Harmondsworth: Penguin.

BACHRACH, P., and BARATZ, M. S. (1963). 'Decisions and Non-Decisions: An Analytical Framework'. *American Political Science Review*, 57(3).

BANKS, O. (1955). *Parity and Prestige in British Education*. London: Routledge & Kegan Paul.

BECKER, H. S., GEER, B., HUGHES, E., and STRAUSS, A. (1969). *Making the Grade*. New York: John Wiley & Sons.

BEN-DAVID, J. (1963). 'The Professions and the Class Structure'. *Current Sociology*, V(12) (1963–4).

BERNSTEIN, B. B. (1967). 'Open Schools, Open Society'. *New Society*, September 14, 1967.

—— (1968). 'On the Curriculum'. (Unpublished.)

—— (1971). 'On the Classification and Framing of Educational Knowledge' in YOUNG, M. F. D. (ed.), *Knowledge and Control*. London: Collier-Macmillan (Chapter 2, this volume).

BIRNBAUM, N. (1970). *The Crisis of Industrial Society*. London: Oxford University Press.

BLAKE, R. (1968). 'Karl Marx and Education'. *Annual Proceedings of the Philosophy of Education Society*.

BLAUG, M., and GANNICOTT, K. (1969). 'Manpower Forecasting since Robbins; a Science Lobby in Action'. *Higher Education Review*, Autumn.

BOTTOMORE, T. B. (1956). 'Some Reflections on *The Sociology of Knowledge*'. *British Journal of Sociology*, 7(1).

BOURDIEU, P. (1967). 'Systems of Education and Systems of Thought'. *International Social Science Journal*, XIX(3), and in YOUNG, M. F. D. (ed.), *Knowledge and Control*. London: Collier-Macmillan. (See Chapter 7, this volume.)

BRAMELD, T. (1967). *Education as Power*. New York: Holt, Rinehart & Winston.

BUCKLEY, W. (1958). 'Social Stratification and the Functional Theory of Stratification'. *American Sociological Review*, 23.

CARTER, M. P. (1967). *A Report of a Survey of Sociological Research in Britain*. British Sociological Association.

CHILD, A. (1943). 'On the Theoretical Possibility of the Sociology of Knowledge'. *Ethics*, 51.

* The term was first suggested by John White (Department of Philosophy, University of London Institute of Education), in an article with that title in *New Society* (March 1969).

CICOUREL, A., and KITSUSE, J. I. (1963a). 'A Note on the Use of Official Statistics'. *Social Problems*, II.

—— (1963b). *The Educational Decision Makers*. Indianapolis: Bobbs-Merrill.

CLARK, B. R. (1960). *The Open Door College*. New York: McGraw-Hill.

COX, C. B. and DYSON, A. E. (1969a). 'The Fight for Education'. *Black Paper* 1 *Critical Quarterly*.

—— (1969b). 'The Crisis in Education'. *Black Paper* 2 *Critical Quarterly*.

CREMIN, L. (1964). *The Transformation of the School*. New York: Alfred A. Knopf.

CROWTHER, G. (1959). *15-18th Report of the Central Advisory Council for Education*. London: H.M.S.O.

DAINTON, F. S. (1968). *Enquiry into the Flow of Candidates in Science and Technology into Higher Education*. London: H.M.S.O.

DAVIE, G.E. (1961). *The Democratic Intellect*. Edinburgh: Edinburgh University Press.

DAVIES, D. I. (1969). 'Education and Social Science'. *New Society*, May 8, 1969.

DAVIES, W. B. (1970). 'On the Contribution of Organizational Analysis to the Study of Educational Institutions'. To be published in the papers of the British Sociological Association Annual Conference, 1970.

DAVIS, K., and MOORE, W. E. (1945). 'Some Principles of Stratification'. *American Sociological Review*, 10(2).

DOUGLAS, J. W. B. (1969). *All Our Future*. London: Weidenfeld & Nicolson.

DURKHEIM, E., and MAUSS, M. (1963). *Primitive Classification* (R. Needham, trans.). London: Cohen & West.

EASTMAN, G. (1967). 'The Ideologizing of Theories; John Dewey, a Case in Point'. *Educational Theory*, I(1).

ESLAND, G. (1970). *Subject and Pedagogical Perspectives in Teaching*. M.A. (Ed.) thesis, University of London. (See YOUNG, M. F. D., *Knowledge and Control*. London: Collier-Macmillan, Chapter 3, this volume.)

FLOUD, J., HALSEY, A. H., and MARTIN, F. M. (1957). *Social Class and Educational Opportunity*. London: Heinemann.

FORD, J. (1969). *Social Class and the Comprehensive School*. London: Routledge & Kegan Paul.

FRIEDMAN, N. L. (1967). 'Cultural Deprivation—A Commentary in the Sociology of Knowledge'. *Journal of Educational Thought*, I, August.

GOODMAN, P. (1969a). 'The Present Moment in Education'. *New York Review of Books*, April.

—— (1969b). 'Can Technology be Human?'. *New York Review of Books*, November 1969.

GOODY, J., and WATT, I. (1962). 'The Consequences of Literacy'. *Comparative Studies in History and Society*, V(3).

GORBUTT, D. A. (1970). *Subject Choice and the 'Swing from Science', a Sociological Critique*. M.A. Thesis, University of London.

GRAMSCI, A. (1957). *The Modern Prince and Other Writings* (translation). New York: Monthly Review Press.

—— (1967). 'In Search of the Educational Principle' (translation). *New Left Review*.

GROSS, N., MASON, W. S., and MCEACHERN, A. (1957). *Explorations in Role Analysis*. New York: John Wiley & Sons.

HABERMAS, J. (1970). 'Knowledge and Interest' in EMMETT, D., and MCINTYRE, A., *Philosophical Analysis and Sociological Theory*. London: Macmillan.

HALSEY, A. H. (1960). 'The Changing Functions of Universities' in HALSEY, A. H., FLOUD, J., and ANDERSON, C. A. (eds.), *Education, Economy and Society*. New York: The Free Press.

HARGREAVES, D. (1968). *Social Relations in the Secondary School*. London: Routledge & Kegan Paul.

HELLERICH, G. (1970). 'Some Educational Implications of Karl Marx's Communism'. *Educational Forum*, May.

HENRY, J. (1960). 'Education, a Cross Cultural Outline'. *Current Anthropology*, I(4).

HIRST, P. H. (1969). 'The Logic of the Curriculum'. *Journal of Curriculum Studies*, I(2), May.

HOARE, Q. (1967). *Education; Programmes and Men.* New Left Review.

HORTON, R. (1967). 'African Traditional Thought and Western Science'. *Africa*, 67, and in YOUNG, M. F. D., *Knowledge and Control.* London: Collier-Macmillan (Chapter 8, this volume).

—— (1968). 'Neo-Tylorianism, Sound Sense or Sinister Prejudice'. *Man*, 3.

KEDDIE, N. (1970). *The Social Basis of Classroom Knowledge—A Case Study.* M.A. thesis, University of London. (See also KEDDIE, N., 'Classroom Knowledge' in YOUNG, M. F. D., *Knowledge and Control*, London: Collier-Macmillan, Chapter 5, this volume.)

KING, M. (1971). 'Reason, Tradition and Progressiveness of Science'. (To be published in *History and Theory*.)

LACEY, C. (1970). *Hightown Grammar.* Manchester: Manchester University Press.

LEFEBVRE, H. (1969). *Explosion; Marxism and the French Upheaval.* New York: Monthly Review Press.

MCPHERSON, A. (1969). ' "Swing from Science", Retreat from Reason?' *Universities Quarterly*, Winter.

MANNHEIM, K. (1936). *Ideology and Utopia* (translated by Wirth and Shib). New York: Harcourt Brace.

MEAD, M. (1938). 'Our Educational Emphases in Primitive Perspective'. *American Journal of Sociology*, 43.

MILES, M. (1964). *Innovation in Education.* New York: Teachers College Press.

MILLS, C. W. (1943). 'The Professional Ideology of Social Pathologists'. *American Journal of Sociology*, 49.

MUSGROVE, F. (1968). 'The Contribution of Sociology to the Study of Curriculum' in KERR, J. (ed.), *Changing the Curriculum.* London: University of London Press.

PETERSEN, A. D. C. (1960). 'The Myth of Subject-Mindedness'. *Universities Quarterly*, 14(3).

REISMAN, D., GUSFIELD, J., and GAMSON, Z. (1970). *Academic Values and Mass Education.* New York: Doubleday.

ROTHBLATT, S. (1969). *The Revolution of the Dons.* London: Faber & Faber.

RYTINA, J. H., and LOOMIS, C. P. (1970). 'Marxist Dialectic and Pragmatism: Power as Knowledge'. *American Sociological Review*, 35(2).

SCHAFFER, H. (1970). 'Alienation and the Sociology of Education'. *Educational Theory*.

SEAMAN, P. (1970). *On Planned Organizational Change.* M.A. thesis, University of London.

SHIPMAN, M. (1968). *Sociology of the School.* London: Longmans.

SWIFT, D. (1969). *The Sociology of Education.* London: Routledge & Kegan Paul.

TAYLOR, W. (1963). *The Secondary Modern School.* London: Faber & Faber.

THOMPSON, E. P. (1970). *Warwick University Ltd.* Harmondsworth: Penguin.

VERNON P. (1957). *Secondary School Selection.* London: Methuen.

WEBER, M. (1952). *Essays in Sociology.* Translated and edited by H. GERTH and C. W. MILLS. London: Routledge & Kegan Paul.

WESTERGAARD, J., and LITTLE, A. (1964). 'The Trend of Social Class Differentials in Educational Opportunity'. *British Journal of Sociology*, XV.

WILKINSON, R. (1964). *The Prefects.* London: Oxford University Press.

—— (1969). *Governing Elites.* London: Oxford University Press.

WILLIAMS, R. (1961). *The Long Revolution.* London: Chatto & Windus.

YOUNG, M. F. D. (1967). *Towards a Sociological Approach to the Curriculum.* M.A. thesis, University of Essex.

# 2. BASIL BERNSTEIN

## On the Classification and Framing of Educational Knowledge*

## INTRODUCTION

How a society selects, classifies, distributes, transmits and evaluates the educational knowledge it considers to be public, reflects both the distribution of power and the principles of social control. From this point of view, differences within and change in the organization, transmission and evaluation of educational knowledge should be a major area of sociological interest (Bernstein, B., 1966, 1967; Davies, I., 1969, 1970; Musgrove, F., 1968; Hoyle, E., 1969; Young, M., 1971). Indeed, such a study is a part of the larger question of the structure and changes in the structure of cultural transmission. For various reasons, British sociologists have fought shy of this question. As a result, the sociology of education has been reduced to a series of input–output problems; the school has been transformed into a complex organization or people-processing institution; the study of socialization has been trivialized.

Educational knowledge is a major regulator of the structure of experience. From this point of view, one can ask: 'How are forms of experience, identity and relation evoked, maintained and changed by the formal transmission of educational knowledge and sensitivities?' Formal educational knowledge can be considered to be realized through three message systems: curriculum, pedagogy and evaluation. Curriculum defines what counts as valid knowledge, pedagogy defines what counts as a valid transmission of knowledge, and evaluation defines what counts as a valid realization of this knowledge on the part of the taught. The term, educational knowledge code, which will be introduced later, refers to the underlying principles which shape curriculum, pedagogy and evaluation. It will be argued that the form this code takes depends upon social principles which

* First published in this volume.

47

regulate the classification and framing of knowledge made public in educational institutions. Both Durkheim and Marx have shown us that the structure of society's classifications and frames reveals both the distribution of power and the principles of social control. I hope to show, *theoretically*, that educational codes provide excellent opportunities for the study of classification and frames through which experience is given a distinctive form. The paper is organized as follows:

1.) I shall first distinguish between two types of curricula: collection and integrated.
2.) I shall build upon the basis of this distinction in order to establish a more general set of concepts: classification and frame.
3.) A typology of educational codes will then be derived.
4.) Sociological aspects of two very different educational codes will then be explored.
5.) This will lead on to a discussion of educational codes and problems of order.
6.) Finally there will be a brief discussion of the reasons for changes in educational codes.

## 1. TWO TYPES OF CURRICULA

Initially, I am going to talk about the curriculum in a very general way. In all educational institutions there is a formal punctuation of time into periods. These may vary from ten minutes to three hours or more. I am going to call each such formal period of time a 'unit'. I shall use the word 'content' to describe how the period of time is used. I shall define a curriculum initially in terms of the principle by which units of time and their contents are brought into a special relationship with each other. I now want to look more closely at the phrase 'special relationship'.

Firstly, we can examine relationships between contents in terms of the amount of time accorded to a given content. Immediately, we can see that more time is devoted to some contents rather than others. Secondly, some of the contents may, from the point of view of the pupils, be compulsory or optional. We can now take a very crude measure of the relative status of a content in terms of the number of units given over to it, and whether it is compulsory or optional. This raises immediately the question of the relative status of a given content and its significance in a given educational career.

We can, however, consider the relationship between contents from another, perhaps more important, perspective. We can ask about any given content whether the boundary between it and another content is clear-cut or blurred. To what extent are the various contents well insulated from each other. If the various contents are well insulated from each other, I shall say that the contents stand in a *closed* relation to each other. If there is reduced insulation between contents, I shall say that the contents stand in an *open* relationship to each other. So far then, I am suggesting that we can go into any educational institution and examine the organization of time in terms of the relative status of contents, and whether the contents stand in an open/closed relationship to each other. I am deliberately using this very abstract language in order to emphasize that there is nothing intrinsic to the relative status of various contents, there is nothing intrinsic to the relationships between contents. Irrespective of the question of the intrinsic logic of the various forms of public thought, the *forms* of their transmission, that is, their classification and framing, are social facts. There are a number of alternative means of access to the public forms of thought, and so to the various realities which they make possible. I am therefore emphasizing the social nature of the system of alternatives from which emerges a constellation called a curriculum. From this point of view, any curriculum entails a principle or principles whereby of all the possible contents of time, some contents are accorded differential status and enter into open or closed relation to each other.

I shall now distinguish between two broad types of curriculum. If contents stand in a closed relation to each other, that is, if the contents are clearly bounded and insulated from each other, I shall call such a curriculum a *collection* type. Here, the learner has to collect a group of favoured contents in order to satisfy some criteria of evaluation. There may of course be some underlying concept to a collection: the gentleman, the educated man, the skilled man, the non-vocational man.

Now I want to juxtapose against the collection type, a curriculum where the various contents do not go their own separate ways, but where the contents stand in an open relation to each other. I shall call such a curriculum an integrated type. Now we can have various types of collection, and various degrees and types of integration.

## 2. CLASSIFICATION AND FRAME

I shall now introduce the concepts, classification and frame, which will be used to analyse the underlying structure of the three message systems, curriculum, pedagogy and evaluation, which are realizations of the educational knowledge code. The basic idea is embodied in the principle used to distinguish the two types of curricula: collection and integrated. Strong insulation between contents pointed to a collection type, whereas reduced insulation pointed to an integrated type. The principle here is the strength of the *boundary* between contents. This notion of boundary strength underlies the concepts of classification and frame.

Classification, here, does not refer to *what* is classified, but to the *relationships* between contents. Classification refers to the nature of the differentiation between contents. Where classification is strong, contents are well insulated from each other by strong boundaries. Where classification is weak, there is reduced insulation between contents for the boundaries between contents are weak or blurred. *Classification thus refers to the degree of boundary maintenance between contents.* Classification focuses our attention upon boundary strength as the critical distinguishing feature of the division of labour of educational knowledge.

It gives us, as I hope to show, the basic structure of the message system, curriculum.

The concept, frame, is used to determine the structure of the message system, pedagogy. Frame refers to the form of the *context* in which knowledge is transmitted and received. Frame refers to the specific pedagogical relationship of teacher and taught. In the same way as classification does not refer to contents, so frame does not refer to the contents of the pedagogy. Frame refers to the strength of the boundary between what may be transmitted and what may not be transmitted, in the pedagogical relationship. Where framing is strong, there is a sharp boundary, where framing is weak, a blurred boundary, between what may and may not be transmitted. Frame refers us to the range of options available to teacher and taught in the *control* of what is transmitted and received in the context of the pedagogical relationship. Strong framing entails reduced options; weak framing entails a range of options. *This frame refers to the degree of control teacher and pupil possess over the selection, organization and pacing of the knowledge transmitted and received in the pedagogical relationship.**

There is another aspect of the boundary relationship between what may be taught and what may not be taught and consequently, another aspect to framing. We can consider the relationship between the non-school everyday community knowledge of the teacher or taught, *and* the educational knowledge transmitted in the pedagogical relationship. We can raise the question of the strength of the boundary, the degree of insulation, between the everyday community knowledge of teacher and taught and educational knowledge. Thus, we can consider variations in the strength of frames, as these refer to the strength of the boundary between educational knowledge and everyday community knowledge of teacher and taught.

From the perspective of this analysis, the basic structure of the message system curriculum is given by variations in the strength of classification and the basic structure of the message system pedagogy is given by variations in the strength of frames. It will be shown later that the structure of the message system evaluation is a function of the strength of classification and frames. It is important to realize that the strength of classification and the strength of frames can vary independently of each other. For example, it is possible to have weak classification and exceptionally strong framing. Consider programmed learning. Here the boundary between educational contents may be blurred (weak classification) but there is little control by the pupil (except for pacing) over *what* is learned (strong framing). This example also shows that frames may be examined at a number of levels and the strength can vary between the levels of selection, organization, pacing and timing of the knowledge transmitted in the pedagogical relationship.

I should also like to bring out (this will be developed more fully later in the analysis) the power component of this analysis and what can be called the 'identity' component. Where classification is strong, the boundaries between the

* It follows that frame strength for teacher and taught can be assessed at the different levels of selection, organization, and pacing of the knowledge.

different contents are sharply drawn. If this is the case then it presupposes strong boundary maintainers. Strong classification also creates a strong sense of membership in a particular class and so a specific identity. Strong frames reduce the power of the pupil over what, when and how he receives knowledge and increases the teacher's power in the pedagogical relationship. However, strong *classification* reduces the power of the *teacher* over what he transmits as he may not over-step the boundary between contents, *and* strong classification reduces the power of the teacher *vis-à-vis* the boundary maintainers.

It is now possible to make explicit the concept of educational knowledge codes. The code is fully given *at the most general level* by the relationship between classification and frame.

## 3. A TYPOLOGY OF EDUCATIONAL KNOWLEDGE CODES*

In the light of the conceptual framework we have developed, I shall use the distinction between collection and integrated curricula in order to realize a typology of types and sub-types of educational codes. The *formal* basis of the typology is the strength of classification and frames. However, the sub-types will be distinguished, initially, in terms of substantive differences.

Any organization of educational knowledge which involves strong classification gives rise to what is here called a collection code. Any organization of educational knowledge which involves a marked attempt to reduce the strength of classification is here called an integrated code. Collection codes may give rise to a series of sub-types, each varying in the relative strength of their classification and frames. Integrated codes can also vary in terms of the strength of frames, as these refer to the *teacher/pupil/student* control over the knowledge that is transmitted.

The diagram sets out general features of the typology. (See page 55.)

A. Collection Codes

The first major distinction *within* collection codes is between specialized and non-specialized types. The extent of specialization can be measured in terms of the number of closed contents publicly examined at the end of the secondary educational stage. Thus in England, *although there is no formal limit*, the student usually sits for three 'A' level subjects, compared with the much greater range of subjects which make up the *Abitur* in Germany, the *baccalaureate* in France, or the *Studente exam* in Sweden.

Within the English specialized type, we can distinguish two varieties: a pure and an impure variety. The pure variety exists where 'A' level subjects are drawn from a common universe of knowledge, e.g. chemistry, physics, mathematics.

* Elaborated codes are *formally* developed in educational institutions. Different educational knowledge codes represent different forms of the institutionalizing of elaborated codes. Thus educational knowledge codes are public regulators of elaborated codes.

The impure variety exists where 'A' level subjects are drawn from different universes of knowledge, e.g. religion, physics, economics. The latter combination, although formally possible, very rarely substantively exists, for pupils are not encouraged to offer—neither does timetabling usually permit—such a combination. It is a matter of interest that until very recently the pure variety at the university level received the higher status of an honours degree, whereas the impure variety tended to lead to the lower status of the general degree.* One can detect the beginnings of a shift in England from the pure to the impure variety, which appears to be trying to work towards the non-specialized type of collection.

Within the non-specialized collection code, we can distinguish two varieties, according to whether a subject or course is the basic knowledge unit. Thus the standard European form of the collection code is non-specialized, *subject* based. The U.S.A. form of the collection is non-specialized, course based.

I have so far described sub-types and varieties of the collection code in simple descriptive terms, and as a consequence it is not easy to see how their distinctive features can be translated into sociological concepts in order to realize a specific sociological problem. Clearly, the conceptual languages here developed has built into it a specific perspective; that of power and social control. In the process of translating the descriptive features into the language of classification and frames, the question must arise as to whether the hypotheses about their relative strength fits a particular case.

Here are the hypotheses, given for purposes of illustration:

1.) I suggest that the European, non-specialized, subject-based form of collection involves strong classification but *exceptionally* strong framing. That is, at levels *below* higher education, there are relatively few options available to teacher, and especially taught, over the transmission of knowledge. Curricula and syllabus are very explicit

2.) The English version, I suggest, involves *exceptionally* strong classification, but relatively weaker framing than the European type. The fact that it is specialized determines what contents (subjects) may be put together. There is very strong insulation between the 'pure' and the 'applied' knowledge. Curricula are graded for particular ability groups. There can be high insulation between a subject and a class of pupils. D stream secondary pupils will not have access to certain subjects, and A stream students will also not have access to certain subjects. However, I suggest that framing, relative to Europe, is weaker. This can be seen particularly at the primary level. There is also, *relative* to Europe, less *central* control over what is transmitted, although, clearly, the various requirements of the university level exert a strong control over the secondary level.†
I suggest that, although again this is *relative*, there is a weaker frame in England

* Consider the recent acrimonious debate over the attempt to obtain permission at Oxford to develop a degree in anthropology, sociology, psychology and biology—a relatively 'pure' combination.

† The content of public examinations between the secondary and the tertiary level is controlled by the tertiary level directly or indirectly, through the control over the various syllabi. Thus, if there is to be any major shift in secondary schools' syllabi and curricula,

between educational knowledge and the everyday community knowledge for certain classes of students: the so-called less able. Finally, relative to Europe, I suggest that there are more options available to the pupil within the pedagogical relationships. The frame as it refers to pupils is weaker. Thus I suggest that framing as it relates to teachers and pupils is relatively weaker, but that classification is relatively much stronger in the English than the European system. Scotland is nearer to the European version of the collection.

3.) The course-based, non-specialized U.S.A. form of the collection, I suggest, has the weakest classification *and* framing of the collection code, especially at the secondary and university level. A far greater range of subjects can be taken at the secondary and university level, and are capable of combination; this suggests weak classification. The insulation between educational knowledge and everyday community knowledge is weaker, as indicated by community control over the schools. The range of options available to pupils within the pedagogical relationships is, I suggest, greater. I would assume then, that classification and framing in the U.S.A. is the weakest of the collection code.

## B.  Integrated Codes

It is important to be clear about the term 'integrated'. Because one subject uses the theories of another subject, this type of intellectual interrelationship does not constitute integration. Such intellectual interrelation may well be part of a collection code at some point in the history of the development of knowledge. Integration, as it is used here, refers minimally to the *subordination* of previously insulated subjects *or* courses to some *relational* idea, which blurs the boundaries between the subjects. We can distinguish two types. The first type is *teacher* based. Here the teacher as in the infant school has an extended block of time with often the same group of children. The teacher may operate with a collection code and keep the various subjects distinct and insulated, or he can blur the boundaries between the different subjects. This type of integrated code is easier to introduce than the second type, which is *teachers* based. Here, integration involves relationships with other teachers. In this way, we can have degrees of integration in terms of the number of teachers involved.

We can further distinguish two varieties according to whether the integration refers to a group of teachers *within* a common subject, or the *extent* to which integration involves teachers of different subjects. Whilst integrated codes, by definition, have the weakest classification, they may vary as to framing. During the initiating period, the frames the teachers enter will be weak, but other factors

---

then this will require changes in the tertiary level's policy, as this affects the acceptance of students. Such a change in policy would involve changes in the selection, organization, pacing and timing of knowledge at the tertiary level. Thus, the conditions for a major shift in the knowledge code at the secondary level is a major shift in the knowledge code at the tertiary level. Changes in the knowledge code at the secondary level are likely to be of a somewhat limited nature without similar changes at the tertiary level. There clearly are other interest groups (industry) which may affect a given curriculum and syllabus.

will effect the final frame strength. It is also possible that the frames the *pupils* enter can vary in strength.

Thus integrated codes may be confined to one subject or they can cross subjects. We can talk of code strength in terms of the range of different subjects co-ordinated by the code, or if this criterion cannot be applied, code strength can be measured in terms of the *number* of teachers co-ordinated through the code. Integrated codes can also vary as to frame strength, as this is applied to teachers or pupils, or both.

Differences within, and between, educational knowledge codes from the perspective developed here, lie in variations in the strength and nature of the boundary maintaining procedures, as these are given by the classification and framing of the knowledge. It can be seen that the nature of classification and framing affects the authority/power structure which controls the dissemination of educational knowledge, and the *form* of the knowledge transmitted. In this way, principles of power and social control are realized through educational knowledge codes, and through the codes they enter into, and shape, consciousness. Thus variations within and change of knowledge codes should be of critical concern to sociologists. The following problems arise out of this analysis:

1.) What are the antecedents of variations in the strength of classification and frames?

2.) How does a given classification and framing structure perpetuate itself? What are the conditions of, and resistance to, change?

3. What are the different socializing experiences realized through variations in the strength of classifications and frames.

I shall limit the application of this analysis to the consideration of aspects of the last two questions. I feel I ought to apologize to the reader for this rather long and perhaps tedious conceptual journey, before he has been given any notion of the view to which it leads.

I shall examine the patterns of social relationship and their socializing consequences which are realized through the European, particularly English, version of the collection code and those which are *expected* to arise out of integrated codes, *particularly those which develop weak framing*. I shall suggest that there is some movement towards forms of the integrated code and I shall examine the nature of the resistance towards such a change. I shall suggest some reasons for this movement.

## 4. CLASSIFICATION AND FRAMING OF DIFFERENT FORMS OF EDUCATIONAL CODE

There will be some difficulty in this analysis, as I shall at times switch from secondary to university level. Although the English system has the distinguishing feature of specialization, it does share certain features of the European system. This may lead to some blurring in the analysis. As this is the beginning of a limited sociological theory which explores the social organization and structuring of educational knowledge, it follows that all statements, including those which have the character of descriptive statements, are hypothetical. The descriptive statements have been selectively patterned according to their significance for the theory.

One of the major differences between the European and English versions of the collection code is that, with the specialized English type, a membership category is established early in an educational career, in terms of an early choice between the pure and the applied, between the sciences and the arts, between having and not having a specific educational identity. A particular status in a given collection is made clear by streaming and/or a delicate system of grading. One nearly always knows the social significance of where one is and in particular, *who* one is with each advance in the educational career. (Initially, I am doing science, or arts, pure or applied; or I am not doing anything; later I am becoming a physicist, economist, chemist, etc.) *Subject loyalty* is then systematically developed in pupils and finally students, with each increase in the educational life and then transmitted by them as teachers and lecturers. The system is self-perpetuating through this form of socialization. With the specialized form of the collection it is banal to say as you get older you learn more and more about less and less. Another, more sociological, way of putting this is to say as you get older, you become increasingly different from others. Clearly, this will happen at some point in any educational career, but with specialization, this happens much earlier.

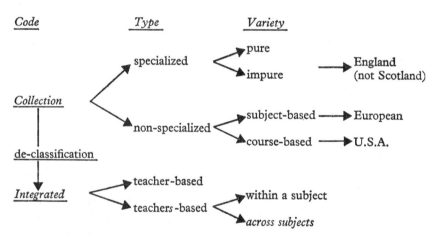

Therefore, specialization very soon reveals *difference from* rather than *communality with*. It creates relatively quickly an educational identity which is clear-cut and bounded. The educational category or identity is pure. Specialized versions of the collection code tend to abhor mixed categories and blurred identities, for they represent a potential openness, an ambiguity, which makes the consequences of previous socialization problematic. Mixed categories such as bio-physicist, psycho-linguist, are only permitted to develop after long socialization into a subject loyalty. Indeed, in order to change an identity, a previous one has to be weakened and a new one created. For example, in England, if a student has a first degree in psychology and he wishes to read for a higher degree in sociology, either he is not permitted to make the switch or he is expected to take a number of papers at first degree level in sociology. In the process of taking the papers, he usually enters into social relationships with accredited sociologists and students through whom he acquires the cognitive and social style particular to the socio-logical identity. Change of an educational identity is accomplished through a process of resocialization into a *new* subject loyalty. A sense of the sacred, the 'otherness' of educational knowledge, I submit does not arise so much out of an ethic of knowledge for its own sake, but is more a function of socialization into subject loyalty: for it is the subject which becomes the linchpin of the identity. Any attempt to weaken or *change* classification strength may be felt as a threat to one's identity and may be experienced as a pollution endangering the sacred. Here we have one source of the resistance to change of educational code.

The specialized version of the collection code will develop careful screening procedures to see who belongs and who does not belong, and once such screening has taken place, it is very difficult to change an educational identity. The various classes of knowledge are well insulated from each other. Selection and differen-tiation are early features of this particular code. Thus, the deep structure of the specialized type of collection code is *strong boundary maintenance creating control from within through the formation of specific identities*. An interesting aspect of the protestant spirit.

Strong boundary maintenance can be illustrated with reference to attempts to institutionalize new forms or attempts to change the strength of classification, within either the European or English type of collection. Because of the excep-tional strength of classification in England, such difficulties may be greater here. Changes in classification strength and the institutionalizing of new forms of knowledge may become a matter of importance when there are changes in the structure of knowledge at the higher levels and/or changes in the economy. Critical problems arise with the question of new forms, as to their legitimacy, at what point they belong, when, where and by whom the form should be taught. I have referred to the 'sacred' in terms of an educational identity, but clearly there is the 'profane' aspect of knowledge. We can consider as the 'profane' the pro-perty aspect of knowledge. Any new form or weakening of classification clearly derives from past classifications. Such new forms or weakened classifications can be regarded as attempts to break or weaken existing monopolies. Knowledge under collection is private property with its own power structure and market situation. This affects the whole ambience surrounding the development and marketing of new knowledge. Children and pupils are early socialized into this concept of knowledge as private property. They are encouraged to work as isolated individuals with their arms around their work. This phenomena, until recently, could be observed in any grammar school. It can be most clearly ob-served in examination halls. Pupils and students, particularly in the arts, appear from this point of view to be a type of entrepreneur.

There are, then, strong inbuilt controls on the institutionalizing of new knowledge forms, on the changing of strength of classification, on the production of new knowledge which derive from both 'sacred' and 'profane' sources.

So far, I have been considering the relationship between strong classification of knowledge, the concept of property and the creation of specific identities with particular reference to the specialized form of the collection code. I shall now move away from the classification of knowledge to its *framing* in the process of transmission.

Any collection code involves an hierarchical organization of knowledge, such that the ultimate mystery of the subject is revealed very late in the educational life. By the ultimate mystery of the subject, I mean its potential for creating new realities. It is also the case, and this is important, that the ultimate mystery of the subject is not coherence, but incoherence; not order, but disorder; not the known, but the unknown. As this mystery, under collection codes, is revealed very late in the educational life—and then only to a select few who have shown the signs of successful socialization—then only the few *experience* in their bones the notion that knowledge is permeable, that its orderings are provisional, that the dialectic of knowledge is closure and openness. For the many, socialization into knowledge is socialization into order, the existing order, into the experience that the world's educational knowledge is impermeable. Do we have here another version of alienation?

Now clearly any history of any form of educational knowledge shows precisely the power of such knowledge to create endlessly new realities. However, socialization into the specific framing of knowledge in its transmission may make such a history experientially meaningless. The key concept of the European collection code is discipline. This means learning to work *within* a received frame. It means, in particular, *learning* what questions can be put at any particular time. Because of the hierarchical ordering of the knowledge in *time*, certain questions raised may not enter into a particular frame.

This is soon learned by both teachers and pupils. Discipline then means accepting a given selection, organization, pacing and timing of knowledge realized in the pedagogical frame. With increases in the educational life, there is a progressive weakening of the frame for both teacher and taught. Only the few who have shown the signs of successful socialization have access to these relaxed frames. For the mass of the population the framing is tight. In a sense, the European form of the collection code makes knowledge safe through the process of socialization into its frames. There is a tendency, which varies with the strength of specific frames, for the young to be socialized into assigned principles and routine operations and derivations. The evaluative system places an emphasis upon attaining *states* of knowledge rather than *ways* of knowing. A study of the examination questions and format, the symbolic structure of assessment, would be, from this point of view, a rewarding empirical study. Knowledge thus tends to be transmitted, particularly to elite pupils at the secondary level, through strong frames which control the selecting, organization, pacing,* and timing of

---

* What is often overlooked is that the pacing of the knowledge (i.e. the rate of expected learning) is implicitly based upon the middle-class socialization of the child. Middle-class

the knowledge. The receipt of the knowledge is not so much a right as something to be won or earned. The stronger the classification and the framing, the more the educational relationship tends to be hierarchical and ritualized and the pupil seen as ignorant, with little status and few rights. These are things which one earns, rather like spurs, and are used for the purpose of encouraging and sustaining the motivation of pupils. Depending upon the strength of frames, knowledge is transmitted in a context where the teacher has maximal control or surveillance, as in hierarchical secondary school relationships.

We can look at the question of the framing of knowledge in the pedagogical relationship from another point of view. In a sense, educational knowledge is uncommonsense knowledge. It is knowledge freed from the particular, the local, through the various languages of the sciences or forms of reflexiveness of the arts which make possible either the creation or the discovery of new realities. Now this immediately raises the question of the relationship between the uncommonsense knowledge of the school and the *commonsense* knowledge, everyday community knowledge, of the pupil, his family and his peer group. This formulation invites us to ask how strong are the frames of educational knowledge in relation to experiential, community-based non-school knowledge? I suggest that the frames of the collection code, very early in the child's life, socialize him into knowledge frames which discourage connections with everyday realities, or that there is a highly selective screening of the connection. Through such socialization, the pupil soon learns what of the outside may be brought into the pedagogical frame. Such framing also makes of educational knowledge something not ordinary or mundane, but something esoteric which gives a special significance to those who possess it. I suggest that when this frame is relaxed to include everyday realities, it is often and sometimes validly, not simply for the transmission of educational knowledge, but for purposes of social control of forms of deviancy. The weakening of this frame occurs usually with the less 'able' children whom we have given up educating.

In general then, and depending upon the specific strength of classification and frames, the European form of the collection code is rigid, differentiating and hierarchical in character; highly resistant to change particularly at the secondary level. With the English version, this resistance to change is assisted by the discretion which is available to headmasters and principals. In England, within the constraints of the public examination system, the heads of schools and colleges

---

family socialization of the child is a hidden subsidy, in the sense that it provides both a physical and psychological environment which immensely facilitates, in diverse ways, school learning. The middle-class child is oriented to learning almost anything. Because of this hidden subsidy, there has been little incentive to change curriculum and pedagogy; for the middle-class child is geared to learn; he may not like, or indeed approve of, what he learns, but he learns. Where the school system is not subsidized by the home, the pupil often fails. In this way, even the *pacing* of educational knowledge is class based. It may well be that frame strength, as this refers to pacing, is a critical variable in the study of educability. It is possible that the weak frame strength (as this refers to *pacing*) of integrated codes indicates that integrated codes presuppose a longer average educational life. Middle-class children may have been potential pupils for progressive schools because of their longer educational life.

have a relatively wide range of discretion over the organization and transmission of knowledge. Central control over the educational code is relatively weak in England, although clearly the schools are subject to inspection from both central and local government levels. However, the relationship between the inspectorate and the schools in England is very ambiguous. To produce widespread change in England would require the co-operation of hundreds of individual schools. Thus, rigidity in educational knowledge codes may arise out of highly centralized *or* weak central control over the knowledge codes. Weak central control does permit a series of changes which have, initially, limited consequences for the system as a whole. On the other hand, there is much stronger central control over the organizational style of the school. This can lead to a situation where there can be a change in the organizational style *without* there being *any* marked change in the educational knowledge code, particularly where the educational code, itself, creates specific identities. This raises the question, which cannot be developed here, of the relationships between organizational change and change of educational knowledge code, i.e. change in the strength of classification and framing.

In general, then, the European and English form of the collection code may provide for those who go beyond the novitiate stage, order, identity and commitment. For those who do not pass beyond this stage, it can sometimes be wounding and seen as meaningless—what Bourdieu calls 'la violence symbolique'.

## Integrated and Collection Codes

I shall now examine a form of the integrated code which is realized through very weak classification and frames. I shall, during this analysis, bring out further aspects of collection codes.

There are a number of attempts to institutionalize forms of the integrated code at different strengths, above the level of the infant school child. Nuffield Science is an attempt to do this with the physical sciences, and the Chelsea Centre for Science Education, Chelsea College of Technology, University of London, is concerned almost wholly in training students in this approach. Mrs Charity James, at Goldsmiths College, University of London, is also producing training courses for forms of the integrated code. A number of comprehensive schools are experimenting with this approach at the middle school level. The S.D.S. in Germany, and various radical student groups, are exploring this type of code in order to use the means of the university against the meaning. However, it is probably true to say that the code at the moment exists at the level of ideology and theory, with only a relatively small number of schools and educational agencies attempting to institutionalize it with any seriousness.

Now, as we said in the beginning of the paper, with the integrated code we have a shift from content closure to content openness, from strong to markedly reduced classification. Immediately, we can see that this disturbance in classification of knowledge will lead to a disturbance of existing authority structures, existing specific educational identities, and concepts of property.

Where we have integration, the various contents are subordinate to some idea which reduces their isolation from each other. Thus integration reduces the authority of the separate contents, and this has implications for existing authority structures. Where we have collection, it does permit in principle considerable differences in pedagogy and evaluation, because of the high insulation between the different contents, However, the autonomy of the content is the other side of an authority structure which exerts jealous and zealous supervision. I suggest that the integrated code will not permit the variations in pedagogy and evaluation which are possible within collection codes. On the contrary, I suggest there will be a pronounced movement towards a common pedagogy and tendency towards a common system of evaluation. In other words, integrated codes will, at the level of the teachers, probably create homogeneity in teaching practice. Thus, collection codes increase the discretion of teachers (within, always, the limits of the existing classification and frames) whilst integrated codes will reduce the discretion of the teacher in direct relation to the strength of the integrated code (number of teachers co-ordinated by the code). On the other hand, it is argued that the increased discretion of the teachers within collection codes is paralleled by *reduced* discretion of the pupils and that the reduced discretion of the teachers within integrated codes is paralleled by *increased* discretion of the pupils. In other words, there is a shift in the balance of power, in the pedagogical relationship between teacher and taught.

These points will now be developed. In order to accomplish any form of integration (as distinct from different subjects focusing upon a common problem, which gives rise to what could be called a *focused* curriculum) there must be some relational idea, a supra-content concept, which focuses upon general principles at a high level of abstraction. For example, if the relationships between sociology and biology are to be opened, then the relational idea (amongst many) might be the issue of problems of order and change examined through the concepts of genetic and cultural codes. Whatever the relational concepts are, they will act selectively upon the knowledge within each subject which is to be transmitted. The particulars of each subject are likely to have reduced significance. This will focus attention upon the *deep* structure of each subject, rather than upon its surface structure. I suggest this will lead to an emphasis upon, and the exploration of, *general* principles and the concepts through which these principles are obtained. In turn, this is likely to affect the orientation of the pedagogy, which will be less concerned to emphasize the need to acquire *states* of knowledge, but will be more concerned to emphasize *how* knowledge is created. In other words, the pedagogy of integrated codes is likely to emphasize various *ways* of knowing in the pedagogical relationships. With the collection code, the pedagogy tends to proceed from the surface structure of the knowledge to the deep structure; as we have seen, only the elite have access to the deep structure and therefore access to the realizing of new realities or to the experiential knowledge that new realities are possible. *With integrated codes, the pedagogy is likely to proceed from the deep structure to the surface structure.* We can see this already at work in the new primary school mathematics. Thus, I suggest that integrated codes will make available from the beginning of the pupils' educational career, clearly in a way appropriate to a given age level, the deep structure of the knowledge, i.e. the principles for the generating of new knowledge. Such emphasis upon various *ways* of knowing, rather than upon the attaining of *states* of knowledge, is likely to affect, not only the emphasis of the pedagogy, but an underlying theory of learning. The underlying theory of learning of collection is likely to be didactic whilst the underlying theory of learning of integrated codes may well be more group or self-regulated. This arises out of a different concept of what counts as having knowledge, which in turn leads to a different concept of how the knowledge is to be acquired. These changes in emphasis and orientation of the pedagogy are initially responsible for the relaxed frames which teacher and taught enter. Relaxed frames not only change the nature of the authority relationships by increasing the rights of the taught, they can also weaken or blurr the boundary between what may or may not be taught, and so *more* of the teacher and taught is likely to enter this pedagogical frame. The inherent logic of the integrated code is likely to create a change in the structure of teaching groups which are likely to exhibit considerable flexibility. The concept of relatively weak boundary maintenance which is the core principle of integrated codes is realized both in the structuring of educational knowledge *and* in the organization of the social relationships.

I shall now introduce some organizational consequences of collection and integrated codes which will make explicit the difference in the distribution of power and the principles of control which inhere in these educational codes. (See page 62 for diagram.)

Where knowledge is regulated through a collection code, the knowledge is organized and distributed through a series of well-insulated subject hierarchies. Such a structure points to oligarchic control of the institution, through formal and informal meetings of heads of department with the head or principal of the institution. Thus, senior staff will have strong horizontal work relationships (that is, with their peers in other subject hierarchies) and strong vertical work relationships within their own department. However, junior staff are likely to have only vertical (within the subject hierarchy) allegiances and work relationships.

The allegiances of junior staff are vertical rather than horizontal for the following reasons. First, staff have been socialized into strong subject loyalty and through this into specific identities. These specific identities are continuously strengthened through social interactions *within* the department *and* through the insulation between departments. Second, the departments are often in a competitive relationship for strategic teaching resources. Third, preferment within the subject hierarchy often rests with its expansion. Horizontal relationships of junior staff (particularly where there is no *effective* participatory administrative structure) is likely to be limited to *non-task based* contacts. There may well be discussion of control problems ('X of 3b is a —— how do you deal with him?' or 'I can't get X to write a paper'). Thus the collection code within the framework of oligarchic control creates for *senior* staff strong horizontal and vertical based relationships, whereas the work relationships of junior staff are likely to be vertical and the horizontal relationships limited to non-work-based contracts. This is a type of organizational system which encourages gossip, intrigue and a conspiracy theory of the workings of the organization, as *both* the *administration* and the *acts of teaching* are *invisible* to the majority of staff.

Now the integrated code will require teachers of different subjects to enter into social relationships with each other which will arise not simply out of non-task areas, but out of a shared, co-operative, educational task. The centre of gravity of the relationships between teachers will undergo a radical shift. Thus, instead of teachers and lecturers being divided and insulated by allegiances to subject hierarchies, the conditions for their unification exists through a common

*Ideal Typical Organizational Structures*

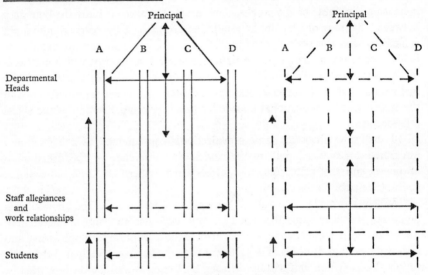

*Key:* Continuous lines represent strong boundaries. Continuous arrows represent direction of strong relationships. Dotted lines represent weak boundaries. Dotted line arrows represent direction of weak relationships.

Collection Code Type = Strong Classification: Strong Frames
Integrated Code Type = Weak Classification: Weak Frames

work situation. I suggest that this changed basis of the relationships, between teachers or between lecturers, may tend to weaken the separate hierarchies of collection. These new work-based horizontal relationships between teachers and between lecturers may alter both the structure and distribution of power regulated by the collection code. Further, the administration and specific acts of teaching are likely to shift from the relative invisibility to *visibility*.

We might expect similar developments at the level of students and even senior pupils. For pupils and students with each increase in their educational life are equally sub-divided and educationally insulated from each other. They are equally bound to subject hierarchies and for similar reasons to staff; their identities and their future is shaped by the department. Their vertical allegiances and work-based relationships are strong, whilst their horizontal relationships will tend to be limited to non-task areas (student/pupil societies and sport) or peripheral non-task based administration. Here again, we can see another example of the strength of boundary maintenance of collection codes; this time between task and non-task areas. Integrated codes may well provide the conditions for strong horizontal relationships and allegiances in students and pupils, based upon a common work task (the receiving and offering of knowledge).* In this situation, we might expect a weakening of the boundary between staff, especially junior staff, and students/pupils.

Thus, a move from collection to integrated codes may well bring about a disturbance in the structure and distribution of power, in property relationships and in existing educational identities. This change of educational code involves a fundamental change in the nature and strength of boundaries. It involves a change in what counts as having knowledge, in what counts as a valid transmission of knowledge, in what counts as a valid realization of knowledge, *and* a change in the organizational context. At the cultural level, it involves a shift from the keeping of categories pure to the mixing of categories; whilst at the level of socialization the outcomes of integrated codes *could* be less predictable than the outcomes of collection codes. This change of code involves fundamental changes in the classification and framing of knowledge and so changes in the structure and distribution of power and in principles of control. It is no wonder that deep-felt resistances are called out by the issue of change in educational codes.

## 5. COLLECTION, INTEGRATED CODES AND PROBLEMS OF ORDER

I shall now turn to aspects of the problem of order. Where knowledge is regulated by collection codes, social order arises out of the hierarchical nature of the authority relationships, out of the systematic ordering of the differentiated knowledge in time and space, out of an explicit, usually predictable, examining procedure. Order internal to the individual is created through the formation of specific identities. The institutional expression of strong classification and framing creates predictability in time and space. Because of strong classification, collection does allow a range of variations between subjects in the organization, transmission and evaluation of knowledge. Because of strong classification, this code does *in principle* permit staff to hold (within limits) a range of ideologies, because conflicts can be contained *within* its various insulated hierarchies. At levels below that of the university, the strong frames between educational knowledge and non-educationally relevant knowledge *in principle* may facilitate diversity in ideology held by staff because it cannot be explicitly offered. At the same time, strong

* It is possible that the weak boundary-maintaining procedures of integrated codes at the level of the organizational structure, knowledge structure and identity structure may increase the pupils/students informal age group affiliations as a source of identity, relation and organization.

framing makes such intrusion highly visible. The range of personal freedoms at the *university* level is symbolized in the ethical system of some collection codes and so forms the basis for the cohesion of the differentiated whole.

Whilst it is usually the case that collection codes, relative to integrated codes, create strong frames between the uncommonsense knowledge of the school and the everyday community-based knowledge of teacher and taught, it is also the case that such insulation creates areas of privacy. For, inasmuch as community-based experience is irrelevant to the pedagogical frame, these aspects of the self informed by such experiences are also irrelevant. These areas of privacy reduce the penetration of the socializing process, for it is possible to distance oneself from it. This still means, however, that the socialization can be deeply wounding, either for those who wish for, but do not achieve, an identity, or for the majority for whom the pursuit of an identity is early made irrelevant.

Order created by integrated codes may well be problematic. I suggest that if four conditions are not satisfied, then the openness of learning under integration may produce a culture in which neither staff nor pupils have a sense of time, place or purpose. I shall comment briefly on these four conditions as I give them. 1.) There must be consensus about the integrating idea and it must be very explicit. (It is ironic that the movement towards integration is going on in those countries where there is a low level of moral consensus.) It may be that integrated codes will only work* when there is a *high* level of ideological consensus among the staff. We have already seen that, in comparison with collection, integrated codes call for greater homogeneity in pedagogy and evaluation, and therefore reduce differences between teachers in the form of the transmission and assessment of knowledge. The teaching process under collection is likely to be invisible to other teachers, unless special conditions prevail. However, when the teaching process is regulated through integrated codes it may well become visible through the greater flexibility in the structure of teaching groups. It is also the case that the weak classification and relaxed frames of integrated codes permits greater expressions of differences between teachers, and possibly between pupils, in the selection of what is taught. The moral basis of educational choices are then likely to be explicit at the initial planning stage. Integrated codes also weaken specific identities. For the above reasons, integrated codes may require a high level of ideological consensus and this may affect the recruitment of staff. Integrated codes at the surface level create weak or blurred boundaries, but at bottom they may rest upon closed explicit ideologies. Where such ideologies are not shared, the consequences will become visible and threaten the whole at every point.

2.) The nature of the linkage between the integrating idea and the knowledge to be co-ordinated must also be coherently spelled out. It is this linkage which will be the basic element in bringing teachers *and* pupils into their working relationship. *The development of such a co-ordinating framework will be the process of socialization of teachers into the code. During this process, the teachers will internalize, as in all processes of socialization, the interpretative procedures of the code*

---

\* In the sense of creating order.

*so that these become implicit guides which regulate and co-ordinate the behaviour of the individual teachers in the relaxed frames and weakened classification.* This brings us to a major distinction between collection and integrated codes. With a collection code, the period of socialization is facilitated by strong boundary maintenance both at the level of *role* and at the level of knowledge. Such socialization is likely to be continuous with the teacher's own educational socialization. With integrated codes, both the role and the form of the knowledge have to be *achieved* in relation to a range of different others, and this may involve resocialization if the teacher's previous educational experience has been formed by the collection code. The collection code is capable of working when staffed by mediocre teachers, whereas integrated codes call for much greater powers of synthesis and analogy, and for more ability to both tolerate and enjoy ambiguity at the level o knowledge *and* social relationships.

3.) A committee system of staff may have to be set up to create a sensitive feed back system and which will also provide a further agency of socialization into the code. It is likely that evaluative criteria are likely to be relatively weak, in the sense that the criteria are less likely to be as explicit and measurable as in the case of collection. As a result, it may be necessary to develop committees for both teachers, students, and where appropriate, pupils, which will perform monitoring functions.

4.) One of the major difficulties which inhere in integrated codes arises over what is to be assessed, and the form of assessment: also the place of specific competencies in such assessment. It is likely that integrated codes will give rise to multiple criteria of assessment compared with collection codes. In the case of collection codes, because the knowledge moves from the surface to the deep structure, then this progression creates ordered principles of evaluation in time. The form of temporal cohesion of the knowledge regulated through the integrated code has yet to be determined, and made explicit. Without clear criteria of evaluation, neither teacher nor taught have any means to consider the significance of what is learned, nor any means to judge the pedagogy. In the case of collection codes, evaluation at the secondary level often consists of the fit between a narrow range of specific competencies and states of knowledge, and previously established criteria (varying in explicitness) of what constitutes a right or appropriate or convincing answer. The previously established criteria together with the specific social context of assessment create a relatively objective procedure. I do not want to suggest that this necessarily gives rise to a form of assessment which entirely disregards distinctive and original features of the pupil's performance. In the case of the integrated code under discussion (weak frames for teacher and taught) then this form of assessment may well be inappropriate. The weak frames enable a greater range of the student's behaviour to be made public and they make possible considerable diversity (at least in principle) between students. It is possible that this might lead to a situation where assessment takes more into account 'inner' attributes of the student. Thus if he has the 'right' attitudes then this will result later in the attainment of various specific competencies. The 'right' attitude may be assessed in terms of the fit between the pupil's attitudes and the current ideology. It is possible, then, that the evaluative criteria of integrated codes with weak frames may be weak as these refer to specific cognitive attributes, but strong as these refer to dispositional attributes. If this is so, then a new range of pupil attributes become candidates for labels. It is also likely that the weakened classification and framing will encourage more of the pupil/student to be made public—more of his thoughts, feelings, and values. In this way more of the pupil is available for control. As a result the socialization could be more intensive and perhaps more penetrating. In the same way as pupils/students defend themselves against the wounds of collection or distance themselves from its overt code, so they may produce new defences against the potential intrusiveness of the integrated code and its open learning contexts.

We can summarize this question of the problem of order as follows. Collection codes have explicit and strong boundary-maintaining features and they rest upon a tacit ideological basis. Integrated codes have implicit and weak boundary-maintaining features and they rest upon an explicit and closed ideological basis. The ideological basis of the collection code is a condensed symbolic system communicated through its explicit boundary-maintaining features. Its covert structure is that of mechanical solidarity. The ideological basis of integrated codes is *not* a condensed symbolic system; it is verbally elaborated and explicit. It is an *overt* realization of organic solidarity and is made substantive through weak forms of boundary-maintenance (low insulations). Yet the covert structure of mechanical solidarity of collection codes creates through its specialized outputs *organic* solidarity. On the other hand the overt structure of organic solidarity of integrated codes creates through its *less* specialized outputs *mechanical* solidarity. And it will do this to the extent to which its ideology is explicit, elaborated and closed, *and* effectively and *implicitly* transmitted through its low insulations. Inasmuch as integrated codes do not accomplish this, then order is highly problematic at the level of social organization and at the level of the person. Inasmuch as integrated codes do accomplish such socialization, then we have the covert deep closure of mechanical solidarity. This is the fundamental paradox which has to be faced and explored.*

## 6. CHANGES OF EDUCATIONAL CODES

I have tried to make explicit the relationships between educational codes and the structure of power and principles of social control. Attempts to change or modify educational codes will meet with resistance at a number of different levels irrespective of the intrinsic educational merit of a particular code. I shall now briefly discuss some reasons for a movement towards the institutionalizing of integrated codes *of the weak classification and weak framing (teacher and taught) type* above the level of the primary school (see postscript).

1.) The growing differentiation of knowledge at the higher levels of thought,

* If educational institutions (following Bourdieu) can be considered as repeating agencies, we can ask the following question. What is the social basis of a repeating agency which attempts to produce unrepeatable or unlikely outcomes?

together with the integration of previously discreet areas, may set up requirements for a form of socialization appropriate to these changes in the structure of knowledge.

2.) Changes in the division of labour are creating a different concept of skill. The inbuilt obsolescence of whole varieties of skills reduces the significance of context-tied operations and increases the significance of general principles from which a range of diverse operations may be derived. In crude terms, it could be said that the nineteenth century required submissive and inflexible man, whereas the twenty-first century requires conforming but flexible man.

3.) The less rigid social structure of the integrated code makes it a potential code for egalitarian education.

4.) In advanced industrial societies which permit, within limits, a range of legitimizing beliefs and ideologies, there is a major problem of control. There is the problem of making sense of the differentiated, weakly co-ordinated and changing symbolic systems and the problem of inner regulation of the person. Integrated codes, with their stress on the underlying unity of knowledge, through their emphasis upon analogy and synthesis, could be seen as a response to the first problem of 'making sense'. The *inter-personal* rather than *inter-positional* control of the integrated code may set up a penetrating, intrusive form of socialization under conditions of ambiguity in the system of beliefs and the moral order.

If these reasons operate, we could consider the movement towards integrated codes as stemming from a technological source. However, it is possible that there is another and deeper source of the movement away from collection. I suggest that the movement away from collection to integrated codes symbolizes that there is a crisis in society's basic classifications and frames, and therefore a crisis in its structures of power and principles of control. The movement from this point of view represents an attempt to declassify and so alter power structures and principles of control; in so doing to unfreeze the structuring of knowledge and to change the boundaries of consciousness. From this point of view integrated codes are symptoms of a moral crisis rather than the terminal state of an educational system.

## CONCLUSION

In this paper, I have tried to explore the concept of boundary in such a way that it is possible to see *both* the power and control components. The analysis focuses directly upon the structuring of transmitted educational knowledge.

Although the concept 'classification' appears to operate on a single dimension, i.e. differences in degrees of insulation between content (subjects/courses etc.), it explicitly points to power and control components. In the same way, the concept 'frame' appears to operate in a single dimension: what may or may not be taught in the pedagogical relationship. Yet the exploration of the concept again points to power and control components. Through defining educational codes in terms of the relationship between classification and framing, these two components are built into the analysis at all levels. It then becomes possible in one framework to derive a typology of educational codes, to show the inter-relationships between organizational and knowledge properties, to move from macro- to micro-levels of analysis, to relate the patterns internal to educational institutions to the external social antecedents of such patterns, and to consider questions of maintenance and change. At the same time, it is hoped that the analysis makes explicit tacit assumptions underlying various educational codes. It attempts to show at a *theoretical* level, the relationships between a particular symbolic order and the structuring of experience. I believe that it offers an approach which is well capable of exploration by diverse methods at the empirical level.

*It should be quite clear that the specific application of the concept requires at every point empirical evidence.* I have not attempted to bolster the argument with references, because in many cases the evidence which is required does not exist in a *form* which bears directly upon the chain of inferences and therefore would offer perhaps spurious support. We have, for example, little *first*-hand knowledge which bears upon aspects of framing as this concept is used in the paper. We also have next to no *first*-hand knowledge of the day-by-day encounters realized by various types of integrated codes.

I hope that the kinds of questions raised by this approach will encourage sociologists of education to explore both theoretically, and empirically, the structure of educational knowledge which I take to be the distinctive feature of this field.

# ACKNOWLEDGEMENTS

I am most grateful to Professor Wolfgang Klafki, and particularly to Mr Hubertus Huppauf of the University of Marburg, for many valuable suggestions and constructive criticism. I should also like to acknowledge many hours of discussion with my colleague Mr Michael Young. I have also learned much from Mr David Adelstein, graduate student in the Department of the Sociology of Education, University of London Institute of Education. I am particularly grateful to Mr W. Brandis, research officer in the Department's Research Unit. I have also benefited from the stringent criticisms of Professor R. Peters, and Mr Lionel Elvin, of the University of London Institute of Education. My greatest debt is to Professor Mary Douglas, University College, London.

I should like to thank the Director of the Chaucer Publishing Company, Mr L. G. Grossman, for a small but vital grant.

# POSTSCRIPT

In the paper, I suggested that integrated codes rest upon a closed explicit ideology. It should then follow that this code would stand a better chance of successful institutionaliza-tion in societies where (a) there were strong and effective constraints upon the development of a range of ideologies and (b) where the educational system was a major agency of political socialization. Further, the weak boundary-maintaining procedures of the integrated code would (a) increase the penetration of the socialization as more of the self of the taught is made public through the relaxed frames and (b) deviancy would be more visible. On the other hand, integrated codes carry a potential for change in power structures and principles of control. I would therefore guess that in such societies, integrated codes would possess weak classification, but the frames for teacher and taught would be strong.

It is a matter of interest that, in England, it is only in the infant school that there is relatively wide-spread introduction of this form of integrated code. This raises the general question of how this level of the educational system was open to such change. Historically, the primary school developed distinct concepts of infant and junior stages, and distinct heads for these two stages. Given the relative autonomy over the transmission of knowledge which characterizes the British system of education, it was in principle possible to have change. Although only a ceiling may separate infant from junior departments, two quite distinct and often incompatible educational codes can develop. We can regard this as a necessary, but not sufficient, condition for the emergence of integrated codes at the infant school level. It was also the case, until very recently, that the selection function started in the junior department, because that department was the gateway to the grammar school. This left the infant school relatively free of control by levels higher than itself. The form of integration in the infant school, again until recently, was *teacher* based, and therefore did not set up the problems which arise out of *teachers*-based integration. Finally, infant school teachers are not socialized into strong educational identities. Thus the English educational system, until recently, has two potential points of openness—the period between the ages of five to seven years, before selection began, and the period post eighteen years of age, when selection is virtually completed. The major control on the structuring of knowledge at the secondary level is the structuring of knowledge at the tertiary level, specifically the university. Only if there is a major change in the structuring of knowledge at this level can there be effective code change at lower levels.

# BIBLIOGRAPHY

BERNSTEIN, B., PETERS, R., and ELVIN, L. (1966). 'Ritual in Education'. *Philosophical Transactions of the Royal Society of London*, Series B, Vol. 251, No. 772.
—— (1967). 'Open Schools, Open Society?' *New Society*, September 14, 1967.
DAVIES, D. I. (1969). 'The Management of Knowledge: a Critique of the Use of Typologies in Educational Sociology'. *Sociology*, 4, No. I. (See also Chapter 9, this volume.)
—— (1970). *Knowledge, Education and Power*. Paper presented to the British Sociological Association Annual Conference, Durham.
DOUGLAS, M. (1966). *Purity and Danger*. London: Routledge & Kegan Paul.
—— (1970). *Natural Symbols*. London: Barrie & Rockliff, The Cresset Press.
DURKHEIM, E. (1947). *On the Division of Labour in Society*. Glencoe (Illinois): The Free Press.
—— (1961). *Moral Education*. Glencoe (Illinois): The Free Press.
—— and MAUSS, M. (1963). *Primitive Classification*. London: Cohen & West.
HOYLE, E. (1969). 'How Does the Curriculum Change? (1) A Proposal for Enquiries (2) Systems and Strategies'. *Journal of Curriculum Studies*, Vol. I, Nos. 2 and 3.
JEFFREY, G. B. (1950). *The Unity of Knowledge: Reflections on the Universities of Cambridge and London*. Cambridge: Cambridge University Press.
KEDDIE, N. G. (1970). *The Social Basis of Classroom Knowledge*. M.A. thesis, University of London Institute of Education. (See also KEDDIE, N. G., 'Classroom Knowledge', Chapter 5, this volume.)
MUSGROVE, F. (1968). 'The Contribution of Sociology to the Study of the Curriculum'; in KERR, J. (ed.), *Changing the Curriculum*. London: University of London Press.
YOUNG, M. F. D. (1971). 'An Approach to the Study of Curricula as Socially Organized Knowledge' in YOUNG, M. F. D. (ed.), *Knowledge and Control*. London: Collier-Macmillan (Chapter I, this volume).

# 3. GEOFFREY M. ESLAND
*Teaching and Learning as the*
*Organization of Knowledge**

## INTRODUCTION

We know little of how knowledge comes to be organized within educational institutions. This applies not merely to the ways in which its institutionalized forms regulate the structures of 'worthwhile' educational experience, but much more so to the realizations of these forms in the realities of individual pupils and teachers. This study is written in the belief that an empirical sociology of knowledge is long overdue, and that it can make a powerful contribution to our understanding of educational processes. The arguments which are here put forward are offered as a possible framework for the analysis of the knowledge which constitutes the life-world[1] of teachers and pupils in particular educational institutions, and the epistemological traditions in which they collectively participate. I would suggest further that the framework provides a means of penetrating the social processes which are leading to disintegration in the plausibility of particular educational principles and the piecemeal adoption of others considered more 'relevant'. The appresentational referents for such relevances are expressive of the bases of power and control in society, and the social distribution of knowledge.

In spite of a number of important developments of the Marxian idea that ideational forms and social structure are dialectically related, the sociology of knowledge has continued to remain marginal to the central concerns of sociology. Due to the wide methodological acceptance among sociologists of what has been called an anti-humanistic scientism[2], there has been a readiness to leave epistemological issues to philosophy, on the assumption that 'knowing' derives from what is verifiable. The sociology of knowledge has thereby been hailed as an extreme and nihilistic form of relativism, likely to disturb the conventions and legitimacies of social order. The theoretical conservatism which lies behind this

* First published in this volume.

has led to an unduly restricted view of what sociology can be expected to explain. One of its notable features in the sociology of education is the lack of enthusiasm for incorporating the ideas of Mead, Mannheim and Schutz into the earlier traditions. The prevalence in sociological research of neo-positivism has perpetuated a view of man as a dehumanized, passive object—an occupant of roles in organizational structures. The point has been made by Berger and Pullberg in their discussion of reified consciousness. They suggest that 'the dehumanization of sociology marks the point at which sociology has lost its own subject. Sociology's task must be the continuing clarification of everyday life. The fulfilling of this task entails a critique of consciousness which is the very stuff of everyday life' (Berger, P. L., and Pullberg, S., 1965).

In his study of institutions and theories of knowledge, Stanley Taylor has argued that this view of man has its antecedents in the Individualism of Bacon, Locke and Kant (Taylor, S., 1956, 1962). Individualism endowed man with an absolute rationality in which the knowing subject is detached from his social context. The world of the theoretical was judged to be autonomous, stripped of the distorting influences of institutional attachments. This individualistic epistemology, which has dominated psychology, and has had wide currency in sociology, produced in the social sciences an empirical concern for the objective, manifested in cross-sectional studies, with semantically rigid categories and a quantifiable symbolic representation. It has become *the* scientific epistemology.

In contrast to this view, this study and the research which it suggests will work within the dialectic epistemology of Marx, Durkheim, Mead and Schutz, a tradition recently articulated by Berger and Luckmann in a newly-formulated view of the sociology of knowledge (Berger, P. L., and Luckmann, T., 1967).

## 1. TEACHING AND LEARNING IN THE SOCIOLOGY OF EDUCATION

In a large number of sociological studies of educational processes, teaching, learning and the organization of knowledge have appeared as separate areas of interest. In view of the fact that teaching essentially involves the intention of changing the consciousness of pupils towards acceptance of the realities marked out in curricula, this is, perhaps, regrettable. It is not, however, surprising. In the first place, for many sociologists these problems are closer to psychology and philosophy than to their own discipline. The second reason, which is related, arises from the dominance of structural functionalist explanations in the sociology of education. Coupled with logico-deductive methodologies, this has ensured that most of the research into teaching has consisted of role studies, with formal rather than substantive theoretical emphasis.[3] The result has been that the content of the role—both the practical activity of teaching and its supporting rationales— are hardly represented in sociological theory. The existential matrix of intentions, cognition and the knowledge on which they are founded, and the situational variants of these are ignored or subsumed under 'beliefs' or 'values', which are then taken as given.

The sociological analysis of teaching is, furthermore, usually undertaken with minimal reference to the learning outcomes for pupils, which are themselves important sources of legitimation for teachers. One of the consequences of the wide plausibility among educational publics of the social welfare ideology is the acquisition by the sociology of learning of the images and rhetoric of anti-poverty programmes. The massively institutionalized emphasis in studies of educability on pupil values and achievement motivation has for a long time chan-nelled the energies of sociologists from the learning processes themselves to the qualities which pupils are thought to bring to the classroom. The lower working-class child has become the arch stereotype of 'social deprivation'. In this respect, the sociology of learning, by its readiness to reify the pupil and his experience, very easily becomes an extension of (reified) educational psychology. We shall here be suggesting that educational opportunity is also conditional on the ideologies and classroom practices of teachers. Through their pedagogy and subject presentation, they are making critical, albeit taken for granted, decisions about the futures of their pupils, the legitimations of which are located in pro-fessional knowledge. Because this is not a unitary or static knowledge, the changing conceptions of the pupil and the learning process which it embraces are important constraints in professional debates about which differentiation procedures, timetabling and pedagogy are appropriate for which schools and which group of pupils. It is because the pupil career is so contingent on the dominant professional legitimacies of teachers that they need to be made explicit, and their structural dependencies clarified.

The situation is by no means improved by the conceptual separation of curriculum research from the study of teaching. Although sociologists have only recently begun to make a theoretical contribution to our understanding of the organization and transmission of knowledge, there has been little indication yet of any attempt to develop an explanatory framework which can relate the know-ledge as it is arranged in the curriculum to the subjective organization of teacher and pupil identity.

The arguments which are set out in this study, therefore, arose partly from a dissatisfaction with existing approaches to the explanation of classroom inter-action, but also from an empirical interest in the ways in which teachers handle the selection and transmission of knowledge during the introduction of new curricula.[4] Particularly important are the pedagogical principles underlying the implementation of innovation and the ways in which the objective existence of new knowledge structures acts back on, and transforms, the teacher's and pupils' subjectively apprehended reality. Surprisingly little is known about the consti-tutive processes of teaching and learning. The relationship between teachers and pupils is essentially a reality-sharing, world-building enterprise. As participants in classroom interaction they inter-subjectively typify and interpret the actions of one another through vocabularies which they take for granted as plausible. In this way, zones of knowledge are constructed and sustained in the transactional processes of school learning, generating the inferential structures which become the co-ordinates of future interpreted experience. Because much of this knowledge is implicit and taken for granted, it is an important component of the structure of a situation.

The ideas of Schutz, Mead, Berger and others from which this analysis is derived are highly applicable to an understanding of teaching and learning. Not only do they point up the implicit ideation contained in what are apparently routine everyday actions, but they also enable the sociologist to consider these ideational complexes in their social and epistemological location. Because they contain the assumptions which lie behind the methodologies and reality tests of teaching, they powerfully define, for teachers and pupils, what 'being educated' means.

In this kind of phenomenological analysis, then, the educational enterprise, the assumptions and definitions of worthwhileness, validity and social order are bracketed and considered in terms of their social-structural and social-psychological realizations. What is being attempted, then, is a view of teaching and learning, not *with* but *as* the organization of knowledge.

In terms of the research which this will generate, not only is it necessary to explore the ideational contents of curriculum and pedagogy as these are constituted in the teacher's perspectives, but also the social infrastructure in which these contents arise. In particular, his career location, in terms of perceived centres of reality definers, and his inter- and intra-professional communications, would be regarded as important social sources of legitimacy in his taken for granted reality as a teacher. The intention is, therefore, to bring together the sociology of knowledge and the sociology of professionalization in an attempt to discover the social-psychological support which professions and associations give to particular *Weltanschauungen*, and to determine the parameters within which reality is defined. It will be argued that occupational perspectives derive much of their cognitive support from institutionalized world views reinforced by the rituals of membership and orthodoxy, and the strategies of loyalty maintenance. It would be particularly important to consider these perspectives in the context of the institutional locales in which teachers perform their jobs. These are the arenas in which they articulate, negotiate and legitimate their ideologies. Case studies of these processes are an obvious first step.

Bernstein has suggested that the changing ideational structures of the curriculum—in moving from closed to open relationships—are related to changes in the social infrastructure which articulates them, and to wider aspects of social change (Bernstein, 1967, 1971). More specifically, they indicate shifts in the commonly-held principles of social order and their plausibility, and, therefore, the changing power relationships of cognitive communities. It is clear that we are witnessing the emergence of curriculum integration as a powerful 'evangelism' in education. It has become ideologized—mainly on pedagogical grounds and the assumed need for 'mentally adaptable' citizens—for all kinds of schools, and particularly for 'less able' pupils. Teachers are becoming committed to integrated studies sometimes without knowing why and with little idea of the problems of management and institutionalization of this knowledge. Quite obviously, integrated projects can be initiated for a variety of pragmatic or philosophical reasons; but the simple fact of their objective reality is sufficient to transform the initial intentionality and to create entirely new subject and pedagogical ideologies. The consequences for teachers, pupils and knowledge are important sociological problems.

The problem of integrating these issues into a theoretical framework is a formidable one. Although the main emphasis of the research being undertaken is to enquire into the social organization of knowledge within individual schools, it is necessary to consider in relation to this the legitimations of the professional and inter-professional epistemic communities outside the institution, and the epistemologies in which they are located.[5] Perhaps the closest formulation we have of this problem is set out in Simmel's essay 'How is Society Possible?' (Wolff, K., ed., 1959). For Simmel, the unity and historical continuity of society is maintained through 'cognitive syntheses', which, through the human capacity for memory and association, create the orientation structures of society. Underlying the heterogeneity of concrete actions are the socially-constructed 'forms' of social life—the nuclear meaning-structures which create uniformities and equivalence. The task of the sociologist is the direct understanding of the emerging 'forms' as they implicitly structure the individual's perception and explanations of the world. We have developed this idea in the concept 'perspective', which has been defined by Mannheim as embracing 'the constitutive categories of thought in terms of which an individual, or an age, attempts to grasp the nature of the world'.[6]

It will be abundantly clear, from the way in which the problem has been set up, that the study has been greatly influenced by the arguments advanced by Berger and Luckmann in *The Social Construction of Reality*, by the work of Alfred Schutz and that of Strauss and his colleagues on professional processes (Strauss, A. L., *et al.*, 1964; Bucher, R., and Strauss, A. L., 1961; Schatzman, L., and Strauss, A. L., 1966). It takes as axiomatic Berger's suggestion that a synthesis between the sociology of knowledge and symbolic interactionism is theoretically and operationally essential in case studies of this nature (Berger, P. L., 1966).

A word, finally, about the use of the word 'subject'. One of the fundamental points of this study is that objective reality as an agglomeration of phenomena external to the body has to be subjectively *realized* before it has any meaning. Quite obviously, therefore, the teacher of English or chemistry has his own realization of these realities as a socially-constructed *nomos* which will be different in many respects from that of anyone else.[7] Thus, his classification of knowledge will recognize its own boundaries. The inverted commas are intended to signify the *subjective* nomos and not simply the taken for granted objective reality.

## 2. THE SOCIOLOGY OF KNOWLEDGE: ITS THEORETICAL POSSIBILITIES FOR THE STUDY OF TEACHING AND LEARNING

Knowledge is usually considered and referred to as a set of abstract structures with intrinsic natures—as particular classifications of problems, data and verification procedures conforming to assumed patterns of coherence. Thus, the naming which confirms the separation between zones of knowledge in a curriculum—called 'subjects' or 'projects'—is thought to represent certain ontologies, essences of human experience. In other words, it is assumed that zones of knowledge are objects which can be considered to have meaning other than in the minds of the individuals in which they are constituted, irrespective of their human realization.

This is the objectivistic view of knowledge. It is the view represented in traditional epistemology and analytic philosophy. It is also how knowledge is conceived in the reality of everyday experience where the taken for granted nature of the world is rarely questioned. The individual consciousness recognizes objects as being 'out there', as coercive, external realities. Their continuing presence provides the probabilities on which rational action can be founded, and their existence can be verified through signals apprested by the senses. Knowledge is thereby detached from the human subjectivity in which it is constituted, maintained and transformed. Such a view implicitly presents man as a passive receiver, as the pliable, socialized embodiment of external facticities. He is represented not as world-producer, but as world-produced. We have, therefore, a reified philosophy in which objectivity is autonomized and which does not regard as problematical for the constituency of the object its constitution in the subjective experience of individuals. One finds it difficult to disagree with the claim that this epistemology is fundamentally dehumanizing.[8] It ignores the intentionality and expressivity of human action and the entire complex process of intersubjective negotiation of meanings. In short, it disguises as given a world which has to be continually interpreted.

Objectivism has been firmly embedded in the norms and rituals of academic culture and its transmission. Through the procedures of psychological testing and school evaluation, the pupil and the curriculum have been reified. 'Bodies of knowledge' are presented for the child to learn and reproduce according to specified objective criteria. Educational psychology has been a powerful legitimating agency and rationalization for objectivism. As such, it has become an important form of social control. In view of the wide public credibility accorded to psychologisms (and, to a lesser extent, sociologisms) in the determination of educational policy, and their institutionalization in teacher education courses, it is perhaps appropriate to question the ideational basis on which their assumptions about human motivation and its pathologies rests. It is arguable that the dereification of much that is taken for granted in educational culture will sensitize to the open human possibilities of creating new knowledge structures and their modes of transmission. For teachers, as for Berger and Pullberg, 'Sociology will only accomplish its task if it studies not merely giveness, but the various processes of becoming giveness'.

The tradition in which the 'passive' view of man is located has itself been the subject of sociological enquiry.[9] We have already referred to the paradigmatic nature of Individualism for modern scientific thought. This tradition which began with Bacon's 'Idols' (in *Novum Organum* 1620) and effectively ended with Kant's *Critique of Pure Reason*, continued to reverberate during the nineteenth century through utilitarianism and positivism, and into the twentieth century through logic, analytic philosophy and behaviourism. In one form or another, it was the dominant social and political concept of the Western world. It inevitably created the validitional parameters of the social sciences—particularly psychology —and has led to the persistence of the objectivistic scientism which lies at the heart of much modern empiricism.

One of the important assumptions of this tradition is the antithesis of the individual and the institution. Objectivity was thought to reside in the cognitive act of the individual who was endowed with an absolute capacity for rationality. Thus, for Kant, the conditions of thought were *a priori*; they cannot be derived from social processes and have no empirical genesis. According to Cartesian 'reason', man would grow out of institutions as a child out of infancy, in the achievement of autonomy. This has been massively reified in the representation of thinking as deriving from the possession of 'intelligence'. Institutions, customs, and belief were the repositories of tradition, prejudice and interest; they were, therefore, non-rational and the source of bias and error in the pursuit of rationality. Objectivity meant the transcending of socio-cultural influences and validation by universal reason. This was echoed in the political ideas of Locke, the *Philosophes* and the *Ideologues*. (It is significant that later 'ideology' came to be synonymous with institutional distortion arising from class and interest.) The political debate between rationality and ideology has been well-documented by Lichtheim (Lichtheim, 1965). 'Objectivism' became very much an optimistic ethic for progressivism and liberalism, and a rationale for the maintenance of political elitism and the gradualness of political emancipation in Britain. It was certainly very much in evidence in the public debates about education—the teacher was, and still is, exhorted to develop the 'rationality' of the learner as if it were a one-dimensional scale and to free him from the 'distortions' of his own commonsense reality. The simplistic notion of 'progressivism' has been preserved in the belief in scientific neutralism, value-freedom, and 'liberal education'.

This intellectual tradition has perpetuated a restricted view of human thought in detachment from the institutional activity in which it arises. According to Mannheim, this tradition has preserved 'the fiction of the isolated and self-sufficient individual'.[10] Its consequences for scientific thought—and in particular, the social sciences—have been tremendous. As Dewey recognized,

We are only beginning to recognize the extent in which the whole British empiricistic philosophy was developed as a method of criticism of institutions, political and ecclesiastical. It became the working creed of the 'liberal' school, because it was originated by Locke in order to provide an analytic method of attack upon beliefs connected with institutions he desired to abolish or reform.[11]

The epistemological sufficiency of objectivism is directly challenged by the sociology of knowledge, which insists that man is seen as existentially related to his social structure. The essential feature of this tradition, which derives from Hegel's *Phenomenology of Spirit* and the *Economic and Philosophic Manuscripts* of 1844 by Marx, is that human sociation is a dialectic phenomenon. Man externalizes himself through physical and mental activity in the process of objectivation. The products which he has created then become his objective world, a reality which confronts him and is available to the definitions of others. This is subjectively appropriated, and the objective structures are transformed into subjective consciousness. The interpretative architecture of the mind is at once an active and a passive agent in the construction of meaning and significance. Through the sedimentation of experience in the memory and objectified products, existence in projected: 'Reconstructed present and reinterpreted past are perceived as a continuum extending forwards into a projected future' (Berger, P. L., and Kellner, H., 1964). The individual biography is, therefore, both a subjective and an institutionalized history of the self: the one acts on the other.

Because this view emphasizes man's active construction of experience, there is a clear challenge to the static, analytic conception of knowledge. The status of knowledge as an entity now becomes problematic and seen as subject to the interpretations of individuals as these are mediated through particular social processes. The preoccupation with knowledge as object masks the extremely complex problems of, and infinite variety in, its realization. The focus, therefore, is now diverted from how man absorbs knowledge so that he can replicate it to how the individual creatively synthesizes and generates knowledge, and what are its social origins and consequences.

It should be emphasized that questions of 'truth' and 'validity' are also problematic. The problems which are thought to reside in a 'body' of knowledge and the rules for their effective solution or verification are themselves socially constructed. The cognitive tradition which generates the problems also, through its relevance system, legitimates the inferential structure which is activated in their solution. Questions and their validation criteria are mutually limiting, and, in a sense, self-fulfilling; the parameters of one are contained within the relevance system of the other; and the logic which binds them is itself dialectically related to them. Thus, as Mills suggests: 'The rules of the game change with a shift in interest'.[12] He goes on to argue that zones of knowledge, through their human constitution, have careers in which the norms of truth change. 'Criteria, or observational and verificatory models are not transcendental. There have been, and are, diverse canons and criteria of validity and truth, and these criteria, upon which determination of the truthfulness of propositions at any time depend, are themselves, in their persistence and change, open to socio-historical relativization.' He explicitly did not exclude the post-Renaissance scientific paradigm from this. This is another way of saying that epistemologies are institutionalized. It is important to emphasize that the cognitive tradition which forms an epistemology can exist only through a supporting community of people.[13] Its members are co-producers of reality and the survival of this reality depends on its continuing plausibility to the community. As will be shown later, this is of particular relevance to teachers and pupils, who, through their joint action, form epistemic communities more or less supporting the cognitive structures which make up the educational culture. In other words, the changing forms and content of knowledge will have social-structural correlates.

What we have attempted is a critique of the conception of knowledge as object. It has been counterposed by a view of man as an agent actively interpreting his world through appresentation and inference. Interpretation, however, does not occur *in vacuo* but through socially-approved categories which are differently legitimated in particular social settings. Thus, truth and validity are not absolutes but derived through certain relevances and legitimacies. The empirical issues for the sociology of knowledge, therefore, are embraced in the dialectic relationship between ideation and its social infrastructure in both its subjective and objective manifestations.

How, then, can it develop our understanding of educational processes?

In general terms, we shall conceptualize teaching and learning as the inter-subjective construction of reality. We shall argue that teachers have certain core assumptions about their 'subjects', about pedagogy, the intellectual status of their pupils, and some idea of what constitutes thinking, including its presence and supposed absence in particular learning situations. They will also have an etiology which is activated in the explanation of deviance or school pathology. These constitute an important part of the knowledge content of the occupational ideology of the teacher.

As Berger has suggested, this will not be a one-dimensional or uniform-quality knowledge, but will be a composite of different kinds of knowledge corresponding to how they are distributed in the different levels of consciousness—broadly distinguished as pre-reflective (or enactive), pre-theoretical, and theoretical. However sedimented and activated, the teacher's stock of knowledge is the relevance system and interpretative grid of both his internal dialogue and the rationales which he feels obliged to give when held accountable by any of his 'publics'. The teacher's behaviour contains tacit and explicit inferential structures through which he intersubjectively constructs his 'natural world' and which themselves are socially located. The joint action of the staff-room and the class-room will confer or withhold legitimation and will thereby create private and public thought structures for the teacher. The degree of correspondence between them will influence the quality of commitment and loyalty which are invested. When a teacher (or a pupil) participates in new curriculum projects, the relationship between the different perspectives with their intentionalities and rationales, will have a crucial effect on the operation and outcome of the project.

The sociology of knowledge can explore the genesis and transformation of these products in the continuing interaction between the teacher and his publics —pupils, colleagues and contemporaries—and can suggest some consequential outcomes for pupils. This is possible through integrated analysis at the different sociological levels of 'subject' and pedagogical perspective content, institutional negotiation between teachers and with 'official' reality defines (e.g. the head-master), and the perceived locations of legitimation and cognitive support. The suggestion is that curriculum and pedagogy should be regarded as professional knowledge, subject to the constraints of inter- and intra-professional organization and negotiation, and accountability. The professional paradigms, rituals of cog-nitive avoidance, loyalty structures, and the legitimations of competing alliances, all have a bearing on the ways in which knowledge is organized and transmitted.

Curriculum change, therefore, has consequences for teacher and pupil identity. Attachments and detachments in the form of new commitments and changing conceptual thresholds will result in new career locations—subjective and objective—for the people involved. And an important expression of this will be the structure of knowledge which evolves. As teaching becomes more pro-fessionalized, it will develop an increasing systematization of theory and a more self-conscious pedagogy. The assumptions which support them, and their connecting logics, and their consequences for social relations can be illuminated by a sociology of knowledge.

It would be appropriate at this stage to consider in more detail the deriva-tions and conceptual dependencies of the theoretical framework which forms the basis of this study. It will be clear that it rests on an all-embracing conception of the sociology of knowledge. Not only does this make possible a sociology of institutions and culture, but also a sociology of mind, language and meaning. Thus, the social phenomenology of Schutz and Husserl, the sociology of know-ledge of Scheler, Mannheim and Mills, and the so-called symbolic interactionist school are all seen as contributing significantly to this perspective. However, we shall be particularly concerned here with the ideas of Schutz, Mills and Kuhn.

One of the most crucial and compelling arguments which Berger has put forward and which we are taking up is that consciousness and identity should be considered in the context of the sociology of knowledge. Only when sociology has its now explanation of psychological reality (that is, the individual's understanding of himself in the processes of his own consciousness), he suggests, can it effect-ively demonstrate, and empirically use the Marxian sub/superstructure dialectic. The notion that man's consciousness arises out of his social being is the central proposition of the sociology of knowledge. But in this structural form, it has no explanation of how ideation or objectified knowledge which arises in social activity is constituted and made plausible in the self. Sociology, therefore, needs an explanation of *realization*—in its existential sense. Berger argues that the theoretical mediation between social structure and consciousness is contained in the ideas of Mead and symbolic interactionism, which he considers to be 'the most important theoretical contribution made to the social sciences in America' (Berger, P. L., 1966). Unlike learning theory and psychoanalysis, which have respectively dominated experimental and clinical psychology, the Meadian epistemology incorporates a dialectic view of man as a world producer as well as a social product. Moreover, not only does this represent the dialectic between self and others, but, also, the inner dialectic which occurs when the individual reflects on his actions. This enables a formulation of consciousness as having different 'tensions', in which the theoretical symbol systems interact with the pre-theoretical and pre-reflective self.[14] Thereby, through language, culture becomes existential.

The contribution of Alfred Schutz to the sociology of knowledge is particularly impressive and is suggestive of several issues which are relevant to an examination of teacher and pupil reality. In combining the phenomenological insights of Husserl with those of Weber, Schutz deepened the conceptual fields of *Verstehen* and 'action', and went some way towards establishing a sociology of mind as a subject of central importance in sociology.

Schutz provided an elaborate critique of consciousness and action, in which the individual act is seen as the visible manifestation of a complex interpretational process within the constituted biography. Intentionality, as embodied in the commitment to a project of action, masks an inner dialectic between 'because of . . .' and 'in order to . . .' motives which occur through the different 'tensions' of consciousness.[15] Hence, both projection and retrospection are contained in the 'vivid present', in which action takes place. Choice for an individual is, therefore, an active process made operational through the interpretational system, which is his biographically-constituted knowledge. The world is apperceived in an immediate experience and appresented to the self through the evocation of associations; these are referred to provinces of meaning which make up the interpretational or contextual scheme. The continuing processes of constitution and accommodation make up the individual's 'stock of knowledge', which is his *Lebenswelt*. This is not, however, held in isolation. It is a social product, held in conjunction with other individuals, who, at varying degrees of distance, occupy his world. Schutz refers to these as consociates, contemporaries, predecessors, and successors. The greatest confirmation of his 'frame of reference' is likely to come from his consociates who inhabit his spatio-temporal world, and with whom he is jointly engaged in reality-construction.[16]

Schutz argues that all individuals are socialized into a pre-existing world which, through the heuristic symbols of its language, is capable of referring experience to particular provinces of meaning. The consciousness is, therefore, structured into symbolic zones. This is essentially what happens when children are introduced to the 'mapped-out' theoretical zones of knowledge called 'subjects'. These are particular theoretical relevance systems which contain certain questions and assumptions about phenomena and a preference system for the testing of reality. They generally consist of the following dimensions:

(i) The unquestioned matrix within which any enquiry starts;
(ii) the elements of knowledge which have to be socially approved;
(iii) which procedures (i.e. sign systems) are appropriate for dealing with the problem;
(iv) the typical conditions under which a problem can be considered solved.[17]

As will be shown later, this framework provides a preliminary basis for the analysis of the content of curriculum units, and the criteria by which they are thought to be coherent entities.

There is an affinity between the ideas of Schutz which we have outlined and Mills's suggestion that intentionality, both imputed and avowed, is related to socially-situated *vocabularies of motive*. These are the epistemologies which contain assumptions about the reality which underlies an individual's action. Theoretically akin to Simmel's 'cognitive syntheses', this concept is operationally of great significance.

We may locate a thinker among political and social co-ordinates by ascertaining what words his functioning vocabulary contains, and what nuances of meaning and value they embody. In studying vocabularies, we detect implicit evaluations and the collective patterns behind them—'cues' for social behaviour. A thinker's social and political rationale is exhibited in his choice and use of words. Vocabularies socially canalize thought.[18]

Mills suggests that in any society or institution, there are dominant vocabularies which form the interpretational matrix of human interaction, and which integrate and stabilize the taken for granted world of different individuals. 'Motives are accepted justification for present, future or past programs or acts'; and, because they *name* the consequences of action, they constrain the range of alternatives open to an individual. Different groups in society have asymmetrical vocabularies of motive, and differential access to motive-imputation procedures. The question of power as control over reality definition and communication is, therefore, central to the social organization of knowledge.

Schutz's interpretational system and Mills's vocabularies of motive can be seen effectively in partnership with Kuhn's idea of 'paradigm'.[19]

Seen in the light of Schutz's appresentational and interpretational schema, rather than in the terms of its own historical perspective, Kuhn's analysis of scientific activity is particularly meaningful. One of the essential points which Kuhn makes about scientific knowledge is its ongoing nature. The conceptual framework has a 'career', and knowledge through time is transformed. His concept 'paradigm' represents the moving parameters which are felt by scientists to legitimately set the inferential co-ordinates of their field of work. It contains the prior knowledge, the projected problems, the frameworks of meaning, criteria of truth and validity; it has assumptions 'as to how entities of the universe interact with each other and with the senses'; and it has a system of methodological rules which can be legitimately employed to find solutions. In Schutz's terms, it constitutes the taken for granted natural world of the scientist. This is 'normal science' where the scientist works out the implications of the paradigm.

It was not Kuhn's intention to discuss science as an institutionalized activity, or to consider the transmutation of a paradigm in the individual perspective. It is clear, however, that he regards the paradigm as professionalized knowledge, and that it is perpetuated through textbooks and teaching programmes. This parallels Berger's notion of the supporting community as a 'plausibility structure' which serves to control the expression of doubt and cognitive dissonance, and to regulate and legitimate change.[20]

While one can acknowledge the heuristic value of 'paradigm', it should be said that it does not explain the pluralism or differentiation of paradigms within scientific activity. The questions which are posed in an analysis of teaching and learning as the organization of knowledge are built on the assumption that within the teacher's stock of knowledge are fragments of multiple paradigms—arising particularly through the interplay of subject and pedagogical knowledge. The relationship between the individual's perspective and its paradigmatic origins are problematic, and will, in any case, represent a unique blend with its own social consequences.

Kuhn's analysis of the break-up of a paradigm which occurs when the scientific community loses confidence in its potential for explanation, is particularly interesting when considered in an institutional context. In Berger's terms, it represents the disintegration of their taken for granted world and the loss of social-psychological support. This process is essentially one of dereification. Certitudes become opaque, and the paradigm is seen as a relative, humanly-produced construction. For some, this experience is anomic, in that it produces a disruption of cognitive order, and a breach in the unity between subject and object. In this situation, argues Kuhn, the practitioners of science often have recourse to philosophy in the effort to clarify their epistemology. Their new paradigm, a new conceptual ordering, then emerges out of the crisis.

The problems of change and resistance to change are closely related to the social distribution of knowledge, which Schutz suggested was one of the central concerns of a sociology of knowledge.[21] These issues are discussed by Holzner in his book, *Reality Construction in Society* (Holzner, B., 1968). He is particularly concerned with the social-structural correlates of the pluralism of cognitive structures, and raises the issues of the social distribution of expertness and its control through professional mandate, and the rules and control of communication by accredited reality definers. Thus, the question of power as control over legitimacy and the labelling of some kinds of knowledge as deviant is critical in the maintenance, transmission and administration of particular symbol systems.

Using the theoretical insights just outlined, we should now return to the central task of this study, which is to suggest ways in which to examine the professional identities of teachers in relation to their subject and pedagogical perspectives. Keeping in mind the dialectic between ideation and its social infrastructure, it should be possible to analyse a classroom situation in which teachers and pupils are engaged in the exchange of knowledge and the construction of reality. Classroom interaction may be conceptualized as the meeting of particular patterns of ideation, the objective reality of which is differently interpreted, realized and justified by the participants. This would provide insights into the social structure of the school, and the constraints which its articulation makes on the consciousness of teacher and pupil. Finally, we can attempt to analyse the assumptions contained in the thought forms themselves—psychologisms, the vocabularies of motive which constitute the rationality contained in the teaching of a subject.

All this should be seen in the context of a decision by a school to introduce an integrated studies programme, a process which could be indicative of a general disaffection with one paradigm, and a psychological openness to a new one. The extraordinary and widespread preoccupation with the 'objectives' of education is only one manifestation of a collective grasping for new symbols of 'relevance' and 'worthwhileness'. It ought to be possible to explain why this is so important a feature of our society, and to offer some suggestion as to where it might be leading.

## 3. PEDAGOGY, SUBJECT PERSPECTIVES AND THE TEACHER'S CAREER

It is a popular belief that teaching cannot be theorized about; that, because it is experienced in the 'vivid present', it is essentially a sensate, existential knowledge, resistant to theoretical explanations.[22] To some extent, this is true—as Durkheim suggested in his distinction between teaching as a 'science' from teaching as an art.[23] Until more is known of the nature of consciousness, particularly its propensity for *ekstasis* (as manifested, for example, in identification, loyalty and commitment), knowledge about teaching (and learning) will only *reflect* the lived experience and not explain it, albeit with varying degrees of refinement.

This popular view has become institutionalized in colleges of education and teaching organizations in requests for greater opportunity for 'on the job' practice as providing the only 'true' knowledge of teaching. This is the practical, pre-theoretical view, which celebrates the activity component of teaching as the acquisition of technique designed to facilitate transfer of knowledge from teacher to pupil.

In the foregoing critique of teaching, this view will be resisted as naïve and limited. It is indicative not only of the general low status of teaching, but the lack, until recently, of studies *of* teaching, as opposed to studies *about* teaching. It ignores the interpenetration of reflective knowledge (whether theoretical or pre-theoretical) and active (or pre-reflective) knowledge. The 'tensions' of consciousness are not autonomous, but react dialectically with each other. This dialectic, which has been expressed by Berger as one between psychological reality (subjective apprehension of reality) and a psychological *model* of reality, induces the regulation of consciousness through the retroactive conferral of meaning on the act. In other words, the summary of infinite acts and communications which occur in a teacher–learner situation represents an appraisal in which meanings are attributed to, and create structures in, the stream of consciousness. The content of the summary, as it is generated in the reflexive analysis within the self, becomes a reference point for future acts, and is a constitutive component of the teacher's perspective. Because the teacher does not merely 'hand on' knowledge, but makes critical choices about sequence, duration, tempo, or, in some cases, appropriate mix of enactive knowledge (e.g. 'pupil dicovery') and theoretical knowledge, the teacher's perspective contains differently legitimated interpretational systems, broadly differentiated as 'subject' and 'pedagogical'. These will contain the inferential structures of public knowledge, the intentionalities, rationales of success and failure labelling, and the verification and validation criteria which constitute evaluation. As Bernstein has suggested (Bernstein, B. B., 1971), curriculum, pedagogy, and evaluation should be considered in their relationship; together, they constitute an epistemology, and vocabularies of motive which will 'dictate broad preferences for the kinds of experiential bases on which knowledge is to be constructed; the epistemological position sensitizes to certain aspects of encountered reality and desensitizes to others'.[24]

Nevertheless, it is important that the constitutive properties of each are kept analytically distinct. The knowledge components which form pedagogy have a different intellectual heritage from the epistemologies which form and sustain 'subjects', and their realization has taken place within different social milieux. Pedagogy was for Durkheim an embodiment of the 'collective fabric of society';[25] as a more or less theoretical rationalization of anthropological assumptions about human nature, it contains within it the anxieties about, and explanations for, the problems of social order (and some strategies for overcoming them). On the basis of these assumptions and anxieties are constructed the rules which control the communication—i.e. the ways of relating and evaluating—between those entrusted with the transmission of knowledge and society's novitiates. The assumptions are the interpretational knowledge to which the child's behaviour is referred. Pedagogy also contains a manipulative dimension in that it suggests strategies for minimizing the resistance between the teacher's world view and that of the pupil.

'Subjects', on the other hand, are the institutionalized symbolic universes oriented around particular questions about different entities within the universe, and man's relationship to them. Contained within them are frames of reference and methodologies which guide the selection of data and the conferral of validity. But, as subjects are reconstituted and transmitted through the social organization of educational institutions, they are dialectically related to pedagogical practices. These help to determine the interpretational shading, and the processes by which the knowledge is categorized and arranged, and whether the ultimate doubts and unknowns are revealed early or late in a school career.

The curriculum is a set of arrangements of knowledge which are assumed to have a purpose: it consists of *intentioned* knowledge. Through their control of the transformations of the child's consciousness, its exponents engineer theoretical world views which are thought to be valid currency in their society. Pedagogy, therefore, can be seen as the rationality of the intention, and evaluation is the verification procedure of the intention.

Unfortunately for the sociologist, however, this abstraction cannot be applied in this form to the intricacies of diverse classroom situations. While we have assumed that teachers hold different kinds of knowledge which make up their occupational ideology, we cannot presuppose the configurations which transpire when teachers meet children in a classroom. The relationships between different pedagogical assumptions and the organization of a subject, even for one teacher, and where the pedagogy can be theoretically justified, are problematical. The outcome of continuing institutional negotiation between teachers with different perspectives, and who are co-producers of an integrated project, is much more so.

The reason for this is that what appears inconsistent to the sociologist may appear acceptably consistent to the teacher, in view of specified contingencies. Furthermore, the interpretational systems of many teachers operate implicitly and sometimes inconsistently (what Polanyi refers to as 'tacit' knowledge). This is only to be expected between different publics—for example, parents, colleagues, pupils, headmaster—when different components of the perspective are suppressed; but it also occurs through time with the same public and even within the individual's internal dialectic. This is particularly likely to be the case with a teacher whose pedagogy is pre-theoretical, where the inferential structures are relatively weak, and the rationale sparse and restricted.

In order to minimize some of these difficulties for the operational working of the research—at least in its early stages—schools have been chosen where a prominent innovation was occurring in curriculum organization. The 'projects of action' which teachers had to undertake in order to carry it through would, it is thought, be more likely to contain documented and articulated rationales which would clarify the reference points by which their perspectives were constructed. The negotiated division of labour and timetable construction are particularly useful sources of data.

It would be convenient at this stage to suggest the main dimensions of the operational model which is being developed for the selection and interpretation of data. It is assumed that all teachers have a 'subject' and a pedagogical per-spective of varying degrees of theoretical consistency and clarity. These are manifested in vocabularies and rationales and the implicit epistemology which supports their control of knowledge and children, and their preference system for evaluating learning outcomes. The visible indication is a teaching style which represents a synthesis of differently perceived, and differentially-operating in-fluences, some of which are in perpetual conflict in the teacher's internal dia-logue. In addition, teachers are being conceptualized as members of epistemic communities which have particular orientations in their explanation of human nature, learning and numerous non-classroom issues. We, therefore, need to know not only the content of legitimations as they are perceived by the teacher, but also their origins and social location. The career location is intended to focus some of the professional and institutional constraints on the teacher's under-standing of his work. To repeat what was said earlier, the perspectives are meant to represent the *constitutive categories of thought* through which a teacher under-stands his occupational world. Their significance should become clear in the later discussion, but for now can be represented in the following way:

## A. Pedagogical Perspective

### 1.) *Assumptions about learning*

   a.) Which psychological theories—explicit or implicit—are dominant?

   b.) What assumptions are held about the qualities of responses from pupils which indicate whether learning is taking place?

c.) How does the teacher define favourable outcomes—the 'good pupil'?

d.) What is the definition of unfavourable outcomes—the 'bad pupil'?

e.) How does the teacher explain the distribution of good and bad pupils?

f.) What are the intentions, embedded in teaching procedures, for favourable outcomes?

2.) *Assumptions about the child's intellectual status*

a.) What is the teacher's implicit model of the child's thinking—psychometric or 'epistemological'? Is the child reified?

b.) Assumptions about age and learning—what are the constraints which chronological age is thought to place on learning?

c.) Assumptions about social class and its relation to thinking.

3.) *Assumptions about teaching style*

a.) Is a didactic or problem-setting technique thought to be most effective in the production of desired outcomes?

b.) Degree of control over communication thought to be necessary.

c.) Degree of legitimation and public emphasis given to pupil-initiated cognitive structures.

d.) Degree of reification of knowledge.

B. Subject Perspective

a.) Which paradigm is defined as crucial, and what is the degree of integration between paradigms? What is the teacher's world view of the subject?

b.) Which problems are defined as important for the subject?

c.) How strongly articulated is the utility dimension of the knowledge—e.g. 'pure' v. applied; the subject content or its technology?

d.) What are the criteria of utility—*extrinsic*: economic, humanitarian, world-improving, social integration; or *intrinsic*: developing particular qualities of awareness?

e.) Assumptions about inferential progression from commonsense to theoretical knowledge.

C. Career Perspective

*Assumptions about career location and relations with epistemic communities*

a.) Degree of public legitimacy for his definition of subject and its methodology.

b.) Perception of crucial diffusion centres of legitimate ideas and degree of access to them.

c.) Significant others who reinforce his reality.

d.) Ethnocentrism of social organization—nature of budgetary and departmental separation within institution.

These categories are by no means exclusive or exhaustive, but are intended as guides for the sorting of data from participant observation and interviews. They suggest the social organization of teachers' perspectives and their grounding in socio-historical epistemologies. Teaching style is likely to reflect changing conceptual thresholds along these dimensions.

## A. Pedagogical Perspective

Several studies have recently documented the social and existential consequences of the bureaucratization of psychological beliefs in Western societies. The social phenomenology of Laing, for example, suggests that the generic 'illnesses' of schizophrenia and depression are the institutionalized definitions of a particular psychological model, which can conveniently be applied to a wide range of human conditions. They are, therefore, an important form of social control (Laing, R. D., 1960). Cicourel and Kitsuse put forward the view that the differentiation of pupils can be regarded as a function of definitional processes which occur within institutional settings (Cicourel, A. V., and Kitsuse, J., 1963). The definitions are part of a larger inferential network of taken for granted assumptions about human nature and social order.

Berger refers to these reified psychological models as 'psychologisms', and suggests that they arise from man's apparent destiny 'not only to experience, but also to explain himself' (Berger, P. L., 1965). He has likened them to the pre-scientific objectifications of mythology and medieval theology; they represent the secularized ideation and secularized consciousness which has accompanied the demonopolization of religious epistemologies as valid explanations of psychological reality. They also provide powerful legitimations in a bureaucratic society for inter-personal manipulation; increasing inroads into the private self are justified in the interests of greater rationality. Cicourel and Kitsuse make the point that it was the desire for a more 'scientific' selection process, in order to maximize a nation's talent, that led to decisions, no doubt plausible to a productivity-conscious society, to employ counsellors.

Little analysis has yet been made of the psychological models which feature in teaching. There is little doubt that they are likely to represent an important part of the pedagogical perspective. As a source of legitimation for a teacher, psychologisms have a crucial influence over his organization of knowledge, and the existential development of pupils.

Psychological models embody the parameters of their enquiry and validation within their assumptions about man, and, as such, are largely self-fulfilling. A particular feature of the exponents of psychological models is their appropriation of the right to define mental health and mental pathology which it follows up with programmes of 'treatment'. In other words, a psychological model contains an etiology and a therapy ideology which are activated in definitions of deviant and normal behaviour. Berger has argued that the power of psychological models lies in their reified appropriation in the subjective consciousness, thereby becoming part of a collectively-held interpretational scheme. Because they change the definitions of self, they become regulative of future action. This is, of course, the point of W. I. Thomas's well-known statement that 'a situation defined as real will be real in its consequences'.

The social distribution of psychological knowledge has led to promiscuous syncretization at pre-theoretical levels, as they are realized in the commonsense, everyday reality; but, at the scientific level, they have tended to remain distinct. In psychiatry, the dominant form is likely to be psychoanalysis, and, in education, the psychometric models of intelligence and personality, and learning theory of 'behaviourist' psychology, and, to a lesser extent, Piagetian or Brunerian cognitive psychology. Kelly's 'personal construct' theory, though not widely known, has also been invoked for the teaching of English.[26]

With the intensification of the teaching of theoretical psychology and sociology in colleges of education, there is a greater likelihood of their appropriation as constitutive categories in the pedagogical perspectives of teachers. Through their relevance penumbra and validation criteria, they will establish the taken for granted preference co-ordinates in the assessment of experience data, notably in responses to the actions of pupils.

One of the difficulties of operationally separating the psychologisms in any analysis of a teacher's pedagogy is that there will be a wide variation in their range and theoretical density. For many teachers, they will consist of little more than the popularized, commonsense views of psychological reality and the means of social control will be implicit. One suspects that teachers approximate to the 'well-informed citizen' discussed by Schutz.[27] Because of their professional isolation the theoretical ideas of their pedagogy are rarely invoked in their work situation. This is likely to produce a sedimentation of pre-theoretical psychology. One suspects also that the social support which a college of education provides for a theoretical psychological interpretational scheme is not sufficiently strong to rob existing pre-theoretical psychologisms of their plausibility. Educational psychology still lacks the prestige of psychiatry and therefore is not as strongly legitimated in courses for student teachers as psychoanalysis and drug therapy are for student psychiatrists. Sociology has even less. Any operational measure of the psychological positions of teachers must, therefore, anticipate a dimension extending from pre-theoretical custodialism to an elaborated phenomenology.[28]

Not all psychological models are of equal significance for the development of pedagogy, that is, for the organization and presentation of 'subject' material. One may broadly distinguish two generic types: a *psychometric* model, and the *epistemological* model of Piaget and Bruner.[29] Each has its own social principles containing fundamentally different assumptions about human nature and consciousness, and its own consequences for the transmission of knowledge. The psychometric model derives from the Individualist, empiricist tradition discussed earlier, and represents the child essentially as object. One of the recent protagonists of this tradition is Bloom, whose taxonomy of 'objectives' is related to the realization of the child's 'innate' potentialities. The other model is explicitly concerned with how the child actively constructs and arranges his knowledge of the world in his developing interpretational schema. This is much closer to the dialectic epistemology of Hegel, Marx and Mead. Even so, as the social nature of reality construction is largely taken as given, it is not, therefore, a true dialectic model. It does, however, have considerable affinity with the sociology of knowledge with which it can be incorporated.

The psychometric model endows the child with an 'intelligence', a capacity of given power within which his thinking develops. He is a novitiate in a world of pre-existing, theoretical forms into which he is initiated and which he is expected to reconstitute. The teacher monitors his progress by means of 'objective' evaluation and he is differentiated from others by its 'objective' criteria. According to the parameters of this model, the teacher is society's surrogate selector; his certified competence to perform this function is not in question. Any criticism which attaches to him as a 'poor' teacher is likely to refer to his enactive *technique*, his charisma, or his ability to maintain 'order'; it is not likely to attack the basic epistemology on which his pedagogy rests.

This view regards the child—by definition—as a deficit system; a passive object to be progressively initiated into the public thought forms which exist outside him as massive, coercive facticities, albeit 'worthwhile' ones. It also legitimates a didactic pedagogy—the 'good pupil' is docile and deferential, cognitively, at least—and it provides particular organizing principles for the selection and transmission of knowledge.

It is possible to regard this epistemology as a reification of both the child and public knowledge; for teachers and pupils, the pedagogy which is founded on it is an agency of alienation, and the knowledge content is an important form of false consciousness.[30]

Access to the 'mysteries' of the subject is controlled by, and made through, the teacher, and is delayed until the pupil is an accredited member of the subject community.[31] A view which sees education as a one-dimensional progressivism, and which regards the properties of knowledge as inert 'things to be mastered', sees the child's achievement in terms of a growing rationality and a result of prior intelligence. This pedagogical perspective is likely to predispose the teacher to limit the range of possible solutions to questions, and to be preoccupied with right answers and 'the right way'. The notion of 'discipline' epitomizes the spartan nature of this ideology. It sensitizes to objectivistic labels, such as I.Q. and age-status (that is, intellectual status)—which are attributed to pupils, and it desensitizes to the intersubjective processes which maintain the assumptions underlying the labels. As Bernstein has suggested, a consequence of this is a clear separation between public and private identities, both for teachers and pupils (Bernstein, B. B., 1971). This is inevitable where there is little concern for the processes of subjective constitution and cognitive accommodation in teacher–pupil interaction. The reality tests of this pedagogy are conducted within its frame of reference and are manifested in the definitions of good and bad pupil. These are usually related to the degree of cognitive symmetry between pupil and the teacher as exponent of the public theoretical knowledge.

This psychologism, and the pedagogy which follows, is founded on several assumptions about children and the human mind, most of which hinge on the attribution to them of a measurable quality called 'intelligence'. The debates about their education have, therefore, centred on a 'more or less' argument. 'Intelligence', in the form of I.Q., is the reified object *par excellence* in this extensively reified psychology, and an immense legitimation for power distribution in society. The assumption that there exists in everyone a latent quality which only needs to be developed has been fostered by the search of psychologists for a professional identity. So pervasive has it become that a good deal of 'sociological' research has been encapsulated within its orbit. In the drive to taxonomize the influences which impede 'learning', various social contingencies have been labelled as being capable of retarding the development of 'achievement motivation', or linguistic/cognitive/affective potential—or even of annihilating them.[32] The continuing argument about the inherited and cultural properties of intelligence is a monument to the individualist epistemology. In reducing the complex processes of thinking to the possession of an innate drive, it fails to consider either the properties of the knowledge which are supposed to demonstrate its presence, or the processes by which individuals interpret and construct their worlds. With great clarity, Durkheim summarized the essence of this developmentalist perspective in his *Education and Sociology*:

Until recently, most pedagogues believed that education was an individual thing, and consequently, they made pedagogy a direct corollary of psychology alone. For Kant, as for Mill, for Herbart as for Spencer, the object of education would be above all to realize in each individual—to their highest perfection—the attributes of the human species in general. They assumed that there is *one* human nature, the forms and properties of which are determinable once and for all, and the pedagogical problem consisted of investigating how the educational influence should be exercised on human nature so defined. They supposed that human growth is only a realization of potentialities and only brings to light the latent energies which existed fully formed, in the physical and mental organism of the child. The educator, then, would have nothing essential to add to the work of nature. He would create nothing new. Therefore, conditions of time and place, the state of the social milieu, lose all interest for pedagogy. Since man carries in himself all the potentialities of his development, it is he, and he alone, who must be observed when one undertakes to determine in what direction and in what manner this development should be guided.[33]

This is not the place to discuss the genesis of this pedagogy, except to suggest that it has close affinities with the empiricist tradition of the nineteenth century from which psychometric techniques derived—and also social Darwinism. Its continuing plausibility is, however, an important sociological problem.

A powerful extension of the psychometric psychologism is the educational programme of 'compensatory education' which is a peculiar reconciliation of social welfare and social Darwinism. As Bernstein and Friedman have argued, the label 'culturally deprived' tends to be conferred on those whose cognition is grossly asymmetrical with that of their teachers. Disjunctive cognitive structures became 'deficit systems' (Bernstein, B. B., 1970; Friedman, N. L., 1967).

Several studies have illustrated the self-fulfilling nature of the assumptions which teachers have of their pupils. Becker suggests that teachers, like the members of other service occupations, tend to differentiate their clients according to the degree of closeness which they achieve to the 'ideal' image (Becker, H. S., 1952). For the Chicago public school teacher, the large number of 'non-ideal' pupils legitimated her low expectations of work and effort, and her 'unproductive' teaching techniques: 'She expects that the amount of work and effort required of her will vary inversely with the social status of her pupils.' Becker also remarks that the lower-class pupil is a source of revulsion and distress to the teacher. 'It is the slum child who most deeply offends the teacher's moral sensibilities'; and, moreover, the teacher is afraid of him. This point is made strongly by Tennenbaum, who argues that revulsion and fear of the slum child's aggression lead the middle-class teacher to homogenize, and negatively stereotype the behaviour of the others, thereby denying the validity of their reality (Tennenbaum, S., 1963). Goodacre also found this to be true of teachers of lower working-class areas. Not only were children regarded as socially homogeneous, but intellectually as well:

More teachers in the lower working-class areas tended to accept that they had no pupils of above average intellectual ability. This suggested that the teachers in the extreme social areas tended to have well-structured stereotypes of the type of pupil and home they could expect. It seemed likely that these expectations were related to their ideas concerning the relationship of occupational level, social conditions and intellectual ability (Goodacre, E. J., 1968).

It is likely that the cognitive distance which characterizes the stereotyping of one life-world by another is related to social separation. Goodacre suggests that definitions of 'good' and 'bad', where teaching groups are large, are likely to be made on a minimal number of cues. 'Teachers who preferred teaching pupils individually rather than in groups, tended to be more favourably disposed towards their pupils and types of background.' This suggests that assumptions about the quality of pupil response are related to a teacher's commitment to individual learning outcomes which, in turn, is related to the size of the teaching groups. Thus, size of teaching groups may have an important relationship with the contents of the pedagogical perspective.

This does not, however, necessarily signify a different pedagogical epistemology. Indeed, the evidence suggests the opposite. The significant key to pedagogical assumptions concerning the child's ultimate intellectual status and the quality of his learning is the organization of knowledge and its perceived status in relation to the total knowledge of the curriculum. It is probable, as Michael Young has suggested, that, in view of the presuppositions of the epistemology, the content of the Schools Council's projects, which are intended for the less able or 'deprived' pupils, is of low status (Young, M. F. D., 1971). This is particularly so of the curriculum for children who have been *Cross'd with Adversity*.[34] The vocabularies of motive of this document suggest a view of the child and the quality of his thinking as not only different, but deficient. His processes of nomization and meaning construction, the content and operation of his interpretational structures, are not considered. The way to get him to learn is to incorporate the familiar and the relevant into his curriculum, thereby trivializing the knowledge which he can learn. There is no suggestion of the sequential cognitive structures which would create the inferential links between 'topics' for the less able and 'subjects' for the able. That it can occur is presumably a matter of faith. One of the features of the Schools Council's programmes has been their failure to recognize the complexity of consciousness, and the problematic relationship between everyday knowledge and theoretical knowledge. The symbolic ordering and extrapolation required for the second is much greater than that needed for the first, where the symbolic rules are more private. It is, of course, the theoretical knowledge which has the higher status, and which is a powerful constraint to learning for the child in whom it is not already constitutive.

What we have suggested is that there is a powerful connection between a reified view of intellectual status (as related to age, I.Q. and attainment) and the reification of school knowledge. John Holt summarizes this well in the following extract from *How Children Fail*, where he distinguishes answer-producers from thinkers:

Practically everything we do in school tends to make children answer-centred. In the first place, right answers pay off. Schools are a kind of temple of worship for 'right answers', and the only way to get ahead is to lay plenty of them on the altar. The chances are good that teachers themselves are answer-centred. What they do, they do because this is what they were, or are, told to do, or what the book says to do, or what they have always done. One ironic consequence is that children are too busy to think (Holt, J., 1964).

Douglas Barnes makes a similar point when he suggests that many lessons have a high factual content and preponderance of 'closed' questions (that is, questions to a predetermined end), and didactic control (Barnes, D., 1969).

In conclusion one could say that the psychometric epistemology, through the credibility attached to educational psychology, has become powerfully institutionalized and constituted in the pedagogical perspectives of teachers as their taken for granted assumptions about intelligence, learning and the 'good pupil'. This model reifies the child and the objects of his learning, so that the school is a massive force of alienation. 'Compensatory education' is a liberal version of the epistemology which has social Darwinism at its opposite end. It is, however, a mystification in that the knowledge associated with its programmes is likely to be low-status knowledge, and accords with a view of 'deprived' children as 'deficit systems'. This epistemology diverts the focus from the knowledge structures associated with the curriculum, and the transformational processes which occur when they are subjectively appropriated in the consciousness —particularly the social nature of these processes.

It is clear that the psychometric epistemology has been paradigmatic for much of the educational practice in Britain. It has set the parameters which have been felt by teachers to legitimate and maintain the inferential co-ordinates of their field of work. Not only has it had the frameworks of meaning and the

criteria of truth and validity which are part of a paradigm, it also has its problems
—one of which is how to get 'unintelligent' children to learn—and the methodological principles which can be legitimately employed to find the solutions (e.g.
compensatory education). This has been a massive constraint on the thinking of
teachers. Their taken for granted, natural world has contained assumptions
about the existence of a substance called 'intelligence', which, like 'phlogiston',
is 'given off' when certain stimuli are applied to the child. If it is not manifested
in certain reality-defining procedures, then the child is deficient. The circularity
of the epistemology thus becomes clear. It is self-defeating and self-contradic-
tory to assume that all children are intellectually deficient until they prove otherwise, and then to spend time and money trying to remedy what one had defined
as inevitable anyway. Lacey provides an excellent illustration of the self-fulfilling nature of the teacher's definition of 'good' pupil. The 'problem pupils'
are so because of the premises on which the differentiation is made (Lacey, C.,
1966). Some teachers, unwilling to accept this inexorable logic, seek to legitimate
their definitions by reference to the social conditions, which, by being thought
capable of retarding or promoting learning, can be held 'responsible' for educational problems—thus producing one of the fundamental dilemmas of the paradigm which is encapsulated in the argument between the conflicting protagonists
of heredity and environment about the constitution of intelligence.

It could be argued that we are witnessing the anomie, that is, the denomiza-
tion, or conceptual dismantling, which accompanies the break-up of a paradigm.
One of the features of this process, Kuhn has argued, is that certainties become
opaque and are seen as relative socio-cultural productions. Reifications are
dereified, and alienation gives way to anomie.[35] The indications are multiple and
diverse. The debate between inherited and acquired characteristics of intelligence is one manifestation; so also is the realization that teachers' expectations
are important in creating pupil identity. Issues like the demise of the eleven plus,
comprehensive education, student unrest over examinations might also be cited.
The work of Henry, Friedenberg, Holt and others are a powerful documentation
of the 'demythologizing' of the main assumptions of the paradigm. One wishes
to avoid over-dramatization, but it is clear that we are witnessing some aspects
of a profound change in the understanding of consciousness.

This has already been documented by Berger for religious institutions which
have for some time had problems of conceptual disorder (for example, the 'death
of God' school). These are underpinned by an increasing tendency to cite
transcendental experience in the subjective consciousness. The 'freak out' and
hippiedom, as features of anomie and the struggle to create a new nomos, may
correspond to the paradigm 'crisis' in education.[36]

What can we suggest are the characteristics of a new paradigm, if indeed
there is one? One of the main features is a preoccupation with subjective experience and its composition, in which man is represented as an active rather
than a passive creature, that is, in the creation of his own objects. It is represented
in the psychological theories of Piaget and Bruner,[37] whose epistemology is
akin to the dialectic scheme of Mead and Schutz. Their emphasis on the

construction of thought forms through sensory and linguistic ordering, and the growth of reflexiveness, amount to an incipient phenomenology. Bruner suggests that learning is the active development of a cognitive technology. Through the grasp and manipulation of various superordinates which epistemically organize the multiple zones of knowledge, the child develops a series of inferential chains which enable him to bring under their control increasing quantities of data. As Bernstein has suggested, when this methodology is applied to teaching, 'the pedagogy is likely to proceed from the deep structure to the surface structure' (Bernstein, B. B., 1971).

Bruner modifies Piaget's stages of development somewhat by suggesting that an epistemology operates at different levels of consciousness and therefore produces different 'textures' of knowledge. He distinguishes three of these—enactive, iconic and symbolic, indicating that the data of the here-and-now experience may, or may not be referred to the interpretational schemes provided by the linguistic ordering of symbolic knowledge. The power to transcend the here and the present lies in the possibilities for extrapolation which lie in the manipulation of symbols. He suggests, therefore, that the strength of the referral system is critical for the development of this power. The acquisition of knowledge is not simply a progressive movement from enactive (or concrete operations) to symbolic (formal operations); it occurs through the routinization of referral sequences and their further elaboration into epistemologies.

A close parallel can be drawn here with the work of Bernstein, who has drawn attention to the different qualities of referral in *particularistic* and *universalistic* frames of reference. The epistemic possibilities of the second are much greater than those of the first because of their more symbolically elaborated inferential chains (Bernstein, B. B., 1970).

For Bruner and for Bernstein, a consideration of the properties of knowledge and their arrangement is crucial for an understanding of consciousness transformation and learning. Bernstein, of course, raises the further question of the relationship between legitimations of particular social groups and the structure of knowledge.

Central to this epistomology, therefore, is a view of human learning, and human sociation generally, as being derived from a dialectic relationship between consciousness and socially-approved, socially-distributed knowledge. This dereifies both the child and knowledge, and necessitates a revision of objectivistic assumptions about 'intelligence'. As John Holt expressed it:

Unintelligence is not what most psychologists seem to suppose—the same thing as intelligence only less of it. It is an extremely different style of behaviour arising out of an entirely different set of attitudes (Holt, J., 1964).

Bruner himself outlines the characteristics of this epistemology in *Towards a Theory of Instruction*:

I suspect that much of growth starts out by our turning around on our traces and recoding in new forms, with the aid of adult tutors, what we have been doing or seeing, then going on to new modes of organization with the new products that have been formed by these. . . . The new models are formed in increasingly powerful representational systems. It is this that leads me to think that the heart of the educational process consists of providing aids and dialogues for translating experience into more powerful systems of notation and ordering. And it is for this reason that I think a theory of development must be linked both to a theory of knowledge and to a theory of instruction, or be doomed to triviality.[38]

Within this paradigm, it is necessary to examine the human propensity for order and *ekstasis*—the power to transform and transcend the active present through existentially different realities. It is also essential to examine the processes of interpenetration between the different tensions of consciousness and the transforming power of social approval and denial. The assumptions, preference system, methodology and reality tests will be fundamentally different from those of the psychometric epistemology.

Other examples of a phenomenological psychology can be cited, although they have not yet been widely diffused. Kelly's 'personal construct' theory is concerned with the generative power of categories which children learn and their effectiveness for organizing experience.[39] Berger also raises these issues in his discussion of 'nomization'—the process of conceptual ordering derived from man's possession of memory. Symmetry, generalization and repeatability provide the stabilizing cognitive reference points for future projects of action. New experiential data can only be meaningful if the individual's nomos can accommodate them. 'Responsiveness', therefore, is seen to be related to the degree of conjunction between the teacher's and the pupil's relevance system (Berger, P. L., and Kellner, H., 1964).

It is clear that this second psychological epistemology will place different constraints on pedagogy, and, therefore, on the knowledge which is taught. For Bruner, the child's appraisal system and its generative power develop dialectically with the teacher's structuring of knowledge. The child 'discovers' chains of experience data which are relevant to his nomos and is encouraged to make them the nuclei around which future knowledge can develop. He is thereby made self-regulative in that he actively controls his sequence of experience. This is the reason for the optimism contained in Bruner's well-known statement that 'any subject can be taught effectively in some intellectually honest form to any child at any stage of development'.[40] The teacher as a guiding significant other induces the child to reflect on the emerging logic, and to use it as a generalizing base for acquiring future knowledge. Because the area of socially-approved knowledge is allowed to be diverse and open-ended, it is expected as a matter of course that the pupil will be able to find some cognitive attachment between himself and his school projects; he is, therefore, expected to become *committed*. 'Intelligence' has, therefore, given way to 'curiosity' as the yardstick of reality tests; and school deviance moves from 'unintelligence' to unwillingness to co-operate, and emotional neutrality. As Bernstein has argued, the child under this pedagogy is likely to find that social distance between himself and his teachers will be difficult to maintain; and that, because his subject nomization is more public, his privacy is eroded (Bernstein, B. B., 1971). The validation criteria for teaching also change: 'bad' teaching is associated with the reification of knowledge—that is, as 'facts to be learned'; and with weak *Verstehen*—the inability to appropriate the consciousness of the child. This is the explicit judgement of Barnes, when he suggests that failures of communication and understanding occur in the inability or unwillingness of teachers to apprehend the commonsense knowledge of their pupils through the reality of their theoretical knowledge. They were unable to recreate the intentionality and subjective reality of pupils in the comments and answers they were offered. Holt makes a similar point when he suggests that teachers and pupils are often talking about different issues while assuming that they are talking about the same thing.

Where these assumptions are constituted, even partly, in the pedagogical perspectives of teachers, not only will the existential outcomes for pupils be different from those of the psychometric position (that is, what constitutes effective learning), but also, the content of 'subjects' themselves as socially-approved knowledge. Within the psychometric paradigm, integrated studies are likely to be regarded as manipulatory (or motivational) devices available to teachers of 'less able', or unwilling, or 'Newsom' children. Subjects are likely to retain their status in the curriculum as knowledge appropriate for able children. This distinction is likely to be one between a curriculum where enactive or concrete knowledge is predominant, and a curriculum based on theoretical provinces of meaning. Thus, handicraft, because of its traditional lack of theoretical knowledge as a school subject, is thought to be a particularly suitable content for 'less able' children. In other words, the psychometric theory of knowledge is limited to a concrete–abstract continuum representing the assumed concrete–abstract progressivism of children's thinking.

The theory of knowledge which is contained in the 'epistemological' psychology is built on different principles of social order. One of its most potent pedagogical implications is that the organization of the curriculum into clearly-bounded zones can no longer be taken as axiomatic. Instead, several different arrangements are possible according to which superordinates are followed. If knowledge is dereified, it is, then, a much more negotiable commodity between teacher and pupil. Its socio-historical relativity is likely to be transparent and the content of knowledge may become subservient to the development of a cognitive technology which is capable of projecting multiple inferential structures containing both enactive and theoretical knowledge. There is no reason to suppose that these will remain within the 'boundaries' of what are now heuristically labelled as 'subjects'. New configurations of knowledge are likely to emerge from the combinations of questions which arise in the learning situations. The problems of objectifying, or naming, these configurations, and of managing the new cognitive structures are great. It is probable that under this pedagogical perspective we shall see the emergence of 'summarizing subjects' which are able to unify what were previously discrete zones—for example, anthropology, communications and linguistics, design and technology, ecology, cybernetics, ethology.

The consequences of this pedagogical epistemology for the social organization of teachers and pupils, and for the future differentiation of knowledge, are very great. It may be possible to detect in the alliances and segmentation occurring within professional associations the generation and growth of new organizing frameworks for knowledge. The intra-professional negotiations which are already occurring indicate the dereification of territoriality. The boundaries are only human constructs and can, therefore, be broken. The psychological correlates of this are likely to be considerable.

For many teachers, the epistemological citing of these assumptions is not possible. They are not aware of the fundamental changes occurring in the basic parameters of their pedagogic reference points. The cognitive and existential anxiety which is induced may amount to anomie and a personal struggle to reintegrate their perspectives. They are experiencing the vertigo of a paradigm break-up in which certitude seems threatened by relativism. This may explain the exotic variety of pedagogical and curriculum arrangements in our present education system, and why anxiety overhangs the outcome and validity of many 'integrated studies' courses. Relativism strikes at the roots of taken for granted reality and is usually resisted, not only because it may lead to an existential vacuum, but because it also relativizes authority and institutionally-convenient divisions of labour.

The result in schools is likely to be confused and inconsistent pedagogical perspectives, particularly in the interrelationships of assumptions about reality, methodology and reality test. This is inevitable, so long as the legitimations are fluid and transient and the social-psychological support of epistemic communities is barely developed.

It would appear, in many cases, that the open-ended organization of knowledge is sometimes inconsistent with a psychometric selection system, and a traditional subject-oriented examination. The rationale of compensatory education may offer the necessary plausibility. Consistency within the pedagogical perspective will be more likely to be present if the legitimations of the reality test and knowledge organization 'fit' the assumptions about consciousness and learning. For some teachers, a critical problem of consistency would arise if their 'epistemological' pedagogical perspective were in conflict with the institutional arrangements of teaching groups and selection processes which upheld psychometric assumptions. The headmaster's reality definition could be important here.

It is also possible, of course, as we shall argue later, that a dereified theory of knowledge is legitimated for a teacher by considerations other than pedagogical ones. He may feel that the paradigms of his subject themselves are inadequate for dealing with questions about 'reality'. However, in view of the intensification of education courses for student teachers, it is probable that for many, their subject perspectives will be heavily influenced by psychological assumptions.

Research into pedagogical perspectives would, therefore, have to be sensitive to the degrees of consistency maintained by teachers who attempt an integrated studies programme, and the relationship between their assumptions and the different legitimations of the school and their professional communities. A comparison of the private and the public rationales of teachers would be particularly illuminating.

It would be necessary, also, to assess the relationship between the implicit psychological model of the pedagogy and its methodology. It is quite probable that many integrated courses will be organized within a psychometric model, in which case, one would expect them to be predominantly pre-theoretical, and clearly separated from the more theoretical 'subjects'.

We have established that the pedagogical perspectives of teachers contain within them the constitutive categories of a psychological epistemology and an incipient theory of knowledge. Not only do they constrain the identity and careers of pupils but they become the interpretative filters in the selection and arrangement of knowledge in the curriculum. The variety of pedagogical and curriculum experiments which is at present being undertaken in schools, testifies to the conceptual opacity of pedagogical intentionality. Various curriculum 'theories' are being invoked and institutionalized as explanations of these phenomena, and legitimations are being hammered out for their validation. These are important data for the sociologist and may provide some indication of the changing nature of social control and the principles of order.

## B. Subject Perspective

One of the great difficulties which is likely to arise in any research into pedagogical and subject perspectives is to phenomenologically reduce to separate analytic categories what is, for teachers, a total, taken for granted classroom praxis. Although there is a continually-operating interrelatedness, it is very necessary that they should be distinguished. If pedagogical assumptions control the intentionality about *how* particular knowledge should be arranged, the subject perspective will contain the rationales for *why* certain knowledge should be taught. The focus of the research will, therefore, be different. Whereas before we were concerned with the continuing relationship between psychological assumptions and pedagogical practice in the teaching of integrated studies, we should here be concerned with the influences, other than pedagogical, which induce teachers to decide that their subject content as a discrete entity was inappropriate for their teaching programme.

We have suggested already that one of the main constraints which pedagogy places on the selection and presentation of knowledge lies in its alternative possibilities for being either answer-oriented or problem-oriented. In the first, the organizing principles and inferential logic are likely to be subservient to solutions; in the second, the organizing principles are likely to be explicitly related to many solutions, or even none at all. One of the reasons for this, it was suggested, is the reduction in plausibility for the Individualist paradigm which reified the child and the socially-approved knowledge which formed the curriculum.

In this section, we shall consider 'subject' perspectives in the light of this second area of plausibility crisis.

It is important to emphasize the institutional and relative nature of teachers' subject perspectives. One of the paradoxes of our analysis is that to refer to knowledge as structures, or 'subjects' is immediately to 'mystify' (and thereby obscure) how knowledge and human thought are reversibly one and the same thing. 'Knowledge' is the external face of subjective reality. The historical reification of knowledge has diverted our attention from the continuing flux of human thought and its power to incarnate itself. It is, therefore, necessary not to consider subjects as given, but to analyse what a teacher *thinks* a subject is. The knowledge which a teacher thinks 'fills up' his subject is held in common with members of a supporting community who collectively approve its paradigms and utility criteria, as they are legitimated in training courses and 'official' statements. It would seem that teachers, because of the dispersed nature of their epistemic communities, experience the conceptual precariousness which comes from the lack of significant others who can confirm plausibility. They are, therefore, heavily dependent on journals, and, to a lesser extent, conferences, for their reality confirmation. The contents and ideologies of these would be important data.

Subject perspectives can be summarized as the biographically-constituted representations of particular symbolizations and meanings which have been institutionally oriented towards particular questions about the universe. They contain the socially-approved methodologies for resolving them and the validation criteria essential for their solution to be considered achieved. Through time, they become the habituated thought forms through which individual reality is constructed; in other words, they become part of the taken for granted stock of knowledge. As Schutz suggests, 'this consists of a set of systems of relevant typifications, of typical solutions for practical and theoretical problems, of typical precepts for typical behaviour. All this knowledge is taken for granted by the respective social group and is thus socially-approved knowledge.'[41]

Bourdieu makes a similar point when he suggests that 'culture is a common set of previously assimilated master patterns from which an infinite number of individual patterns directly applicable to specific situations are generated' (Bourdieu, P., 1967).

According to this view, subjects are mystifications which arbitrarily differentiate and objectify the physical and symbolic universes. They thereby constrain the subjective identities of the individuals in a society, and obscure their realization that they are humanly produced. They are, furthermore, maintained and distributed through their institutionalized transmission in schools where 'through the very logic of its functioning, the school modifies the content and the spirit of the culture it transmits; and above all, its express function is to transform the collective heritage into a common individual unconscious' (Bourdieu, P., 1967).

This is, however, a rather simplified view. Schools and universities do not have a monopoly over the generation and transmission of theoretical knowledge.

In a society characterized by a pluralism of 'knowledge-producing' and knowledge-validating agencies, critical problems of choice and accommodation arise for educational institutions. Industrial organizations are powerfully able to affirm or deny the validity of an epistemology and are, therefore, particularly important as plausibility structures. This is maintained through the problem orientation of industry which ideologizes knowledge as technology. The bureaucratization of knowledge and research which accompanies economic rationalization is partly responsible for the contemporary plausiblity crisis, and the reality disintegration of subject identities. The territorial disputes between the members of subject communities indicate that certain zones of knowledge are no longer appropriate for the analysis of the universe, and that 'the boundaries of species whereby men sort them, are made by men'. This quotation from Locke was used by Jevons to explain the cognitive mergers which are developing in the various scientific subjects (Jevons, F. R., 1969).

Jevons argues that there are, in many instances, greater differences within scientific 'disciplines' than between them, and that 'physical science' has provided the main overarching framework for their integration. A concern for the social and economic content of problems has led to a pluralistic approach to their solution which can be better provided within the new framework.

This process is essentially one of dereification, characterized by a questioning of the basic assumptions about the central explanatory axes of a subject, and the sufficiency of its problem validation. This can only be remedied by a widening of the data admitted to the problem and incorporating the experimentation of other 'subjects'. The point which should be made is not that knowledge contents are necessarily moving to open relationships with each other, but that this is a feature of the nomization process to larger and more stabilized structures. As pragmatic openness becomes institutionalized, it is likely to be followed by ideologized closure. We may, in fact, be seeing the crystallization of large overarching fields of knowledge which summarize and integrate previously discrete zones. Some possible candidates have already been suggested—anthropology, ecology and ethology.

There are several reasons for this phenomenon, some of which are central to an understanding of the constitutive categories of teachers' subject perspectives.

Bernstein has related the changing organization of knowledge to the Durkeimian analysis of social change (Bernstein, 1967). Differentiation of knowledge within and between subjects arises out of the intensification of the division of labour. Individuals relate increasingly through differences, and cognitive symmetry is reduced. This does not, however, say sufficient about the social infrastructures in which new ideational complexes are propagated. The question which remains, and which is central to the sociology of knowledge, is *what* are the social-structural and social-psychological processes which are leading to and sustaining the increased integration of knowledge? In other words, how does one explain the continuing plausibility of and social support given to the integrationist ideology?

An important key to this lies in the vocabularies of motive which are contained in subject perspectives, whether articulated by teachers or research workers. Accompanying the reappraisal of subject content is a profoundly strong utility ideology. The pluralism of knowledge-producing, and knowledge-ratifying agencies inevitably promotes the operation of market forces on the limited supply of resources made available for research. In consequence, requests which are submitted are likely to be couched in vocabularies which emphasize the world-improving, humanity-aiding nature of the research. One of the most notable utility criteria is that of economic benefit. This is particularly true of research which is controlled and sponsored by industrial organizations. Economic nationalism generates sensitivity towards the economic return of knowledge—a feature of contemporary industrial societies which has been massively ideologized in 'technology', and the euphemism 'industrial needs'. Educational institutions are induced to structure their overt motives in terms of the use to which knowledge can be put in the solution of material problems. It could be argued that this has always been so. Merton's analysis of the topics chosen by scientists in seventeenth-century England shows clearly the relatedness of research to particular social and economic problems.[42] But the difference between that situation and the present day is that the bureaucratization of knowledge has been manifestly conducive to the institutionalization of an integrationist ideology, which is now confronting educators as a powerful objective reality. Growing economic rationalization produces rationalized knowledge to the extent that means–ends connections between problems and their solution are sharpened. The instrumental integrationist ideology is a necessary consequence of the primacy of problems and their solubility, and the synchronization of the multiple methodologies of 'interdisciplinary' teams is an essential feature of industrial management. The contemporary faith in the 'generalist', the 'adaptive personality', the 'divergent thinker', and the 'scientific administrator', is powerfully plausible in a context of economic and political nationalism. Furthermore, an integrated province of knowledge becomes a powerful base for the generation of larger and more embracing problems, and, thereby, becomes self-justifying. The dialectic between identified problems and the methodologies for their solution creates a spiral of 'integrated' knowledge.

McDermott has noted the monopolistic tendencies of many American industrial and political institutions over the use of knowledge (McDermott, J., 1969). 'The great institutions have become generalists, increasingly able to integrate the discrete information of the specialists into technical and organizational systems.'

Daniels has suggested that the democratic control of educational and scientific institutions has been an important feature of the decline of 'purity' as a realizable ideal for scientists (Daniels, G. H., 1967).

The socio-psychological correlates of the bureaucratization of knowledge are formidable. The dissemination of multiple-paradigm solutions through the communications media produces problems of conceptual assimilation which threaten the ethnocentric organization of knowledge. Educational and professional institutions are faced with critical problems of choice in their criteria for the admission of new knowledge, and difficult decisions about their plausibility. Rationalization in the form of ecumenism and integrated studies is a probable consequence. Not only is this a means of redefining the co-ordinates of the taken for granted world—thereby reducing existential anxiety; but it is also a response to the visible inadequacy of particular frames of reference as explanations of material problems.

A research programme enquiring into the parameters of teachers' subject perspectives should focus particularly on the utility criteria of certain zones of knowledge as they are formulated in teachers' vocabularies of motive. These could be considered as either predominantly *intrinsic*—that is, stressing the propensity of the knowledge for developing a particular quality of awareness in the child; or *extrinsic*—emphasizing its world-improving, humanity-aiding potential. An analysis of problems as they are stated in professional journals and conferences, etc., could be used to trace the changing focus of the 'subject'. It is likely that the curriculum will have an increasing social problem orientation and that justifications for the inclusion of knowledge will contain a technology rationale. A recent example of a social problem legitimation for science in the curriculum is Dyer's argument for an integrated biology course (Dyer, 1967). He suggests that the utilitarian function of biology has been seriously underestimated in educational planning, and that this is reflected in the inadequate financial resources and publicity allocated to it. He lays out the operational possibilities for the curriculum of fields as varied as marine biology, biochemistry, and genetics, and he is critical of the separation of zoology and botany in 'A'-level courses, and of universities for failing to include genetics, ecology and cell biology. His solution is a total reorganization of the subject around 'the study of mankind', in order that its 'direct social and economic application' can be realized.

A similar claim was made by Mikesell for geography.[43] He argues that there is little justification for the intellectual and social separation of the diverse fields which comprise geography: 'It is a mosaic within a mosaic.' The geographic epistemology is connected with the 'locational and spatial configuration of matter'; this is wide enough to admit not only parasitology and geology, but also, sociology, psychology, economics and political science. He suggests that the embracing framework could be 'cultural ecology'.

Dineen makes a similarly ambitious suggestion that linguistics, because it comprises history, culture, communication and psychology, is '*the* interdisciplinary subject'.[44]

The social utility ethic is reinforced on intrinsic grounds also: that is, through the pedagogical assumption that 'effective learning' requires an explicit emphasis on knowledge as technology. This is the conclusion produced after a survey carried out in the United States in 1957 for the American Association for the Advancement of Science.[45] 48,000 high-school children were questioned in order to ascertain the popular image of science. The report noted that the practice of science as reflected in science teaching, had a poor image, and recommended a massive public relations campaign which would stress 'the real human rewards of science'. It was thought to be desirable that the mass media should present an image of science which emphasized human interest, group work and the relationship between science and technology. Within the classroom, the pedagogy should emphasize pupil participation and the interdependence of scientific subjects, including the behavioural sciences. It was significant that the final paragraph of the summary refers to the fact that an unfavourable image 'is an indication of the climate of opinion in which citizens may be expected to vote funds for new laboratories, and voters may be expected to judge Congressional appropriations for science education'.

There is a parallel here with the current concern in this country about the so-called decline in the popularity of science in schools and higher education. The 'need' for science tends to be couched in vocabularies which emphasize its economic and world-improving utility—notably in the interests of economic nationalism. Thus, the Dainton Report suggests that 'breadth, humanity and up-to-dateness must be infused into the science curriculum and its teaching'; and teachers are exhorted to make scientific knowledge 'attractive' and 'relevant'.[46] The word 'relevant' is an acceptable cachet which signifies that, on both pedagogical and economic grounds, it is *useful* knowledge—i.e. knowledge as technology—which is important. As such, it is a powerful form of social control.

We have argued, then, that the processes of democratization and bureaucratization of knowledge have contributed to the ideologization of technology, and thus to the displacement of 'subject' boundaries. The first is creating an open-market situation where the members of subject communities are induced to appeal in competition with others for public support and scarce resources, in order to justify their existence and desired expansion. 'Ecumenism' strengthens the hand and increases relevance. The other is producing a rationalization of knowledge in the attempt to match solutions to the material problems of economically-competing industrial units. Unless teachers are, therefore, prepared to modify their subject perspectives and pedagogy and accommodate these demands, their teaching is likely to be considered as 'irrelevant'. How they reconcile the different rationales of pedagogy and subject content in the creation of integrated studies and its intentionality is a large question. We have argued in this and the previous section that ideological support for the relocation of subject boundaries and the institutionalization of integrated studies is being provided by two distinguishable processes of social and ideational change. These are the development of a subjectivistic and 'epistemological' approach to the human mind, and the ideologization of technology, derived from economic rationality and political democracy. How far teaching perspectives, curriculum organization and the social structure of the school embody and confirm these broad ideational patterns is the subject of the research. It is likely that, in a large number of schools, they are forming the substance of elaborate processes of definition, negotiation and justification which are centred on the school time-table and the content of examinations. It is also probable that they are creating acute problems of personal identity. Because they undermine their everyday reality, these ideational complexes will be interpreted by many as a threat to the established authority, and as creating problems of institutional classification and resource allocation. The logistic battles are being fought in the attempts of teachers to articulate and control the integrationist ideology. Whether integrated projects are a temporary step towards fewer but more inclusive 'subjects' is an interesting empirical question. If this is the case—and one is tempted to suggest that it is—the organization of power in reality definition will be a significant key to the institutionalization of new epistemologies. The teacher's career location —both inside and outside his place of work—is likely to establish for him the cognitive co-ordinates and legitimations of his subject perspectives. His career perspective, in terms of his degree of access to the perceived reality-defining centres, and his interpretation of their rationales, will provide a fruitful framework for discerning the changing criteria of valid school experience.

## C. Career Perspective: The Institutional and Professional Organization of Knowledge

One of the main purposes of this study has been to show the social nature of teachers' knowledge—that the frames of reference and constitutive categories of pedagogy and subjects rest in, and are legitimated through, the socio-historical contexts in which they arise.

This section will seek to amplify this theoretically and operationally— through a synthesis of the sociology of knowledge with the ideas of the Chicago School on the sociology of professions.

It is, of course, impossible to do justice here to the conceptual richness of the substantive theory and research of the Chicago sociologists. We can, however, suggest particular ideas which could be developed further in the research. It would be convenient to isolate two main threads which have been an important feature of their work. The first relates to the concept 'career' as—in Hughes's words—'the moving perspective in which a person sees his life as a whole and interprets the meaning of his various attributes, actions and the things which happen to him' (Hughes, E. C., 1937). We should include here the ideas of Becker and others on commitment and situational adaptation and the constraints of joint action on individual reality definition.[47] The other is the work on professional processes and ideologies. This has been superbly summarized by Schatzman and Strauss in their typology for the study of psychiatry (Schatzman, L., and Strauss, A. L., 1966). This could well be prototypical for a research programme into the subject and pedagogical knowledge of teaching.

Greenwood, in an article on professionalization, suggests that the folk concept of 'profession' is usually applied to an occupation which has developed a systematic body of theory and culture.[48] This 'serves as a base in terms of which the professional rationalizes his operations in concrete situations.' Schatzman and Strauss make clear that this knowledge, and the processes by which it is maintained and transformed, can be the subject of sociological analysis, and put forward a set of models as a way in which this could be systematically directed. They summarize these models in this way:

1.) *Interprofessional process*—providing a view of an institution as 'a professional arena involving confrontation and negotiation'.
2.) *Professional process*—'a perspective on professions emphasizing organizational and ideological segmentation and branching over time'.
3.) *Public process*—'a view of public rhetorics in terms of who understands what' about the work of a profession;
*Socio-cultural processes*—'a perspective on institutional forms as affecting professional practice, ideologies and careers'.

It would be useful at this stage to consider how this framework could be applicable to the study of teaching.

The subject and pedagogical perspectives of teachers form a large part of their professional knowledge. Colleges of education devote much of their teaching to the inculcation of 'subject' knowledge and the dissemination of psychological theories which are thought to have a bearing on child development and learning. There are obviously significant variations between different colleges. These may occur in the particular theories thought to be most relevant; or they may occur in the degree of constraint which pedagogical assumptions are allowed over subject knowledge; and there will also be different attachments to the paradigms which make up a subject.

It is not the purpose of this study to offer a sociological critique of the knowledge thought to be relevant by colleges of education, but to suggest that, through their control of the professional education, and entry of intending teachers, they are powerful epistemic communities, and, as such, are worthy of a sociological critique.

If we take each of the models in turn, it should be possible to show the configurations of influence and negotiation as they are represented in the individual teacher identity; and to suggest how the general points made about subject and pedagogical perspectives can be incorporated into the research programme.

## 1.) *Interprofessional process*

The analysis at this level would be carried out in case studies of particular schools and would explore the ways in which professionals, representing different subjects and pedagogy, negotiated a division of labour within their work situations. As Schatzman and Strauss express it, this concerns the 'ways in which emergent operations, developing operational philosophies and styles of work modify professional, institutional and ideological commitments'. Professional knowledge is negotiable currency. Research would attempt to suggest the dominant patterns of negotiation and the structural contingencies which modified them. More substantively, it would seek to identify the pedagogical assumptions of particular teachers, along the lines of the theoretical model already outlined, to penetrate the intentionality behind arrangements of knowledge, and to trace the inferences between pedagogy, subject and evaluation.

Justifications for divisions of time for sequences of knowledge; the distribution between answer-seeking and problem-finding procedures; the classification constraints placed on symbolic knowledge—these would be some of the empirical indicators of a pedagogical perspective.

How those of a number of teachers meshed together would be an important problem for the research. So, too, would the justifications for particular subject content in the project as indicators of subject ideology.

The research carried out by Strauss and his colleagues into psychiatric ideologies and institutions is particularly relevant to this problem (Strauss A. L., et al., 1964). Mental hospitals were conceptualized as 'arenas' in which debates were held between widely different perspectives about the nature of mental illness and its therapies. The differences, which penetrated all levels of patient management, diagnosis, etiology and treatment, arose from the competing inferential structures of the three main analytic systems of psychiatry—psychoanalysis, somatotherapy, and milieutherapy. The form which was dominant in an institution tended to be related to certain structural factors: for example, the perspectives of the senior and administrative staff, the number and status of the patients, and the ecology of the hospital. The spatial separation of wards and ward shape signified particular conceptions of patients which acted as a powerful structural reality in the definition of health. An administrative classification which admitted only two types of patient, chronic and acute, was able to obliterate finer classifications that were contained in the ideologies.

The relationship between the ecology of an institution and the conceptual maps of its inmates is implicit in an article by Campbell.[49] His concern is the relationship between cognitive ethnocentrism and social-structural separation as maintained through the administrative assumptions and decisions of an institution. He is specifically interested in the curriculum and the structural contingencies which maintain the segregation of subjects in academic institutions. He maintains that definitions of centrality and marginality arise through the superimposition of departmental boundaries on speciality boundaries. One of the significant consequences of this is a budgetary separation which creates competitive groups. Boundaries are rationalized through decisions taken about what is central and what is peripheral as they are exemplified in allocation of space, time, money and staff, and even students. 'This promotes the basis of an ingroup identification against competitive outgroups.' Linguistic separation is reinforced by the competitive nature of the structural organization. Campbell points to the demise of the interdisciplinary work of the Yale Institute of Human Relations as being a consequence of administrative ethnocentrism. It was not supported in the departmentalism of budgetary and promotional units. A similar lack of institutional support for an integrated course characterized the seventeen-year experiment of Northwestern University's 'interdisciplinary' courses. Campbell makes the point that 'there were no institutional rewards to the faculty for doing the job of integrating and preparing the common language', and makes the important distinction between a truly interdisciplinary course and 'multi-disciplinary' courses such as these.

An important connection can be made here with Becker's idea of career and commitment. An ethnocentric administrative classification is likely to impede the generation of side bets and commitment for de-ethnocentric subject perspectives. The degree to which critical reality definers—in schools, the headmaster and deputy—are prepared to modify departmentalism will have a significant effect on the emergence and maintenance of commitment to new curricula. It should also be possible to consider the formation of pupil commitments and the relationship between particular perspectives and pupil fates.

## 2.) *The professional process*

This model enables the sociologist to focus on the formation of segments as social movements within a profession, and on the resulting conflicts and accommodations of ideation as they evolve through time. It was first put forward by Bucher and Strauss to represent the processual formation of alliances and 'deviant' subgroups, which occur in most professions, and as a criticism of the functionalist view of professions as homogeneous entities (Bucher, R., and Strauss, A. L., 1961). Thus, they identify them as 'loose amalgamations of segments pursuing different objectives in different manners, and more or less delicately held together under a common name at a particular period in history'. Disagreements between the members of different segments may be fundamental; not only do they concern the methodology and technique thought to be most characteristic of the profession, but even, in some cases, the most typical professional act. These produce different conceptions of the main paradigms of its work activity, and different professional vocabularies. Bucher and Strauss argue that segments are likely to form around new centres of interest—or 'unorthodox missions'—and identification of new problems as important for the profession. This may be accompanied by the establishment of public relations media for their articulation and legitimation and, possibly, alliances with segments of the same or another profession.

This model is particularly useful in its application to the changing conceptualizations of 'subjects' in teaching. The subject associations of the teaching profession may be theoretically represented as segments and social movements involved in the negotiation of new alliances and rationales, as collectively-held reality constructions become transformed. Thus, applied to the professional identities of teachers within a school, it would be possible to reveal the conceptual regularities and changes which are generated through membership of particular subject communities, as they were manifested in textbooks, syllabi, journals, conference reports, etc. 'Subjects' can be shown to have 'careers' which are dependent on the social-structural and social-psychological correlates of membership of epistemic communities. The individual career and set of appropriate commitments are worked out within the frames of reference which these allow.

Empirically, this model should enable one to discover the colleagueship network of teachers and their sense of legitimate centres of interest of the subjects they teach. Their career location will historically and socially frame the conceptual structures which are thought to be valid. It would also be useful in examining the institutionalization of segments and alliances as these are made visible through publications and training courses. In some ways, the segments of professions develop in the way in which Berger has suggested religious sects emerge, that is, as a voluntaristic obeisance to charismatic individuals (Berger P. L., 1954). One could argue, for example, that the formation of epistemic communities around the ideas of Leavis and Holbrook for English, and Namier for history, had some of the features of a sectarian movement which later became institutionalized. Davie's study of the transformations of mathematics courses at Edinburgh University, and Ben-David's of the origins of psychology are excellent illustrations of processes which lead to the emergence of some individuals as critical reality definers for an area of knowledge, and therefore of a supporting community (Davie, G. E., 1961; Ben-David, J., and Collins, R., 1966).

One study of professional membership which is relevant to the operational elaboration of this model is that by Mills of the professional ideology of social pathologists.[50] He suggests that the sales and distribution of textbooks are an important constraint on professional knowledge. Because textbooks embody prevailing ideologies and notions of the appropriate paradigms and boundaries, they make likely the perpetuation and reification of particular subject contents for the aspiring entrants to a profession who have to 'master' them. They are, therefore, useful sources of data for the sociologist.

Diana Crane's study of the 'invisible college' network in the organization of scientific perspective and practice is also relevant. She suggests that research scientists are located in a 'social circle' which, through its processes of indirect interaction, constrains the definitions which individual scientists make about relevant problems and methodologies. She makes the point that critical changes in the content of a subject may come from the influence of 'outsiders', whose perspectives form the nucleus of a new professional segment. This is particularly likely under the constraints of a competitive ethos which rewards the originality which often results from hybridization (Crane, D., 1969). Although neither of these studies specifically consider the differentiation of knowledge within and between communities, they offer ways of considering professional segmentation which could usefully be applied to teaching communities.

It is not envisaged that an analysis of professional alliances and segments would occupy more than a small part of the research. Its use lies in the means which it provides to consider the teacher's perspectives in their cognitive location.

3.) *Public process and socio-cultural processes*

Schatzman and Strauss use these categories to distinguish two important sources of data in the analysis of occupational ideologies, and which, they suggest, should be included in the theoretical and operational models. They present great problems for research in that the conceptualization of 'publics' will inevitably be arbitrary, and socio-cultural processes much more so. Furthermore, what little material exists on these is generally non-sociological and widely dispersed. One could, however, work from the work situation outwards—that is, from the dominant 'forms' of inference and plausibility in the professional perspectives of teachers attempting to cite them in their wider epistemologies and the processes by which they are communicated.

The concept 'public' was elaborated by Blumer to refer to the groups or aggregates who collectively view or use a particular service in society, and, therefore, contribute to public debate about it. Thus, particular orientations in educational practice are located in the ideologies of the dominant publics, and their 'rhetorics of legitimation'.[51] It would seem necessary, for example, to consider the Schools Council and educational research bodies in this context; similarly, numerous industrial organizations which hold views on education; various parents' organizations, and even the news media. The question one would be asking about these publics is what characterizes their thinking about education? How are changing conceptual thresholds for defining valid school experience communicated and made plausible to the teacher and to other publics? How is the dialogue between consumers of education and its professional exponents indicative of changing concepts of order and control? The institutional correlates of these processes will be manifested in the career flow of teacher and pupil and the definitions which are attached to particular mental states and experiences.

The rhetorics and ideologies of 'publics' are, of course, located in the sociocultural processes which support and label particular kinds of enterprise as educationally 'worthwhile'. Their analysis is one of the significant contributions which the sociology of knowledge can make to the study of educational practices. We have suggested earlier that the subject and pedagogical perspectives of teachers contain 'preferences' which become operative in their explanation of the world, and that these are part of the wider, historical, educational epistemologies. It is important that the research incorporates them into the discussion of perspectives. Strauss suggests, for example, that the philosophical ambivalence which is evident in conflicting definitions of psychiatric practice is partly derived from the uncertain coexistence of social Darwinism, social welfare and positivism. It is likely, as we suggested earlier, that the psychological assumptions contained in pedagogy embody a similar set of ideological presuppositions.[52]

We have, in this section, outlined several points of departure which a study of teachers' work processes, perspectives and career flow might take. It is obvious that the task of abstracting the perspectival styles and cognitive 'forms' from the multiple processes of interaction—direct and indirect—in which teachers are collectively located is not to be underestimated. The power of the suggested indicators to elucidate and generalize is not yet known; one can only venture the hope that they are at present sensitive enough to collate a sufficient range of data to make their inadequacy apparent.

## CONCLUSION

Integrated Studies: Some Specific Issues for Research

We have tried to show that the decision by teachers in a school to launch an integrated studies programme is a socio-culturally located 'project of action'.

Its vocabularies of intention and rationale are fragments of conceptual traditions which create stabilities and collectively-shared means of apprehending the world. The configurations—social and ideational—of such projects of action, their origins and consequences, are what the research will be about. We have presented the theoretical model with its operational indicators; it may now be useful to spell out in more detail some of the questions which are expected to guide the early stages of data collection through participant observation, interviews, and, later, questionnaires.

Fundamentally, we are asking questions about the decision of teachers to innovate in their curriculum and pedagogical presentation—that is, their conscious rejection of a previous arrangement and their choice of another. We are then limiting the area of innovation to the initiation and ongoing maintenance of integrated studies courses. At this stage, it is not important to delineate the many possible structural arrangements of what is usually referred to as team teaching. The critical point of interest is the relationship between the structure selected and the intentionalities of the participating teachers, that is, their paradigmatic location in curriculum and pedagogy. We shall then be able to suggest ideational consistencies and conflicts which are developed in the negotiated division of labour, and how, in the resulting transformations, teachers and pupils rationalize their experience.

The research programme can be differentiated into three levels representing qualitively different sorts of data which follow the different questions which are being asked. These are, first, issues at the level of ideology, which would include the paradigms, vocabularies of motive, public and private rationales, psychologisms and sociologisms, and a philosophy of 'subject'. We should be attempting here to explain the teacher's knowledge as an epistemologically-located interpretational system on which particular actions are grounded. The second set of problems is at the level of institutional interaction and structural constraint in which we should be observing the operation of innovation as process. The relevant issues here would arise out of the negotiated division of labour between teachers and between teachers and pupils. They would, for example, include the intended learning outcomes and the labels attached to them; also, the institutional organization of knowledge into the structural units of time and space, and the constraints which they impose on the ideational content of the curriculum. At the third level, we should attempt to locate the 'publics' and epistemic communities outside the school from which the teachers derived their cognitive support.

Within these levels we should specifically be asking such questions as the following:

1. Why they decided to introduce integrated studies in the first place;
2. how the division of material into teaching units was negotiated, and for what reasons a particular distribution was accepted;
3. which forms of pedagogy were evident; which was dominant, and in what ways it related to the arrangement of knowledge;
4. what forms did the institutionalization of the project take? Were any structural changes in the school classification system indicated?

5. What criteria were used to assess the success and failure of the project, and the individual contribution of pupils?
6. How was the relationship between the knowledge of the project and the remaining curriculum content defined?
7. What were the subsequent rationales and commitments—public and private—of those taking part in integrated studies?
8. Was there any communication about it with other institutions and/or professional associations?
9. What are the subjective and objective changes in career location?
10. Which publics are perceived as the sources of legitimation for the project?

These questions would not necessarily be formalized, but would be used implicitly to orient the interpretation of the data.

The 'project' is, therefore, being conceptualized as a world-building enterprise negotiated by pupils and teachers in which outcomes are uncertain and precarious, but which may be indicative of changing principles of social order and control. Its ongoing objectivation, its communication to others, significant and otherwise, and its consequences for the subjective identities and distribution of the school's reality definers, will be reflected in the changing knowledge which teachers and pupils have of each other, and the task structure in which they participate.

In his discussion of the 'sociological imagination', C. Wright Mills presents a view of modern man as an anomic being confronted by uncontrollable change and the massive dissolution of his cherished symbols, searching, in an existential vacuum, for a new identity. He suggests that the sociologist, through his understanding of 'the larger historical scene in terms of its meanings for the inner life and external career of . . . individuals' is able to illuminate the causes of personal unease and to empirically investigate the possible solutions and renewals of plausibility being undertaken (Mills, C. W., 1959). A recent book by Orrin Klapp takes up the same theme. Klapp argues that modern society, because of technological change, is preoccupied with identity search, and, in consequence, is throwing up numerous agencies and devices which support the collective groping for new mystiques and symbols (Klapp, O. E., 1969). Perhaps it would not be too fanciful to argue that symbolic loss and conceptual dislocation are widely apparent in many of our educational institutions, bringing to the teacher and pupil consequential problems of inadequate self-symbolism and a distrust of previously acceptable legitimations. This study, in trying to focus the individual biography in its socio-historical context is in a very real sense attempting to penetrate the symbolic drift of school knowledge, and the consequences for the individuals who are caught up in it, and attempting to construct their reality through it. Hopefully, one is seeking explanations—and even description—of the sources and the processes of change, and the continual restructuring of consciousness and ideation, as it occurs in the pupil and teacher career. The task is daunting, but essential if we are to understand the complex relationship between school and society as being more than a system within a system. Perhaps, also, it may offer to the teacher a way towards a deeper understanding of his work than sociology has so far shown itself able to provide.

# ACKNOWLEDGEMENTS

This article is based on material presented in 1970 for the degree of M.A. in the University of London, Institute of Education. In both its forms, it owes much to the ideas and guidance of Michael Young, to whom I am especially grateful. I am indebted to John Hayes, of King's College, London, for his many insights concerning the applicability of Schutz's writings to the sociology of education. I am particularly grateful to my friend and former colleague Peter Seaman, of Enfield College of Technology, for many valuable hours of discussion and for contributing in so many ways to the development of this study. I should also like to thank Nell Keddie for helpful comments and criticism. I have bene-fited from discussion with Roger Dale, of the Open University, of many of the issues of the study. And I owe a great debt of thanks to my fellow-members of the graduate seminar in the Department of Sociology, at the Institute of Education, London.

# NOTES

[1] For a discussion of the concept 'life world' see Schutz, A. (1964), *Collected Papers* The Hague: Martinus Nijhoff, Vol. 1, pp. 120–39; and pp. 207–59.

[2] See Berger, P. L., and Pullberg, S. (1965), 'Reification and the Sociological Critique of Consciousness', *History and Theory*, Vol. 4, No. 2.

[3] For a full discussion of this distinction see Glaser, B., and Strauss, A. L. (1967), *The Discovery of Grounded Theory*, London: Weidenfeld & Nicolson.

[4] This part of a research programme into curriculum innovation currently being developed in the Department of Sociology, University of London, Institute of Education.

[5] For a discussion of 'epistemic communities', see Holzner, B. (1968), *Reality Construction in Society*, Cambridge (Mass.): Schenkman, p. 60.

[6] Mannheim, K. (1956), *Ideology and Utopia*, London: Routledge & Kegan Paul, p. 244.

[7] The concept 'nomos' is elaborated by Berger to refer to man's propensity for creating meaningful order out of discrete phenomena; he suggests also the biological—as well as the social—dimensions of this process. See Berger, P. L. (1969), *The Social Reality of Religion*, London: Faber & Faber, pp. 19–25; see also Berger, P. L., and Kellner, H. (1964), 'Marriage and the Construction of Reality', *Diogenes*, Vol. 46, pp. 1–24.

[8] This is the position of Berger and Pullberg, *op. cit.*

[9] See, particularly, Horton, J. (1966), 'Order and Conflict Theories of Social Problems', *American Journal of Sociology*, Vol. 71, No. 6, May; Dawe, A. (1970), 'The Two Sociologies', *British Journal of Sociology*, Vol. 21, No. 2. See also Bruyn, S. T. (1966), *The Human Perspective in Sociology*, Englewood Cliffs (N.J.): Prentice-Hall.

[10] See Mannheim, K. *op. cit.*, p. 25.

[11] Dewey, John, 'Philosophy' in Gee Wilson (ed.) (1929), *Research in the Social Sciences*, New York: Macmillan. This reference is cited in Taylor, S. (1956), *Conceptions of Institutions and Theories of Knowledge*, New York: Twayne, p. 160.

[12] See Mills, C. W. (1939), 'Language, Logic and Culture', *American Sociological Review*, 4(5). Reprinted in Horowitz, I. (ed.) (1969), *Power, Politics and People, The Collected Papers of C. Wright Mills*, London: Oxford University Press, p. 429.

[13] See Holzner, B., *op. cit.* See also Berger, P. L., *The Social Reality of Religion*, London: Faber & Faber.

[14] 'Tensions' of consciousness refer to the different appraisals which an individual makes of an event occurring in the external world. Through his possession of reflective power, he is able to convert the spontaneous, non-inferential awareness of the 'vivid present' into a theoretical symbolic system. See Schutz, A., 'On Multiple Realities' in *Collected Papers*, Vol. 1, *op. cit.*

[15] *Ibid.* See also Schutz, A. (1967), *The Phenomenology of the Social World*, Evanston (Illinois): Northwestern University Press, p. 25.

[16] See on this, Schutz, A. (1964), 'Symbol, Reality and Society', *Collected Papers*, Vol. 1, pp. 287–356; and 'On Multiple Realities'.

[17] Schutz, A., 'Symbol, Reality and Society', pp. 351–2.

[18] Mills, C. W. (1940), 'Situated Actions and Vocabularies of Motive', *American Sociological Review*, Vol. 5, December. Reprinted in Horowitz, I., *op. cit.*

[19] Kuhn, T. S. (1962 and 1970), *The Structure of Scientific Revolutions*, Chicago: University of Chicago Press.

[20] The concept 'plausibility structure' is developed by Berger in his *Rumours of Angels* (1970), Harmondsworth: Allen Lane, The Penguin Press, to explain the diverse and competing patterns of thought within and between institutions.

[21] Schutz, A., *Collected Papers*, Vol. 2, p. 121.

[22] For a discussion of the concept 'vivid present' see Schutz, A., *Collected Papers*, Vol. 1, pp. 207–29.

[23] Durkheim, E. (1956), *Education and Sociology*, Glencoe (Illinois): The Free Press, Chap. 2.

[24] This quotation is from Holzner, B., *op. cit.*

[25] Durkheim, E., *op. cit.*

[26] Britton, J., and Newsome, B. (1968), 'What is Learnt in English Lessons', *Journal of Curriculum Studies*, Vol. 1, No. 1.

[27] Schutz, A., 'The Well-Informed Citizen' *Collected Papers*, Vol. 2, pp. 120–34.

[28] A. L. Strauss has argued in *Psychiatric Ideologies and Institutions*, New York: The Free Press, 1964, Chap. 5, that 'custodialism' is a prominent feature of pre-theoretical psychotherapy and is still widely represented in some state mental institutions in America. It is suggested here that because the epistemology which underlies custodialism is common to teaching and medical care, this is the case for some teachers.

[29] It should be pointed out, however, that the psychometric model has been so pervasive that Piaget's work is frequently incorporated within it. Piaget's 'developmental' model easily lends itself to the assumption that the child becomes progressively more rational as concrete images 'give way' to abstract. For a discussion of Piaget's epistemological interest see Bruner, J. S. (1966), *Toward a Theory of Instruction*, New York: Norton & Co., and Furth, H. G. (1969), *Piaget and Knowledge*, Englewood Cliffs (N.J.): Prentice-Hall.

[30] It should be stated clearly that the definition of 'alienation' intended here is that provided by Berger in *The Social Reality of Religion*, Chap. 4: 'Alienation is the process whereby the dialectical relationship between the individual and his world is lost to consciousness. The individual "forgets" that this world was and continues to be co-produced by him. Alienated consciousness is undialectical consciousness.' As Kon has pointed out in his review of the various uses of the concept in 'The Concept of Alienation of Modern Sociology' in Berger, P. L. (ed.) (1969), *Marxism and Sociology*, New York: Appleton-Century-Crofts, this particular ideology of alienation is a statement of the Marxian position without the utopian assumptions of Marx. It is represented in educational writing in the works of Henry and Friedenberg.

[31] See Bernstein (1971).

[32] This view is contained in the arguments of the Plowden Report, Chaps. 2 and 3. Not all the theoretical views of intelligence, however, are reifications. Becker refers to studies which view test scores as artefacts of the test constuction, but few of them go beyond the general statement. Becker, H. S.. 'Education and the Lower Class Child' in Gouldner, A. W., and Gouldner, H. P. (eds.) (1963), *Modern Sociology*, London: Hart-Davis.

[33] Durkheim, E., *op. cit.*, p. 115.

[34] See Schools Council Working Paper 27, *Cross'd with Adversity*, Evans Methuen Educational, 1970.

[35] See Berger's discussion of this issue in relation to the changing ideation of religious institutions in *The Social Reality of Religion* and *Rumor of Angels*, New York: Anchor Books.

[36] *Ibid.*

[37] Bruner, J. S. (1960), *The Process of Education*, Cambridge (Mass.): Harvard University Press (1966), *Toward a Theory of Instruction*, New York: Norton & Co. For a review and summary of Piaget's numerous writings see Flavell, J. H. (1963), *The Developmental Psychology of Jean Piaget*, New York: Van Nostrand-Reinhold, and Furth, H. G., *op. cit*

[38] Bruner, J. S., *Toward a Theory of Instruction*, p. 21.

[39] For a discussion of Kelly's 'Personal Constructs' see Bannister, D., and Mair, J. M. M. (1968), *The Evaluation of Personal Constructs*, London: Academic Press.

[40] Bruner, J. S., *The Process of Education*, p. 32.

[41] Schutz, A., *Collected Papers*, Vol. 1., p. 348.

[42] Merton, R. K. (1957), 'Science and Economy of Seventeenth-century England', *Social Theory and Social Structure*, Glencoe (Illinois): The Free Press, pp. 607–27.

[43] Mikesell, M. W. (1969), 'The Borderlands of Geography as a Social Science', in Sherif, M., and Sherif, C. W. (eds.), *Interdisciplinary Relationships in the Social Sciences*, Chicago: Aldine.

[44] Dineen, F. P., 'Linguistics and the Social Sciences', in Sherif, M., and Sherif, C. W., *op. cit.*

[45] Mead, M., and Metraux, R. (1957), 'Image of the Scientist Among High-School Students', *Science*, Vol. 126, pp. 384–90.

[46] *Enquiry into the Flow of Candidates in Science and Technology into Higher Education* (Dainton Report) (1968), paragraphs 160–90. H.M.S.O.

[47] See particularly Becker, H. S. (1964), 'Personal Change in Adult Life', *Sociometry*, Vol. 27, pp. 40–53. See also Becker, H. S., and Carper, J. (1965), 'Development of Identification with an Occupation', *American Journal of Sociology*, Vol. 61, No. 4., January; and (1956), 'The Elements of Identification with an Occupation', *American Sociological Review*, Vol. 21. Becker H. S. (1961), 'Notes on the Concept of Commitment', *American Journal of Sociology*, Vol. 66.

[48] Greenwood, E., 'The Elements of Professionalization', *Social Work*, Vol. 2, No. 3, 1957. Reprinted in Vollmer, H. M., and Mills, D. M. (eds.), *Professionalization*, Englewood Cliffs (N.J.): Prentice-Hall. The notion of 'profession' as a 'folk concept' is Becker's—see Becker, H. S. (1962), 'The Nature of a Profession', *National Society for the Study of Education Year Book*, pp. 27–46.

[49] Campbell, D. T., 'Ethnocentrism of Disciplines and the Fish-scale Model of Omniscience', in Sherif, M., and Sherif, C. W., *op. cit.*

[50] Mills, C. W., 'The Professional Ideology of Social Pathologists', in Horowitz, I., *op. cit.*

[51] This concept is used by Ball, D. W. (1967), 'An Abortion Clinic Ethnography', *Social Problems*, Vol. 14, pp. 293–301.

[52] A recent study which has developed this approach in the study of deviance and which could well be extended into educational knowledge is Anthony Platt's book (1970), *The Child Savers*, Chicago: University of Chicago Press.

# BIBLIOGRAPHY

BARNES, D. (1969). 'Language in the Secondary Classroom' in *Language, the Learner and the School*. Harmondsworth. Penguin.

BECKER, H. S. (1952). 'Social Class Variations in Teacher–Pupil Relationships'. *Journal of Educational Sociology*, Vol. 25.

BEN-DAVID, J., and COLLINS, R. (1966). 'Social Factors in the Origins of a New Science, the Case of Psychology'. *American Sociological Review*, Vol. 31, No. 4.

BERGER, P. L. (1954). 'The Sociological Study of Sectarianism'. *Social Research*, Winter.

—— (1965). 'Towards a Sociological Understanding of Psychoanalysis'. *Social Research*, Vol. 32.

—— (1966). 'Identity as a Problem in the Sociology of Knowledge. *European Journal of Sociology*, Vol. 7, pp. 105–15.

—— and KELLNER, H. (1964). 'Marriage and the Construction of Reality'. *Diogenes*, Vol. 46, pp. 1–24.

—— and LUCKMANN, T. (1967), *The Social Construction of Reality*. Harmondsworth: Allen Lane, The Penguin Press.

—— and PULLBERG, S. (1965). 'Reification and the Sociological Critique of Consciousness'. *History and Theory*, Vol. 4, No. 2.

BERNSTEIN, B. B. (1967). 'Open Schools, Open Society?' *New Society*, September 14, 1967.

—— (1970). 'A Critique of the Concept of Compensatory Education' in RUBIN-STEIN, D., and STONEMAN, C. (eds.), *Education for Democracy*. Harmondsworth: Penguin.

—— (1971). 'On the Classification and Framing of Educational Knowledge' in YOUNG, M. F. D. (ed.), *Knowledge and Control*. London: Collier-Macmillan. (Chapter 2, this volume.)

BOURDIEU, P. (1967). 'Systems of Education and Systems of Thought'. Vol. 19, pp. 338–58. Reprinted this volume, Chapter 7.

BUCHER, R., and STRAUSS, A. L. (1961). 'Professions in Process', *American Journal of Sociology*, January.

CICOUREL, A. V., and KITSUSE, J. (1963), *The Educational Decision Makers*. Indianapolis: Bobbs-Merrill.

CRANE, D. (1969). 'Social Structure in a Group of Scientists: A Test of the "Invisible College" Hypothesis'. *American Sociological Review*, Vol. 34, No. 3.

DANIELS, G. H. (1967). 'The Pure Science Ideal and Democratic Culture'. *Science*, Vol. 156, pp. 1699–1706.

DAVIE, G. E. (1961). *The Democratic Intellect*. Edinburgh; Edinburgh University Press.

DYER, K. F. (1967). 'Crisis in Biology'. *Journal of Biology Education*, Vol. 1, No. 2.

FRIEDMAN, N. L. (1967). 'Cultural Deprivation: A Commentary in the Sociology of Knowledge'. *Journal of Educational Thought*, I, August, pp. 88–99.

GOODACRE, E. J. (1968). *Teachers and Their Pupils' Home Background*. Slough: National Foundation for Educational Research.

HOLT, J. (1964). *How Children Fail*. Harmondsworth: Penguin.

HOLZNER, B. (1968). *Reality Construction in Society*. Cambridge (Mass.): Schenkman.

HUGHES, E. C. (1937). 'Institutional Office and the Person'. *American Journal of Sociology*, Vol. 43.

JEVONS, F. R. (1969). 'The Content of Science Courses'. *Higher Education Review*, Vol. 1, No. 2.

—— (1969). *The Teaching of Science*. London: Allen & Unwin.

KLAPP, O. E. (1969). *The Search for Collective Identity*. New York: Holt, Rinehart & Winston.

LACEY, C. (1966). 'Some Sociological Concomitants of Academic Streaming'. *British Journal of Sociology*, XVII(3).

LAING, R. D. (1960). *The Divided Self*. Harmondsworth: Penguin.

LICHTHEIM, G. (1965). 'The Concept of Ideology'. *History and Theory*, Vol. 4, No. 2.

MCDERMOTT, J. (1969). 'Knowledge is Power'. *The Nation*, April 14.

MILLS, C. W. (1959). *The Sociological Imagination*. Harmondsworth: Penguin.

SIMMEL, G., et al. (1959). *Essays on Sociology, Philosophy and Aesthetics*. Edited by K. H. WOLFF. New York: Harper & Row.

SCHATZMAN, L., and STRAUSS, A. L. (1966). 'A Sociology of Psychiatry'. *Social Problems*, Vol. 14.

STRAUSS, A. L., SCHATZMAN, L., BUCHER, R., ERLICH, D., and SABSTEIN, M. (1964). *Psychiatric Ideologies and Institutions*. New York: The Free Press.

TAYLOR, S. (1956). *Conceptions of Institutions and the Theory of Knowledge*. New York: Twayne.

—— (1962). 'Social Factors and the Validation of Thought'. *Social Forces*, Vol. 41(1), pp. 76–82.

TENNENBAUM, S. (1963). 'The Teacher, the Middle Class, the Lower Class'. *Phi Delta Kappan*, November, pp. 82–6.

YOUNG, M. F. D. (1971). 'Curricula as Socially Organized Knowledge' in YOUNG, M. F. D. (ed.), *Knowledge and Control*. London: Collier-Macmillan. (see this volume, Chapter 1).

# PART TWO

*SOCIAL DEFINITIONS OF KNOWLEDGE*

## 4. ALAN F. BLUM

*The Corpus of Knowledge as a
Normative Order: Intellectual
Critiques of the Social Order
of Knowledge and Commonsense
Features of Bodies of Knowledge*\*

Our intention in this paper is to examine several variants of one method which has been used historically by thinkers to characterize, criticize and revise the authoritative bodies of knowledge of their disciplines.

While bodies of knowledge have been found deficient on a variety of grounds, one method of criticizing knowledge has been used persistently by a variety of thinkers. This method describes the producers of bodies of knowledge as commonsense actors;[1] such a description is essentially equivalent to faulting such knowledge as lacking objectivity. In this paper we shall inspect three different ways of accomplishing such a demonstration and examine some of the implications of this critical method.

To begin, we shall give general characterizations of the intellectual critiques developed by Descartes, Hobbes and Marx, followed by fairly close discussions of each of their critiques. Our intention throughout is to demonstrate the ways in which these critiques play off a common theme: that the social organization of knowledge is describable not in terms of the 'structural' properties of events-in-the-world which the knowledge is intended to formulate, but rather as a product of the informal understandings negotiated among members of an organized intellectual collectivity. The social organization of knowledge, then, is viewed not as a product of the 'factual', 'real' character of the world, but rather, as an outcome of the commonsense theorizing that occurs in the process of organizing and applying some description of the world.

\* This paper first appeared in *Theoretical Sociology* (1970), McKinney, J., and Tiryakian, E. (eds.), New York: Appleton-Century-Crofts.

## DEPICTIONS OF BODIES OF KNOWLEDGE AS PROBLEMATIC

Descartes' dissatisfaction with the corpus of knowledge which he confronted was pre-eminently occasioned by the 'varied opinion' which seemed to him to characterize it.[2] Descartes presumed that the features of controversy and argumentation indicated the presence of varied and differing opinions as to the nature of things and thus reflected an absence of certain knowledge. If there were certain knowledge, opinion would not be varied, and there would be no controversy because there would be nothing over which to argue. Certainty indicates a body of knowledge warranted by indubitably clear standards which anyone can recognize as furnishing distinct and unambiguous knowledge. Throughout history, men have characterized bodies of knowledge in this way—and have found them deficient. Their position derives from the supposition that knowledge differs from belief as fact differs from opinion; knowledge is true and not really arguable.

In Hobbes we note a different and perhaps more complex confrontation with the normative order of knowledge.[3] It is recognized that Hobbes' depiction of the corpus of knowledge changed over time and that this was reflected in his changing preference for Plato rather than Aristotle as the pre-eminent philosopher of antiquity.

Essentially, Hobbes conceived of the corpus of knowledge as the body of norms and precepts laid down by classical philosophy. While in the earlier period he originally did not question the validity of these norms and precepts, he did ask himself whether the mere enumeration of precepts constitutes the most efficient format for organizing knowledge. Hobbes took as problematic the format for presenting knowledge and was thus led to reassign meaning to the corpus; he did not accept the meaning which classical philosophy had assigned to the corpus of political philosophy.

One variation of Hobbes' view is found in Machiavelli, who characterized the classic tradition of political philosophy as guided by speculation and 'ideals' rather than by empirical descriptions of political experience. In their respective ways, then, Hobbes and Machiavelli both depicted the traditional corpus of knowledge reflected in classical political thought as unrealistic, inapplicable and conjectural. Their choice of such descriptions suggests that they had developed their own conceptions of the criteria which the corpus of political knowledge could be expected to fulfil. Such conceptions were based upon their notions of the uses for which political knowledge is designed.

The complexity of Marx's view stems from the fact that he depicted not one but many bodies of knowledge, and found them each problematic on quite different grounds.[4] One of his most important contributions was his argument that knowledge is not disinterested and that the construction of a corpus of knowledge is inextricably linked to the interests of those who produce it. Thus, a critique of knowledge is necessarily a critique of producers of knowledge. Moreover, he attempted to demonstrate that knowledge, in principle, cannot be disinterested and hence must be evaluated with reference to practical demonstrations of its efficacy.

Marx characterized at least three bodies of knowledge at various times—history, philosophy and classical economics—and he tended to treat each of them as a separate corpus. Of all the problematic features which he located, the most important was this: all previous bodies of knowledge tended to generate their own self-justifying standards of evaluation which were so closely linked to the interests of the creators that any evaluation of the corpus must take these interests as a point of departure.

Moreover, Marx located the dominant feature of all bodies of knowledge in the fact that since this knowledge was constructed to serve the interests of its producers, while the producers did not share the interests of the objects of knowledge (that is, the masses), such knowledge was controlled by the interests of its creators and was necessarily a distortion of reality (under the premise that reality = the interests of the masses). Thus, Marx saw the corpus as biased and invalid. The strength of his indictment derived principally from the tactic of attributing deficiencies in the corpus not to the lack of certainty, but to the organized features of intellectual activity as an interest group.

In the case of each of these three thinkers, we may note that the depiction of a corpus of knowledge originates in his feelings that the corpus is, in certain respects, deficient. Thus, his description of the corpus inevitably appears as a description of its inadequacy in some respect. This deficiency is used by the thinker to ascribe problematic status to the corpus, to criticize it in such ways as to make its problematic character explicit. We are dealing, then, with the common 'signs' or cultural insignia of a deficient corpus of knowledge which thinkers 'see' from within a tradition and which they accredit as legitimate evidence of the inadequate state of knowledge. Our point is that all of these 'signs' are furnished by the thinker's recognition of the commonsense character of the corpus.

## REVISING OF BODIES OF KNOWLEDGE

### Hobbes' Revision

Hobbes introduced a programme for redefining the corpus of knowledge of political philosophy. Recall that his objection was to the inapplicability of the traditional corpus as reflected in the work of Aristotle. Hobbes did not appreciate the efficacy of the traditional corpus in providing men with knowledge that was useful for facilitating their attainment of political prudence. Hobbes sought to replace theory by the primacy of practice; he sought the justification of knowledge in its practical benefit to man.

What device did Hobbes use to reassert the primacy of practical political knowledge as the distinguishing feature of the corpus? What are the standard resources which a thinker has available for redefining a corpus of knowledge in order to adapt it to the requirements of practicality?

Note that Hobbes did not—in his early period—find the *content* of the corpus problematic. What he did find questionable was the way in which the corpus was organized. It was not organized in such a way that men would find believable; since knowledge must facilitate man's adaptation to the practical circumstances of his polity, it should be organized in a way that he could find usable. Hobbes' question now became: How does one redefine a corpus of knowledge so that men will find it usable?

In this respect, Hobbes decided that the most important characteristic of an adequate body of knowledge lies in the procedures which are provided for its determinate application. Since the only men of theoretic import were aristocrats, the question became one of redesigning the corpus of knowledge in such a way that the aristocracy would find it usable. According to Hobbes, such a corpus should not be organized around general precepts, but rather in terms of examples.[5]

Thus he urged that the corpus of knowledge be redefined in terms of examples rather than general precepts. He then searched for a format which would suitably organize knowledge around a set of examples which would provide an educative influence. To this end he stated that history properly read and utilized would provide the substance of this new corpus of knowledge. Why history? Because it provides the empirical cases which are more compelling to men than general precepts are. Men could understand, believe, and find useful a corpus organized in such a way because such a body of knowledge provides them with more appropriate guidelines in particular cases than does an enumeration of norms and precepts. According to Hobbes, an adequate body of knowledge was one that a member could use as a set of instructions in particular instances. Examples are instructive in such cases, and history provides the empirical substance of such examples.[6] How may we then summarize the particular strategy introduced by Hobbes for his purposes of revising the traditional corpus of knowledge?

Beyond the obvious characterization of Hobbes' tactic as being organized around some version of an 'applicability' criterion, we may note a much more powerful feature. Hobbes' proposal amounted to the assertion that a corpus of knowledge cannot be defined and warranted unless the objects of knowledge (societal members) are able to use such knowledge as normative orders in formulating routine courses of action. This means that producers of knowledge can be expected to meet criteria of adequacy only if they respect (and perhaps, share) the points of view of those societal members who will employ such knowledge. Thus, adequate bodies of knowledge are usable bodies of knowledge, and usable bodies of knowledge are those which both producers and consumers respect within the same community of meanings.

The defect of the traditional corpus of classical political philosophy was not to be found in the fact that it was insensitive to the problem of facilitating the political prudence of societal members, for it was aware of such a problem as the central task of political philosophy.[7] Rather, its defect sprang from the fact that the creators of knowledge did not understand the kinds of meanings which such members were likely to assign to knowledge, and thus could not properly execute this task. To put it another way, classical political philosophy's failure was a failure to respect the points of view of its subjects as political actors. Hobbes proposed that a satisfactory understanding of actors would indicate that they do not find knowledge in the form of general precepts usable and employable, while such would not be the case for knowledge organized in terms of empirical cases and instances.

We find in Hobbes one of the great styles of challenging a corpus of knowledge: by accusing it of sterility, formalism and abstractness, he indicted its creators for their failure adequately to respect the points of view of their subjects.

In retrospect, Hobbes' final position closely resembled the programme of Machiavelli. The traditional corpus was rejected by both for roughly similar reasons; the new corpus was seen as needing to satisfy the criterion of usability by particular segments of the population, and the most effective way to attain usability was thought to be through the empirical study of human motivation.

## Descartes' Revision

Perhaps the most famous philosophic strategy introduced for the purposes of revising a corpus of knowledge was Descartes' programme of methodical doubt. Essentially, this programme was organized around a systematic and self-conscious distrust of commonsense knowledge. It specified the in-principle suspension of commonsense knowledge for the purpose of 'cleansing one's mind' in order to arrive at certainty. (Recall that his search for certainty derived from his recognition of the discontinuities within the corpus of knowledge.)

Descartes' programme for such a reconstruction was this: by screening out all influences, one may arrive at a description of an indubitably clear state of affairs; then, given such a description, one proceeds by systematically unravelling all of the derivations which are concealed within this description.

The inconsistencies of the previous corpus were attributed to the fact that thinkers were responsive to sense data, and sense data were unreliable and deceptive. In other words, a corpus of knowledge based upon descriptions of sense data is problematic, since it rests upon spurious foundations.

Descartes proposed that the state of the world as it appeared to the thinker's senses be considered problematic, and offered instead a programme based upon the discovery of simple, immediate and certain truths by systematically distrusting what was known through the senses. We might summarize Descartes' programme thus: suspend all knowledge, start with particular and certain instances, and derive systematically.

In part, Descartes' critique may be read as follows: since the corpus of knowledge is normatively stipulated (that is, since it serves intellectuals as a normative order), the act of doubting it can be seen as deviation. Descartes then proposed various justifications for his repudiation of the corpus of knowledge as a normative order. As methods for discovering new principles, he proposed intuition (immediate intellectual awareness) and deduction (correct inference from those facts known with certainty). He prescribed the following rules: 1) avoid all prejudice and accept nothing as true which cannot be clearly recognized as such; 2) divide each problem into as many parts as possible; 3) develop an orderly connection of thinking, starting with simple facts and gradually leading to more complex problems; and 4) make complete enumerations.

Descartes recommended that everything be distrusted unless it could be clearly recognized as true. He proposed the utilization of new criteria for warranting factual descriptions for, according to him, what was lacking was a procedure for collecting and systematizing thought in an orderly, efficient manner. He was doing nothing more than providing rules for disciplining thought.

Now, there are two interesting notions in this strategy of criticizing and revising a corpus of knowledge. In the first place, the corpus was indicted because it was generated by scholars who were not thinking efficiently. This is almost a pedagogical critique. But certain knowledge was possible if only the thinker would apply himself vigorously to specific rules. In following such rules, the thinker would be able to discover certain truth. Descartes' programme, thus, was aimed at the psychological reconstruction of the mind of the thinker.

The second strategy was a variation on a recurrent theme in intellectual innovation: the reconstruction proceeds in terms of the rules furnished by an alternative or competing corpus of knowledge. One is not only encouraged to doubt, in order to free the mind from 'clutter', but with a small nucleus of 'certain' facts in hand which are collected as a residual effect of total doubt, one proceeds 'constructively' in terms of specific rules. Whereas Hobbes used history as his alternative, Descartes used the model of inference and reasoning derived from mathematics and geometry.

The strategy of invoking an alternative corpus of knowledge to reconstruct a corpus which is quite different has been frequently utilized. In these cases the thinker generally proposes that the 'new' corpus has demonstrated that it can resolve the same class of problems more effectively than the traditional corpus. Since Descartes conceived of the central problem of philosophy as establishing certain truth, he searched out other disciplines with the same concerns but with a different set of substantive problems. After all, he reasoned, certainty is certainty, and the methods productive of it in one domain should be useful in another.

## Marx's Revision

We shall begin with Marx's indictment of the corpus of historical knowledge: '. . . we do not set out from what men say, imagine, conceive, nor from men as narrated, thought of, imagined, conceived, in order to arrive at men in the flesh. We set out from real, active men.'[8]

Marx characterized the corpus of historical knowledge as deficient because historians had accepted the assertions of societal members and their theorizing as factually descriptive of the historical epoch. He accused historians of accepting and codifying such commonsense knowledge, and of treating it as 'given' and factual, rather than as problematic.

Marx claimed that the basic fact of history—the relation of man to nature—could not be grasped by taking the theories of these men as given; rather the actions of men in relating to nature should be studied directly and empirically. Previous historians had developed an abstract conception of social organization based upon sets of ideas which members had asserted, with such ideas being used as the data of history. On the contrary though, it should not be the theories of societal members which are consulted, but the actual activities of such members.

History does nothing; it 'does not possess immense riches', it 'does not fight battles'. It is men, real living men who do all this, who possess things and fight battles. . . . History is nothing but the activities of men in pursuit of their ends . . .'[9]

The corpus is problematic because the data upon which it is based are derivative and of peripheral relevance to the actual forces of change in society. The abstractions of historians were seen as commonsense descriptions which were inaccurate depictions of the 'real' character of society. The immediate remedy to such abstract and misleading descriptions of society is the empirical observation of men as actors, relating to nature. Thinkers will manage to produce such descriptions, however, only when they are able to free themselves from the interests which control them.

The way to proceed is to anchor one's descriptions in 'real' (that is, empirical) descriptions. A 'real' description shows some aspect of man's relation to nature. Thus, we should begin with real premises and deduce our knowledge from them. The historical corpus of knowledge began with arbitrary premises.[10]

Marx found the historical corpus of knowledge and the philosophical corpus of knowledge deficient on two essential grounds: 1) they were abstract and disconnected from empirical description, and 2) they accepted commonsense conceptions of events as 'given' without treating them as problematic, as mere commonsense descriptions whose formal character remained to be observed and explicated. Both bodies of knowledge, but particularly history, tended to conceal 'real' factors, and to accept commonsense conceptions of members as factual. He also indicted these bodies of knowledge for their speculative character, since their descriptions did not afford practical demonstration of their warrant. His was one of the most articulate examples of discrediting a corpus of knowledge because of the difficulty in demonstrating its factual character.

It is instructive to compare Marx's critiques of history and philosophy with his indictment of the corpus of knowledge produced by the classical economists. Marx characterized this corpus as deficient not because it ignored real factors, but because it conceived of them inadequately: classical economics treated the totality of economic laws, relations and institutions as a cluster of isolated, objective facts and called these facts by neutral, abstract names (such as commodity, value, ground rent). Such conceptualization deprived economic facts of their social meanings.

He proposed to translate these terms into factors 'determinative of human existence', with labour serving as his medium of translation. Since he conceived of labour as the existential, or basic, activity of man, his conceptualization of the economy was specifically addressed to the problem of how the economy realizes man's basic nature.

In introducing the concept of labour, Marx was embarking upon a fundamental enterprise in reconceptualizing economics. He proposed that the abstract terminology of economics be translated into a terminology organized around man's nature and his potentialities. In this way, conceptualization became radical rather than abstract.[11]

To conceive of this enterprise in its proper perspective—as a grand tactic in reconceptualization—imagine a modern sociologist responding to behaviourist descriptions by contending that they do not assign appropriate sociological meaning to their terms; or, think of Durkheim attempting to reconceptualize a variable like 'season of the year' or 'time of day' by reassigning to it a sociological meaning. Marx was seeking to reconceptualize economics from the point of view of sociology; his polemic charged that every term must be conceived as an instance of social action and related to the typical mind of a typical actor. His particular medium, in this sense, was labour.

Thus, while his emphasis changed as he turned his attention to different bodies of knowledge, Marx's indictment was generally organized around his description of each corpus as inadequately conceptualized. The tactics he proposed for correcting such a state were designed to demonstrate how meaning should be reassigned to events from the perspective of one who is interested in 'real' description. The device which Marx proposed for this purpose was the dialectic method.

The dialectic can be restated as a series of rules. Start with the premise that men are born to be free; to be rational decision-makers functioning in harmony with constraints that fit their potentialities. Then reflect upon the fact that, historically, men have never met this description, have never lived in socially organized environments which have fulfilled this intrinsic potential. Following this, conceive of every act, activity, event, relationship and object as mere factuality, as a datum which is not to be endorsed just because it is, but which, rather, because it is, is somehow imperfect. The mere existence of things in certain ways does not make them real except on a factual level. What is real is latent, concealed underneath mere factual appearance, for what is real is a potential essence which is attributed to man by virtue of his being human. Thus, one examines every fact in a spirit of negation, with a view to locating the contradiction. The world of mere factuality is a contradiction because it conceals the realization of what really is (or inhibits the development, expression, cultivation of rationality). Dialectic thought then begins with the premise that man is unfree, that man and nature exist in conditions of alienation or as other than they 'really' are.

Thought and the objects of thought are judged in terms of a standard which the theorist ascribes intrinsically to the very nature of thought and objects. This standard is reason: thought and its objects both are judged in reference to this standard of rationality. The essence of thought is reason; this is the criterion used to assign the status of reality to thought and its objects. Rationality is real, that is, essences and purposes are real. The real, then, is not the existent or the factual, but lies 'in the nature of things'.

Marx's tactics for treating the social world as problematic can be characterized as follows: the comprehension of the world by commonsense thought and by scholars is often misleading and fails to reveal things 'as they really are'. Our task is to develop a tactic for transcending appearances in order to get at reality. Unlike Descartes, Marx did not propose the suspension of all knowledge, for he felt that the theorist using the dialectical method operates with a standard of reality that serves as a presupposition. To Marx, making the world problematic meant taking things as they appeared and then subverting them to expose their 'real' character.

The use of the dialectic proceeds through the demonstration that a systematic examination of the actor's lot reveals him to be unfree, contrary to factual appearance. The actor generally does not know that he is unfree, but this is not important theoretically—one only grasps oneself in such a self-conscious way when one is free, and since men are unfree (creatures of a system into which they have no insight) they cannot attain such self-consciousness.

How does the sociologist demonstrate that despite factual appearances, men are not free? He can show that actors are controlled by stimuli and impulses which they cannot freely manipulate, and that such controls are generated by the organization of the system. He can also demonstrate that all actions assembled by members can be reinterpreted within some schema as contributing to the irrationality of the system by preventing actors from recognizing their potentialities. Thus, all social structures can be analysed in terms of the way in which they contribute to the perpetuation of the ignorance, or alienation, of the actors.

## THE SOCIAL ORGANIZATION OF KNOWLEDGE

We can better understand the methodology of criticism in these three cases if we see each of the critiques as directed to the question: How is this particular body of knowledge possible? What this amounts to is asking how the assembly of a corpus of knowledge can be described as a sociological event. Discussion of this question requires some attention to the social order problem. Each of these three thinkers was able (to a degree that most of us are not) to conceive of a body of knowledge as a socially organized set of activities; each of them tried to show how the organized features of the corpus were in some sense a function of the taken for granted and unanalysed commonsense stipulations negotiated by the thinkers. These were the grounds which permitted each to accuse the corpus of lacking 'objectivity'.

To find a corpus of knowledge problematic is equivalent to challenging the rules to which members of a collectivity subscribe. More than this, the challenge amounts to saying that the rules available for organizing the production of this particular corpus of knowledge are insufficient for reproducing such knowledge, and that therefore the producers *went outside of the rules* in various unspecified ways to settle the problem of adequate description. Descartes, Hobbes and Marx do not assert that thinkers can do otherwise (for rules do have to be 'interpreted' in ways for which the rules themselves do not apply), but they argue that thinkers avoid describing precisely how they do such interpretive work by imputing an artificial stability to events-in-the-world. Such imputations allow the thinker to avoid the problem of describing his methods and procedures for the production of such stability. Thus, Descartes, Hobbes and Marx could each argue that behind every corpus's conception of a factual, stable, real world there lies an unanalysed, socially organized set of methods for producing such conceptions.

Let us conceive of the tasks of these three critics as the description of traditions of knowledge in the following way. They were confronted with bodies of knowledge as empirical data which they judged to be inadequate, and on the basis of such judgements each presented a description of the course of action which he presumed to be the necessary conditions and causes of such bodies of knowledge. Thus each theorized about the development of knowledge, and presented a sociological description of intellectual activity as the organization of social actions.

A conception of intellectual activity as a course of social action presupposes a conception of enquiry as rule-guided. These three thinkers—like all those who reflect on their intellectual traditions—conceived of the previous bodies of knowledge as the assembled products of the methodical treatments of intellectuals acting upon their symbolic environments. They differed, though, in their manner of depicting the rule-guided character of intellectual activity as a course of action.

Thus, the intellectuals as actors were depicted by Hobbes as dopes in the sense in which scholars, academics and pedants are dopes: they were dopes who imposed their own theoretic models upon their subjects and who confused their own points of view with the points of view of these subjects. When their subjects failed to behave in ways congruent with the descriptions, they attributed this to the imperfections of the 'real' world and to the irrationality of actors in this world.[12] Thus, the problem of previous learned men was the fact that they did not adapt their intellectual behaviour to the contingencies of the concrete circumstances. They narcissistically manipulated their own theories while remaining indifferent to the necessity of consulting the world in which their subjects existed.

Descartes depicted his intellectual predecessors as dopes in another way, and in a manner quite distinct from Marx. We can note this distinction clearly in comparing the two.

To Descartes, the assembly of the pre-existing corpus of knowledge was almost anomic; he had a *laissez-faire* vision of the process of generating knowledge. He depicted intellectuals as a collection of autonomous particles, each of whom followed his own path in sensing, experiencing and producing knowledge. The body of knowledge thus appeared as a concerted effect produced by independent and autonomous intellectuals, and such a production had in common only the negative feature that it was produced through the independent exercise of commonsense theorizing. Intellectuals were seen as dopes in the sense that any man who does not formulate his activity in terms of a consensually shared normative order is a dope. Dopes are those actors whose behaviour is governed exclusively by what Weber called usage, rather than by orientation to a normative order.[13]

Marx also saw intellectual activity as socially governed and socially controlled. Such activity could be accurately described as action oriented to a normative order; however, it was oriented to the order furnished by rational self-interest rather than by criteria of 'truth'. In this respect, Marx was one of the first thinkers to present a developed sociological description of intellectual activity as an organized interest group. Intellectuals appeared as dopes in Marx's indictment because they were chained to their theories and were not free to alter these theories. Such unfreedom was a necessary consequence of their positions within the social organization of society. Thus, while the intellectual predecessors of Hobbes and Descartes were depicted as special kinds of intellectual dopes, Marx's predecessors were portrayed as dopes precisely because they were no different in character from the average normal members of society. To Marx, dopes were intellectuals whose theoretical activities were controlled by the same forces that controlled the thoughts of normal members of society.

In order to demonstrate the commonsense character of knowledge, one need only describe a producer of knowledge as an actor whose organized practices themselves become features of the knowledge he is producing.

Marx had no difficulty in conceiving of such producers as actors. The only way in which to characterize social theory as bourgeois is to depict social theorists as typical societal members who are controlled by the same forces and interests as any man in society. Such a depiction says in effect that the activity of theorizing can be reproduced simply by virtue of knowledge of the theorist's social position and interests in the world. The objectivity of such knowledge is at issue because members' theories and practices have more to do with assembling the completed description than does the so-called factual character of the world which the description is intended to display or mirror or depict. In this way Marx repudiated his predecessors, for they had failed to free themselves from their ordinary theories and to inspect the intrinsic features of events-in-the-world. To transcend their positions as ordinary societal members in order to consult the world empirically constituted an impossible feat for them because their culturally accredited practices of seeing, observing, and recording were inexorably tied to their interests.

Descartes proceeded somewhat differently but with much the same result. If there was a factual, stable, regular and standard world 'out there', a world which was discovered rather than created by investigative procedures, then all descriptions of this world should converge independently of the methods and procedures for accomplishing such descriptions. Descartes seized upon this classic notion of objectivity—that there are elements of experience which are invariant across all methods and procedures for finding and reporting them—as the standard by which he found previous knowledge deficient.

This deficiency was a consequence of the fact that different investigative procedures produced different factual worlds. Intellectuals failed to suspend their commonsense knowledge of the world sufficiently, and so their descriptions varied with their diverse ways of conceiving of the world which they tacitly utilized as culturally accredited investigative assumptions.

Both Marx and Descartes accused intellectuals of assembling treatments of their environments of cultural objects (ideas) whose methodical and regular features were as much a function of their unanalysed practices as of the stable character of these objects themselves.

Hobbes' critique was based upon different grounds, but it also resulted in a criticism of the objectivity of the pre-existing corpus. Such knowledge failed to be objective because it was not empirical. By this, Hobbes meant that theorists did not consult events in the world before describing them, but rather, by first imposing their own descriptions upon the world, inspected events by measuring them with the yardstick of 'reality' established by their descriptions.

Hobbes reasoned somewhat as follows: knowledge which men cannot use is not objective knowledge, because if it is not usable it must not be relevant to them. Descriptions which are formulated in such ways as to be irrelevant to the actions of members are not reproducible because men do not act under their auspices.

## CONCLUSION: THE SOCIAL ORDER PROBLEM OF SOCIOLOGY

Let us try to pull together the various important threads of this chapter. What is perhaps ostensibly an essay in this history of ideas is actually intended as a discussion of intellectual methodology and of the social organization of knowledge. We intend 'social organization of knowledge' in this sense: that knowledge is organized and assembled methodically by actors acting under the auspices of some conception of an adequate corpus of knowledge as a maxim of conduct.

Scholars who have traditionally sought to discover 'objective' knowledge have had to contend with the fact that the search for and discovery of such knowledge is socially organized. Philosophically, this has often constituted a dilemma. Sociologically, it is not so much a dilemma as an inescapable fact of enquiry. The implication is this: if objective knowledge is taken to mean knowledge of a reality independent of language, or presuppositionless knowledge, or knowledge of the world which is independent of the observer's procedures for finding and producing the knowledge, then there is no such thing as objective knowledge.

Hobbes, Descartes and Marx each seized upon some feature of knowledge which reflected this lack of 'pure' objectivity and used such a deficiency as grounds for their respective critiques. Yet it is interesting to note that each of these men, in producing his own corpus, could be held accountable and criticizable on similar grounds, for producing knowledge which could not stand the test of 'pure' objectivity.

In point of fact, sociologists among others are able to produce accredited knowledge which they regard as 'objective enough'. The question then is how do sociologists decide the status of knowledge as objective enough?

In order to begin to establish criteria for answering such a question sociologists must come to grips with the issue of the interaction between their investigative procedures and their findings. This means that sociologists must begin to treat as problematic the unanalysed features of their methods and procedures which become constitutive properties of the events-in-the-world as in themselves describable events-in-the-world.

In this sense, it is important to note that sociological investigation is essentially a topic of sociological enquiry. To put it more clearly, the methods and procedures of sociology are applicable to the empirical practices of sociology as an event-in-the-world.

The import of this is not often appreciated, for sociologists like to assume that their various gambits, such as standardization, hypothetico-deductive procedure or scientific method serve to insulate them from potential describability with their own principles. On the contrary, it can be demonstrated quite easily that at every point within the course of sociological enquiry, the sociologist has to decide on the basis of his tact and his commonsense knowledge how to settle various matters which require resolution before the enquiry can be consummated.

It is not that sociologists fail to recognize this fact of life; rather, they treat it as irrelevant, as a problem to be either controlled or evaded. Yet when sociologists follow methodological canons as maxims of conduct, they invariably find it impossible to proceed unless they raise as problematic what the canons mean as describable practices.

When Homans instructs us in the proper ways of theorizing, when Merton gives us the rules for doing a functional analysis, when Lazarsfeld tells us how to 'move from concepts to indicators', they rely upon our co-operation and willingness to make sense of what they are saying when such sensibility rests in every case upon unanalysed and problematic features of an investigation which are waiting to be described. The fact that we can understand their counsel and make sense of their arguments, the fact that we often reproduce such counsel in our practices, means only that we share with them a common culture, a culture which is rarely described and analysed. The challenge then is how to make this culture problematic and describable. One way to begin is to conceive of the sociologist as an actor whose descriptions of events-in-the-world stand as assembled products of his methods and procedures of describing as a socially organized activity. It is at this point that we can start to see the sociologist's relation to his corpus as an actor's relationship to maxims of conduct. We can begin to appreciate the ways in which the problematic relationship between knowing rules and following them operates in the case of sociological practice.

In fact, it is through an examination of sociology as an event-in-the-world that we come to recognize the commonsense character of sociological description.

If sociology is an activity like any other, it is describable in the same ways as any other, and such description faces the problems encountered in all describing. Thus, describing the activity of sociology as a paradigmatic instance of sociological description, we can better understand the resources available for a description when we apply them to our activity of describing. We illuminate a range of problems involved in description when we attempt to describe ourselves doing the activity of describing, and in so doing we teach ourselves how to describe.

We know that sociology is possible because it is done, it is *played* in Wittgenstein's sense. The production and circulation of sociological descriptions attests to the fact that sociology is done and that it constitutes an observable and reportable set of activities. We *do* produce such descriptions in regular, standard and stable ways, and they are accredited by our colleagues as legitimate. The fact that sociology as an activity is assembled in regular, standard and typical ways suggests that sociology is describable, and also serves to raise in another form the problem of social order: given the existence of a set of observable practices called sociology, how are they possible?

The prevailing conceptions of sociological description fail to provide adequate solutions to the social order problem of sociology, which in turn suggests that because of their failure to account for the existence of sociology in a satisfactory way, they cannot be expected to account for other events of conduct.

One such solution is organized around a conception of sociological enquiry as completely circumscribed by rules. This conception is typically articulated in the authoritative canons of hypothetico-deductive theorizing and philosophy of science texts. As a solution to the social order problem of sociology, this position implies that the existence of sociology as a set of activities in the world can be accounted for by the appeal to 'common norms', 'rules', and their 'internalization'. Levy's programme[14] for adequate theorizing, for example, consists of a set of rules which we are instructed to follow to produce the describable state of affairs which he strongly recommends—ideal, elegant, scientific theory. We contend that while such rules can be enumerated *ad infinitum*, the statement of them does not describe how they are done in such a way that an actor in the world can follow them as instructions so as to produce Levy's desirable state of affairs. The programme is then not adequately descriptive; it is an elliptic and persuasive solution to the problem of social order.

The second solution differs in emphasis but derives from the same conception of sociological description. We could account for sociology in terms of the events which sociological descriptions depict. Thus, the methodically produced character of human activities is seen as controlling the existence of sociology as an activity.

It is because marriages, wars and suicides are done regularly and methodically that the activity of describing them is possible. Under this view, we have the strongest possible argument for the 'pure' scientific status of sociology. Thus, sociology exists because it describes an objective, pure and incorrigible 'real' world; we can account for sociology by enumerating and 'pointing to' the objects in the world to which sociological names and descriptions refer.

On the other hand, it is easy to see that the methodical character of marriage, war and suicide is only seen, recognized and made possible through the organized practices of sociology. These regularities do not exist 'out there' in pristine form to which sociologists functionally respond, but rather, they acquire their character as regularities and their features as describable objects only through the grace of sociological imputation. Thus, it is not an objectively discernible, purely existing external world which accounts for sociology; it is the methods and procedures of sociology which create and sustain that world.

How then is sociology possible? How may we resolve the social order problem of sociology? How is this activity—doing sociology—achieved? Sociology exists because sociologists have managed to negotiate a set of practices for creating and acting upon external worlds. We shall have adequately described sociology and accounted for its existence when we have described these commonsense practices.

## NOTES AND REFERENCES

[1] The notion of the commonsense character of bodies of knowledge was developed from my readings of the works of Alfred Schutz and Harold Garfinkel. I must particularly record my indebtedness to the tremendous corpus of published and unpublished writings of Garfinkel, which, while not being responsible for what follows, nevertheless provided me with a number of usable conceptions for organizing the materials.

[2] For my discussion of Descartes, I used his *Discourse on Method*, trans. Arthur Wollaston (Baltimore: Penguin Books, 1960).

[3] For my discussion of Hobbes, see Molesworth's edition of the English works, *The Elements of Law*, ed. Tönnies (Cambridge: The University Press, 1928), L. Strauss, *The Political Philosophy of Hobbes* (Chicago: University of Chicago Press, 1952).

[4] All of Marx's writings are useful for this discussion, but the following have the greatest relevance: K. Marx, *The Poverty of Philosophy* (New York: International Publishers, 1963); K. Marx and F. Engels, *The German Ideology* (New York: International Publishers, 1947); K. Marx, *A Contribution to the Critique of Political Economy* (Chicago: Charles Kerr, 1904); T. B. Bottomore and M. Rubel, eds., *Karl Marx: Selected Writings in Sociology and Social Philosophy* (New York: McGraw, 1964). We have also used H. Marcuse, *Reason and Revolution* (Boston: Beacon, 1960).

[5] Think of academic political scientists who insist that the most adequate corpus of political knowledge is that which is intelligible to practising politicians.

[6] Bear in mind that we are discussing Hobbes' critique and programme of revision for only one point in his career; he subsequently found the *content* of the traditional corpus inadequate, and came to distrust history as providing the most adequate empirical grounds. Thus in the end he contested both the validity and the applicability of the traditional corpus, and saw the possibility of developing an applicable corpus of knowledge based upon the direct study of human nature (his theory of motives) rather than upon history.

[7] For a compelling description of this 'central task' see Leo Strauss, *What is Political Philosophy?* (Glencoe: Free Press, 1959).

[8] *German Ideology*, p. 14.

[9] Bottomore and Rubel, *Karl Marx*, p. 63.

[10] Note how both Marx and Descartes use a notion of the 'real', 'hard' starting points of enquiry.

[11] In this sense, 'radical' means 'sociological'.

# 5. NELL KEDDIE
## Classroom Knowledge*

One consequence of the particular normative orientation of much sociology of education has been its definition of educational failure: explanations of educational failure are most often given in terms of pupils' ethnic and social class antecedents[1] and rely on a concept of social pathology rather than one of cultural diversity.[2] It is only recently that attention has been given to the defining processes occurring within the school itself[3] and to the social organization of curriculum knowledge.[4] The studies suggest that the processes by which pupils are categorized are not self-evident and point to an overlooked consequence of a differentiated curriculum: that it is part of the process by which educational deviants are created and their deviant identities maintained.[5] Here I hope to raise questions about these processes by considering two aspects of classroom knowledge: what knowledge teachers have of pupils, and what counts as knowledge to be made available and evaluated in the classroom. This involves casting as problematic what are held to be knowledge and ability in schools rather than taking either as given.

The empirical data on which this account is based[6] were collected by observation, tape recording and questionnaire in a large mixed comprehensive school with a fairly heterogeneous social class intake, although in the school, as in its catchment area, social class III is over-represented. Pupils from social classes I and II tend to be placed in A streams and those from social classes IV and V in C streams.[7] The study is focused on the humanities department which in 1969/70 introduced an examination course based on history, geography and social science to fourth-year pupils. The course was constructed to be taught as an undifferentiated programme across the ability range, and to be examined by mode 3 at ordinary level and C.S.E. at the end of the fifth year.[8] The course is described as 'enquiry based' and is taught by 'key lessons' to introduce a topic, and a workcard system to allow children to work individually and at their own speed. In the fifth year the work is often organized around topics; in the

* First published in this volume.

fourth year it is generally organized in 'blocks' of different subjects. This study is concerned with the first social science block which has socialization as its theme and follows directly after a geographical study of regions of Britain. Both were taught from material prepared by the department's teachers (in this case sociologists, a psychologist, an economist and geographers), so that each class keeps the same teacher for both geographical and social science studies.

The school is probably atypical of secondary schools in this country in its high degree of institutionalized innovation (every subject is now examined by mode 3 at C.S.E.) and therefore if the data has any claim to generality it must be because the school stands as a critical case and illustrates the fate of innovatory ideals in practice. Throughout this account references to teachers and pupils are specifically references to teachers and pupils of this one school.

A central issue for teachers in the school is whether or not the school should unstream. Bourdieu[9] points out that conflict indicates consensus about which issues are deemed worthy of conflict. In this debate consensus that is not articulated is the most interesting because it is not questioned and includes, as I shall show, evaluations of what constitutes knowledge and ability and thus evaluations of what pupils are and ought to be like in critical respects. In the fourth year pupils are divided into three broad ability bands, A, B and C, and some departments stream rigidly within these bands. The humanities department divides pupils into parallel groups within each band and looks forward to teaching completely mixed ability groups.

In casting as problematic what counts as knowledge and ability, I begin with what teachers themselves find problematic: the teaching of C stream pupils. C stream pupils present teachers with problems both of social control and in the preparation and presentation of teaching material. By their characterization of C stream pupils as 'that type of child' and 'these children', teachers tell that they feel that C stream pupils are unlike themselves. By inference, teachers feel that A stream pupils are more like themselves, at least in ways that count in school. Teaching A stream pupils seems to be relatively unproblematic for teachers: they take the activities in these classrooms for granted, they rarely make explicit the criteria which guide the preparation and presentation of teaching material for these pupils, and what counts as knowledge is left implicit, and, apparently, consensual. The 'question' to which C. Wright Mills[10] refers rarely arises: the empirical problem is the phenomen on which Garfinkel calls the 'unavailability' of the 'formal structures of practical actions'.[11] The assumption underlying my interpretation of data is that C stream pupils disrupt teachers' expectations and violate their norms of appropriate social, moral and intellectual pupil behaviour. In so far as C stream pupils' behaviour is explicitly seen by teachers as inappropriate or inadequate, it makes more visible or available what is held to be appropriate pupil behaviour because it provokes questions about the norms which govern teachers' expectations about appropriate pupil behaviour.

## THE IDEAL PUPIL

Becker[12] developed the concept of the *ideal pupil* to refer to that set of teacher expectations which constitute a taken for granted notion of appropriate pupil behaviour. In examining discrepancies between what I shall call *educationist* and *teacher* contexts I shall argue that it is in the likeness of the images of the ideal pupil from one context to the other that the relation and the disjunction between the views expressed by teachers in these contexts is explained.

The fundamental discrepancy between the views of teachers as they emerge in these contexts can be expressed as that between theory and practice, or what Selznick calls doctrine and commitment:[13]

Doctrine, being abstract, is judiciously selective and may be qualified at will in discourse, subject only to restrictions of sense and logic. But action is concrete, generating consequences which define a sphere of interest and responsibility together with a corresponding chain of commitments. Fundamentally, the discrepancy between doctrine and commitment arises from the essential distinction between the interrelation of ideas and the interrelation of phenomena.

This is a distinction between 'words' and 'deeds'[14] and it is necessary to remember that words like deeds are situated in the ongoing interaction in which they arise. 'Doctrine' as the ideology and theory of the humanities department is enunciated in the educationist context, which may also be called the context of *discussion* of school politics, in particular discussion which evokes interdepartmental conflicts, especially those about streaming. (The actual context of school politics, for example, heads of departments' meetings, may provoke something else again.) The other aspect of the educationist context is the discussion of educational theory, and here talk of the department's policy often evokes statements about its alignment with or opposition to other humanities programmes[15] constructed by other course makers. The educationist context may be called into being by the presence of an outsider to whom explanations of the department's activities must be given or by a forthcoming school meeting which necessitates discussion of policy of how things *ought* to be in school.

By contrast, the teacher context is that in which teachers move most of the time. It is the world of *is* in which teachers anticipate interaction with pupils in planning lessons, in which they act in the classroom and in which when the lesson is over they usually recount or explain what has happened. I shall elaborate on the characteristics of both contexts to suggest their relation to each other and the implications for the possible fate of educational innovation in schools.

## THE EDUCATIONIST CONTEXT

The educational policy of the course and of the department draws selectively and consciously on educational theory and research, and is seen by at least some of the department as an informed and expert view of education, as opposed to the lay and commonsense views advanced by other departments. The 'pure' educational policy of the department seems to contain the following as its components:

1. Intelligence is not primarily determined by heredity. Differential educational performance may be accounted for by differential motivation rather than differential intelligence. Ability is to be accounted for as much by motivation as by intelligence and is largely determined by the child's social class antecedents.

2. Streaming by ability weights the school environment against those whose family background has already lessened their chances of educational achievement, because it 'fixes' the expectations that both teachers and pupil have of a pupil's performance and is thereby likely to lower the motivation of pupils with low achievement-orientation who have been assigned to low streams.

3. The criteria by which pupils are allocated to streams or sets when they enter the school (the mathematics department, for example, are said to use verbal I.Q. scores) have been discredited by both psychologists and sociologists; but their lack of reliability is not understood by those who use them.

4. Streaming perpetuates the distinction between grammar and secondary modern school under one roof, and creates or maintains social divisiveness, since like the grammar school it favours middle-class children.

5. A differentiated curriculum divides pupils. The school should try to unite them.

Those in the school who favour streaming oppose the views given above on the grounds that the individual child is best helped by being placed in a stream with those like himself so that he can receive teaching appropriate to his pace and level.

I have insufficient data about the extent to which teachers in the humanities department hold this educational policy in its 'pure' form. Probably most select out of it aspects of it that are most relevant to them. Outwardly at least, all members of the department are in favour of the mixed ability teaching which the department has introduced into the first and second years. The department is committed eventually to teaching mixed ability groups in the higher forms, but sees the matter as sufficiently problematic to delay until a new teaching block is ready in a couple of years' time. The main point, however, is that those teachers who will advance the educationist view in the discussion of school and educational policy will speak and act in ways that are discrepant with this view when the context is that of the *teacher*. While, therefore, some educational aims may be formulated by teachers as *educationists*, it will not be surprising if 'doctrine' is contradicted by 'commitments' which arise in the situation in which they must act as *teachers*.

The way in which the course is set up reveals how teachers can hold discrepant views without normally having to take cognizance of the contradictions which may arise. For example, a resolution is partially effected by shifting the meaning of motivation from an assertion of the desirable in the educationist context to an explanation of the desirable in the teacher context. Thus the educationist assumes that in the ideal environment of the unstreamed school with an undifferentiated curriculum, the differential motivation which now leads to under-achievement will be greatly reduced. In the teacher context, in which teachers move in their everyday activities as teachers, motivation becomes an explanation of pupils' behaviour. In this exchange, two teachers who also hold the educationist's view in part are talking about the A stream class of the teacher who speaks first:

TEACHER J: [Some of the class] have written to Oldham Town Council for material for the New Town project.
TEACHER C: They're really bright, are they?
TEACHER J: Mostly from middle-class families, well motivated.

Here the relationship between initiative, intelligence, social class and motivation is the assumption taken for granted that makes the exchange of comments possible, and also illustrates well the portrayal of social skills as cognitive ones.

In the educationist's view, motivation is subsumed in a notion of rationality as leading to autonomy for the individual. The ideal pupil in the educationist context is the one who can perceive and rationally evaluate alternatives. He will become the ideal man of a society which embraces consensus politics and a convergence thesis of social class. In an interview[16] the head of department spoke of the 'qualities of mind' that the course will attempt to develop:

'I think mainly rationality—this is the essence of what we're trying to teach. Not, I hope, a belief that rationality will always . . . produce good moral answers because it won't, clearly; but a person who is prepared to weigh evidence. . . . This is the last opportunity many of them get for a structured view of society. This is political education . . . a participating society does not mean to my mind a population that is attending lots of planning meetings. It's a population that's aware of what's involved in planning. . . . It's educating people to be aware of what's involved in making political decisions. . . .'

Whether or not all the department's teachers share these educational aims and subscribe to this image of society, the course is set up with intentions of developing in pupils modes of work and thought which will help them to become more autonomous and rational beings. That is, it is set up in the hope that the conception of enquiry-based work will help to create the ideal pupil. I select three main aspects of the course to show how it also in fact caters for a pupil who already exists: the A stream academic and usually middle-class pupil. Thus the course embodies not only an image of what the ideal pupil ought to be, but also what he already is. These three aspects are:
1.) 'Working at your own speed'—this notion is very firmly embedded in the ideology of the course and it is significant that a teacher I heard 'selling' the course to pupils described it as 'self-regulating work which allows you to get ahead'. The corollary of this is that others fall behind, at least in relation to the pace of the course. Teachers were constantly urging pupils: 'You must finish that this week because next week we're going on to a new topic.' Teachers frequently remarked how much more quickly A pupils work than C pupils, and A pupils generally expressed approval of the notion of 'working at your own speed'—it is *their* speed. It would seem inevitable that the principle of individual speeds should be incompatible with a course that moves in a structured way from topic to topic. The only leeway is for some pupils to work through more workcards than others.

2.) All the studies on achievement orientation stress the middle-class child's tendency to thrive on an individualistic and competitive approach to learning. It follows that a workcard system which puts a premium on the individual working by himself rather than in a group, is probably set up in advance for the success of some pupils rather than others because they already value that kind of autonomy. Observation suggested that the result of this was that while pupils worked or rested from working, they talked in the peer group about matters like football and boy friends. Talk about work tended to be of the order: 'Do you know the answer to question 2?' Thus the content of the work rarely becomes the content of peer-group interaction but becomes separate from it. An analogy might be drawn with the doing of repetitive industrial tasks, where satisfaction derives from group interaction rather than from the work which brings in the money (or grades). The possibility for pupils of continuous interaction with friends may, however, be an important element in reducing social control problems for teachers.

3.) Teachers express regret that a problem in motivating C stream pupils is their tendency to see education in vocational terms. It was never made explicit (if realized at all by some teachers) that the educational aims of a course like this one also fulfil the vocational purposes of the more successful pupils. A stream pupils have been told, and they told me, that learning to work independently (of teacher and textbook) will help them 'in the sixth form and at university'. I also heard a teacher telling a B group that 'any worker who can think for himself is worth his weight in gold to his employer'. It is likely that lower stream pupils know this to be a highly questionable statement and do not look forward to this kind of satisfaction from their work. Thus while teachers do not, on the whole, perceive higher education as vocational, C stream pupils do not find the vocational rationale of the course commensurate with their expectations of what work will be like.

Both 1.) and 2.) suggest that the short-term aims of the course, where it impinges immediately on the pupils' work situation, are weighted in favour of A stream pupils, giving priority to skills and attitudes they are most likely to possess. In its long-term aims the same pattern emerges. It seems likely that an undifferentiated course will be set up with an image of the pupil in mind. Because in the educationist context the perspective is one of how things *ought* to be, it is not so obvious to teachers that they are drawing, albeit selectively, on what already *is*. As I shall show, in the teacher context teachers organize their activities around values which as educationists they may deny. These values arise from the conjunction of social class and ability in the judgements teachers make on pupils. It is by exploring what is judged to be appropriate behaviour that it becomes clear how ability and social class which are held separate in the educationist context are confounded in the teacher context.

## THE TEACHER CONTEXT

1.) Normal Pupils

In this context what a teacher 'knows' about pupils derives from the organizational device of banding or streaming, which in turn derives from the dominant organizing category of what counts as ability. The 'normal' characteristics (the term is taken from Sudnow[17]) of a pupil are those which are imputed to his band or stream as a whole. A pupil who is perceived as atypical is perceived in relation to the norm for the stream: 'She's bright for a B' (teacher H); or in relation to the norm for another group: 'They're as good as Bs' (teacher J of three hardworking pupils in his C stream group). This knowledge of what pupils are like is often at odds with the image of pupils the same teachers may hold as educationists, since it derives from streaming whose validity the educationist denies.

Although teachers in the humanities department might express disagreement with other teachers over teaching methods, evaluations of pupils and so on, there seems, in the teacher context, to be almost complete consensus about what normal pupils are like. It is probable, given the basis of categorization, that members of the department are, in terms of 'what everyone knows' about pupils, much closer to other teachers in the school than they themselves commonly imply. As house tutors, most of their negotiations with teachers outside the department must be carried on in terms of shared meanings. Because these meanings are taken for granted both within and outside the department they are not made explicit as a set of assumptions because they continue to refer to an unquestionable reality 'out there'. It is possible to disagree about an individual pupil and to couch the disagreement in terms of his typical or atypical 'B-ness', but in the teacher context it would be disruptive of interaction and of action-to-be-taken to question that 'B-ness' exists. Like the concept of ability from which it derives it is unexamined in the teacher context since it belongs to the shared understandings that make interaction possible. In the educationist context, where other interests are at stake, 'ability' and 'streaming' shift into new categories of meaning. Although the teacher may be the same person in both contexts, what he 'knows' as educationist about pupils may not be that which he as teacher 'knows' about them. The frame of reference shifts from a concern with 'things as they *are*' to 'things as they *ought* to be',[18] and in this context both ability and streaming may become problematic as they cannot be for the practical ongoing purpose of the teacher.

The imputation of normal attributes to pupils by teachers does not tell us objectively about pupils. Rather it is the case that in certain areas of school life teachers and different groups of pupils maintain conflicting definitions of the situation. For the teacher, social control may depend on his being able in the classroom to maintain publicly his definition of the situation. He may do this by attempting to render pupil definitions invalid. Thus he may treat pupils' complaints about the course with scepticism and subsume them under normal categories like: 'he's trying to get out of work', 'it's just a bit of "agro" ', 'they'll try anything on'. These explanations may or may not coincide with pupils' explanations of their motives. The general effect of teachers' explanations is to recognize the situation as conflictual, but to render invalid the particular point the pupil is making and thus to delineate the extent of pupils' rights. Equal rights are not granted to all pupils since the 'same' behaviour may have different meanings attributed to it, depending on the normal status of the pupil. In one C stream lesson a pupil asked the teacher:

PUPIL: This is geography, isn't it? Why don't we learn about where countries are and that?
TEACHER: This is socialization.
PUPIL: What's that? I'd rather do geography. . . . Netsilik Eskimo—I don't know where that is.
TEACHER [ironically:] After the lesson we'll go and get the atlas and I'll show you. (Teacher D)

A few days earlier I had asked this teacher whether any pupil had asked in class (as they had in some other classes): 'Why should we do social science?' and had had the reply:

TEACHER: No, but if I were asked by Cs I would try to sidestep it because it would be the same question as 'Why do anything? Why work?'
OBSERVER: What if you were asked by an A group?
TEACHER: Then I'd probably try to answer.

For me, as observer, learning how to recognize normal pupils was an important aspect of my socialization as observer from the teachers' point of view. Teachers took some care that I should understand what pupils were like, especially C pupils. In my first days in the school they frequently prepared me for what I should expect when I attended their lesson, and they afterwards explained to me why the lesson had gone as it had. These explanations tended to take the form: 'C stream pupils are . . .' or 'low ability pupils are . . .' This aspect of 'learning the ropes'[19] is presumably an important element in the socialization of student and probationary teachers.

The 'normalization' of pupils tends to produce a polarity between A and C pupils in which they reflect reversed images of each other. The B stream pupil is left in the middle and tends to shift around in the typology. Generally when special workcards are prepared it is for C groups and it is assumed that Bs will follow the same work as A pupils. On the other hand, teachers often see B pupils as posing the same social control problems as C streams. One teacher saw this as the *result* of their undefined status and characterized B stream pupils as suffering from identity problems. His characterization could as well refer to teachers' problems in being unable to define clearly the normal B pupil, as to the perspective of the pupils themselves, who may have quite clear notions of their own position and status, though they are liable to be defined out by the teachers. Similarly A pupils who present discipline problems to teachers are likely to be described as pupils who 'are really Bs'. This characterization is not necessarily applied to those A pupils who will probably be entered for C.S.E. and not 'O' level in the humanities examinations and might therefore be seen as right for a B stream. This is in keeping with the tendency not only for normative judgements to predominate—teachers speak more about the 'moral' and 'social' qualities of pupils than of their cognitive skills—but for the former qualities to be presented as though they were cognitive skills:

TEACHER K: If you want, you can go on to the Depression later in the term. There's also material on America in the twenties.

TEACHER B: Isn't it true to say that although it's C material in a sense, the level of response depends on the level of intelligence. For example, some of the moral problems you pose—it would take an A child really to see the implications. Some of the girls would find it interesting.

TEACHER K: Yes, it could be used at all levels.                      (At a staff meeting)

## 2.) Ability and Social Class

Most children enter secondary schools with their educational identities partially established in the records, and by the fourth year the question is rather how these identities are maintained than how they were established. Teachers appear to have two principal organizing categories: ability and social class. Social class, however, tends to be a latent and implicit category for sorting pupil behaviour. On occasion though, some teachers appear to use social class as an explanation of educational performance:

Teacher B of a group of boys he described as 'working class who belong to a B group':

'they don't work but they came up high in a test which tested their grasp of concepts'.

On another occasion he spoke of the same boys as

'really from a higher stream—able but they don't work'.

Teacher H distinguished between the performance of two 'bright' girls in his A stream class:

'one is the daughter of a primary school headmaster; a home with books and lots of encouragement . . . [the other one] comes from quite a different kind of home which doesn't encourage homework . . .'

He felt that the latter had potential ability she was not using to the full.

Another teacher (L) characterized a girl whom he thought 'works only for grades' as a 'trade unionist'.

Teacher J had a threefold typology of his C stream class (which he told me before I observed his class for the first time) in which he linked certain kinds of psychological disturbance with a working-class culture. It is possible to identify two types of pupil in what follows: the remedial child and the pathologically disturbed child:

TEACHER: The difficulties with the least able child are those of remedial children: children who don't work in normally accepted ways in school—with these children I'm not succeeding, humanities aren't succeeding. The Cs who fail can't meet [the head of department's] criteria [of autonomous work]. They need to be in a group with only a few teachers. . . . Many have working-class parents—Jane's got problems. Her father's a not-very-bright milkman and her mother ran away. Lots of difficult children have disturbed backgrounds and this is often more important than innate abilities.

OBSERVER: What do you mean by disturbed?

TEACHER: Fathers who beat mothers, nervous breakdowns in the family, that sort of thing.

He speaks of 'that kind of child' and says they 'fluctuate in behaviour' . . . 'Jane has little idea of how to behave generally . . . [but Susan] is a big mouthing fishwife who can, on occasion, work solidly and be pleasant.'

The third type of child was identified only after the lesson: the quiet child who works fairly hard through most lessons. In terms of social control this pupil is not a problem and this is why the casual listener-in to teachers' talk might get the impression that all C stream pupils are constant problems for teachers.

After the lesson this teacher, like others, wondered if he were too lenient with the problem pupils; he said of Jane 'Perhaps she gets away with too much . . . [but] she can't concentrate and needs the teacher all the time.' The key phrase in his general description is probably the reference to 'children who don't work in normally accepted ways in school'. These pupils' behaviour can be seen as generally inappropriate. Like the concept of the disadvantaged child the reference contains a notion of 'under-socialization' and instability originating in the social disorganization[20] of the 'background' of the pupil. The dominant notion here seems akin to some social psychological accounts of delinquency[21] which specify a multiplicity of factors like a 'bad' home as a cause of deviance without making it clear what a bad home is, how it causes deviance or why other homes, which should on the same criteria be 'bad', do not produce delinquents. Because the social pathology approach allows explanations of pupil behaviour to be made in terms of discrete factors, teachers tend not to perceive the collective social class basis of pupils' experience but to fragment that experience into the problems of individual (and 'disadvantaged') pupils. This makes it likely that the pupils' collective definition of the educational situation will be rendered invisible to teachers,[22] and failure individualized.

This teacher's (J) normal C pupil is probably cast in a more explicit model of psychological disturbance than many, but this does not affect the essential outline of the image, in which instability plays a large part and is frequently linked with aggression. In terms of social control instability means unpredictability and the social control problems as perceived by the teacher are demonstrated in the remark of this teacher who said that many C stream pupils are 'awkward customers' and are allowed to get away with too much: 'it's important if you're to get anywhere not to antagonize these children.' This teacher, like most of the teachers in the department, expects his C pupils to behave differently in class from his A pupils: for example, he expects and allows them to make more noise and to achieve a great deal less work than A pupils. It is not possible to estimate the degree to which his expectations are instrumental in creating the situation as he defines it.

Frequently C, and occasionally, B pupils become 'characters'; for example: 'Clare will envelop Dick one of these days. The girls think Dick is very sexy.' A stream pupils are not spoken of in this way. This is linked with another normal characteristic of C pupils—their immaturity.[23] Thus after showing a film called *The First Fifteen Minutes of Life* to groups of pupils, the noise made by B and C groups was described as 'covering up embarrassment' and as 'the back row of the cinema', indicating the pupils' response had been characterized as contextually inappropriate. A pupils who were much more silent (but were also hushed quite systematically) were characterized as more 'mature' in their response, although the comments of a girl to her friends: 'they shouldn't show films like that to fifteen year olds', suggested that some of these pupils, at least, found the film difficult to accept. It may have been relevant to the C pupils' response that they were quite unable to see a rationale for the showing of the film since the label 'socialization' had no explanatory significance for them. Many defined the film as 'biology' and said 'we've done it before'.

Clearly, A stream pupils' definition of appropriate behaviour in the situation was taken over from or coincided with that of the teachers. It is already clear that teachers are most concerned with what they perceive as the negative characteristics of C pupils' behaviour and that this is to some extent linked with expectations of appropriate behaviour that have a social class basis and differentiation. C stream pupils are often seen to lack those qualities which are deemed by teachers desirable in themselves and appropriate to school,[24] whereas A stream pupils appear to possess these qualities. The negative aspects of the normal C pupil emerge whenever a teacher compares C and A pupils:

'It's amazing how much quicker As are than Cs. The As have almost caught Cs now.' (Teacher D)

'I did it slightly differently with the As because they're rushed for time. With the As I used the pink card more, but I still put diagrams on the board. But it was still quicker.' (Teacher J)

'I meant to find out [what "ulu" an Eskimo word, meant] but I knew the Cs wouldn't ask. It's remarkable how they can read through and not notice words they don't understand.' (Teacher D)

'I didn't know any more than was on the workcard—this was all right with Cs, but it wouldn't be with As.' (Teacher G)

These comments indicate that teachers have notions about the organization of time and material (and the degree of preparation necessary) in the classroom which depend on the normal characteristics of the ability group they are teaching. Thus what teachers 'know' about pupils as social, moral, and psychological persons is extended to what they know about them as intellectual persons, which as I shall show leads to the differentiation of an undifferentiated curriculum.

3.) Ability and Knowledge

One of the remarkable features of the tendency to attribute to pupils the normal characteristics of their ability band is that what is held to constitute ability is rarely made explicit. When teachers discuss whether material is suitable for teaching to A, B or C streams, the criteria on which they make judgements remain largely implicit and consensual. Throughout it is difficult to separate out references to cognitive skills from imputed social and moral characteristics on the one hand and from characterization of teaching material on the other. This comment on teaching material about the Depression is typical:

'Some of the economic implications are difficult—it's O level type of material . . . but some of the human elements may be C material.' (Teacher at staff meeting)

Material is categorized in terms of its suitability for a given ability band and, by implication, ability is categorized in terms of whether or not these pupils can manage that material. Like the pupils who are categorized in terms of levels of ability, knowledge in school is categorized in terms of its supposed hierarchical nature with reference to criteria of age and ability. I shall be concerned with how teachers organize knowledge in relation to the normal attributes of the pupils they are teaching, according to criteria used to establish the hierarchies of ability and knowledge. This approach involves starting from the assumption that not only is ability not a given factor but also that we do not know what the knowledge to be got or the subject to be mastered properly is. We can only learn what they are by learning what teachers and pupils who are involved in defining that knowledge claim to be doing: subjects are what practitioners do with them.

Within the course itself, the enquiry-based mode is intended to change the emphasis from mastery of given contents of a subject to mastery of the method of enquiry itself. The workcards are to some extent structured around the 'concepts' it is desirable for pupils to acquire through working through the material. Thus the teacher who speaks of the 'working-class' boys in his B group who are 'able but don't work, but come up high in a test which tested their grasp of concepts', is using the term concept partly in the in-language of the course. The term derives from Bloom,[25] who uses it in his taxonomy of the hierarchical organization of knowledge where each level subsumes, under more general categories, the categories of the level below. The head of the humanities department here shows how the notion of concept, which appears to be glossed as 'idea' or 'structure', is embedded in the organization of the teaching material:

'When you begin to think in terms of drawing things together, although, as I say, there are certain contents more important than other contents, and that's why we do the British economy rather than endless regional studies of Britain or endless historical studies of the treaties of the nineteenth century, the most important element in the work is teaching the children how to work. Teaching them a mode of enquiry is, I think, fundamental to the whole thing. Because this is the common ingredient of the historian's work, the geographer's work, the social scientist's work and this is the lasting influence on the child, not the memory of a particular date, and I regard as part of the teaching of that mode of enquiry the development of concepts and ideas which obviously increases the degree of sophistication in their mode of enquiry. The more ideas they've got, the more ideas of structures they've got, the better equipped they are to think in an orderly mode of enquiry.'[16]

It appears from this that what he is describing is not so much a change from an emphasis on contents to an emphasis on method, but a change in content in terms of how that content is organized. It may not be intrinsic to the way the course is set up that teachers treat the teaching material as a body of knowledge or 'facts' to be got across to pupils, rather than as ways of organizing facts or contents in relation to each other. In the classroom it often seems that pupils are more enquiry-minded than teachers, whose presentation of material does not allow concepts to be distinguished from content because the concept is presented in terms of its content. This relationship is also clearly illustrated in the end-of-topic test where many questions ask the pupil to match a content to a term or 'concept', for example:

In some experiments hungry animals are given a food pellet each time they produce a particular response, such as pressing a bar or pecking at a disc. This is called: *stimulus, extinction, motivation, reinforcement.*

Thus although the course was deliberately set up by teachers as educationists to counteract what they saw as an inappropriate exercise of authority by the teacher in the traditional talk-and-chalk presentation of material, in the teacher context enquiry for the pupil is still heavily teacher directed.

In the following extract from a C stream lesson, the teacher (E)—who is not a sociologist and has to rely on prepared material on a pink card[26] which includes a description of the joint family, but not of the extended family as it is defined in Britain today—rejects alternative definitions to the nuclear family suggested by pupils because his reading of the material leads him to see common residence as a critical criterion:

TEACHER: Now who'd like to tell me what we mean by the family? [Pause] It's not as obvious as you might think. What is a family? Derek?
DEREK: A mother, a daddy.
TEACHER: Yeah.
DEREK: A couple of kids if they got them.
TEACHER: Yes.
DEREK: A granddaddy, a grandmummy.
TEACHER: Yes.
DEREK: An aunt, an uncle.
TEACHER: You'd include that in the family.
BOY: Yes, you would.
GIRL: [untranscribable]
TEACHER: Anybody disagree with that—that in a family you'd include grandparents?
DEREK: Well they are 'cos they're your mother's and father's mothers and fathers.
TEACHER: And it's all part of one family?
BOY: Yeah.
TEACHER: Anybody disagree or like to add to it at all? What we mean by the family?
GIRL [she has probably been reading the pink card]: It's also a group of people living under one roof.
GIRL: No, it's not. [Other pupils agree and disagree].
TEACHER: Ah, a group of people living under one roof—aah—that differs from what Derek said, isn't it? Because the group—ssh, Derek . . .

DEREK [his voice emerges above the teacher's voice]: . . . would still be the same as your mum, wouldn't it? It'd still be your family.

TEACHER: Yeah, the group that Derek mentioned doesn't live under one roof. Now we can limit the family to say its a group of people related by blood, er, who live under one roof; or we can extend its meaning to include what Derek said: grandparents, aunts and uncles and so on, who may in individual cases live under the same roof, but it's not normal. The British family, I say the British family because the idea of families differs, as we shall see, over the world. Peter and Derek, you're not listening.

PETER: I am.

TEACHER: . . . British family is parents and children, that is what you might call the, er, nuclear family; in other words, the core of the family. They tend to live together until the children have developed, matured, if you like, into adults. . . .

The way the exchange goes is not entirely a matter of 'how much' sociology this teacher knows; it is also a question of the relation between the categories he is using to structure this knowledge in the classroom and those used by the boy which derive from his everyday knowledge of 'what everyone knows' about families. The teacher moves outside this everyday knowledge since there must be occasions when he refers to his own relations as 'family' even if his ties with them are less close than those of Derek with his extended kin. The teacher cues the class that he wants them to move into another reality[27] with the words: 'It's not as obvious as you might think.' The C girls who said to me 'why should we learn about families? I mean we know about families, we live in them,' have not made this shift to seeing that the family might be viewed as problematic. It appears at this point, and I discuss the matter further below, that the ability to 'grasp a concept' in the context of the course and probably in its wider sense, refers to a pupil's willingness or ability to take over or accept the teacher's categories. This may mean, as it would have done for Derek, having to make a choice between apparently contradictory sets of statements unless he can see a reason for shifting his perspective to another set of categories. I shall suggest that Derek's stance is common among C pupils and differs from that of A stream pupils, who assume that the knowledge the teacher will purvey to them has a structure in which what they are asked to do has some place. This does not mean that the A pupil expects that knowledge to be relevant to his everyday experience. The argument is that A and C pupils tend to approach classroom knowledge from different positions and with different expectations. This argument makes no assumptions about the hierarchical status of the knowledge they are being asked to 'grasp' or about the degree of generalization or 'abstraction' involved. The concept of intelligence as a differential ability to deal with abstractions is implicit in the teachers' frequent reference to the 'levels' of difficulty in the material and the 'levels' of pupils' response.

I turn now to teachers' discussion of teaching material before and after use in the classroom, and follow this with a consideration of the data provided by pupils' responses to a questionnaire and to the teaching material in the classroom.

## 4.) The Teaching Material: 'Subjects' and Pupils

When teachers talk about how they have or will teach material they speak nearly always about the problems of teaching C stream pupils. Teaching the material to the A stream pupils for whom it is primarily prepared and who stand in some sense as ideal pupils appears relatively unproblematic; although, as I shall argue, there are reasons why it might be regarded as highly problematic. I have already quoted comments from staff meetings which showed the difficulty of 'economic implications' as opposed to 'human elements' (p. 144). Similarly the comments showed a link between the level of response to 'moral problems' and the 'level of intelligence' (p. 141). The following extracts from teachers' comments bring out these points more clearly:

'Yes, worth bringing out with the more able group.' (Teacher B)

'I envisage problems with 4Cs in understanding unusual relationships. The meaning of relationships, it's going to be very difficult to get this over to them.' (Teacher J)

'Yes, um, when we did it with the 4Cs before they, er, didn't seem particularly interested that, er, other people had family groups of their own. Because it wasn't real to them, it was so far removed, it didn't seem of complete . . . of any relevance to them.' (Teacher L)

'I think if you're dealing with it purely in terms of kinship diagrams and white sheets,[26] again you're actually reducing the interest again, if you make it too intellectual. What illustrative material is there on this? . . . I think I've said this before . . . that sociology has its validity in its abstractions and in its intellectual [untranscribable] . . . to what extent the 4Cs will take that or to what extent it will remain a series of stories about families . . .' (Teacher J—not himself a sociologist)

The picture that emerges from these comments which are highly representative, is one of oppositions that describe material and pupils: 'intellectual' is opposed to 'real', and 'abstractions' to 'stories'. One teacher implies that so long as the material is accessible only in terms of kinship diagrams and buff cards it will be too 'intellectual'. To make it 'real', illustrative material is needed. The points they make are not ones simply of method, but are about methods relating to C stream pupils, and so questions arise not only about why C pupils are believed to need non-intellectual material, but also why A pupils are believed not to need illustrative material and not to have problems in understanding 'the meaning of relationships'. The suggestion in these comments is that there is something in the material which 'it might be possible to bring out with the As'. The phrases 'bring it out', 'make explicit', the 'implications of moral problems', 'economic implications', seem to point to a range of understanding that is not available to C pupils who can engage only marginally with the material. Teacher J provides a further gloss[28] on this when he says after a lesson with a C group:

'This stuff [on language] is much too difficult for them. . . . On the other hand they could cope with the family stuff. They could say something in their own words about different kinds of family, because they already knew something about them even if they did not know the correct term.'

'The correct term' implies something about how status may be attributed to knowledge. The pupils' ignorance of the 'correct term' suggests their deficiency. In the following discussion it is further suggested that the range of understanding that is available to C stream pupils must be rooted in their 'experience', and that this is linked with another phrase teachers often use about adapting teaching material for C pupils: 'putting it in language they can understand':

TEACHER J:  How about the family for the Cs? It may have more in it for them because it's nearer home.

TEACHER B:  There'll be a lot of visual stimulus for discussion. . . . The Cs should be able to get somewhere with discussion . . . we won't do the history of the family with them, it's too difficult, probably too difficult for anyone.

What seems to emerge overall from the way teachers discuss teaching material in relation to pupils' abilities is an assumption that C pupils cannot master subjects: both the 'abstractions of sociology' and the 'economic implications' are inaccessible to them. The problem then in teaching C pupils is that you cannot teach them subjects. When A pupils do subjects it can be assumed by teachers that they do what, in terms of the *subject*, is held to be appropriate, and material is prepared with regard to what is seen as the demands of the *subject*. In teaching C pupils modifications must be made with regard to the *pupil*, and it is as though the subject is scanned for or reduced to residual 'human elements' or a 'series of stories'.

The clearest statement of the differential emphasis on subject and pupils is that made by Teacher K. He is describing how he is able to 'gear' his study of the British economy for a C pupil at 'quite a different level' from the level at which he teaches it to his A group. He says:

'I can streamline it so it's got various grades of content and I can, I hope, do things which are very useful and valuable to the C child which I don't feel are as necessary for the A child. But they're all doing economics, they're all doing certain vital basic studies in how the economy works. . . .'

He describes how the study is dealing with 'land, labour and capital . . . in answer to what we call the "for whom" question in economics':

'Well, that leads on to a special study of labour for the Cs. Rewards for labour—wages. Wages can then be considered for girls in terms of why they're paid often lower than men's pay and what sorts of factors determine the different wages rates for different sorts of employment—something that's very immediate for these children.'

Later he says:

'Looking at a mixed economy he can angle that study much more towards taxation and the practical elements of how to fill in tax forms and what you get relief for, whereas . . . I'd be much more concerned with how the different types of taxation work, with the higher ability child: the difference between direct and indirect taxation and S.E.T. and so on. And also the effects that different forms of taxation have on the rates of economic growth—the more sophisticated elements which the lower ability child, it may not be possible for him to grasp the ideas that are part of that type of study but he's still able to study taxation and at a simpler level; but he's not being discriminated against.'

Here it is clear that one consequence of a differential treatment of the economy is the way in which categories of analysis are made available to or withheld from pupils. This teacher held the educationist view in almost its pure form, and the political implications of his teaching of economics should probably be seen as an unintentional and unrecognized manifestation of consensus politics arising from an image of society as consensus. The teaching cannot be said to be intentionally prescriptive: it is presented as an objective account of the economic system rather than one of a number of possible accounts. He is not deliberately restricting the categories that are available to A pupils, since his teaching reflects his own thinking. When he further restricts C stream pupils to a study of labour and that in terms of differential wages, he sees this as 'valuable' for the C pupils in terms of their ascribed status as workers. He does not intentionally withhold the framework which would allow the pupil to raise questions about the taxation policy as a whole, but he does effectively prevent, by a process of fragmentation, the question of how such knowledge becomes available.[29]

## 5.) The Pupils' Response

I shall now attempt some account of the relation between teachers' and pupils' definitions of the classroom situation. The main contention is that the differences attributed to A and C pupils by teachers are substantive, but they may be open to interpretations other than those habitually made by teachers. In presenting the data I look at the ways in which teachers and pupils scan each others' activities in the classroom and attribute meaning to them.

The first indication of a differentiated response of A and C pupils comes from the responses to a questionnaire administered to the whole fourth year which sought information on the degree to which pupils have access to or have taken over the teachers' definitions of the humanities course.

A pupils all knew the terminology of the course and did not have to ask what 'key lesson' or pink card meant. Question 2 is quite open-ended: 'Do you think key lessons are a good idea or not, and why?' The majority of A pupils chose to answer it in terms of the structure of the course as teachers defined it, with answers that indicate that they saw the key lesson as an introduction to a new topic suggesting the nature of the work to follow:

'It introduces you to the topic.'
'It helps you to understand the topic better.'
'You see what a subject is about.'
'You're not dropped into a mass of facts.'

The table (p. 150) shows the pattern of responses to questions 2 and 3 of the questionnaire. Question 3 asked pupils to explain what a pink card, a buff card and a yellow workcard are respectively. A pupils show a much higher tendency to distinguish the 'blue sheet' from the 'white sheet' as a 'summary', 'an introduction to a topic' or 'a key lesson on paper', and not to describe both simply as 'information sheets'.

Percentages of those accepting the teachers' definition of:

| Stream | (a) The course | (b) Pink cards | (c) Yellow workcards |
|--------|----------------|----------------|----------------------|
| A | 68 | 68 | 40[3] |
| B | 50[1] | 44 | 23 |
| C | 8[2] | 19 | 3 |

Total number of respondents: A—111; B—102; C—112.

[1] Nearly half of these responses, 23 from a class of 29, came from one class, which suggests that the teacher is in some way acting differently with this B group.

[2] C pupils' answers are very diverse and no distinct trend emerges, although they tend to be more concerned with how the lesson is organized for learning, and the showing of films is contrasted favourably with 'just talking' and workcards as teaching methods.

[3] It is likely that A pupils are more often encouraged to think of the yellow workcards as a 'guide' to using other workcards rather than as just 'questions on the white sheet'.

A pupils were also more likely to pick up and use the terms 'social science' or 'sociology' as an overall label for their studies and were more likely to characterize the film, *The First Fifteen Minutes of Life*, which introduced the study of socialization, as about 'learning' rather than as 'biology' or as well as 'biology'; although they were generally unable, when asked, to gloss[28] the term 'learning' despite the fact that they had written up notes on it.

A pupils are generally more sensitive to what they have been told *about* the course. Thus when I asked them what they thought of the course, typical responses were:

'It's very good; you can disagree with the teacher.'
'You can link up subjects.'
'You can think out things for yourself.'
'It's good for learning how to work at university.'

It seems likely they had accepted definitions received from teachers, because when I asked these pupils to tell me about a time they had disagreed with the teacher or about a time when they had been able to link up between subjects, they could recall no instances of either. There appears to be a discrepancy between their definition and their experience of the course of which they were not aware.

It seems probable that the pupils who come to be perceived by teachers as the most able, and who in a streamed school reach the top streams, are those who have access to or are willing to take over the teachers' definition of the situation. As A pupils' behaviour is generally seen by the teachers as appropriate, so also is their handling of what is presented as knowledge. Appropriate pupil behaviour here seems to be defined by the pupil's ability to do a subject. This is not necessarily a question of the ability to move to higher levels of generalization and abstraction so much as an ability to move into an alternative system of thought from that of his everyday knowledge. In practical terms this means being able to work within the framework which the teacher constructs and by which the teacher is then himself constrained, as the position of the teacher (E) teaching the family (already quoted on page 145) suggests. In teacher E's lesson pupils' definitions of the family which stemmed from their everyday knowledge of families conflicted with the teacher's 'expert' definition. The following extracts are from a lesson on the same material with A pupils and teacher D:

TEACHER: Ninety per cent of British families are nuclear families.
BOY: What are the other ten per cent?
TEACHER: We're going on to those. . . .

BOY: What are joint families?
TEACHER: Where you have two or more related families living in the same house. There may be three generations.
GIRL: If you have your granny and grandad living with you is that a joint family?
TEACHER: Yes. . . .

PUPIL: What about single people?
TEACHER: They're not really a family unless they have children. . . .

TEACHER: Another group that's rare throughout the world but is found among the Netsilik Eskimo is the polyandrous group. . . .
PUPIL: What country is that found in? . .

Here the questions from the pupils take the framework the teacher presents for granted, and the pupils show a willingness to accept the terminology (the 'correct term') as part of that framework. The scepticism of many C pupils, which leads them to question the teachers' mode of organizing their material, means that they do not learn what may be taken for granted within a subject, which is part of the process of learning what questions may be asked within a particular subject perspective.[30]

It would appear that the willingness to take over the teacher's definition of what is to constitute the problem and what is to count as knowledge may require pupils to regard as irrelevant or inappropriate what they might see as problems in a context of everyday meaning. (In this they resemble the teacher who made irrelevant the everyday use of the term 'family'.) This means that those pupils who are willing to take over the teachers' definitions must often be less rather than more autonomous (autonomy being a quality or characteristic the enquiry mode is intended to foster) and accept the teacher's presentation on trust. One unit of the socialization theme was work on isolated children, intended to show the necessity of socialization by presenting a negative case. In one account of an isolated child, Patrick, the description did not make clear that he was isolated in a henhouse because he was illegitimate and that the woman who put him there was his mother. In doing this workcard, A pupils generally did not raise problems about why the boy's mother treated him as she did, but got on with the workcard, although it emerged when they were questioned that they had not realized that the child was illegitimate. Some C pupils who wanted first to know why the woman had treated the child like this were told by their teacher: 'Well, we're not too interested in that but in the actual influence on the development of the child.' Here not only is there a clear resemblance between the way that A pupils and the teacher had each shifted categories of meaning so that enquiry into the question 'Why would anyone treat a child like that?' becomes inappropriate, but also that the material is already in some sense 'real' and 'immediate' to C pupils, but that the teacher took no cognizance of this. It is often assumed by teachers that the comprehension of everyday meaning of material will be obvious to A pupils. Here it is suggested that this cannot be taken for granted. It may be clear to C pupils, whose first concern is likely to be with this kind of meaning.

It may be that the important thing for A pupils is the belief that the knowledge is structured and that the material they are asked to work with has sufficient closure to make 'finding the answer' possible. They are usually willing to work within the framework outlined by the teacher and within his terms. Thus a new term like 'social science' is at first a label with little meaning but is self-legitimating, and A pupils seem content to wait and let the content emerge so long as they can undertake the immediate task of completing a workcard. This means they frequently do not understand the generalizations teachers make to explain the theme which links several units of work, but this is not apparent to teachers or pupils so long as the work is structured in more or less self-contained units.

Because A pupils are prepared to take over teachers' definitions on trust, they were much quicker to accept social science as a new 'subject' within the course, while C pupils continued to refer to the material on socialization in terms of subjects they already knew, like geography or biology, and to question the validity of what they saw as an unjustifiable change of content. A pupils were not generally able to explain the rationale of the socialization theme as teachers had explained it to them[31] but they accepted that the study could be legitimated and were prepared to operate within the 'finite reality' of the subject as the teacher established it. This enabled them to move more quickly into what Blum[32] calls the 'common culture' of the subject and to use its terminology. A striking example of this mastery of the language of the subject comes from an A class taught by a psychologist where pupils have acquired a set of terms they can use without gloss.[28] This is from a discussion of Patrick, the child shut in the henhouse:

TEACHER: So we should, when he was found at the age of eight and a half, have been able to teach him to speak?
GIRL: Yes.
BOY: Yes, it was like he'd, um, he'd, um, been sort of lost for ages and had difficulties in speaking.
TEACHER: It's not quite the same. Yes, er . . .
BOY: He's just regressed in er er er in understanding things like.
TEACHER: Mm, but he has been using his vocal chords in some way, as Graham pointed out. He's been imitating chickens. Do you think this could retard his development at all?
BOY: Yes, associating—if you asso—if we associate foreign language words with one of those, it does mean the same thing in his language——
TEACHER: Do you th——
BOY: —he'd be able to speak but he wouldn't think in that language.

The following extract from a C lesson makes an interesting contrast since it may be that the mastery of terms like 'regression' represents closure in the questions likely to be asked. In the following, the boy is able to pose the 'commonsense' question about 'unlearning' because the material has suddenly enabled him to see something taken for granted as problematic:

BOY: Who knew he was in there, then?
TEACHER: Only his mother.
BOY: Where was his father, then?
TEACHER: His mother had separated from his father—she pretended to be a respectable widow. . . . The interesting thing is that the boy was fostered out. He was illegitimate, you see. If you think about it he must have learnt to walk and probably had the beginnings of speech—so what do you think happened?
BOY: The woman who put him in the chicken coop had made him go backwards.
TEACHER: Very good . . .
BOY 2: Well done . . .
BOY: How do you unlearn?
TEACHER: Well you simply forget—in school—tests show that.
BOY: [makes some objection—untranscribable].
TEACHER: You need to keep practising skills.

A noticeable feature of this sequence is that the teacher's response renders the question unproblematic: 'Well you simply forget'. Here is another extract where the same process can be seen. The group is a C group, the teacher has been through the pink cards with the class as a whole and the pupils are now working with workcards. Most pupils are having difficulty with a question which runs: 'Is it biologically absolutely necessary that this division of labour (between the sexes) should be as rigid as it is?'

TEACHER: Yeah, in other words is it bio-um-physically impossible for the women to do the men's tasks. . . . Well, supposing you said is it biologically necessary for that division. . . . It is *not* biologically necessary. It's um er social reasons.
BOY: Will you come and tell us that, sir, please.
TEACHER: Well it's obviously not biologically necessary. I mean there's no physical reason why the women can't do the men's jobs; they wouldn't be able to do it as well because they're not as strong.
BOY: Aren't women the stronger sex?
TEACHER: Not in the [. . .] sense. The [. . .] says that they have more resistance to pain usually, and so on, and tend to live longer—they're stronger in that sense.
BOY: [untranscribable] . . . feel it.
TEACHER: No, they feel the same pain but they have a greater resistance to it.
BOY: What they always crying for?
TEACHER: Well, that's temperament, isn't it? Anyway we're getting away from the point about the Eskimos, aren't we?

In each of the last two sequences the material had led the pupil to pose as problematic an event he had probably previously taken for granted, and in each case the teacher closes the question in such a way as to render it (for himself if not for the pupil) unproblematic again, apparently because he is not able to accommodate it within the structure he is using. In the first instance the pupil's question could have opened up major issues about learning, in the second about the relative strength of heredity and environment. In neither instance was the pupil's enquiry integrated into the unfolding of the lesson although very germane to its theme.

153

The matter is complicated here by the teacher's unfamiliarity with the material, but it seems that what counts is whether the pupil's comment or question may be seen as having meaning within the relevance structure[33] the teacher is using, which derives from his notion of what counts as knowledge within a given subject. This relevance structure may, however, shift with respect to the knowledge the teacher has about the pupil, so that the pupil's questions and comments are seen by the teacher as deriving from different relevance structures depending on the statues of the pupil with respect to his imputed ability. Thus both the 'knowledge' the teacher has of his subject and the 'knowledge' he has of the pupil must be seen as variables in the organization and evaluation of what counts as knowledge in the classroom. This may mean that when similar questions are asked by A and C pupils they are categorized differently by the teacher. This is a consequence of the implied notion that A pupils can master subjects while C pupils cannot. The A pupils' questions will be seen as relevant if they can be seen as helping to make explicit the implications of the subject. C pupils' questions are seen as ends in themselves: they arise out of 'experience' or everyday reality, beyond which these pupils supposedly cannot go, and are therefore scanned for different kinds of meaning. It seems likely that it is here that teachers' expectations of pupils most effectively operate to set levels of pupil achievement: C pupils are not expected to progress in terms of mastering the nature of a subject, and so their questions are less likely to be seen as making a leap into the reality of the subject. These expectations seem to be implied in the remarks of teachers who said they could get away with not preparing work for C pupils but would not risk that with A pupils. The questions of the latter will require the knowledge of the teacher as 'expert'.

It seems that in considering what might be involved in the pupil's educational career it would be necessary to specify possible interactional sequences between teacher and pupil in which the pupil's educational identity is established in terms of the expectations the teacher has of him. It is likely that one of the crucial differences in the 'latent cultures'[34] from which pupils come is in providing children with modes of acquiring knowledge that leads to differential access to the ways in which teachers structure knowledge: not so much to the particular structures as to the notion that it will be structured in ways that may make it remote from everyday experience. It may be that it is this remoteness from everyday life that is an important element in legitimating academic knowledge in schools. Pupils who have easy access to this knowledge need an ability to sustain uncertainty about the nature of the learning activity in the belief that some pattern will emerge. This requires a willingness to rely on the teacher's authority in delineating what the salient areas of a problem are to be. This will often mean a pupil putting aside what he 'knows' to be the case in an everyday context. Children who demonstrate this facility are likely to be regarded as more educable, and to find their way into high-ability groups or to be defined as of high ability, since these are pupils with whom teachers can feel they are making progress. It is likely, as C pupils' questions demonstrate, that all pupils can move between 'common sense' and 'finite provinces of meaning', but that the particular shifts that the school requires and legitimates are based on a social organization of knowledge that is most likely to be achieved by the predominantly middle-class pupils in A streams.

Once pupils are placed in high-ability groups the wish to achieve at school in the school's terms is confirmed and situated in school activities, and is reinforced by their long-term vocational expectations. These are the pupils in the study who when asked about the humanities course in general terms show they tend to see it in the terms in which teachers define it. These pupils are more likely to move towards using the language of the subject as the teacher presents it and, equally important, their behavioural style is more likely to seem to the teacher appropriate to the occasion, than the style of C pupils.[35] Once pupils are accredited by streaming or some other device as of high ability, their questions are likely to be scanned by teachers for a different kind of meaning and to be used to a different end from those of C pupils. Teachers will also tend to assume for A pupils that the ability to move into the structure of a subject presupposes that understanding at a 'lower', 'concrete', 'experiential' level which they attribute to C pupils as the limits of their ability. However, it can be argued that A pupils do not necessarily have this understanding, which may involve a different mode of thought and not a simple hierarchical progression from low- to high-order generalizations as teachers seem often to suppose, at least implicitly. It was assumed, for example, that A pupils had a commonsense understanding of why Patrick had been isolated, which in many cases they did not. They had, like the teacher of the C stream group who asked why he had been isolated, apparently defined it out of what it was relevant to enquire into, because neither teacher nor workcard referred to it.

Teachers also tend to assume that A pupils grasp the rationale of the subject in terms of the way teachers indicate progression of linkage from one piece of work to the next. In view of the fact that A pupils generally did not seem to have grasped what the linkage was except in the most general terms, it appears that teachers make assumptions about A pupils' ability to master subjects that are not justified; but because they present and evaluate material in discrete units, this assumption is not often tested.

## CONCLUSIONS

In the presentation and discussion of data an attempt has been made to examine what teachers 'know' about their pupils and how that knowledge is related to the organization of curriculum knowledge in the classroom. Ability is an organizing and unexamined concept for teachers whose categorization of pupils on the grounds of ability derives largely from social class judgements of pupils' social, moral and intellectual behaviour. These judgements are frequently confounded with what are held to be rational values of a general nature. There is between teachers and A pupils a reciprocity of perspective which allows teachers to define, unchallenged by A pupils, as they may be challenged by C pupils, the nature and boundaries of what is to count as knowledge. It would seem to be the failure of high-ability pupils to question what they are taught in schools that contributes in large measure to their educational achievement.

It seems that one use to which the school puts knowledge is to establish that subjects represent the way about which the world is normally known in an 'expert' as opposed to a 'commonsense' mode of knowing. This establishes and maintains normative order[32] in and within subjects, and accredits as successful to the world outside school those who can master subjects. The school may be seen as maintaining the social order through the taken for granted categories of its superordinates who process pupils and knowledge in mutually confirming ways. The ability to maintain these categories as consensual, when there are among the clients in school conflicting definitions of the situation, resides in the unequal distribution of power. There is a need to see how this enters into and shapes the interactional situation in the classroom. Clearly there is also a need to examine the linkages between schools and other institutions, and attempt to understand the nature of the relationship between what counts as knowledge in schools and what counts as knowledge in other relevant societal areas. In particular, there is a need to understand the relationship between the social distribution of power and the distribution of knowledge, in order to understand the generation of categorizations of pupil, and categories of organization of curriculum knowledge in the school situation. (Because these linkages are unspecified here, the comments I have made about teachers may at times appear to be critical of the 'failures' of individuals.)

In the wider context of educational discussion, two panaceas currently put forward to reform the educational system are unstreaming and an undifferentiated curriculum. It seems likely that these prescriptions overlook the fact that streaming is itself a response to an organizing notion of differential ability. It seems likely that the hierarchical categories of ability and knowledge may well persist[36] in unstreamed classrooms and lead to the differentiation of undifferentiated curricula, because teachers differentiate in selection of content and in pedagogy between pupils perceived as of high and low ability. The origins of these categories are likely to lie outside the school and within the structure of the society itself in its wider distribution of power. It seems likely, therefore, that innovation in schools will not be of a very radical kind unless the categories teachers use to organize what they know about pupils and to determine what counts as knowledge undergo a fundamental change.

## ACKNOWLEDGEMENTS

My thanks are first and foremost to the teachers and pupils of the school of the study. The teachers in the humanities department were, throughout the time I was at the school, unfailingly helpful in giving me their time and allowing me into their lessons with a tape recorder. I am indebted to Gillian Frost, who was also carrying out research at the school, both for the discussions we had, and for the data she made available to me.

The London Borough of Bromley made it possible for me to study for the Master's Degree of the University of London, by seconding me for a year, giving me the time to carry out the study on which this paper is based. I should like to thank Professor Basil Bernstein for his encouragement and for his assistance in getting the tape recordings transcribed. My thanks are also due to John Hayes and Michael Young with whom I discussed the material at various stages and to whom I owe very many insights that helped me to organize the data. I owe similar thanks to my fellow graduate students, in particular to John Bartholomew, and also to John Beck. My thanks are also to Michael Young for reading this paper in an earlier draft and making many detailed and constructive comments which helped me to clarify confusions and inconsistencies.

## NOTES AND REFERENCES

[1] The direction of mainstream sociology of education in this respect can be seen in the very comprehensive account of available studies in Chapters 3, 4 and 5 of Olive Banks's *The Sociology of Education*, 1968.

[2] Baratz and Baratz (1970).

[3] Cicourel and Kitsuse (1963); Dumont and Wax (1969); Wax and Wax (1964).

[4] Bernstein (1971); Young (1971).

[5] Cicourel and Kitsuse (1963) show the importance in this context of the processes by which students are allocated to college or non-college courses. The Schools Council's acceptance of a differentiated curriculum, like the Newsom Report, maintains a distinction between the 'academic' and the 'non-academic' child.

[6] Keddie (1970).

[7] I have to thank Gillian Frost for making this information available to me.

[8] This mode of examination allows teachers to construct and examine their own courses with moderation from an external examiner.

[9] Bourdieu (1967).

[10] Wright Mills (1940).

[11] Garfinkel and Sacks (1970).

[12] Becker (1952).

[13] Selznick (1949), p. 70. I have to thank John Bartholomew for bringing this to my notice.

[14] Deutscher (1966).

[15] For example, the Humanities Curriculum Project of the Schools Council directed by Lawrence Stenhouse.

[16] An interview with Gillian Frost, whom I thank for making it available to me.

[17] Sudnow (1968).

[18] 'Is' and 'ought' are not necessarily discrepant. There is no reason why there should not be a fit between them.

[19] Geer, *et al.* (1968).

[20] Cohen, A. K. (1959).

[21] Deutsch (1963).

[22] Dumont and Wax (1969) make a similar point about the culture of the Cherokee Indian. There is clearly a relationship between individualization of failure and the psychologistic notion of a curriculum based on pupils' 'needs'. See also Friedman (1967).

[23] This relationship is also apparent in the data of Hargreaves (1967), p. 95: 'On one occasion a teacher left the room to investigate some noise in the corridor. "Who are you lot?" he cried. "3B, sir", came the reply. "You sound more like 1E than 3B", was the master's crushing retort.'

[24] Wax and Wax (1964) find the same situation in what they call a 'vacuum ideology' which is attributed to the Cherokee Indian by white teachers.

[25] Bloom (1956).

[26] Workcards for pupils are of three kinds: pink cards written by a member of staff which give an overview of the topic to be studied ('concepts' are generally printed in capital letters to point the organization of material to the pupils); buff cards which are also referred to as 'documents' because they often reproduce original sources and deal with

areas of the topic in more detail; yellow workcards which have questions intended to guide pupils in the use of the other workcards. Many pupils treated these straightforwardly as question sheets.

[27] The concept here is that of 'multiple realities' developed by Schutz (1967). In organizing the data I have also been greatly influenced by the distinction between 'common-sense' and 'expert' knowledge made by Horton (1967). I have also used this article in attempting to conceptualize A and C pupils' approaches to knowledge as the outcome of alternative thought systems, as opposed to seeing the differences in terms of a hierarchical relationship.

[28] Garfinkel and Sacks (1970), pp. 342–5 and 362–6.

[29] There is a need for studies of the models of society inherent in subjects as they are taught in schools and in textbooks. T. S. Kuhn (1970) suggests how an authoritarian model of science is built into science subjects as they are taught and the textbooks as they are used. Other studies might cast light on how a normative order is transmitted through the contents of subjects in schools and, in relation to this, what counts as 'objectivity' in that subject and how it operates to maintain that normative order.

[30] One exposition of a subject from this point of view is made by Merton (1959).

[31] For example, most teachers explained to pupils that the film showed how early the human child begins to learn, and that the study of isolated children showed how necessary it is for a child to be brought up among human beings if his learning is to proceed and he is to become human. Nevertheless most pupils were unable to point to any link between the two units of study. At the most they were able to say both were 'about learning'.

[32] Blum (1970).

[33] Schutz (1967), p. 5 following.

[34] The concept here is that the school represents the *manifest* culture. See Becker (1960).

[35] It seems likely that teachers frequently pay more attention to the style than to the content of pupils' comments. Clearly this is linked to problems of social control. C pupils in particular tend to call out in class. There is probably also a problem for teachers in how C pupils actually phrase their comments or questions. When I reported to the humanities department on the research, I gave as examples of pupils asking questions from the point of view of their own commonsense views of the world, one question already quoted: 'What are they [women] always crying for then?' and another from the key lesson in which pupils were shown slides of the foetus in the womb, when a C boy asked about the foetus: 'How does it go to the toilet then?' This latter question, which seems to be an intelligent one, probably could not be asked more precisely without a concept of the body's 'functions'. When I gave these two questions as examples one teacher said the boys 'must have been joking'. At the least he implies that these questions are not appropriate to the business of learning and it is likely that his response is to the pupil's language and has a social class basis. Probably this teacher made explicit what many teachers feel: that the C pupil's attitudes and manners are inappropriate to the classroom; similar attitudes of teachers are to be found in: Hargreaves, *op. cit.*, and Werthman.

[36] Barker Lunn (1970) suggests that teachers often carry attitudes appropriate to streaming into unstreamed classes and that this is particularly damaging for the 'low-ability' working-class child.

# BIBLIOGRAPHY

BANKS, O. (1968). *The Sociology of Education.* London: Batsford.

BARATZ, S., and BARATZ, J. (1970). 'Early Childhood Intervention: the Social Science Basis of Institutionalized Racism'. *Harvard Educational Review*, 40, February.

BARKER LUNN, J. C. (1970). *Streaming in the Primary School.* Slough: National Foundation for Educational Research.

BECKER, H. S. (1952). 'Social Class Variations in the Teacher–Pupil Relationship'. *Journal of Educational Sociology*, Vol. 25, April 1952. Also in BELL, R., and STUBB, H. (eds.) (1968), *The Sociology of Education: A Sourcebook.* Homewood (Illinois): The Dorsey Press.

BECKER, H. S. and GEER, B. (1960). 'Latent Culture: a Note on the Theory of Latent Social Roles'. *Administrative Science Quarterly*, 5(2).

BERNSTEIN, B. B. (1971). 'On the Framing and Classification of Educational Knowledge' in YOUNG, M. F. D. (ed.) (1971), *Knowledge and Control*. London: Collier-Macmillan. (Chapter 2, this volume.)

BLOOM, B. S. (1956). *Taxonomy of Educational Objectives*. New York: David McKay.

BLUM, A. (1970). 'The Corpus of Knowledge as a Normative Order'. Reprinted in YOUNG, M. F. D. (ed.) (1971), *Knowledge and Control*. London: Collier-Macmillan. (Chapter 4, this volume.)

BOURDIEU, P. (1967). 'Systems of Education and System of Thought'. *International Social Science Journal* XIX(3), and reprinted in YOUNG, M. F. D. (ed.) (1971), *Knowledge and Control*. London: Collier-Macmillan. (Chapter 7, this volume.)

CICOUREL, A. V., and KITSUSE, J. I. (1963). *The Educational Decision Makers*. Indianapolis: Bobbs-Merill.

COHEN, A. K. (1959). 'The Study of Social Disorganization and Deviant Behaviour' in MERTON, R. K., BROOM, L., and COTTRELL, L. S. (eds.), *Sociology Today: Problems and Prospects*. New York: Basic Books.

DEUTSCH, M. (1963). 'The Disadvantaged Child and the Learning Process' in PASSOW, H. (ed.), *Education in Depressed Areas*. New York: Teachers College Press.

DEUTSCHER, I. (1966). 'Words and Deeds: Social Science and Social Policy'. *Social Problems*, 13 (Winter).

DUMONT, R. V., and WAX, M. L. (1969). 'Cherokee School Society and the Intercultural Classroom'. *Human Organization*, 28(3), Fall.

FRIEDMAN, N. L. (1967). 'Cultural Deprivation: A Commentary in the Sociology of Knowledge'. *Journal of Educational Thought*, I, August.

GARFINKEL, H., and SACKS, H. (1970). 'On Formal Structures of Practical Actions' in MCKINNEY, J., and TIRYAKIAN, E., *Theoretical Sociology: Perspectives and Development*. New York: Appleton-Century-Crofts.

GEER, B., HAAS, J., VIVONA, C., MILLER, S. J., MILLER, C., and BECKER, H. S. (1968). 'Learning the Ropes: Situational Learning in Four Occupational Training Programmes' in DEUTSCHER, I., and THOMPSON, E. J., *Among the People: Encounters with the Poor*. New York: Basic Books.

HARGREAVES, D. (1967). *Social Relations in a Secondary School*. London: Routledge & Kegan Paul.

HORTON, R. (1967). 'African Traditional Thought and Western Science'. *Africa*, 67. Reprinted in YOUNG, M. F. D. (ed.) (1971), *Knowledge and Control*. London: Collier-Macmillan. (Chapter 8, this volume.)

KEDDIE, N. G. (1970). *The Social Basis of Classroom Knowledge: A Case Study*. M.A. thesis, University of London.

KUHN, T. S. (1970). *The Structure of Scientific Revolutions*, 2nd ed. Chicago: University of Chicago Press.

MERTON, R. K. (1959). 'Notes on Problem-Finding' in MERTON, R. K., BROOM, L., and COTTRELL, L. S. (eds.), *Sociology Today: Problems and Prospects*. New York: Basic Books.

MILLS, C. W. (1940). 'Situated Action and Vocabularies of Motive'. *American Sociological Review*, (IV)5.

SCHUTZ, A. (1967). *Collected Papers. Volume I: The Problem of Social Reality*. The Hague: Martinus Nijhoff.

SELZNICK, P. (1949). *T.V.A. and the Grass Roots: a Study in the Sociology of Formal Organizations*. Berkeley and Los Angeles: University of California Press.

SUDNOW, D. (1968). 'Normal Crimes: Sociological Features of the Penal Code in a Public Defender Office'. *Social Problems*, 15 (Winter).

WAX, M. L., and WAX, R. H. (1964). 'Formal Education in an American Indian Community'. *Social Problems Monograph*, II, Spring.

WERTHMAN, C. (1963.) 'Delinquency in Schools'. A Test for the Legitimacy of Authority'. *Berkeley Journal of Sociology*, VIII.

YOUNG, M. F. D. (1971). 'An Approach to the Study of Curricula as Socially Organized Knowledge'. In YOUNG, M. F. D. (ed.) (1971), *Knowledge and Control*. London: Collier-Macmillan. (Chapter I, this volume.)

Obviously this approach can only be justified in so far as the object to which it is applied, that is, the intellectual field (and thus the cultural field) possesses the relative autonomy which authorizes the *methodological auto-nomization* operated by the structural method when it *treats* the intellectual field *as* a system which is governed by its own laws. It is possible to see, from the history of Western intellectual and artistic life, how the intellectual field (and at the same time the intellectual, as distinct from the scholar, for instance) gradually came into being in a particular type of historical society. As the areas of human activity became more clearly differentiated, an intellectual order in the true sense, dominated by a particular type of legitimacy, began to define itself in opposition to the economic, political and religious powers, that is, all the authorities who could claim the right to legislate on cultural matters in the name of a power or authority which was not properly speaking intellectual. Intellectual life was dominated throughout the Middle Ages, during part of the Renaissance, and in France (with the importance of the court) throughout the classical period, by an *external* legitimizing authority. It only gradually became organized into an intellectual field as creative artists began to liberate themselves economically and socially from the patronage of the aristocracy and the Church and from their ethical and aesthetic values. There began to appear *specific authorities of selection and consecration* that were intellectual in the proper sense (even if, like publishers and theatre managers, they were still subjected to economic and social restrictions which therefore continued to influence intellectual life), and which were placed in a situation of *competition for cultural legitimacy*. As L. L. Schücking has shown, the dependence of writers on the aristocracy and its canons of taste persisted far longer in the domain of literature than in the theatre, since 'anyone who wished to get his works published did well to seek the patronage of a great lord.' To win the approval of a patron and of the aristocratic public the writer was obliged to conform to their cultural ideal, to their taste for difficult and artificial forms, for the esotericism and classical humanism peculiar to a group anxious to distinguish itself from the common people in all its cultural habits. In contrast the writer for the stage in the Elizabethan period was no longer exclusively dependent on the goodwill and pleasure of a single patron. Unlike the theatre of the French court which, as Voltaire reminded an English critic who praised the naturalism of the line 'not a mouse stirring' in *Hamlet*, was confined to a language as noble as that of the high-ranking persons to whom it was addressed, the Elizabethan dramatist owed his freedom of expression to the demands of the various theatre managers and, through them, to the entrance fees paid by a public of increasingly diverse origin.[1] And so institutions of intellectual and artistic consecration proliferated and diversified increasingly. Examples were the academies and salons (where especially in the eighteenth century, with the eclipse of the court and court art, the nobility fraternized with the bourgeois intelligentsia, adopting its patterns of thought and its artistic and moral conceptions), as well as the institutions of consecration and cultural diffusion such as publishing houses, theatres, cultural and scientific associations. Simultaneously the public was extended and diversified. Thus the intellectual field in becoming increasingly independent of external influences (which from this point on must pass through the mediating structure of the field) becomes a field of relations governed by a specific logic: competition for cultural legitimacy. 'Historically regarded,' notes L. L. Schücking, 'the publisher begins to play a part at the stage at which the patron disappears, in the eighteenth century.'[2] There is no uncertainty about this among the poets. Thus Alexander Pope, when writing to Wycherley on May 20, 1709, sounds a mocking note at the expense of Jacob Tonson, the celebrated publisher and editor of an authoritative anthology. Jacob, he declares, creates poets in the same way as kings used to create knights. Another publisher, Dodsley, was later to exercise similar powers and so become the target of Richard Graves's witty verses:

> In vain the poets from their mine
> Extract the shining mass,
> Till Dodsley's Mint has stamped the coin
> And bids the sterling pass.

And indeed such publishing firms gradually became a source of authority. Who could conceive the English literature of that century without a Dodsley, or the 'German of the following century without a Cotta? . . . Once Cotta had succeeded in assembling some of the most eminent "classic" writers in his publications, it became for decades a sort of title to immortality to be published by him.'[3] And Schücking points out that the influence of theatre managers was even greater, since after the fashion of an Otto Brahm, they could by their decisions mould the taste of an age.[4]

Everything leads one to suppose that the constitution of a relatively autonomous intellectual field is the condition for the appearance of the independent intellectual, who does not recognize nor wish to recognize any obligations other than the intrinsic demands of his creative project. One tends rather too much to forget that the artist did not always display towards all external restraints the impatience which for us appears to be a definition of the creative project. Schücking tells us that Alexander Pope, who was considered a very great poet throughout the eighteenth century read his masterpiece, a translation of Homer, which his contemporaries thought incomparable, to his patron Lord Halifax, in the presence of a large gathering and, according to Samuel Johnson, accepted without murmur the alterations suggested by the noble lord. Schücking cites many examples which go to prove that this practice was far from exceptional:

Chaucer's famous disciple Lydgate evidently regarded it as entirely natural when his patron Duke Humphrey of Gloucester, brother of Henry V (1413-22), corrected his manuscript; and we know of exact parallels to this in the life of Spenser, who was contemporary with Shakespeare. Shakespeare himself, in Sonnet 78, declares that his Maecenas 'mends the style' of others, and in his *Hamlet* shows us a prince who instructs actors like an experienced director.[5]

As the intellectual field gains in autonomy, the artist declares more and more firmly his claim to independence and his indifference to the public. It is undoubtedly with the nineteenth century and the romantic movement that the development towards the emancipation of the creative intention started which was to find in the theory of art for art's sake its first systematic statement.[6] This revolutionary redefinition of the intellectual's vocation and of his function in society is not always recognized as such, because it leads to the formation of the system of concepts and values that go to make up the social definition of the intellectual which is regarded by our society as self-evident. According to Raymond Williams, 'the radical change . . . in ideas of art, of the artist and their place in society' which with the two generations of romantic artists, Blake, Wordsworth, Coleridge and Southey on the one hand, and Byron, Keats and Shelley on the other, coincides in England with the industrial revolution, presents five fundamental characteristics:

first, that a major change was taking place in the nature of the relationships between a writer and his readers; second, that a different habitual attitude towards the 'public' was establishing itself; third, that the production of art was coming to be regarded as one of a number of specialized kinds of production subject to much the same conditions as general production; fourth, that a theory of the 'superior reality' of art as the seat of imaginative truth was receiving increasing emphasis; fifth, that the idea of the independent creative writer, the autonomous genius, was becoming a kind of rule.[7]

But should we see the aesthetic revolution contained in the theory of the superior reality of art and of the autonomous genius merely as a compensatory ideology, provoked by the threat which industrial society and the industrialization of intellectual society constitute for the autonomy of artistic creation and the irreplaceable singularity of the cultivated man? If we did so, it would be to substitute for a total explanation of reality a part of the total reality to be explained. Instead of the select circle of readers with whom the artist had personal contacts, and whose advice and criticism he was accustomed, from prudence, deference, goodwill or interest, or all of these at the same time, to accept, he now is confronted with a public, an undifferentiated, impersonal and anonymous 'mass' of faceless readers. These readers are a market composed of potential buyers able to give to a work that economic sanction which, in addition to assuring the artist's economic and intellectual independence, is not always entirely lacking in cultural legitimacy. The existence of a 'literary and artistic market' makes possible the establishment of a body of properly intellectual professions—either by the appearance of new roles or by existing roles taking on new functions—that is, the creation of a real field in the form of a system of relations built up between the agents of the system of intellectual production.[8] The specificity of the system of production combined with the specificity of its product, a two-dimensional reality, both merchandise and meaning, whose aesthetic value cannot be reduced to its economic value even when economic viability confirms intellectual consecration, leads to the specificity of the relations which are established within it. The relations between each of the agents of the system and the agents or institutions which are entirely or partly external to the system are always mediated by the relations established within the system itself, that is, inside the intellectual field. The competition for cultural legitimacy, in which the public is both prize, and in appearance at least, arbitrator, can never be completely identified with the competition for commercial success. The invasion of methods and techniques borrowed from the commercial world in connection with the commercialization of the work of art, like commercial advertising for intellectual products, coincides with the glorification of the artist and of his quasi-prophetic mission, and with the systematic attempt to separate the intellectual and his universe from the everyday world, if only by sartorial extravagance. This is parallelled by the artist's declared intention of refusing to recognize any but the ideal reader, who must be an *alter ego*, that is, another intellectual, present or future, able to assume in his creation or comprehension of works of art the same truly intellectual vocation which characterizes the autonomous intellectual as one who recognizes only intellectual legitimacy. 'That is beautiful which corresponds to an inner necessity', Kandinsky said. The declaration of the autonomy of the creative intention leads to a morality of conviction which tends to judge works of art by the purity of the artist's intention and which can end in a kind of terrorism of taste when the artist, in the name of his conviction, demands unconditional recognition of his work. So from this point on, the ambition for autonomy appears as the specific tendency of the intelligentsia. The exclusion of the public and the declared refusal to meet popular demand which encourages the cult of form for itself, of art for art's sake— an unprecedented accentuation of the most specific and irreducible aspect of the act of creation, and thus a statement of the specificity and irreducibility of the creator—are accompanied by the contraction and intensification of the relations between members of the artistic society. And so what Schücking calls mutual admiration societies, small sects enclosed in their esotericism,[9] begin to appear, while at the same time there are signs of a new solidarity between the artist and the critic or journalist.

The only recognized critics were those who had the entry to the arcana and had been initiated—persons, that is to say, who had been more or less won over to the group's aesthetic outlook. . . . It follows . . . that each of these esoteric groups grew into a sort of mutual admiration society. The contemporary world wondered why the critics, who had usually represented a conservative state, suddenly threw themselves into the arms of the practitioners of a new art.[10]

Inspired by the conviction—so profoundly embedded in the social definition of the intellectual's vocation that it tended to be taken for granted—that the public is irretrievably doomed to incomprehension, or at best to belated comprehension, this 'new criticism' (in the true sense of the word for once) leans over backwards to justify the artist. Feeling it is no longer authorized, as representative of the cultivated public, to pronounce a peremptory verdict in the name of an undisputed code, it places itself unconditionally at the artist's service and endeavours scrupulously to decipher his intentions and reasons in what is intended to be merely an expert interpretation. This is clearly excluding the public altogether: and in fact there begin to appear from the pens of theatre or art critics, who are gradually omitting references to the attitude of the public at premières and openings of exhibitions, such eloquent phrases as 'the play was well-received by the public'.[11]

To recall that the intellectual field as an autonomous system, or claiming to be so, is the result of a historical process of autonomization and internal differentiation, is to justify the methodological autonomization that authorizes the search for the specific logic of the relations established within this system and which constitute it as such. It also means dispelling illusions born of familiarity by demonstrating that since it is the product of history, this system cannot be dissociated from the historical and social conditions under which it was established. Any attempt to consider propositions arising from a synchronic study of a state of the field as essential, transhistoric and transcultural truths is thereby condemned.[12] Once the historic and social conditions which make possible the existence of an intellectual field are known—which at the same time define the limits of validity of a study of a state of this field—then this study takes on its full meaning, because it can encompass the concrete totality of the relations which constitute the intellectual field as a system.

## THE BIRDS OF PSAPHON

The full implications of the fact that an author writes for a public have never been completely explored. Few social actors depend as much as artists, and intellectuals in general, for what they are and for the image that they have of themselves on the image that other people have of them and of what they are. 'There are some qualities', writes Jean-Paul Sartre, 'that come to us entirely from the judgements of other people.'[13] This is the case with the quality of writer, a quality which is socially defined and which is inseparable in every society and every age from a certain social demand which the writer must take into account; it is even more clearly the case with the writer's reputation, that is, the idea a society forms of the value and truth of the work of a writer or artist. The artist may accept or reject this image of himself which society reflects back at him, he cannot ignore it: by the intermediary of the social image which has the opacity and inevitability of an established fact, society intervenes at the very centre of the creative project, thrusting upon the artist its demands and refusals, its expectations and its indifference. Whatever he may want and whatever he may do, the artist has to face the social definition of his work, that is, in concrete terms, the success or failure it has had, the interpretations of it that have been given, the social representation, often stereotyped and over-simplified, that is formulated by the amateur public. In short, haunted by the anguish of salvation, the artist is condemned to watch in suspense for signs, always ambiguous, of an election which is perpetually in the balance. He may experience failure as a sign of true success or immediate, brilliant success as a warning of damnation (by reference to a historically dated definition of the consecrated or damned artist). He must of necessity recognize the truth of his creative project as reflected by the social reception of his work, because the recognition of this truth is contained within a project which is always seeking to be recognized.

The creative project is the place of meeting and sometimes of conflict between the *intrinsic necessity of the work of art* which demands that it be continued, improved and completed, and *social pressures* which direct the work from outside. Paul Valéry distinguished between 'works which are *as it were created by their public*, in that they fulfil its expectations and are thus almost determined by knowledge of these expectations, and works which on the contrary *tend to create their own public*'.[14] And one could no doubt establish all the intermediary stages between works almost exclusively determined and dominated by the image (whether intuitive or scientifically established) of the public's expectations, such as newspapers, magazines and best-selling works, and those works which are entirely subordinate to the intentions of their creator. Important methodological consequences follow from this: the more autonomous the works to which methodology is applied (at the cost of the methodological autonomization by which it postulates its object as a system) the more rewarding internal analysis of these works will be. But it is in danger of becoming unreal and *misleading* when applied to those works 'intended to act powerfully and brutally on the sensibility, to win over a public which wants strong emotions and strange adventures' of which Valéry speaks. Such works are created *by* their public because they are created expressly *for* their public, such as, in France, *France-Soir*, *France-Dimanche*, *Paris-Match* or such descriptions in *Parisiennes*, which can be attributed almost entirely to the economic and social conditions of their manufacture and are therefore entirely amenable to external analysis. Those who are known as 'best-selling authors' are obviously the most accessible material for traditional sociological methods, since one is entitled to assume that social pressures (willingness to keep to a style that has served them well, fear of losing popularity, etc.) carry more weight in their intellectual project than the intrinsic necessity of the work of art. The Jansenist mystique of the intellectual who can never view overnight success without some suspicion is perhaps partly justified by experience. It might be possible for creative artists to be more vulnerable to success than to failure, and indeed they have been known to fail to conquer their own success, and to subordinate themselves to the pressures imposed by the social definition of a work of art which has received the consecration of success. Conversely, these methods are correspondingly less helpful when applied to works of art whose authors, in refusing to conform to the expectations of actual readers, impose the demands which the necessity of the work enforces on them, without conceding anything to the idea, anticipated or experienced, that readers form or will form of their work.

Nevertheless, even the 'purest' artistic intention cannot completely escape from sociology, because, as we have seen, for it even to exist depends on certain particular, historical and social conditions and also because it is obliged to make some reference to the objective truth reflected back from the intellectual field. The relationship between the creator and his creation is always ambiguous and sometimes contradictory. This remains true in so far as the cultural work, as a symbolic object intended to be communicated, as a message to be received or refused, and with it the author of the message, derives not only its value —which can be measured by the recognition it receives from the writer's peers or the general public, by his contemporaries or by posterity—but also *its significance and truth* from those who receive it just as much as from the man who produces it. While social pressures may sometimes reveal themselves in the direct and brutal form of financial pressures or legal obligations, for example, when an art dealer insists that a painter keeps to the manner that has brought him success,[15] they usually work in a more insidious way. Even the author most indifferent to the lure of success and the least disposed to make concessions to the demands of the public is surely obliged to take account of the social truth of his work as it is reported back to him by the public, the critics or analysts, and to redefine his creative project in relation to this truth. When he is faced with this objective definition, is he not encouraged to rethink his intentions and make them explicit, and are they not therefore in danger of being altered? More generally, does not the creative project inevitably define itself in relation to the projects of other creators? There are few works which do not contain some indications of the idea the author had formed of his enterprise, of the concepts in which he thought out his originality and novelty, that is, what distinguished him, in his own eyes, from his contemporaries and predecessors. For instance, as Louis Althusser observes.

Marx as he went along left us, in the text or the footnotes of *Das Kapital*, a whole series of judgements on his own work, critical comparisons with his predecessors (the Physiocrats, Smith, Ricardo, etc.), and finally very precise methodological observations, which bring his analytical method close to that of the sciences— mathematical, physical, biological, etc., as well as to the dialectical method as defined by Hegel. . . . When speaking of his work and his discoveries Marx makes reflections in philosophically equivalent terms on the novelty and therefore the specific distinction of his aims.[16]

Doubtless not all intellectual creators have formulated such a conscious idea of what they were trying to acheve: one thinks of Flaubert, for instance, sacrificing at the request of Louis Bouilhet, many 'parasitic sentences' and 'extras, which slow down the narrative' but which may have been the expression of some of the most profound currents of his genius:

This reversal, this relating of speech to its other, silent face which is for us today the chief concern of literature, Flaubert was clearly the first to attempt—but the attempt was almost always, as far as he was concerned, either unconscious or shamefaced. His literary consciousness was not, nor could it have been, at the same level as his work and his experience. . . . Flaubert does not give us (in his correspondence) a true theory of his practice which, in so far as it was revolutionary, remained completely obscure to the writer himself. He himself thought *L'Éducation sentimentale* an aesthetic failure for lack of action, perspective and construction. He did not see that this book was the first to carry out that *de-dramatization*, one is tempted to say *de-novelization* of the novel, which was to be the starting point for all modern literature, or rather he felt to be a fault what is for us its greatest quality.[17]

It is sufficient to think of what Flaubert's work would have been like (and we can imagine this by comparing the different versions of *Madame Bovary*) if he had not had to reckon with a censorship which was hardly calculated to make it easier for him to discover the true character of his artistic intention. If, instead of being obliged to refer to an aesthetic theory in which the proper concern of the novel is the psychology of the characters and the successful construction of the plot, he had come into contact, among critics and the public, with the theory of the novel that is available for novelists of our time, in the light of which theory contemporary readers read his work and all that is left unsaid, his whole life's work would no doubt have been profoundly altered.

Since *Last Year in Marienbad* came out [Gérard Genette has observed], there has been an extraordinary change of perspective in the reputation of Alain Robbe-Grillet. Until then, in spite of the perceptible strangeness of his first books, Robbe-Grillet had passed for a realistic and objective writer, turning on everything the impassive eye of a sort of writing ciné-camera, outlining in the visible world, for each of his novels, a field of observation which he would not abandon until he had exhausted the descriptive possibilities of its *being-there*, without regard for the action nor for the characters. Roland Barthes had pointed out the revolutionary aspect of this form of description (in *Les Gommes* and *Le Voyeur*) which, by reducing the perceived world to a series of surfaces, got rid of both the 'classical object' and 'romantic sensibility': adopted by Robbe-Grillet himself, simplified and popularized in many different forms, this analysis eventually became the Vulgate with which we are all familiar of the 'nouveau roman' and the 'visual school of writing'. Robbe-Grillet then seemed to be definitely established in his role of fastidious quantity surveyor, execrated and therefore adopted as such by both official criticism and public opinion. *Last Year in Marienbad* changed all that in a way which was given added force by the publicity accompanying a cinematographic event: overnight Robbe-Grillet had become a kind of author of fantasy, an explorer of the world of imagination, a seer, a thaumaturge. Lautréamont, Bioy Casarès, Pirandello and surrealism quickly replaced the railway time-table and the *Catalogue des armes et cycles* in the arsenal of references. . . . Was this a conversion, or should the 'Robbe-Grillet case' be reconsidered? Hastily re-read in this new light, the earlier novels now revealed a disturbing unreality, previously unsuspected, which it suddenly seemed easy to identify: space which is unstable yet obsessive, anxious, stumbling progress, false resemblances, confusion of people and places, expanding time, generalized feelings of guilt, secret fascination with violence—who could fail to recognize them: Robbe-Grilbet's world was the world of dreams and hallucinations and it was simply careless reading on our part, inattentive or ill-directed, which had distracted us from this evident fact. . . . Robbe-Grillet has ceased to be the symbol of a 'chosiste' neo-realism, and the public meaning of his work has swung over to the side of the imaginary and subjective. One may object that this change in meaning only affects the 'Robbe-Grillet myth' and remains external to his work; but a parallel development can be seen in the theories propounded by Robbe-Grillet himself. Between the man who declared in 1953: '*Les Gommes* is a descriptive and scientific novel' . . . and the man who said in 1961 that the descriptions in *Le Voyeur* and *La Jalousie* 'are always given by someone' . . . and to conclude that these descriptions are 'entirely subjective' and that this subjectivity is the essential characteristic of what has been called the 'new novel', who could fail to detect one of those shifts of emphasis which indicates both a turning point in the writer's thought and the desire to re-align his previous works in the new perspective?[18]

Gérard Genette concludes this analysis (which deserves to be quoted in full for its ethnographic precision) by claiming for the writer 'the right to contradict himself'. But although he goes on to demonstrate by a fresh reading of the novels themselves the legitimacy of the two concurrent interpretations, he is surely dodging the sociological problem posed by the fact that Robbe-Grillet has given his blessing in succession to two contradictory versions of the truth. The simultaneous evolution of the creator's writings about his work, of the 'public myth' of his work and perhaps even of the internal structure of the work, leads one to wonder whether between the initial claims of objectivity and the later conversion to pure subjectivity there did not take place a realization and self-admission of the objective truth of the work and of the creative project. In other words, a realization and admission which were prepared and encouraged by the opinions of literary critics and even by the public version of these opinions. Indeed it has not often enough been pointed out that, today at any rate, what a critic says about a work appears to the creator himself not so much a critical judgement on the value of the work as an *objectivization of the creative project* in so far as it can be deduced from the work itself. It is therefore essentially distinguishable from the work as a pre-reflective expression of the creative project and even from the theoretical remarks the creator may make about his work. It follows that the relation connecting the creator (or, more precisely, the more or less conscious representation the creator forms of his creative intention) and criticism seen as an effort to recapture the creative project by studying the work, in which it reveals itself only by concealing itself (even from the eyes of the creator himself), cannot be described as a relation of cause and effect however much the concomitant evolution of the critic's opinion and the author's opinion of his work may incline one in this direction. Is that to say that the words of the critic have no effect at all? In fact critical writing which the creator recognizes because he feels himself recognized and, because he recognizes himself in it, does not amount to a pleonasm with the work, because it expresses the creative project by putting it into words, and thus encourages it to be what is expressed.[19]

By its nature and ambition, the objectivization achieved by criticism is undoubtedly predisposed to play a particular role in the definition and development of the creative project. But it is in and through the whole system of social relations which the creator maintains with the entire complex of agents composing the intellectual field at any given moment of time—that the progressive objectivization of the creative intention is achieved. This complex of agents includes other artists, critics, and intermediaries between the artist and the public such as publishers, art dealers or journalists whose function is to make an immediate appreciation of works of art and to make them known to the public (not to make a scientific analysis of them as does the critic in the proper sense). It is also in this way that the *public meaning* of the work and of the author is established by which the author is defined and in relation to which he must define himself. To enquire into the origins of this public meaning is to ask oneself who judges and who consecrates, and how the selection process operates so that out of the undifferentiated and undefined mass of works which are produced and even published, there emerge works which are worthy of being loved, admired, preserved and consecrated. Should one fall in with the widely-held opinion that this task is the responsibility of a few 'taste makers' who are fitted by their

INTELLECTUAL FIELD AND CREATIVE PROJECT

audacity or by their authority to shape the taste of their contemporaries? It is often in the name of a charismatic conception of his task that the *avant-garde* publisher, acting as a 'master of wisdom', assigns himself the mission of discovering in the works and in the persons of those who come to him the imperceptible signs of grace, and to reveal to themselves those he has recognized among those who have recognized him. The same conception frequently inspires the enlightened critic, the adventurous art-dealer or the inspired amateur. What is the real situation? In the first place the manuscripts received by the publisher are subject to various determining forces. Most frequently they already bear the mark of the intermediary (who is himself situated in the intellectual field as the director of a series, a publisher's reader, one of the publishing houses' 'own' authors, a critic well known for his accurate or daring judgement, etc.) through whom they reached the publisher.[20] Secondly they are the result of a sort of pre-selection which the authors themselves operate by reference to the idea they have of the publisher, of the literary tendency he represents—the 'new novel' for example—which may have guided their creative project.[21] What are the criteria of selection operated by the publisher, within the situation of pre-selection? He knows he does not possess the key which will reveal infallibly the works that deserve to last, and he may profess simultaneously the most radical aesthetic relativism and the most complete faith in a kind of absolutism of 'flair'. In fact the conception he has of his specific vocation as an *avant-garde* publisher, aware of having no aesthetic principles except a distrust of all established canons, necessarily takes into account the image which the public, critics and authors have of his function in the division of intellectual labour. This image, which is defined by contrast with the image of other publishers, is confirmed in his eyes by the range of authors who select themselves in relation to it. The idea the publisher has of his own practice (as audacious and innovating for instance) which directs his practice at least as much as it expresses it, the intellectual 'posture' which can very roughly be described as '*avant-gardiste*' which is doubtless the ultimate and often indefinable principle on which his choices are made, are established and confirmed by reference to the idea he has of ideas and postures different from his own and of the social representation of his own posture.[22] The situation of the critic is not very different: the already pre-selected works he receives now bear a further mark, that of the publisher (and sometimes that of the preface which may be by a creative writer or another critic) so that his reading of any particular work must take into account the social representation of the typical characteristics of books brought out by the publisher concerned ('new novel', 'objectal literature', etc.), a representation for which he and his fellow critics may be in part responsible.[23] Do we not sometimes see the critic acting as initiated disciple, sending the interpreted revelation back to its originator, who, in return, confirms him in his vocation of privileged de-coder by confirming the accuracy of the interpretation? Literature and painting have often witnessed this kind of perfect couple, perhaps today more than ever before. The publisher acting as a businessman (which he also is) can technically use the public image of his publications—for example the Vulgate of the 'new novel'—

in order to launch a book. The kind of thing he may say to the critic, who has been selected not only as a function of his influence but also as a function of the affinities he may have with the book, which may go as far as declared allegiance, is an extremely subtle mixture in which the idea he has of the work compounds with the idea he has of the idea which the critic will have of the book, given that he has a certain conception of the house's publications.

Is the publisher not making a sound sociological observation when he concludes that the 'new novel' is no more or less than the sum total of novels published by the Éditions de Minuit. It is significant that what has become the name of a literary school, adopted by the authors themselves, was originally, like 'impressionists', a pejorative label attached by a traditionalist critic to the novels published by the Éditions de Minuit. But the authors have not been content merely to assume this public definition of their enterprise; they have been defined by it inasmuch as they have had to define themselves in relation to it. Just as the reading public was encouraged to look for and imagine links that might connect books published under the same format, so too, the authors, it could be said, have been encouraged to think of themselves as constituting a school, and not simply a fortuitous group, by the necessity of taking account of each other and of conforming to the image that the public had formed of them? What has in fact happened is that they have adopted not only the title but also the version of their work by which their public image was defined, identifying themselves with a social identity imposed from the outside and originally arising out of a mere coincidence that they have turned into a collective project. From being encouraged to situate themselves in relation to the others in the group, to see in each of the others a form of expression of their own truth, to recognize themselves in those whom they recognize as authentic members of the school, have they not been led to establish explicitly the principle of what should unite them since they were seen by other people as forming a single unit? And at the same time as the group becomes apparent to itself and affirms itself more clearly as a school, does it not encourage critics and the public to incline increasingly to look out for signs of what unites the members of the school and distinguishes them from other schools, that is, to separate what might be brought together and to bring together what might be kept apart? The public is also invited to join in the game of images reflected *ad infinitum* which eventually come to exist as real in a universe where reflection is the only reality. The *avant-gardiste* position (which is not necessarily attributable to snobbism) is under an obligation to formulate, to welcome and to deal in 'theories' which can provide a rational basis for an adherence that owes nothing to their reasons. We must go to Proust again:

Because she thought she was 'advanced' and (in art only) 'never far enough to the left', as she said, [Madame de Cambremer] had the idea not only that music progresses, but that it does so along a straight line, and that Debussy was in a way a super-Wagner, a little more advanced even than Wagner. She did not realize that while Debussy was not as independent of Wagner as she herself was to believe a few years later, because after all one uses conquered arms to rid oneself of the other whom one has momentarily defeated, he was nevertheless searching, after the weariness that was already beginning to be felt for over-complete works in which everything is expressed, to fulfil the opposite need. Of course there were theories to support this reaction for the moment, similar to those which in politics are brought in to support laws against the congregations, wars in the East (teaching against nature, yellow peril, etc.). They said that an age of speed required a rapid form of art, exactly as they would have said that the war that was to come would not last a fortnight, or that when the railway came it would cut off those little places where the coach stopped.[24]

So the public meaning of the work, as an objectively instituted judgement on the value and truth of the work (in relation to which any individual judgement of taste is obliged to define itself), is necessarily collective. That is to say, that the subject of an aesthetic judgement is a 'one' which may take itself for an 'I'. The objectivization of the creative intention which one might call 'publication' (in the sense of 'being made public') is accomplished by way of an infinite number of particular social relationships, between publisher and author, between author and critic, between authors, etc. In each of these relationships, each of the agents employs the socially established idea he has of the other partner to the relationship (the representation of his position and function in the intellectual field, of his public image as a consecrated or damned author, as an *avant-garde* or traditional publisher, etc.). Each agent also employs the idea of the idea that the other partner of the relationship has of him, that is of the social definition of his truth and his value as constituted in and through the whole network of relationships between all the members of the intellectual world. It follows that the relationship the creator has with his work is always mediated by the relationship he has with the public meaning of his works. This meaning is concretely recalled to him with regard to all the relationships he has with all the other members of the intellectual world. It is the product of the infinitely complex interactions between intellectual acts seen as judgements which are both determined and determining of the truth and value of works and of authors. Thus, the most singular and personal aesthetic judgement has reference to a common meaning already established. The relationship with any work, even one's own, is always a relationship with a work which has been judged. The *ultimate* truth and value of a work can never be anything but the sum of potential judgements of it which all the members of the intellectual world would formulate by reference in all cases to the social representation of the work as the integration of individual judgements of it. Because the particular meaning must always be defined in relation to the common meaning, it necessarily contributes to the definition of what will be a new version of this common meaning. The judgement of history, which will be the final pronouncement on the work and its author, is already begun by the judgement of the very first reader; posterity will have to take into account the public meaning bequeathed to it by contemporary opinion. Psaphon, the young Lydian shepherd, trained birds to repeat: 'Psaphon is a god.' When they heard birds speaking, and the words they said, Psaphon's fellow-citizens hailed him as a god.

## PROPHETS, PRIESTS AND SORCERERS

Although each part of the intellectual field is dependent on all the others, not all depend on the others to the same extent. In chess the future of the queen may depend on the most insignificant pawn, but the queen nevertheless continues to be much more powerful than any other piece. Similarly the constituent parts of the intellectual field which are placed in a relationship of functional interdependence are nevertheless distinguished by differences in *functional weight* and contribute in very unequal measure to give the intellectual field its particular structure. In fact, the dynamic structure of the intellectual field is none other than the network of interactions between a plurality of forces. These may be isolated agents like the intellectual creator, or systems of agents like the educational systems, the academies or circles. These forces are defined, basically at any rate, both in their existence and their function, by the *position* they occupy in the intellectual field. They are also defined by the *authority*, more or less recognized, that is more or less forceful and far-reaching (and in all cases mediated by their interaction), which they exercise or claim to exercise over the public. This authority represents both the prize and at the same time to some extent the empire of the competition for intellectual consecration and legitimacy.[25] It may be the upper classes who, by their social standing, sanction the rank of the works they consume in the hierarchy of legitimate works. Also, it may be specific institutions such as the educational system and academies which by their

| The sphere of legitimacy claiming universality | The sphere of what is in process of legitimation | The sphere of the arbitrary as regards legitimacy (or the sphere of sectional legitimacy) | |
|---|---|---|---|
| Music | Cinema | Dress design Cosmetics | Cookery |
| Painting Sculpture | Photography | | |
| Literature Theatre | Jazz | Interior decoration Furnishing | Other daily aesthetic choices (sporting events, etc.) |
| Legitimate legitimation authorities (universities, academies) | Legitimation authorities in competition with each other and claiming legitimacy (critics, clubs) | Non-legitimate legitimation authorities (*haute couture* designers, advertising) | |

authority and their teaching consecrate a certain kind of work and a certain type of cultivated man. Equally it may be literary or artistic groups, coteries, critical circles, 'salons' or 'cafés' which have a recognized role as cultural guides or 'taste-makers'. Whatever the form, a plurality of social forces almost always exists in all societies, sometimes in competition, sometimes co-ordinated, which by reason of their political or economic power or the institutional guarantees they dispose of, are in a position to impose their cultural norms on a larger or smaller area of the intellectual field. These social forces claim, *ipso facto*, cultural legitimacy whether for the cultural products they manufacture, for the opinions they pronounce on cultural products manufactured by others, or for the works and cultural attitudes they transmit. When they clash they do so in the name of the claim to be the fount of orthodoxy, and when they are recognized it is their claim to orthodoxy which is being recognized. Any cultural act, whether creation or consumption, contains the implicit statement of the right to express oneself legitimately. It thereby involves the position of the person concerned in the intellectual field and the type of legitimacy he claims to represent. Thus it is that the creator may have a completely different relationship towards his work—and his work inevitably bears the mark—depending on whether he occupies a position which is marginal (in relation to the university, for example) or official. When a friend advised him to apply for a university chair Feuerbach replied: 'I am only somebody as long as I am nobody', betraying both his nostalgia for integration into the official institution and the objective truth of a creative project which is obliged to define itself by contrast with the official philosophy which has rejected it. Banned by the university after his *Thoughts on Death and Immortality*, he escaped the restrictions of the state only to assume the role of free philosopher and revolutionary thinker which, by its refusal, that same official philosophy had assigned him.

The structure of the intellectual field maintains a relation of interdependence with one of the basic structures of the cultural field, that of cultural works, established in a hierarchy according to their degree of legitimacy. One may observe that in a given society at a given moment in time not all cultural signs—theatrical performances, sporting spectacles, recitals of songs, poetry or chamber music, operettas or operas are equal in dignity and value, nor do they call for the same approach with the same degree of insistence. In other words, the various systems of expression from the theatre to television, are objectively organized according to a hierarchy independent of individual opinions, that defines cultural legitimacy and its degrees.[26] Faced with signs situated outside the sphere of legitimate culture the consumers feel they are authorized to remain purely consumers and to judge freely, in the domain of consecrated culture on the other hand they feel they are subject to objective norms and are obliged to adopt an attitude which is pious, ceremonial and ritualistic. That is why jazz, cinema and photography, for example, do not occasion (because they do not insist upon it to the same extent) the reverence which is commonly found in the presence of works of learned culture. It is true that some virtuosi are carrying over, into these arts in the process of becoming legitimate, models of behaviour which are current in the domain of traditional culture. But in the absence of an institution devoted to teaching them systematically and methodically and thereby giving them the seal of respectability as constituent parts of legitimate culture, most people experience them in an entirely different way. If learned knowledge of the history of these arts and familiarity with the technical rules or theoretical principles that characterize them are only found in exceptional circumstances, it is because people do not feel bound, as they do elsewhere, to make the effort to acquire, retain and transmit the corpus of knowledge which goes to make up the necessary condition and ritual accompaniment of learned consumption.

One passes then by degrees from the entirely consecrated arts—the theatre, painting, sculpture, literature or classical music (among which hierarchies are also established that may vary in the course of time), to system of signs which (at first sight anyhow) are left to individual judgement, whether interior decorating, cosmetics or cookery. The existence of sanctified works and of a whole system of rules which define the sacramental approach assumes the existence of an institution whose function is not only to transmit and make available but also to confer legitimacy. In fact, jazz and the cinema have at their disposal means of expression which are at least as powerful as those of more traditional cultural works. There are groups of professional critics who have the use of learned journals and platforms on radio and television, who also (and this is a sign of their pretentions to cultural legitimacy) often ape the learned and tedious tones of academic critics and take from them the cult of erudition for erudition's sake, as if, haunted by doubts about their legitimacy, they had no other course than to adopt and exaggerate the external signs by which can be recognized the authority of those who control the monopoly of institutional legitimation, that is, the professors. Often relegated to the 'marginal' arts by their marginal position in the intellectual field, these individuals, isolated and deprived of all institutional guarantees, who in a competitive situation are inclined to make very disparate, even uncomparable judgements, are never heard outside the limited assemblies of fans, such as jazz groups or cinema clubs. So for instance the position of photography on the hierarchy of legitimate works and activities, halfway between 'vulgar' activities abandoned apparently to the anarchy of individual preferences, and noble cultural activities subject to strict rules, explains the ambiguity of the reactions it arouses, especially among members of the cultivated classes. Unlike a legitimate activity, an activity which is only in the process of becoming legitimate puts the question of its own legitimacy to those who indulge in it. Those who want to break with the rules of common practice and refuse to assign to their activity and to its product the customary significance and function are obliged somehow to provide a substitute (which cannot fail to appear as such) for what is given in the nature of immediate certainty, to the faithful worshippers of legitimate culture. This 'certainty' is a conviction of the cultural legitimacy of the activity and all the supporting reassurances from technical models to aesthetic theories. It is evident that the form of the relationship of participation which each subject maintains with the field of cultural works and, in particular, the content of his artistic or intellectual intention and the form taken by his creative project (for example the degree to which it is thought out and made explicit) closely depend on his position in the intellectual field. The same is the case for the themes and problems which define the specificity of the thought of an intellectual, which a lexicological analysis, among other methods, might bring to light. According to the position he occupies in the intellectual field each intellectual is conditioned to direct his activity towards a certain area of the cultural field. This is in part the legacy of previous generations and in part recreated, reinterpreted and transformed by his contemporaries. Likewise he is conditioned to maintain a certain type of relation which may be more or less easy or difficult, natural or dramatic, with the cultural signs, themselves either more or less respectable, more or less noble, more or less marginal or possibly more or less original, which make up this region of the cultural field. A methodical analysis of references made to other authors, measuring their frequency, their homogeneity or diversity (which would indicate the degree of auto-didacticism), the extent and range of the regions of the field to which they refer, the position in the hierarchy of legitimate values of the authorities or sources invoked, the tacit or unacknowledged references (which might be the height of sophistication or the height of naïveté), paying at the same time special attention to the particular manner in which quotation is made, whether irreproachably academic or casual, reverent or condescending, ornamental or necessary, would reveal the existence of 'families of thought' that are really cultural families. These families could easily be attached to typical positions, whether actual or potential, acquired or professed, in the intellectual field, and more precisely, to typical relations, past or present, with the university establishment.[27]

The structure of the intellectual field may be more or less complex and diversified according to the society or the age and the functional weight of the various authorities which have or claim to have cultural legitimacy. However, it remains true that certain fundamental social relationships are established whenever an intellectual society exists which is relatively independent of the political, economic and religious authorities. These may be relationships between creators whether contemporaries or of different periods, equally or unequally sanctified by different publics and by authorities of varying degrees of legitimacy or legitimating power, or relationships between creators and various authorities of legitimacy. There may be legitimate granters of legitimacy or claiming to be so, such as academies, learned societies, coteries, circles or small groups. They may be accepted or rejected in varying degrees, authorities of legitimation or transmission such as the educational system, or authorities of transmission alone such as scientific journalists—with all the possible combinations and double affinities this permits. It follows that the relations which each intellectual can maintain with each other member of intellectual society or with the public and, *a fortiori*, with all social reality outside the intellectual field (such as his social class or origin, or the one he belongs to, or economic forces such as dealers or buyers) are mediated by the structure of the intellectual field. More precisely his relations are mediated by his position relative to the properly cultural authorities whose powers organize the intellectual field: cultural acts or judgements always contain a reference to orthodoxy. But, more profoundly, within the intellectual field as a structured system, all individuals and all social groups that are specifically and permanently devoted to the manipulation of cultural goods (to adapt one of Weber's formulae) maintain not only competitive relationships but relationships of functional complementarity. This happens in such a way that each of the agents or systems of agents which make up the intellectual field derives a greater or smaller proportion of its characteristics from the position it occupies in this system of positions and oppositions.

The school is required to perpetuate and transmit the capital of consecrated cultural signs, that is, the culture handed down to it by the intellectual creators of the past, and to mould to a practice in accordance with the models of that culture a public assailed by conflicting, schismatic or heretical messages—for example, in our society, modern communication media. Further it is obliged to establish and define systematically the sphere of orthodox culture and the sphere of heretical culture. Simultaneously it defends consecrated culture against the continual challenge offered by the mere existence of new creators (or by deliberate provocation on their part) who can arouse in the public (and particularly in the intellectual classes) new demands and rebellious doubts. Thus the school is invested with a function very similar to that of the Church which, according to Max Weber, must 'establish and systematically define the new victorious doctrine or defend the old one against prophetic attacks, lay down what has and what has not sacred value and make it penetrate the faith of the laity.' It follows that the educational system as an institution specially contrived to conserve, transmit and inculcate the cultural canons of a society, derives a number of its structural and functional characteristics from the fact that it has to fulfil these particular functions. It also follows that a number of the characteristic traits of the teaching and the teacher which the most critical commentators mention only as grounds for condemnation, properly belong to the very definition of the function of education. So, for instance, it would be easy to demonstrate that the routine and routine-engendering activity of the school and the teachers, as frequently attacked by great cultural prophecies as by small heresies (often consisting simply of this denunciation alone), are without doubt unavoidably implicit in the logic of an institution which is fundamentally entrusted with a function of cultural conservation.

What is frequently described as competition for success is in reality a competition for consecration waged in an intellectual world dominated by the competition between the authorities which claim the monopoly of cultural legitimacy and the right to withhold and confer this consecration in the name of fundamentally opposed principles: the personal authority called for by the creator and the institutional authority favoured by the teacher. It follows that the opposition and complementarity between creators and teachers (that is to say 'between *auctores* who state their own doctrine, and *lectores* who explain the doctrines of others'—according to Gilbert de La Porrée's differentiation) undoubtedly constitutes the fundamental structure of the intellectual field. Likewise, the opposition between priest and prophet (with the secondary opposition between priest and sorcerer) dominates, according to Max Weber, the religious field. The curators of culture responsible for cultural propaganda and for organizing the apprenticeship which produces cultural devotion, are opposed to the creators of culture, *auctores* who can impose their *auctoritas* in artistic and scientific matters (as others can in ethical, political or religious matters). This is similar to the way that the permanence and omnipresence of the legitimate, organized institution are opposed to the unique, irregular lightning flashes of a creation which has no legitimation principle but itself. These two types of creative project are so clearly opposed that the condemnation of professorial routine which is in a way consubstantial with prophetic ambitions, often acts as a substitute for a diploma of qualification as a prophet. A conflict between priest and sorcerer may present itself as a conflict between priest and prophet or—who knows?—between two rival prophets. The debate about the 'new criticism' which was carried on between Raymond Picard and Roland Barthes, provides the best illustration of this analysis. Has the intellectual project of either contestant any other content besides opposition to the other's project? The priest condemns the 'oracular revelations' and 'systematic spirit', in brief the prophetic and 'vaticinal' spirit of the sorcerer;[28] the sorcerer condemns the archaism and conservatism, the routine and routine-mindeness, the pedantic ignorance and fussy prudence of the priest.[29] Each has his role: on one side academic dead calm, on the other the wind of change.[30]

Every intellectual brings into his relations with other intellectuals a claim to cultural consecration (or legitimacy) which depends, for the form it takes and the grounds it quotes, on the position he occupies in the intellectual field. In particular the claim depends on his relation to the university, which, in the last resort, disposes of the infallible signs of consecration. The Academy claims the monopoly of consecration of contemporary creators. It contributes to the organization of the intellectual field in respect of orthodoxy by a type of jurisprudence which combines tradition and innovation. On the other hand the university claims the monopoly of transmission of the consecrated works of the past, which it sanctifies as 'classics' as well as the monopoly of legitimation and consecration (by granting degrees amongst other things) of those cultural consumers who most closely conform. In these circumstances, the ambivalent aggressiveness of the creators is understandable—waiting for the signs of their academic consecration, they cannot fail to be aware that confirmation can only come in the last resort from an institution whose legitimacy is disputed by their entire creative activity. Similarly, several of the attacks against academic orthodoxy come from intellectuals situated on the fringes of the university system who are prone to dispute its legitimacy, thereby proving that they acknowledge its jurisdiction sufficiently to reproach it for not approving them.[31]

Indeed we each have a suspicion that a number of disputes which are apparently situated in the pure realm of principle and theory derive the least mentionable aspects of their *raison d'être* and sometimes their entire existence from the latent or patent tensions in the intellectual field. How else are we to explain why so many ideological quarrels of the past are incomprehensible to us today? The only real participation possible in past disputes is perhaps the kind that is authorized by similarity of position between intellectual fields of different periods. When Proust attacks Saint-Beuve, is this not Balzac fulminating against the man he called 'Sainte-Bevue' ('bévue' = blunder)? The ultimate cause of the conflicts, real or invented, which divide the intellectual field along its lines of force and which constitute beyond any doubt the most decisive factor of cultural change, must be sought at least as much in the objective factors determining the position of those who engage in them as in the reasons they give, to others and to themselves, for engaging in them.

## THE CULTURAL UNCONSCIOUS

Finally it is by the extent to which he forms part of an intellectual field by reference to which his creative project is defined and constituted, by the extent to which he is, as it were, the contemporary of those with whom he wishes to communicate and whom he addresses through his work, referring implicitly to a whole code he shares with them—themes and problems of the moment, methods of argument, manners of perception, etc.—that the intellectual is socially and historically situated. His most conscious intellectual and artistic choices are always directed by his own culture and taste, which are themselves interiorizations of the objective culture of a particular society, age or class. The culture which enters into the composition of the works he creates is not something added on as it were to an already existing intention and thereby irreducible to the realization of that intention. On the contrary it constitutes the necessary precondition for the concrete fulfilment of an artistic intention in a work of art, in the same way that language as the 'common treasury' is the precondition for the formulating of the most individual word. Because of this the work of art is always elliptical—it leaves unsaid the essential, it implicitly assumes what forms its very foundations, that is the axioms and postulates which it takes for granted, the axiomatics of which should be the study of the science of culture. What is betrayed by the eloquent silence of the work is precisely the culture (in the subjective sense) by means of which the creator participates in his class, his society and his age, and which he unwittingly introduces into the works he creates, even into those which appear most original. This culture consists of credos which are so obvious that they are tacitly assumed rather than explicitly postulated. Examples are ways of thought, forms of logic, stylistic expressions and catchwords (yesterday's existence, situation, authenticity, today's structure, unconscious and praxis) which seem so natural and inevitable that they are not properly speaking the object of a conscious choice. They can be likened to what Arthur O. Lovejoy speaks of as the 'metaphysical pathos'[32] or what might be called the tonality of mood which characterizes all the means of expression of an age, even those furthest apart in the cultural field, for example, literature and landscape gardening. Agreement on the implicit axiomatics of understanding and affectivity forms the basis for the logical integration of a society and an age. The 'philosophy without a subject', which is today returning with so much stir to the forefront of the intellectual scene in the form of structural linguistics or anthropology, seems to exercise a veritable fascination over people who only recently stood at the very opposite pole of the ideological horizon and who used to combat it in the name of the unquestioned rights of consciousness and subjectivity. This is because, unlike Durkheimian thought, which it is reviving in a new form, it does not reveal all the anthropological consequences of its discoveries in such a brutal and systematic fashion which made it possible to forget that what is true of uncivilized thought is true of all cultivated thought.

For the judgements and arguments of witchcraft to have any validity [wrote Mauss], they must have a principle which cannot be submitted to examination. One may discuss whether the mana is present in such and such a place or not, but one does not question its existence. Now the principles on which these judgements and arguments are founded, without which one does not believe them to be possible, are what in philosophy are called categories. Always present in language, without necessarily being explicit, they ordinarily exist rather in the form of habits governing consciousness, which are themselves unconscious.[33]

Our common apprehension of the world is also founded on principles not open to examination and unconscious categories of thought which constantly threaten to insinuate themselves into the scientific vision. Bachelard is speaking the same language as Mauss when he notes that 'rational habits', whether 'the Euclidian mentality', the 'geometric unconscious' connected with the apprenticeship to Euclidian geometry, or 'the dialectic of form and matter' 'are so many scleroses over which we must triumph before we can find the spiritual movement of discovery.'[34] But since the scientific project and the very progress of science presuppose a reflective return to the foundations of science and the making explicit of the hypotheses and operations which make it possible, it is undoubtedly in works of art that the social forms of the thought of an age find their most naïve and complete expression. So, as Whitehead observes: 'It is in literature that the concrete outlook of humanity receives its expression. Accordingly it is to literature that we must look, particularly in its most concrete forms . . . if we hope to discover the inward thoughts of a generation.'[35] Thus to take a single example, the relation which the creator maintains with the public, which is closely linked as we have seen with the situation of the intellectual field within the society and with the position of the artist within this field, obeys models which are profoundly unconscious. This is insofar as it is a relationship of communication naturally subject to the rules governing interpersonal relationships in the social world of the artist or of those whom he is addressing. As Arnold Hauser observes, ancient Oriental art with its frontal representation of the human face is an 'art which displays and demands respect', it offers the viewer an expression of deference and courtesy which conforms to a pattern of etiquette. All courtly art is a courteous art which by its submission to the principle of frontal representation displays its refusal of the straining after effect of a facile illusionist art.

This attitude finds expression later on but still quite clearly in the conventions of the classic court theatre where the actor, without conceding anything to the demands of scenic illusion, addresses the audience directly, apostrophizes it in a way with each of his words and gestures. He is not content merely to avoid turning his back on the audience but demonstrates in every possible way that the entire action is pure fiction, a *divertissement* presented according to agreed rules. The naturalist theatre is a transitional step towards the complete opposite of this 'frontal' art, that is the film, which mobilizes the audience, brings it to the action instead of bringing and presenting the action to it, and attempts to present the action in such a way as to suggest that the actors are being observed in a real-life situation, thus reducing the fiction to a minimum.[36]

These two types of aesthetic intention which the work of art reveals by the way it addresses the spectator are in elective affinity with the structure of the societies in which they are established and with the structure of social relationships, aristocratic or democratic, favoured by those societies. When Scaliger finds it ridiculous that 'the characters never leave the stage and that those who remain silent are considered as if they were present', when he considers it absurd 'to behave on stage as if one cannot hear what one person is saying about another,'[37] it is because he no longer understands the theatrical conventions which the men of the Middle Ages took for granted because they confirmed a system of implicit choices. These same choices, according to Panofsky, were expressed in the 'composite'[38] space of pictorial or plastic representation in the Middle Ages. This juxtaposition in space of successive scenes was entirely different from the theatrical and plastic conventions of the Renaissance and the classical age, with their 'systematic' representation of space and time which is expressed equally in perspective and in the rule of the three unities.

It may seem surprising to ascribe to the cultural unconscious the attitudes, aptitudes, knowledge, themes and problems, in short the whole system of categories of perception and thought acquired by the systematic apprenticeship which the school organizes or makes it possible to organize. This is because the creator maintains with his acquired culture, as with his early culture, a relationship which might be defined according to Nicolaï Hartmann as both 'carrying' and 'being carried' and that he is not aware that the culture he possesses possesses him. Thus as Louis Althusser points out,

it would be most imprudent to reduce the influence of Feuerbach in Marx's writings between 1841 and '44 to those places only where he is explicitly mentioned. For numerous passages in these texts reproduce or directly denote developments of Feuerbach's thought, without his being quoted by name. . . . But why should Marx have to put quotation marks round Feuerbach when everyone knew about him, and above all when Marx had *appropriated his thought* and thought in Feuerbach's concepts as if they were his own?[39]

Unconscious borrowings and imitations are clearly the most obvious expression of the cultural unconscious of an age, of that general sense which makes possible the particular sense in which it finds expression.

For this reason, the relationship which an intellectual maintains of necessity with the school and his educational past is a determining weight in the system of his most unconscious intellectual choices. Men formed by a certain school have in common a certain cast of mind; shaped in the same mould they are predisposed to enter into an immediate complicity with like souls.[40] What individuals owe to the school is above all a fund of commonplaces, not only a common language and style but also common meeting grounds and grounds for agreement, common problems and common methods of tackling them. The cultivated men of a given age may have different opinions on the subjects about which they quarrel but they are at any rate agreed on quarrelling about certain subjects. What attaches a thinker to his age, what situates and dates him, is above all the kind of problems and themes in terms of which he is obliged to think. As we know, historical analysis often finds it difficult to distinguish between what can be attributed to the particular manner of a creative individuality and what is to be accounted for by the conventions and rules of a genre or an art form, and even more, to the taste, ideology and style of an age or a society. The themes and manner which are personal to a creator always draw in part on topics and rhetoric as the common source of themes and forms which define the cultural tradition of a society and an age. It is because of this that the work is always objectively oriented in relation to the literary milieu, its aesthetic demands and intellectual expectations, its categories of perception and thought. For example let us consider the distinctions between literary genres with the notions of epic, tragic, comic and heroic, between styles according to categories such as the pictorial or plastic, or between schools with oppositions such as those between classical and naturalist, bourgeois and populist, realist and surrealist. Such distinctions direct both the creative project, which they define by making it possible for it to define itself differentially and for which they provide its essential resources. By depriving it of the resources which other creators in other ages will derive from their ignorance of these distinctions, the public are led to desire subjects of a determined type and a typical manner, which is regarded as the 'natural' and 'reasonable' way to treat these subjects, because it conforms to the social definition of the natural and the reasonable.[41]

In the same way that linguisticians have recourse to the criterion of inter-comprehension in order to determine linguistic areas, one might also determine intellectual and cultural areas and generations by locating the networks of questions and compulsory themes which define the cultural field of an age. It would be superficial to conclude that in all cases of patent divergences between intellectuals of an age over what are sometimes called 'the great problems of the time' there must be a failure of logical integration. The open conflicts between tendencies and doctrines tend to mask, from the participants themselves, the underlying complicity which they presuppose and which strikes the observer from outside the system. This complicity can be expressed as a consensus within the dissensus which constitutes the objective unity of the intellectual field of a given period. This unconscious consensus on the focal points of the cultural field is formed by the school when it forms the unthought element common to all individual thought.

The essential fact is undoubtedly that intellectual schemas which are laid down in the form of automatic reflexes can only be grasped, in most cases, by the retrospective study of operations already completed. It follows that they may govern and regulate intellectual operations without being consciously perceived and controlled. It is above all through the cultural unconscious which he retains from his intellectual training and particularly from his schooling that a thinker participates in his society and his age: schools of thought may bring together, more commonly than it might be supposed, thoughts of school. This hypothesis is confirmed in an exemplary fashion by the analysis of the relationship between Gothic art and Scholasticism which was proposed by Erwin Panofsky. What the architects of Gothic cathedrals unconsciously borrowed from the school was a '*principium importans ordinem ad actum*' or a '*modus operandi*', that is, 'that peculiar method of procedure which must have been the first thing to impress itself upon the mind of the layman whenever it came in touch with that of the schoolman'.[42] Thus for example, the principle of clarification (*manifestatio*), the schema of literary presentation discovered by Scholasticism which requires the author to make plain and explicit (*manifestare*) the order and logic of his words—we should say his 'plan'—also governs the action of the architect and sculptor, as can be seen by comparing the Last Judgement on the tympanum at Autun with those of Paris and Amiens, where despite the increased richness of motifs, the greatest clarity is maintained by the balance of symmetry and correspondences.[43] If this is so, it is because the builders of cathedrals were under the constant influence of Scholasticism—the 'habit-forming force'—which between 1130-40 and about 1270 'held the virtual monopoly of education' over an area of about 150 kilometres around Paris.

It is not very probable that the builders of Gothic structures read Gilbert de la Porrée or Thomas Aquinas in the original. But they were exposed to the Scholastic viewpoint in innumerable other ways, quite apart from the fact that their own work automatically brought them into a working association with those who devised the liturgical and iconographic programmes. They had gone to school, they listened to sermons, they could attend the public *disputationes de quolibet*, which, dealing as they did with all imaginable questions of the day, had developed into social events not unlike our operas, concerts or public lectures; and they could come into profitable contact with the learned on many occasions.[44]

It follows, Panofsky observes, that the connection between Gothic art and Scholasticism is 'more concrete than a mere "parallelism" and yet more general than those individual (and very important) "influences" which are inevitably exerted on painters, sculptors or architects by erudite advisers'. This connection is a 'genuine cause-and-effect relation' which operates by the spreading 'of what may be called, for want of a better term, a mental habit—reducing this overworked cliché to its precise Scholastic sense as a principle that regulates the act, *principium importans ordinem ad actum*.'[45] As a 'habit-forming force' the school provides those who have undergone its direct or indirect influence not so much with particular and particularized schemes of thought as with that general disposition which engenders particular schemes, which may then be applied in different domains of thought and action, a disposition that one could call the cultivated *habitus*.

Thus in order to explain the structural homologies that he finds between domains of intellectual activity as far removed from each other as architecture and philosophic thought, Erwin Panofsky refuses to be satisfied with invoking a 'unitary world vision' or a 'spirit of the times', which would amount merely to giving a name to what one is seeking to explain, or worse, putting forward as an explanation that which requires explaining. He suggests what is apparently the most obvious and certainly the most persuasive explanation. In a society where the transmission of culture is the monopoly of a school, the underlying affinities uniting works of learned culture (and at the same time behaviour and thought) are governed by the principle emanating from the educational institutions. These institutions are entrusted with the function of transmitting consciously (and also in part unconsciously) the unconscious. More precisely, the school produces individuals who possess this system of unconscious (or extremely obscure) schemes constituting their culture. Obviously it would be naïve to stop looking for an explanation at this point, as if the school was an empire within an empire, and as if culture had its absolute beginnings there. But it would also be naïve to take no account of the fact that the school by the very logic of its functioning, modifies the content and spirit of the culture it transmits, or to forget that its express function is to transform the collective heritage into an individual and common unconscious. To relate the works produced by an age to the educational practices of the time is therefore to provide oneself with one means of explaining not only what they say but also what they betray in so far as they participate in the symbolic aspects of an age or a society.

Thus the sociology of intellectual and artistic creation must take as its object the creative project as a meeting point and an adjustment between determinism and a determination. That is, if it is to go beyond the opposition between an internal aesthetic theory, obliged to treat a work as if it were a self-contained system with its own reasons and *raison d'être*, itself defining the coherent principles and norms necessary for its interpretation, and an external aesthetic theory which at the cost often of detrimentally diminishing the work, attempts to relate it to the economic, social and cultural conditions of artistic creation. In fact, all influence and constraint exercised by an authority outside the intellectual field is always refracted by the structure of the intellectual field. This is why for instance the relationship which an intellectual has with the social class he comes from or belongs to is mediated by the position he occupies in the intellectual field. It is in terms of this intellectual field that he feels authorized to claim that he belongs to that class (with the choices that implies), or on the other hand, is inclined to repudiate it and to conceal it with shame. Thus forces of determinism can only become a specifically intellectual determination by being reinterpreted, according to the specific logic of the intellectual field, in a creative project. Economic and social events can only affect any particular part of that field, whether an individual or an institution, according to a specific logic, because at the same time as it is restructured under their influence, the intellectual field obliges them to undergo a conversion of meaning and value by transforming them into objects of reflection or imagination.

# NOTES

[1] L. L. Schücking, *The Sociology of Literary Taste*, translated by B. Battershaw, London: Routledge, 1966, pp. 13–15.

[2] With, as Schücking notes (*ibid.*, p. 16), a transition phase when the publisher is dependent on subscriptions, which in turn depend largely on the relations between the author and his patrons.

[3] *Ibid.*, pp. 50–1.

[4] *Ibid.*, p. 52.

[5] *Ibid.*, p. 27. Elsewhere (p. 43) Schücking tells us that Churchyard, a contemporary of Shakespeare's, wrote in one of his prefaces with cynical frankness that, taking the fish as his exemplar he swam with the stream; Dryden admitted openly that he was concerned only to win the public to his side and if the public wanted a rather low kind of comedy or satire, he would not hesitate to give it.

[6] It is true that we can find in earlier periods, from the sixteenth century on, and perhaps even before that, declarations of the artist's aristocratic disdain for the public's bad taste, but before the nineteenth century they never constitute a *profession de foi* of the creative intention and a sort of collective doctrine.

[7] R. Williams, *Culture and Society, 1780–1950*, 3rd ed., Harmondsworth: Penguin Books, 1963, pp. 49–50.

[8] Raymond Williams also brings to light the interdependent relations linking the appearance of a new public, belonging to a new social class, of a group of writers coming from the same class, and of institutions or art forms invented by that class. 'The character of literature is also visibly affected, in varying ways, by the nature of the communication system and by the changing character of audiences. When we see the important emergence of writers of a new social group, we must look not only at them, but at the new institutions and forms created by the wider social group to which they belong. The Elizabethan theatre ... as an institution was largely created by individual middle-class speculators, and was supplied with plays by writers from largely middle-class and trading and artisan families, yet in fact was steadily opposed by the commercial middle class and, though serving popular audiences, survived through the protection of the court and nobility. .... The formation in the eighteenth century of an organized middle-class audience can be seen as in part due to certain writers from the same social group, but also, and perhaps mainly, as an independent formation which then drew these writers to it and gave them their opportunity. The expansion and further organization of this middle-class audience can be seen to have continued until the late nineteenth century, drawing in writers from varied social origins but giving them, through its majority institutions, a general homogeneity' (R. Williams, *The Long Revolution*, Harmondsworth: Pelican Books, 1965, p. 266).

[9] A description of the chief tendencies of the 'aesthetic movement' can be found in Schücking, *op. cit.*, pp. 28–30.

[10] *Ibid.*, p. 30. There is also (p. 55) a description of the functioning of these societies and in particular of the 'mutual services' they made possible.

[11] *Ibid.*, p. 62.

[12] It goes without saying that the propositions which emerge from the study of an established intellectual field can provide the basis for a structural interpretation either of intellectual fields which arose from a different historical evolution, such as the intellectual field of fifth-century Athens, or even of intellectual fields in the process of becoming established.

[13] J.-P. Sartre, *Qu'est-ce que la littérature?*, Paris: Gallimard, 1948, p. 98.

[14] P. Valéry, *Œuvres*, I, Paris: Gallimard, Bibliothèque de la Pléiade, p. 1442.

[15] R. Moulin, *Le marché de la peinture en France, essai de sociologie économique*, Paris: Éd. de Minuit, 1967.

[16] L. Althusser, *Lire le Capital*, II, Paris: Maspero, 1965, pp. 9–10.

[17] G. Genette, *Figures*, Paris: Éd. du Seuil, Collection 'Tel quel', 1966, pp. 242–3.

[18] *Ibid.*, pp. 69–71.

[19] Only an analysis of the actual structure of the works would make it possible to establish whether the conversion of the creative project which appears in the creator's writings about his work is also demonstrated in his most recent works, which if this is so, ought—as a mere reading of them appears to suggest—to present the most *accomplished* and the most *systematic* expression of this creative intention.

[20] Schücking's observations allow us to make this proposition of more general relevance: 'As regards getting published, one fact has been observable since at least the eighteenth century—the fortunate situation of anyone who is in personal touch with writers who are well known and have their public and a certain prestige with the publishers. Their recommendation may carry sufficient weight to smooth away the main difficulties for the newcomer. Thus it is almost a rule that the beginner's work does not pass direct from him to the appropriate authority but takes the indirect and often difficult course past the desk of an artist of repute' (op. cit., p. 53).

[21] Thus we see how the meeting between author and publisher may be experienced and interpreted in the logic of pre-established harmony and predestination: 'Are you pleased to be published by the Éditions de Minuit?—If I had done as I wanted I'd have gone to them straight away. . . . But I didn't dare, it seemed too grand for me. So I sent my manuscript to X Éditions first. That doesn't sound very complimentary for X Éditions! Then they turned down my book and I took it to the Éditions de Minuit just the same.— How do you get on with the publisher?—First of all he told me what my book was about. He saw things in it I hadn't dared to hope I could do, everything about time, the coincidences' (Quinzaine littéraire, September 15, 1966).

[22] To exist, in the system of symbolic relations which constitutes the intellectual field, is to be known and recognized by distinctive features (a manner, a style, a specialty, etc.), differential divisions which can be expressly looked for and which serve to lift one out of anonymity and insignificance.

[23] 'Except for these opening pages which appear to be a more or less conscious pastiche of the new novel, L'Auberge espagnole tells a fantastic but perfectly comprehensible story, whose action obeys the logic of dreams, not of reality' (É. Lalou, L'Express, October 26, 1966). Here, the critic who suspects the young novelist of having wandered consciously or unconsciously into a hall of mirrors falls into the trap himself by describing what he considers as a reflection of the new novel in the light of a common reflection of the new novel.

[24] M. Proust, A la recherche du temps perdu: Sodome et Gomorrhe, Paris: N.R.F., 1927, II, 2, pp. 35–6. Choices frequently admit of even more summary justifications; the pendulum mechanism by which each generation tends to reject the implicit propositions which provided the basis for the consensus of the previous generation, owes part of its effectiveness to the social fear of appearing to be attached to a bygone age and thereby to be situated in a devalued position in the intellectual field; many taboos even in the least cumulative subjects have no other foundation ('pre-war literature', 'Third-Republic sociology' or 'old-fashioned art').

[25] 'Like politics, artistic life consists of a struggle to win support.' The analogy suggested by Schücking (op. cit., p. 197) between the political field and the intellectual field is based on an intuition which is partly correct but which over-simplifies the question.

[26] Legitimacy is not legality; if individuals from those classes which are least favoured in cultural matters almost always pay at least lip-service to the legitimacy of the aesthetic rules proposed by learned culture, that does not exclude the possibility of their spending their lives, de facto, outside the sphere of application of the rules without the rules losing thereby any of their legitimacy, that is, their claim to be universally recognized. The legitimate rule may not in any way determine modes of conduct situated within its sphere of influence, it may have only exceptions to its application, but it nevertheless defines the modality of the experience which accompanies these modes of conduct and it is not possible for it not to be thought and recognized, especially when it is contravened, like the rule of cultural conducts when they wish to be considered as legitimate. In short, the existence of what I call cultural legitimacy lies in every individual, whether he wants to or not, whether he admits it or not, being placed, and knowing he is placed, in the sphere of application of a system of rules which make it possible to qualify and stratify his behaviour in a cultural context.

[27] It hardly needs saying that the perception of the intellectual field as such and the sociological description of that field are more or less accessible to the individual depending on the position he himself occupies in the field.

[28] Cf. R. Picard, Nouvelle critique ou nouvelle imposture, Paris: Jean-Jacques Pauvert, Collection 'Libertés', pp. 24, 35, 58 and 76.

[29] Cf. Barthes, op. cit.: 'The reasonable critic does his best to bring everything down a peg: what is banal in life must not be disturbed; what is not banal in a book should on

the contrary be made to appear banal' (p. 22); 'what does he know about Freud except what he has read in the "Que sais-je?" series?' (p. 24).

³⁰ 'True, these demanding and modest tasks remain absolutely indispensable; but the wind of change of M. Barthes and his friends should also be for everyone the opportunity for a very serious heart-searching' (Picard, *op. cit.*, p. 79).

³¹ This type of ambivalent attitude is particularly widespread among the lower strata of the intelligentsia, among journalists, popularizers, disputed artists, radio and television producers, etc.: many opinions and modes of conduct have their origins in the relationship which these intellectuals have with early education and thereby with the educational establishment.

³² A. O. Lovejoy, *The Great Chain of Being: A Study of the History of an Idea*, Cambridge: Mass., Harvard University Press, 1961, p. 11.

³³ M. Mauss, 'Introduction à l'analyse de quelques phénomènes religieux', in: *Mélanges d'histoire des religions*, XXIX.

³⁴ G. Bachelard, *Le Nouvel Esprit scientifique*, Paris: P.U.F., 1949, pp. 31 and 37-8.

³⁵ A. N. Whitehead, *Science and the Modern World*, 1926, p. 106.

³⁶ A. Hauser, *The Social History of Art*, I, translated by Godman, New York: Vintage Books, 1957, pp. 41-2.

³⁷ Quoted *ibid.*, II, pp. 11-12.

³⁸ E. Panofsky, 'Die Perspektive als symbolische Form', *Vorträge der Bibliothek Warburg, 1924-1925*, Leipzig–Berlin, 1927, p. 257 *sqq.*

³⁹ L. Althusser, *Pour Marx*, Paris: Maspero, 1965, p. 62.

⁴⁰ Obviously, in a society of intellectuals formed by the educational system, the autodidact necessarily has certain properties, all negative, which he must take into account and whose mark is borne by his creative project.

⁴¹ Schücking shows how deeply and permanently the school marks its pupils: 'The greatest creative artists and the greatest revolutionaries of history form no exception here, but remain set in their respect for the achievements which they admired in adolescence and which they had actually been educated to appreciate. Often it takes much time for that respect to disappear; in some cases it never disappears at all. It is indeed astonishing how often it is the great poets themselves who look reverently upward to their predecessors whom posterity not only ranks well below their level, but regards as their artistic antipodes. Thus it seemed to Rousseau an act of extraordinary daring when he placed his *Nouvelle Héloïse* next to the *Princesse de Clèves* . . .; thus throughout his life Byron continued to worship the neo-classic work of Pope to which positively divine honours were accorded in the century in which he himself had been born. The strength of this department of impressions gathered during school years upon even the greatest and freest of spirits is nowhere more clearly shown than in the case of Martin Luther, who declared that "a page of Terrence" whom he had to study at school was worth all the dialogues of Erasmus put together' (*op. cit.*, p. 79).

⁴² E. Panofsky, *Gothic Architecture and Scholasticism*, New York, 1957, p. 28.

⁴³ *Ibid.*, p. 40.

⁴⁴ *Ibid.*, p. 24.

⁴⁵ *Ibid.*, pp. 20-3.

# PART THREE

*COGNITIVE STYLES IN COMPARATIVE PERSPECTIVE*

## 7. PIERRE BOURDIEU
### Systems of Education and Systems of Thought*

Speaking of the course of his intellectual development in *A World on the Wane*, Claude Lévi-Strauss describes the techniques and rites of philosophy teaching in France:

It was then that I began to learn how any problem, whether grave or trivial, can be resolved. The method never varies. First you establish the traditional 'two views' of the question. You then put forward a commonsense justification of the one, only to refute it by the other. Finally you send them both packing by the use of a third interpretation, in which both the others are shown to be equally unsatisfactory. Certain verbal manœuvres enable you, that is, to line up the traditional 'antitheses' as complementary aspects of a single reality: form and substance, content and container, appearance and reality, essence and existence, continuity and discontinuity and so on. Before long the exercise becomes the merest verbalizing, reflection gives place to a kind of superior punning, and the 'accomplished philosopher' may be recognized by the ingenuity with which he makes ever-bolder play with assonance, ambiguity and the use of those words which sound alike and yet bear quite different meanings.

Five years at the Sorbonne taught me little but this form of mental gymnastics. Its dangers are, of course, self-evident: the mechanism is so simple, for one thing, that there is no such thing as a problem which cannot be tackled. When we were working for our examinations and, above all, for that supreme ordeal, the *leçon* (in which the candidate draws a subject by lot, and is given only six hours in which to prepare a comprehensive survey of it), we used to set one another the bizarrest imaginable themes. . . . The method, universal in its application, encouraged the student to overlook the many possible forms and variants of thought, devoting himself to one particular unchanging instrument. Certain elementary adjustments were all that he needed. . . .[1]

This admirable ethnological description of the intellectual and linguistic patterns transmitted—implicitly rather than explicitly—by French education, has its counterpart in the description of the patterns that direct the thinking

* This paper first appeared in the *International Social Science Journal*, Volume XIX, Number 3, 1967.

and behaviour of the Bororo Indians when they build their villages to a plan every bit as formal and fictitious as the dualistic organization of the *agrégation* exercises, patterns whose necessity, or, to put it another way, whose function is recognized in this case by the ethnologist, probably because he is, at once, more detached and more intimately involved:

... The wise men of the tribe have evolved a grandiose cosmology which is writ large in the lay-out of their villages and distribution of their homes. When they met with contradictions, those contradictions were cut across again and again. Every opposition was rebutted in favour of another. Groups were divided and re-divided, both vertically and horizontally, until their lives, both spiritual and temporal, became an escutcheon in which symmetry and asymmetry were in equilibrium. . . .[2]

As a social individual, the ethnologist is on terms of intimacy with his culture and therefore finds it difficult to think objectively about the patterns governing his own thought; the more completely those patterns have been mastered and have become a part of his make-up—and therefore coextensive and consubstantial with his consciousness—the more impossible is it for him to apply conscious thought to them. He may also be reluctant to admit that, even though acquired through the systematically organized learning processes of the school, and therefore generally explicit and explicitly taught, the patterns which shape the thinking of educated men in 'school-going' societies may fulfil the same function as the unconscious patterns he discovers, by analysing such cultural creations as rites or myths, among individuals belonging to societies with no educational institutions, or as those 'primitive forms of classification' which are not, and cannot be, the subject of conscious awareness and explicit, methodical transmission. Do the patterns of thought and language transmitted by the school, e.g. those which treatises of rhetoric used to call figures of speech and figures of thought, actually fulfil, at any rate among members of the educated classes, the function of the unconscious patterns which govern the thinking and the productions of people belonging to traditional societies or do they, because of the conditions in which they are transmitted and acquired, operate only at the most superficial level of consciousness? If it be true that the specificity of societies possessing a scholarly, cumulative, accumulated culture lies, from the point of view that concerns us here, in the fact that they have special institutions to transmit, explicitly or implicitly, explicit or implicit forms of thought that operate at different levels of consciousness—from the most obvious which may be apprehended by culture, like the metaphors and parallels inspired by Greek or Roman history, play a part comparable in all respects with that which traditional societies allot to proverbs, sayings and gnomic poems. If it be accepted that culture and, in the case in point, scholarly or academic culture, is a common code enabling all those possessing that code to attach the same meaning to the same words, the same types of behaviour and the same works and, conversely, to express the same meaningful intention through the same words, the same behaviour patterns and the same works, it is clear that the school, which is responsible for handing on that culture, is the fundamental factor in the cultural consensus in as far as it represents the sharing of a common sense which is the prerequisite for communication. Individuals owe to their schooling, first and foremost, a whole collection of commonplaces, covering not only common speech and language but also areas of encounter and agreement, common problems and common methods of approaching those common problems: educated people of a given period may disagree on the questions they discuss but are at any rate in agreement about discussing certain questions. A thinker is linked to his period, and identified in space and time, primarily by the conditioning background of problem approach in which and by which he thinks. Just as linguists have recourse to the criterion of inter-comprehension for determining linguistic areas, so intellectual and cultural areas and generations could be determined by identifying the sets of dominant conditioning questions which define the cultural field of a period. To conclude in all cases, on the basis of the manifest divergences which separate the intellectuals of a given period on what are sometimes known as the 'major problems of the day', that there is a deficiency of logical integration would be to allow ourselves to be misled by appearances; disagreement presupposes agreement on the areas of disagreement, and the manifest conflicts between trends and doctrines conceal from the people concerned in those conflicts the implied basic concurrence which strikes the observer alien to the system. The consensus in dissensus, which constitutes the objective unity of the intellectual field of a given period, i.e. participation in the intellectual background of the day—which is not to be confused with submission to fashion—is rooted in the academic tradition. Authors having nothing else at all in common are yet contemporary in the accepted questions on which they are opposed and by reference to which at least one aspect of their thought is organized: like the fossils that enable us to date prehistoric eras, the subjects of discussion—crystallized remains of the great debates of the day—indicate, though probably with certain shifts in time, the questions which directed and governed the thinking of an age. We might, for instance, in the recent history of philosophic thought in France, distinguish a period of dissertation on judgement and concept, a period of dissertation on essence and existence (or fear and anxiety) and finally, a period of dissertation on language and speech (or nature and culture). A comparative study of the commonest subjects of academic essays or treatises and of lectures in different countries at different periods would make an important contribution to the sociology of knowledge by defining the necessary frame of problematic reasoning, which is one of the most fundamental dimensions of the intellectual programming of a society and a period. This was what Renan foreshadowed when he wrote:

Will it be believed that, at ceremonies similar to our prize-givings, when in our country oratory is essential, the Germans merely read out grammatical treatises of the most austere type, studded with Latin words? Can we conceive of formal public meetings taken up with readings of the following: On the nature of the conjunction; On the German period; On the Greek mathematicians; On the topography of the battle of Marathon; On the plain of Crissa; On the centuries of Servius Tullius; On the vines of Attica; Classification of prepositions; Clarification of difficult words in Homer; Commentary on the portrait of Thersites in Homer, etc.? This implies that our neighbours have a wonderful taste for serious things and perhaps, too, a certain capacity for facing up bravely to boredom when circumstances require.[3]

There may be coexisting in the thought of a given author, and *a fortiori* of a given period, elements which belong to quite different scholastic periods;[4] the cultural field is transformed by successive restructurations rather than by radical revolutions, with certain themes being brought to the fore while others are set to one side without being completely eliminated, so that continuity of communication between intellectual generations remains possible. In all cases, however, the patterns informing the thought of a given period can be fully understood only by reference to the school system, which is alone capable of establishing them and developing them, through practice, as the habits of thought common to a whole generation.

Culture is not merely a common code or even a common catalogue of answers to recurring problems; it is a common set of previously assimilated master patterns from which, by an 'art of invention' similar to that involved in the writing of music, an infinite number of individual patterns directly applicable to specific situations are generated. The *topoi* are not only commonplaces but also patterns of invention and supports for improvisation: these *topoi*—which include such particularly productive contrasting pairs as thought and action, essence and existence, continuity and discontinuity, etc.—provide bases and starting points for developments (mainly improvised), just as the rules of harmony and counterpoint sustain what seems to be the most inspired and the freest musical 'invention'. These patterns of invention may also serve to make up for deficiency of invention, in the usual sense of the term, so that the formalism and verbalism criticized by Lévi-Strauss are merely the pathological limit of the normal use of any method of thought. Mention may be made, in this context, of what Henri Wallon wrote about the function of thinking by pairs in children; 'contrasts of images or of speech result from such a natural and spontaneous association that they may sometimes override intuition and the sense of reality. They are part of the equipment constantly available to thought in the process of self-formulation and they may prevail over thinking. They come under the head of that "verbal knowledge" whose findings, already formulated, are often merely noted, without any exercise of reflective intelligence and whose workings often outlast those of thought in certain states of mental debilitation, confusion or distraction.'[5]

Verbal reflexes and thinking habits should serve to sustain thought but they may also, in moments of intellectual 'low tension', take the place of thought; they should help in mastering reality with the minimum effort, but they may also encourage those who rely on them not to bother to refer to reality. For every period, besides a collection of common themes, a particular constellation of dominant patterns could probably be determined, with as many epistemological profiles (taking this in a slightly different sense from that given to it by Gaston Bachelard) as there are schools of thought. It may be assumed that every individual owes to the type of schooling he has received a set of basic, deeply interiorized master-patterns on the basis of which he subsequently acquires other patterns, so that the system of patterns by which his thought is organized owes its specific character not only to the nature of the patterns constituting it but also to the frequency with which these are used and to the level of consciousness at which they operate, these properties being probably connected with the circumstances in which the most fundamental intellectual patterns were acquired.

The essential point is probably that the patterns which have become second nature are generally apprehended only through a reflective turning-back —which is always difficult—over the operations already carried out; it follows that they may govern and regulate mental processes without being consciously apprehended and controlled. It is primarily through the cultural unconscious which he owes to his intellectual training and, more particularly, to his scholastic training, that a thinker belongs to his society and age—schools of thought may, more often than is immediately apparent, represent the union of thinkers similarly schooled.

An exemplary confirmation of this hypothesis is to be found in the famous analysis by Erwin Panofsky of the relationship between Gothic art and Scholasticism. What the architects of the Gothic cathedrals unwittingly borrowed from the schoolmen was a *principium importans ordinem ad actum* or a *modus operandi*, i.e. a 'peculiar method of procedure which must have been the first thing to impress itself upon the mind of the layman whenever it came in touch with that of the schoolman'.[6] Thus, for example, the principle of clarification (*manifestatio*), a scheme of literary presentation discovered by Scholasticism, which requires the author to make plain and explicit (*manifestare*) the arrangement and logic of his argument—we should say his plan—also governs the action of the architect and the sculptor, as we can see by comparing the Last Judgement on the tympanum of Autun Cathedral with the treatment of the same theme at Paris and Amiens where, despite a greater wealth of motifs, consummate clarity also prevails through the effect of symmetry and correspondence.[7] If this is so, it is because the cathedral-builders were subject to the constant influence—to the habit-forming force—of Scholasticism, which, from about 1130–40 to about 1270, 'held a veritable monopoly of education' over an area of roughly 100 miles around Paris.

It is not very probable that the builders of Gothic structures read Gilbert de la Porrée or Thomas Aquinas in the original. But they were exposed to the Scholastic point of view in innumerable other ways, quite apart from the fact that their own work automatically brought them into a working association with those who devised the liturgical and iconographic programs. They had gone to school; they listened to sermons; they could attend the public *disputationes de quolibet* which, dealing as they did with all imaginable questions of the day, had developed into social events not unlike our operas, concerts or public lectures; and they could come into profitable contact with the learned on many other occasions.[8]

It follows, according to Panofsky, that the connection between Gothic art and Scholasticism is 'more concrete than a mere "parallelism" and yet more general than those individual (and very important) "influences" which are inevitably exerted on painters, sculptors or architects by erudite advisors'. This connection is 'a genuine cause-and-effect relation' which 'comes about by the spreading of what may be called, for want of a better term, a mental habit—reducing this overworked cliché to its precise Scholastic sense as "a principle that regulates the act", *principium importans ordinem ad actum*'.[9] As a habit-forming force, the school provides those who have been subjected directly or indirectly to its influence not so much with particular and particularized patterns of thought as with that general disposition, generating particular patterns that can be applied in different areas of thought and action, which may be termed cultured *habitus*.

Thus, in accounting for the structural homologies that he finds between such different areas of intellectual activity as architecture and philosophical thought, Erwin Panofsky does not rest content with references to a 'unitarian vision of the world' or a 'spirit of the times'—which would come down to naming what has to be explained or, worse still, to claiming to advance as an explanation the very thing that has to be explained; he suggests what seems to be the most naïve yet probably the most convincing explanation. This is that, in a society where the handing on of culture is monopolized by a school, the hidden affinities uniting the works of man (and, at the same time, modes of conduct and thought) derive from the institution of the school, whose function is consciously (and also, in part, unconsciously) to transmit the unconscious or, to be more precise, to produce individuals equipped with the system of unconscious (or deeply buried) master-patterns that constitute their culture. It would no doubt be an over-simplification to end our efforts at explanation at this point, as though the school were an empire within an empire, as though culture had there its absolute beginning; but it would be just as naïve to disregard the fact that, through the very logic of its functioning, the school modifies the content and the spirit of the culture it transmits and, above all, that its express function is to transform the collective heritage into a common individual unconscious. To relate the works of a period to the practices of the school therefore gives us a means of explaining not only what these works consciously set forth but also what they unconsciously reveal inasmuch as they partake of the symbolism of a period or of a society.

## SCHOOLS OF THOUGHT AND CLASS CULTURES

Apart from collective representations, such as the representation of man as the outcome of a long process of evolution, or the representation of the world as governed by necessary and immutable laws instead of by an arbitrary and capricious fate or by a providential will, every individual unconsciously brings to bear general tendencies such as those by which we recognize the 'style' of a period (whether it be the style of its architecture and furniture, or its style of life) and patterns of thought which organize reality by directing and organizing thinking about reality and make what he thinks thinkable for him as such and in the particular form in which it is thought. As Kurt Lewin remarks, 'Experiments dealing with memory and group pressure on the individual show that what exists as "reality" for the individual is, to a high degree, determined by what is socially accepted as reality. . . . "Reality" therefore, is not an absolute. It differs with the group to which the individual belongs.'[10] Similarly, what is a 'topical question' largely depends on what is socially considered as such; there is, at every period in every society, a hierarchy of legitimate objects for study, all the more compelling for there being no need to define it explicitly, since it is, as it were, lodged in the instruments of thought that individuals receive during their intellectual training. What is usually known as the Sapir–Whorf hypothesis is perhaps never so satisfactorily applicable as to intellectual life; words, and especially the figures of speech and figures of thought that are characteristic of a school of thought, mould thought as much as they express it. Linguistic and intellectual patterns are all the more important in determining what individuals take as worthy of being thought and what they think of it in that they operate outside all critical awareness. 'Thinking . . . follows a network of tracks laid down in the given language, an organization which may concentrate systematically upon certain phases of reality, certain aspects of intelligence, and may systematically discard others featured by other languages. The individual is utterly unaware of this organization and is constrained completely within its unbreakable bounds'.[11]

Academic language and thought effect this organization by giving prominence to certain aspects of reality thinking by 'schools' and types (designated by so many concepts ending in 'ism') which is a specific product of the school, makes it possible to organize things pertaining to the school, i.e. the universe of philosophical, literary, visual and musical works and, beyond or through them, the whole experience of reality and all reality. To use the terms of Greek tradition, the natural world becomes meaningful only when it has been subject to *diacrisis*—an act of separation introducing the 'limit' (*peras*) into indeterminate chaos (*apeiron*). The school provides the principle for such organization and teaches the art of effecting it. Basically, is taste anything other than the art of differentiating—differentiating between what is cooked and what is raw, what is insipid and what has savour, but also between the classical style and the baroque style or the major mode and the minor mode? Without this principle of separation and the art of applying it that the school teaches, the cultural world is merely an indeterminate, undifferentiated chaos; museum visitors not equipped with this basic stock of words and categories by which differences can be named and, thereby, apprehended—proper names of famous painters which serve as generic categories, concepts designating a school, an age, a 'period' or a style and rendering possible comparisons ('parallels') or contrasts —are condemned to the monotonous diversity of meaningless sensations. In the words of a workman from Dreux: 'When you don't know anything about it, it's difficult to get the hang of it. . . . Everything seems the same to me . . . beautiful pictures, beautiful paintings, but it's difficult to make out one thing from another.' And another workman, from Lille this time, comments: 'It's difficult for someone who wants to take an interest in it. All you can see are paintings and dates. To see the differences, you need a guide, otherwise everything looks the same.'[12] As the systems of typical pre-knowledge that individuals owe to the school grow richer (in other words, as the standard of education rises), familiarity with the organized universe of works becomes closer and more intense. The school does not merely provide reference marks: it also maps out itineraries, that is to say methods (in the etymological sense) or programmes of thought. The intellectual and linguistic master-patterns organize a marked-out area covered with compulsory turnings and one-way streets, avenues and blind alleys; within this area, thought can unfurl with the impression of freedom and improvisation because the marked-out itineraries that it is bound to follow are the very ones that it has covered many a time in the course of schooling. The order of exposition that the school imposes on the culture transmitted—which, most of the time, owes at least as much to school routines as to educational requirements—tends to gain acceptance, as being absolutely necessary, from those acquiring the culture through that order. By its orderly treatment of the works of culture the school hands on, at one and the same time, the rules establishing the orthodox manner of approaching works (according to their position in an established hierarchy) and the principles on which that hierarchy is founded. Because the order of acquisition tends to appear indissolubly associated with the culture acquired and because each individual's relationship with his culture bears the stamp of the conditions in which he acquired it, a self-taught man can be distinguished straightaway from a school-trained man. Having no established itineraries to rely on, the autodidact in Sartre's *La Nausée* sets about reading, in alphabetical order, every author possible. It is perhaps only in its decisive rigidity that this programme seems more arbitrary than the usual syllabus sanctioned by the school and based on a chronological order which, though apparently natural and inevitable, is in fact equally alien to considerations of logic and teaching; nevertheless, in the eyes of people who have gone through the ordered sequence of the *cursus*, a culture acquired by such a curious process would always contrast as sharply with an academic culture as a tangled forest with a formal garden.

Being responsible for instilling these principles of organization, the school must itself be organized to carry out this function. If it is to hand on this programme of thought known as culture, it must subject the culture it transmits to a process of programming that will make it easier to hand on methodically. Whenever literature becomes a school subject—as among the Sophists or in the Middle Ages—we find emerging the desire to classify, usually by genre and by author, and also to establish hierarchies, to pick out from the mass of works the 'classics' worthy of being preserved through the medium of the school. Collections of excerpts and textbooks are typical of such works designed to serve the school's allotted function of ordering and emphasizing. Having to prepare their pupils to answer academic questions, teachers tend to plan their teaching in accordance with the system of organization that their pupils will have to follow in answering those questions; in the extreme case, we have those prose composition manuals providing ready-made essays on particular subjects. In the organization of his teaching and sometimes of his whole work every teacher is obliged to make some concessions to the requirements of the educational system and of his own function. Georgias's *Encomium of Helen* is perhaps the first historic example of a demonstration of professorial skill combined with something like a 'crib'; and surely many of Alain's essays are but consummate examples of what French students in *rhétorique supérieure* (the classical upper sixth), whom he taught for the best part of his life, call *topos*, i.e. lectures or demonstrations closely tailored to the letter and spirit of the syllabus and meeting perfectly, in themes, sources, style and even spirit, the examination requirements for admission to the École Normale Supérieure. The programme of thought and action that it is the school's function to impart thus owes a substantial number of its practical characteristics to the institutional conditions in which it is transmitted and to specifically academic requirements. We therefore cannot hope fully to understand each 'school of thought', defined by its subjection to one or other of these programmes, unless we relate it to the specific logic governing the operation of the school from which it derives.

It follows that the gradual rationalization of a system of teaching geared more and more exclusively to preparation for an increasing variety of occupational activities could threaten the cultural integration of the educated class if, so far as that class is concerned, education, and more particularly what is known as general culture, were not at least as much a matter for the family as for the school, for the family in the sense of parents and their progeny and also in that of the fields of knowledge (many scientists are married to women with an arts background) and if all types of training did not allot a place, always a fairly important one, to classical, liberal education. The sharing of a common culture, whether this involves verbal patterns or artistic experience and objects of admiration, is probably one of the surest foundations of the deep underlying fellow-feeling that unites the members of the governing classes, despite differences of occupation and economic circumstances. It is understandable that T. S. Eliot should regard culture as the key instrument in the integration of the elite:

A society is in danger of disintegration when there is a lack of contact between people of different areas of activity—between the political, the scientific, the artistic, the philosophical and the religious minds. The separation cannot be repaired merely by public organization. It is not a question of assembling into committees representatives of different types of knowledge and experience, of calling in everybody to advise everybody else. The elite should be something different, something much more organically composed, than a panel of bonzes, caciques and tycoons. Men who meet only for definite serious purposes and on official occasions do not wholly meet. They may have some common concern very much at heart, they may, in the course of repeated contacts, come to share a vocabulary and an idiom which appear to communicate every shade of meaning necessary for their common purpose; but they will continue to retire from these encounters each to his private social world as well as to his solitary world. Everyone has observed that the possibilities of contented silence, of a mutual happy awareness when engaged upon a common task, or an underlying seriousness and significance in the enjoyment of a silly joke, are characteristics of any close personal intimacy; and the congeniality of any circle of friends depends upon a common social convention, a common ritual, and common pleasures of relaxation. These aids to intimacy are no less important for the communication of meaning in words than the possession of a common subject upon which the several parties are informed. It is unfortunate for a man when his friends and his business associates are two unrelated groups; it is also narrowing when they are one and the same group.[13]

Intimacy and fellow-feeling, congeniality, based on a common culture are rooted in the unconscious and give the traditional elites a social cohesion and continuity which would be lacking in elites united solely by links of professional interest: 'They will be united only by a part, and that the most conscious part, of their personalities; they will meet like committees.'[14] It would not be difficult to find, within the ruling class, social units based on the 'intimacy' created by the same intellectual 'programming'—affinities of schooling play an extremely important part once a body can be recruited by co-option.

Unlike the traditional type of education, setting out to hand on the integrated culture of an integrated society—all-round education producing people equipped for their various roles in society in general—specialized education, imparting specific types of knowledge and know-how, is liable to produce as many 'intellectual clans' as there are specialized schools. To take the most obvious and crudest example, the relations between arts people and science people are often governed, in present-day society, by the very laws to be seen in operation in the contacts between different cultures. Misunderstandings, borrowings removed from their context and reinterpreted, admiring imitation and disdainful aloofness—these are all signs familiar to specialists on the situations that arise when cultures meet. The debate between the upholders of literary humanism and the upholders of scientific or technological humanism is usually conducted in relation to ultimate values—efficiency or disinterestedness, specialization or general liberal education—just because each type of schooling naturally tends to be shut into an autonomous and self-sufficient world of its own; and because any action for the handing on of a culture necessarily implies an affirmation of the value of the culture imparted (and, correlatively, an implicit or explicit depreciation of other possible cultures); in other words, any type of teaching must, to a large extent, produce a need for its own product and therefore set up as a value, or value of values, the culture that it is concerned with imparting, achieving this in and through the very act of imparting it.[15] It follows that individuals whose education condemns them to a kind of cultural hemiplegia, while at the same time encouraging them to identify their own worth with the worth of their culture, are inclined to feel uneasy in their contacts with people with an alien and sometimes rival culture; this uneasiness may be reflected in a compensatory enthusiasm serving as a means of exorcism (we need only think, for example, of the fetishism and Shamanism to be seen among certain specialists in the sciences of man with regard to the formalization of their findings) as well as in rejection and scorn.

The primary causes of the opposition between 'intellectual clans', of which people in general are aware, are never all to be found in the content of the cultures transmitted and the mentality that goes with them. What distinguishes, for example, within the large 'arts' group, a graduate of the École Normale Supérieure from a graduate of the École Nationale de l'Administration or, within the 'science' group, a graduate of the École Polytechnique from a graduate of the École Centrale is perhaps, quite as much as the nature of the knowledge they have acquired, the way in which that knowledge has been acquired, i.e. the nature of the exercises they have had to do, of the examinations they have taken, the criteria by which they have been judged and by reference to which they have organized their studies. An individual's contact with his culture depends basically on the circumstances in which he has acquired it, among other things because the act whereby culture is communicated is, as such, the exemplary expression of a certain type of relation to the culture. The formal lecture, for instance, communicates something other, and something more, than its literal content: it furnishes an example of intellectual prowess and thereby indissolvably defines the 'right' culture and the 'right' relation to that culture; vigour and brilliance, ease and elegance are qualities of style peculiar to the act of communication which mark the culture communicated and gain acceptance at the same time as the culture from those receiving it in this form.[16] It could be shown in the same way how all teaching practices implicitly furnish a model of the 'right' mode of intellectual activity; for example, the very nature of the tests set (ranging from the composition, based on the technique of 'development', which is the predominant form in most arts examinations, to the 'brief account' required in advanced science examinations), the type of rhetorical and linguistic qualities required and the value attached to these qualities, the relative importance given to written papers and oral examinations and the qualities required in both instances, tend to encourage a certain attitude towards the use of language—sparing or prodigal, casual or ceremonious, complacent or restrained. In this way the canons governing school work proper, in composition or exposition, may continue to govern writings apparently freed from the disciplines of the school—newspaper articles, public lectures, summary reports and works of scholarship.

Taking it to be the fact that educated people owe their culture—i.e. a programme of perception, thought and action—to the school, we can see that, just as the differentiation of schooling threatens the cultural integration of the educated class, so the *de facto* segregation which tends to reserve secondary education (especially in the classics) and higher education almost exclusively to the economically and, above all, culturally most favoured classes, tends to create a cultural rift. The separation of those who, around the age of ten or eleven, embark on a school career that will last many years, from those who are shot straight into adult life, probably follows class divisions much more closely than in past centuries. Under the *ancien régime*, as Philippe Ariès points out, 'schooling habits differed not so much according to rank as according to function. Consequently, attitudes to life, like many other features of everyday life, differed not much more', notwithstanding 'the rigidly diversified social hierarchy'.[17] On the other hand, 'since the eighteenth century, the single school system has been replaced by a dual educational system, each branch of which is matched not to an age group but to a social class—the *lycée* or the *collège* (secondary schooling) for the middle classes and the elementary (or primary) school for the common people'.[18] Since then, the distinct quality of education has been matched by a duality of culture. 'The whole complexion of life', to quote Philippe Ariès again, 'has been changed by the difference in schooling given to middle-class children and working-class children.'[19] Culture, whose function it was if not to unify at least to make communication possible, takes on a differentiating function. 'It is not quite true', writes Edmond Goblot, 'that the bourgeoisie exists only in the practice of society and not in law. The *lycée* makes it a legal institution. The *baccalauréat* is the real barrier, the official, state-guaranteed barrier, which holds back the invasion. True, you may join the bourgeoisie, but first you have to get the *baccalauréat*.'[20] The 'liberal' culture of the humanist traditions with Latin its keystone, and the social 'signum' *par excellence*, constitutes the difference while at the same time giving it the semblance of legitimacy.

When, instead of thinking of his individual interests, he (a member of the bourgeoisie) thinks of his class interests, he needs a culture that marks out an élite, a culture that is not purely utilitarian, a luxury culture. Otherwise, he would fast become indistinguishable from the section of the working classes that manages to gain an education by sheer hard work and intelligence and goes on to lay siege to the professions. The educational background of a middle-class child who will not work, despite the educational resources of the *lycée*, will not bear comparison with that of a working-class child who studies hard with nothing but the resources of the senior primary school. Even when schooling leads nowhere professionally, therefore, it is still useful in maintaining the barrier.[21]

The school's function is not merely to sanction the *distinction*—in both senses of the word—of the educated classes. The culture that it imparts separates those receiving it from the rest of society by a whole series of systematic differences. Those whose 'culture' (in the ethnologists' sense) is the academic culture conveyed by the school have a system of categories of perception, language, thought and appreciation that sets them apart from those whose only training has been through their work and their social contacts with people of their own kind. Just as Basil Bernstein contrasts the 'public language' of the working classes, employing descriptive rather than analytical concepts, with a more complex 'formal language', more conducive to verbal elaboration and abstract thought, we might contrast an academic culture, confined to those who have been long subjected to the disciplines of the school, with a 'popular' culture, peculiar to those who have been excluded from it, were it not that, by using the same concept of culture in both cases, we should be in danger of concealing that these two systems of patterns of perception, language, thought, action and appreciation are separated by an essential difference. This is that only the system of patterns cultivated by the school, i.e. academic culture (in the subjective sense of personal cultivation, or *Bildung* in German), is organized primarily by reference to a system of works embodying that culture, by which it is both supported and expressed. To speak of 'popular' culture suggests that the system of patterns that makes up the culture (in the subjective sense) of the working classes could or should, in circumstances that are never specified, constitute a culture (in the objective sense) by being embodied in 'popular' works, giving the populace expression in accordance with the patterns of language and thought that define its culture (in the subjective sense). This amounts to asking the populace to take over the intention and means of expression of academic culture (as the prole- tarian writers do, whether of middle-class or working-class extraction) to express experience structured by the patterns of a culture (in the subjective sense) to which that intention and those means are essentially alien. It is then quite obvious that 'popular' culture is, by definition, deprived of the objectification, and indeed of the intention of objectification, by which academic culture is defined.

## SCHOOLING AND THE INTELLECTUAL MAKE-UP OF A NATION

Like a great many features by which 'schools of thought' and 'intellectual clans' in the same society may be recognized, many national characteristics of intellectual activity must be referred back to the traditions of educational systems which owe their specific character to national history and, more especially, to their specific history within that national history. In the absence of a comparative study of the specific history of different educational systems, a history of the intellectual patterns (or, to put it another way, of the patent and latent pro- grammes of thinking), that each school transmits implicitly or explicitly in every age (history of curricula, of teaching methods and of the ecological conditions in which teaching is carried out, of the types and subjects of exercises, of treatises of rhetoric and stylistics, etc.), we are obliged to make do with a partial treatment bearing on the French educational system alone. To account for such traits as the fondness for abstraction or the cult of brilliance and dis- tinguished performance that are commonly regarded as part of the 'intellectual make-up' of the French, we must surely relate them to the specific traditions of the French educational system. At the end of a study in which he shows the extent of the influence of Aristotle's thought on French seventeenth-century literature, Etienne Gilson concludes: 'Abstraction is, for Aristotle and the Schoolmen, the distinctive act of human thought and . . . if the essence of the classical spirit was the tendency to generalize and abstract the essence of things, it was perhaps because, for several centuries, young Frenchmen had been taught that the very essence of thought was to abstract and generalize.'[22] Similarly, instead of relating the professorial cult of verbal prowess to the national cult of artistic or military prowess, as J. R. Pitts does,[23] should we not rather look for the cause in teaching traditions? Ernest Renan does so:

The French educational system has patterned itself too closely on the Jesuits, with their dull eloquence and Latin verse; it is too reminiscent of the rhetoricians of the later Roman Empire. The weakness of the French, which is their urge to hold forth, their tendency to reduce everything to declamation, is encouraged by the persistence of the French educational system in overlooking the substance of knowledge and valuing only style and talent.[24]

Renan foreshadows what Durkheim was to say in his *Evolution Pédagogique en France*, where he sees in the 'pseudo-humanistic teaching' of the Jesuits and the 'literary-mindedness' that it encourages one of the basic ingredients of the French intellectual temperament.

Protestant France in the first half of the seventeenth century was in process of doing what Protestant Germany did in the second half of the eighteenth century. All over the country there was, as a result, an admirable movement of discussion and investigation. It was the age of Casaubon, Scaliger and Saumaise. The revocation of the Edict of Nantes destroyed all this. It killed studies in historical criticism in France. Since the literary approach alone was encouraged, a certain frivolity resulted. Holland and Germany, in part thanks to our exiles, acquired a near-monopoly of learning. It was decided from then on that France should be above all a nation of wits, of good writers, brilliant conversationalists, but inferior in knowledge of things and liable to all the blunders that can be avoided only by breadth of learning and maturity of judgement.[25]

And Renan, like Durkheim after him, notes that 'the system of French education created after the Revolution under the name of *université* in fact derives far more from the Jesuits than from the old universities',[26] as can be seen from its handling of literary material.

It (the university) uses a superabundance of classical material but without applying the literary spirit that would bring it to life; the ancient forms are in daily use, passing from hand to hand; but antiquity's sense of beauty is absolutely lacking . . .; never does the arid exercise of the intellect give place to a vital nourishment of the spiritual man. . . . All that is learnt is a remarkable skill in concealing from oneself and others that the dazzling shell of high-flown expression is empty of thought. A narrow, formalistic outlook is the characteristic feature of education in France.[27]

This is the very language used by Durkheim:

The tremendous advantage of a scientific education is that it forces man to come out of himself and brings him into touch with things; it thereby makes him aware of his dependence on the world about him. The 'arts' man or the pure humanist, on the other hand, never in his thinking comes up against anything resistant to which he can cling and with which he can feel at one: this opens wide the door to a more or less elegant dilettantism but leaves man to his own devices, without attaching him to any external reality, to any objective task.[28]

This literary teaching, based on the idea that human nature is 'eternal, immutable, independent of time and space, since it is unaffected by the diversity of circumstances and places', has, according to Durkheim, left its stamp on the intellectual temperament of the French, inspiring a 'constitutional cosmopolitanism', 'the habit of thinking of man in general terms' (of which 'the abstract individualism of the eighteenth century is an expression') and 'the inability to think in any other than abstract, general, simple terms'.[29]

Renan also points out how the institutional conditions in which teaching was given after the Revolution helped to strengthen the tendency towards literary showing-off.[30]

Twice a week, for an hour at a stretch, the professor had to appear before an audience made up at random and often changing completely from one lecture to the next. He had to speak without any regard for the special needs of the students, without finding out what they knew or did not know. . . . Long scientific deductions, necessitating following a whole chain of reasoning, had to be ruled out. . . . Laplace, if he had taught in such establishments, would certainly not have had more than a dozen students. Open to all, having become the scene of a kind of rivalry inspired by the aim of drawing and holding the public, what kind of lectures were therefore given? Brilliant expositions, 'recitations' in the manner of the declamators of the later Roman Empire. . . . A German visitor attending such lectures is astounded. He arrives from his university, where he has been accustomed to treat his professor with the greatest respect. This professor is a *Hofrat* and some days he sees the Prince! He is an earnest man whose utterances are all worth attention, and takes himself extremely seriously. Here, everything is different. The swing-door which, throughout the lecture, is forever opening and closing, the perpetual coming and going, the casualness of the students, the lecturer's tone, which is hardly ever didactic though sometimes declamatory, his knack for finding the sonorous commonplace which, bringing nothing new, is unfailingly greeted with acclaim by his audience—all this seems queer and outrageous.[31]

And we can only agree with Renan once more when, reviewing a book by a German observer, Ludwig Hahn,[32] he shows that such a procedure for selection as the competitive examination merely accentuates the weight and advantage given to qualities of form:

It is most regrettable that the competitive examination is the only means of qualifying for a teaching post in secondary schools, and that practical skill allied to sufficient knowledge is not accepted for this purpose. The men with the most experience of education, those who bring to their difficult duties not brilliant gifts, but a sound intellect combined with a little slowness and diffidence will always, in public examinations, come below the young men who can amuse their audience and their examiners but who, though very good at talking their way out of difficulties, have neither the patience nor the firmness to be good teachers.[33]

Renan finds everywhere signs of this tendency to prefer eloquence to truth, style to content.

The institution to which France has committed the recruitment of its secondary and university teachers, the École Normale, has, on the arts side, been a school of style, not a school where things are learnt. It has produced delightful journalistic writers, engaging novelists, subtle intellects in the most varied lines—in short, everything but men possessing a sound knowledge of languages and literatures. On the pretext of keeping to general truths concerning ethics and taste, minds have been confined to the commonplace.[34]

It is indeed in the traditions of the school, and in the attitude to scholastic matters that the school fosters, that the first cause of what Madame de Staël called 'le pédantisme de la légèreté' should be sought. To quote Renan again:

The word pedantry, which, if not clearly defined, can be so misapplied and which, to superficial minds, is more or less synonymous with any serious scholarly research, has thus become a bogey to sensitive and discriminating people, who have often preferred to remain superficial rather than to lay themselves open to this most dreaded charge. This scruple has been taken to such a point that extremely distinguished critics have been known deliberately to leave what they are saying incomplete rather than use a word smacking of the schools, even though it is the appropriate one. Scholastic jargon, when there is no thought behind it or when it is merely used, by people of limited intelligence, to show off, is pointless and ludicrous. But to seek to proscribe the precise, technical style which alone can express certain fine or deep shades of thought is to fall into an equally unreasonable purism. Kant and Hegel, or even minds as independent of the schools as Herder, Schiller and Goethe, would certainly not, at this rate, escape our terrible accusation of pedantry. Let us congratulate our neighbours on their freedom from these shackles, which would nevertheless, it must be said, be less harmful to them than to us. In their country, the school and learning touch; in ours, any higher education which, in manner, still smacks of the secondary school is adjudged bad form and intolerable; it is thought to be intelligent to set oneself above anything reminiscent of the classroom. Everyone plumes himself a little on this score and thinks, in so doing, to prove that he is long past the school-teaching stage.[35]

Because they always relate the 'intellectual make-up' of the French to the institutional conditions in which it is formed, Renan's and Durkheim's analyses represent a decisive contribution to the sociology of the intellectual make-up of a nation. Although the school is only one socializing institution among others, the whole complex of features forming the intellectual make-up of a society—or more exactly of the educated classes of that society—is constituted or reinforced by the educational system, which is deeply marked by its particular history and capable of moulding the minds of those who are taught and those who teach both through the content and spirit of the culture that it conveys and through the methods by which it conveys it. A good many of the differences dividing intellectual universes—differences in intellectual and linguistic patterns, like the techniques of composition and exposition, and more especially in the intellectual frame of reference (discernible, for example, through implicit or explicit, optional or inevitable quotations)—could be linked up with the academic traditions of the various nations and, more specifically, with the creative thinker's relationship with his national academic tradition, which depends, basically, on his educational background. Many of the distinguishing features of English 'positivism' or French 'rationalism' are surely nothing other than the tricks and mannerisms of the schools? Does not the ranking of intellectual activities (according to the degree of formalization, accessibility, abstraction and generality, or according to literary quality), which is implicitly and even explicitly conveyed and sanctioned by each scholastic tradition and finds concrete expression in the ranking of academic disciplines at any given point in time, govern intellectual productions just as much as the precepts of rhetoric inspired by the same values, which encourage or discourage, for instance, abstract treatment not based on examples, conceptual and syntactic esoterism, or stylistic elegance? Similarly, in each historical society, the ranking of questions worthy of interest determines a great many choices that are felt as 'vocations' and directs the keenest intellectual ambitions towards the subjects of study carrying most prestige. American sociologists regard the sociology of knowledge as 'a marginal speciality with a persistent European flavour'[36] because this branch of science is still dominated by an 'original constellation of problems', by a tradition perpetuated by education in Europe and still alive for European sociologists, who are more often inclined, because of their philosophical training, to state in sociological terms the traditional philosophical problem of the conditions in which objective knowledge is possible and the limits to such knowledge. The same logic should no doubt apply to many of the 'influences' that the historians of literature delight in detecting between authors, schools or periods, presupposing affinities at the level of thought patterns and problem approach and also, in some cases, a collective interest in groups or nations which are implicitly credited with legitimacy. The feeling of familiarity conveyed by certain works or certain intellectual themes, and conducive to their wide dissemination, is probably largely due to the fact that minds organized in accordance with the same programme have no difficulty in 'finding their bearings' with them. Would Heisenberg's Uncertainty Principle have had such a success in textbook literature if it had not landed, just at the right time, on a terrain already marked out between the determinism and the freedom of philosophy dissertations?[37]

Because we were all children before reaching man's estate, and for a long time were governed by our appetites and our tutors, often at variance with one another, neither, perhaps, always giving us the best of advice, it is almost impossible for our opinions to be as clear or as sound as they would have been had we had full use of our reason from the moment of our birth and had we never been guided by anything other than it.[38]

Descartes' utopia of innate culture, of natural culture, leads to the core of the contradiction defining the individual's relationship with his culture. As the light dove might imagine that it would fly better in a vacuum, the thinking individual likes to dream of thinking free from this unthought deposit that has formed within him, under the rod of his mentors, and which underlies all his thoughts.

'I received', says Husserl, 'the education of a German, not that of a Chinaman. But my education was also that of the inhabitant of a small town, with a home background, attending a school for children of the lower middle class, not that of a country landowner's son educated at a military college.[39] Like Descartes, Husserl invites his readers to think about the paradoxes of finitude. The individual who attains an immediate, concrete understanding of the familiar world, of the native atmosphere in which and for which he has been brought up, is thereby deprived of the possibility of appropriating immediately and fully the world that lies outside. Access to culture can never be more than access to one culture—that of a class and of a nation. No doubt someone born outside who wishes to understand the universe of the Chinese or of the Junker class can start his education again from scratch on the Chinese or Junker model ('for example by trying', as Husserl says, 'to learn the content of the curriculum of the military college'), but such mediate, knowing acquisition will always differ from an immediate familiarity with the native culture, in the same way as the interiorized, subconscious culture of the native differs from the objectified culture reconstructed by the ethnologist.

## NOTES

[1] C. Lévi-Strauss, *A World on the Wane*, London: Hutchinson, 1961, pp. 54–5.

[2] *Ibid.*, p. 230.

[3] E. Renan, *L'Avenir de la science*, Paris: Calmann Lévy, 1890, pp. 116–17.

[4] Because of its own inertia, the school carries along categories and patterns of thought belonging to different ages. In the observance of the rules of the dissertation in three points, for example, French schoolchildren are still contemporaries of St Thomas. The feeling of the 'unity of European culture' is probably due to the fact that the school brings together and reconciles—as it must for the purposes of teaching—types of thought belonging to very different periods.

[5] H. Wallon, *Les Origines de la pensée chez l'enfant*, Paris: Presses Universitaires de France, 1945, Vol. I, p. 63.

[6] E. Panofsky, *Gothic Architecture and Scholasticism*, New York, 1957, p. 28.

[7] *Ibid.*, p. 40.

[8] *Ibid.*, p. 23.

[9] *Ibid.*, pp. 20–1.

[10] K. Lewin, *Resolving Social Conflicts*, New York: Harper & Brothers, 1948, p. 57.

[11] B. L. Whorf, 'Language, Mind and Reality', in *Language, Thought and Reality*, p. 256.

[12] Cf. P. Bourdieu and A. Darbel, with D. Schnapper, *L'Amour de l'art, les musées et leur public*, Paris: Éditions de Minuit, 1966, pp. 69–76. (Coll. 'Le Sens commun'.)

[13] *Notes towards the Definition of Culture*, London: Faber & Faber, 1962, pp. 84–5.

[14] *Ibid.*, p. 47.

[15] As disparagement of the rival culture is the most convenient and surest means of magnifying the culture being imparted and of reassuring the person imparting it of his own worth, the temptation to resort to this means is all the greater in France because of the teachers' leaning towards charismatic instruction (which leads them to feel that subjects and teachers are on competitive teams), towards the charismatic ideology that goes with it, which encourages them to regard intellectual careers as personal vocations based upon 'gifts' so obviously mutually exclusive that possession of one rules out possession of the other: to proclaim that you are no good at science is one of the easiest ways of assuring others and yourself that you are gifted on the literary side.

[16] Although there is no necessary link between a given content and a given way of imparting it, people who have acquired them together tend to regard them as inseparable. Thus, some people regard any attempt to rationalize teaching as threatening to desacralize culture.

[17] P. Ariès, *L'Enfant et la vie familiale sous l'Ancien Régime*, Paris: Plon, 1960, p. 375.

[18] *Ibid.*

[19] *Ibid.*, p. 376.

[20] E. Goblot, *La Barrière et le niveau, étude sociologique sur la bourgeoisie française*, Alcan, 1930, p. 126.

[21] E. Goblot, *op. cit.*, pp. 125–6.

[22] E. Gilson, 'La Scolastique et l'esprit classique', in *Les Idées et les lettres*, Paris: Vrin, 1955, p. 257.

[23] J. R. Pitts, *A la recherche de la France*, Paris: Seuil, 1963, p. 273.

[24] E. Renan, *Questions contemporaines*, Paris: Calmann-Lévy, n.d., p. 79.

[25] E. Renan, *op. cit.*, p. 80.

[26] *Ibid.*, p. 81, No. 1.

[27] *Ibid.*, p. 277.

[28] E. Durkheim, *L'Évolution pédagogique en France*, Alcan, Vol. II, p. 55.

[29] *Ibid.*, II, pp. 128–32.

[30] By making the formal lecture the type of teaching with the highest prestige, the French system of education encourages works of a certain kind and intellectual qualities

of a certain kind, pre-eminent importance being attached to qualities of exposition. Consideration should be given to the question whether an institution such as the British lecture system is associated with other habits of thought and other values.

[31] E. Renan, *op. cit.*, pp. 90–1.

[32] L. Hahn, *Das Unterrichtwesen in Frankreich, mit einer Geschichte der Pariser Universität*, Breslau, 1848.

[33] E. Renan, 'L'Instruction publique en France jugée par les Allemands', *Questions Contemporaines*, Paris: Calmann-Lévy, n.d., p. 266. It would be easy to show how the values involved in the selection system govern the whole of intellectual life owing to the fact that, since, as they are deeply interiorized, they dominate the relationship of every creator with his work. This would explain, for example, the evolution of the thesis for the doctorate: individuals fashioned by a system requiring from each the unmatchable perfection that can give top place in competitive examinations are inclined to make steadily greater demands on themselves; thus, despite the ritual character of the actual ordeal of upholding the thesis, the authors of 'theses for the doctorate' set out, as it were, to outdo each other in intellectual ambition, erudition and lengthiness, devoting ten to fifteen years to producing their professional masterpiece.

[34] E. Renan, *op. cit.*, p. 94. It would be easy to show that there are affinities between the values directing educational activity and the values of the educated classes (cf. P. Bourdieu and J. C. Passeron, *Les Héritiers, les étudiants et la culture*, Paris: Éditions de Minuit, 1964).

[35] E. Renan, *L'Avenir de la science*, Paris: Calmann-Lévy, 1890, p. 116.

[36] 'The sociology of knowledge remained of peripheral concern among sociologists at large, who did not share the particular problems that troubled German thinking in the 1920s. This was especially true of American sociologists who have in the main looked upon the discipline as a marginal speciality with a persistent European flavour. More importantly, however, the continuing linkage of the sociology of knowledge with its original constellation of problems has been a theoretical weakness even where there has been an interest in the discipline' (P. L. Berger and Thomas Luckmann, *The Social Construction of Reality*, New York: Doubleday & Co., 1966, p. 4).

[37] However great the affinities, borrowings are always reinterpreted by reference to the structures into which they are incorporated, that is, in this instance, to the patterns of thought peculiar to each national tradition (we need only think, for example, of the changes undergone by Hegel's philosophy in France), even when, as in the case of the philosophical writings of phenomenological inspiration which flourished in France after 1945, the native forms of thought and indeed of language follow, even in their detail, the linguistic and verbal patterns of the imported philosophy, to such a point that they seem to be aping the laborious clumsiness of literal rather than literary translations.

[38] R. Descartes, *Discours de la méthode*, Part II.

[39] E. Husserl, A VII, 9, p. 15, quoted by R. Toulemont, *L'Essence de la société selon Husserl*, Paris: Presses Universitaires de France, 1962, p. 191.

# 8. ROBIN HORTON
*African Traditional Thought and Western Science*[*][1]

## I. FROM TRADITION TO SCIENCE

The first part of this paper seeks to develop an approach to traditional African thought already sketched in several previous contributions to this journal.[2] My approach to this topic is strongly influenced by the feeling that social anthropologists have often failed to understand traditional religious thought for two main reasons. First, many of them have been unfamiliar with the theoretical thinking of their own culture. This has deprived them of a vital key to understanding. For certain aspects of such thinking are the counterparts of those very features of traditional thought which they have tended to find most puzzling. Secondly, even those familiar with theoretical thinking in their own culture have failed to recognize its African equivalents, simply because they have been blinded by a difference of idiom. Like Consul Hutchinson wandering among the Bubis of Fernando Po, they have taken a language very remote from their own to be no language at all.

My approach is also guided by the conviction that an exhaustive exploration of features common to modern Western and traditional African thought should come before the enumeration of differences. By taking things in this order, we shall be less likely to mistake differences of idiom for differences of substance, and more likely to end up identifying those features which really do distinguish one kind of thought from the other.

Not surprisingly, perhaps, this approach has frequently been misunderstood. Several critics have objected that it tends to blur the undeniable distinction between traditional and scientific thinking; that indeed it presents traditional thinking as a species of science.[3] In order to clear up such misunderstandings, I propose to devote the second part of this paper to enumerating what I take to be the salient differences between traditional and scientific think-

* This paper first appeared in *Africa*, Vol. XXXVII, 1967.

ing and to suggesting a tentative explanation of these differences. I shall also explore how far this explanation can help us to understand the emergence of science in Western culture.

In consonance with this programme, I shall start by setting out a number of general propositions on the nature and functions of theoretical thinking. These propositions are derived, in the first instance, from my own training in biology, chemistry, and philosophy of science. But, as I shall show, they are highly relevant to traditional African religious thinking. Indeed, they make sense of just those features of such thinking that anthropologists have often found most incomprehensible.

1.) *The quest for explanatory theory is basically the quest for unity underlying apparent diversity; for simplicity underlying apparent complexity; for order underlying apparent disorder; for regularity underlying apparent anomaly*

Typically, this quest involves the elaboration of a scheme of entities or forces operating 'behind' or 'within' the world of commonsense observations. These entities must be of a limited number of kinds and their behaviour must be governed by a limited number of general principles. Such a theoretical scheme is linked to the world of everyday experience by statements identifying happenings within it with happenings in the everyday world. In the language of philosophy of science, such identification statements are known as correspondence rules. Explanations of observed happenings are generated from statements about the behaviour of entities in the theoretical scheme, plus correspondence-rule statements. In the sciences, well-known explanatory theories of this kind include the kinetic theory of gases, the planetary-atom theory of matter, the wave theory of light, and the cell theory of living organisms.

One of the perennial philosophical puzzles posed by explanations in terms of such theories derives from the correspondence-rule statements. In what sense can we really say that an increase of pressure in a gas 'is' an increase in the velocity of a myriad of tiny particles moving in an otherwise empty space? How can we say that a thing is at once itself and something quite different? A great variety of solutions has been proposed to this puzzle. The modern positivists have taken the view that it is the things of common sense that are real, while the 'things' of theory are mere fictions useful in ordering the world of common sense. Locke, Planck and others have taken the line that it is the 'things' of theory that are real, while the things of the everyday world are mere appearances. Perhaps the most up-to-date line is that there are good reasons for conceding the reality both of commonsense things and of theoretical entities. Taking this line implies an admission that the 'is' of correspondence-rule statements is neither the 'is' of identity nor the 'is' of class-membership. Rather, it stands for a unity-in-duality uniquely characteristic of the relation between the world of common sense and the world of theory.

What has all this got to do with the gods and spirits of traditional African religious thinking? Not very much, it may appear at first glance. Indeed, some modern writers deny that traditional religious thinking is in any serious sense theoretical thinking. In support of their denial they contrast the simplicity, regularity and elegance of the theoretical schemas of the sciences with the unruly complexity and caprice of the world of gods and spirits.[4]

But this antithesis does not really accord with modern field-work data. It is true that, in a very superficial sense, African cosmologies tend towards proliferation. From the point of view of sheer number, the spirits of some cosmologies are virtually countless. But in this superficial sense we can point to the same tendency in Western cosmology, which for every commonsense unitary object gives us a myriad of molecules. If, however, we recognize that the aim of theory is the demonstration of a limited number of *kinds* of entity or process underlying the diversity of experience, then the picture becomes very different. Indeed, one of the lessons of such recent studies of African cosmologies as Middleton's *Lugbara Religion*, Lienhardt's *Divinity and Experience*, Fortes's *Oedipus and Job* and my own articles on Kalabari, is precisely that the gods of a given culture do form a scheme which interprets the vast diversity of everyday experience in terms of the action of a relatively few *kinds* of forces. Thus in Middleton's book, we see how all the various oppositions and conflicts in Lugbara experience are interpreted as so many manifestations of the single underlying opposition between ancestors and *adro* spirits. Again, in my own work, I have shown how nearly everything that happens in Kalabari life can be interpreted in terms of a scheme which postulates three basic *kinds* of forces: ancestors, heroes and water-spirits.

The same body of modern work gives the lie to the old stereotype of the gods as capricious and irregular in their behaviour. For it shows that each category of beings has its appointed functions in relation to the world of observable happenings. The gods may sometimes appear capricious to the unreflective ordinary man. But for the religious expert charged with the diagnosis of spiritual agencies at work behind observed events, a basic modicum of regularity in their behaviour is the major premise on which his work depends. Like atoms, molecules and waves, then, the gods serve to introduce unity into diversity, simplicity into complexity, order into disorder, regularity into anomaly.

Once we have grasped that this is their intellectual function, many of the puzzles formerly posed by 'mystical thinking' disappear. Take the exasperated, wondering puzzlements of Levy-Bruhl over his 'primitive mentality'. How could primitives believe that a visible, tangible object was at once its solid self and the manifestation of an immaterial being? How could a man literally see a spirit in a stone? These puzzles, raised so vividly by Levy-Bruhl, have never been satisfactorily solved by anthropologists. 'Mystical thinking' has remained uncomfortably, indigestibly *sui generis*. And yet these questions of Levy-Bruhl's have a very familiar ring in the context of European philosophy. Indeed, if we substitute atoms and molecules for gods and spirits, these turn out to be the very questions cited a few paragraphs back—questions posed by modern scientific theory in the minds of Berkeley, Locke, Quine and a whole host of European philosophers from Newton's time onwards.

Why is it that anthropologists have been unable to see this? One reason, as I suggested before, is that many of them move only in the commonsense world of Western culture, and are unfamiliar with its various theoretical worlds. But perhaps familiarity with Western theoretical thinking is not by itself enough. For a thoroughly unfamiliar idiom can still blind a man to a familiar form of thought. Because it prevents one from taking anything for granted, an unfamiliar idiom can help to show up all sorts of puzzles and problems inherent in an intellectual process which normally seems puzzle-free. But this very unfamiliarity can equally prevent us from seeing that the puzzles and problems are ones which crop up on our own doorstep. Thus it took a 'mystical' theorist like Bishop Berkeley to see the problems posed by the materialistic theories of Newton and his successors; but he was never able to see that the same problems were raised by his own theoretical framework. Again, it takes materialistically inclined modern social anthropologists to see the problems posed by the 'mystical' theories of traditional Africa; but, for the same reasons, such people can hardly be brought to see these very problems arising within their own theoretical framework.

2.) *Theory places things in a causal context wider than that provided by common sense*

When we say that theory displays the order and regularity underlying apparent disorder and irregularity, one of the things we mean is that it provides a causal context for apparently 'wild' events. Putting things in a causal context is, of course, one of the jobs of common sense. But although it does this job well at a certain level, it seems to have limitations. Thus the principal tool of common sense is induction or 'putting two and two together', the process of inference so beloved of the positivist philosophers. But a man can only 'put two and two together' if he is looking in the right direction. And common sense furnishes him with a pair of horse-blinkers which severely limits the directions in which he can look. Thus commonsense thought looks for the antecedents of any happening amongst events adjacent in space and time: it abhors action at a distance. Again, common sense looks for the antecedents of a happening amongst events that are in some way commensurable with it. Common sense is at the root of the hard-dying dictum 'like cause, like effect'. Gross incommensurability defeats it.

Now one of the essential functions of theory is to help the mind transcend these limitations. And one of the most obvious achievements of modern scientific theory is its revelation of a whole array of causal connections which are quite staggering to the eye of common sense. Think for instance of the connection between two lumps of a rather ordinary-looking metal, rushing towards each other with a certain acceleration, and a vast explosion capable of destroying thousands of people. Or think again of the connection between small, innocuous water-snails and the disease of bilharziasis which can render whole populations lazy and inept.

Once again, we may ask what relevance all this has to traditional African religious thinking. And once again the stock answer may be 'precious little'. For a widely current view of such thinking still asserts that it is more interested in the supernatural causes of things than it is in their natural causes. This is a misinterpretation closely connected with the one we discussed in the previous section. Perhaps the best way to get rid of it is to consider the commonest case of the search for causes in traditional Africa—the diagnosis of disease. Through the length and breadth of the African continent, sick or afflicted people go to consult diviners as to the causes of their troubles. Usually, the answer they receive involves a god or other spiritual agency, and the remedy prescribed involves the propitiation or calling-off of this being. But this is very seldom the whole story. For the diviner who diagnoses the intervention of a spiritual agency is also expected to give some acceptable account of what moved the agency in question to intervene. And this account very commonly involves reference to some event in the world of visible, tangible happenings. Thus if a diviner diagnoses the action of witchcraft influence or lethal medicine spirits, it is usual for him to add something about the human hatreds, jealousies and misdeeds that have brought such agencies into play. Or, if he diagnoses the wrath of an ancestor, it is usual for him to point to the human breach of kinship morality which has called down this wrath.

Although I do not think he has realized its full significance for the study of traditional religious thought, Victor Turner has brought out this point beautifully in his analyses of divination and the diagnosis of disease amongst the Ndembu people of Central Africa.[5] Turner shows how, in diagnosing the causes of some bodily affliction, the Ndembu diviner not only refers to unseen spiritual forces, but also relates the patient's condition to a whole series of disturbances in his social field. Turner refers to divination as 'social analysis', and says that Ndembu believe a patient 'will not get better until all the tensions and aggressions in the group's interrelations have been brought to light and exposed to ritual treatment'. Although Turner himself does not refer to comparable material from other African societies, Max Gluckman, drawing on data from Tiv, Lugbara, Nyakyusa, Yao and several other traditional societies, has recently shown that the kind of analysis he has made of divination among the Ndembu is very widely applicable.[6] The point in all this is that the traditional diviner faced with a disease does not just refer to a spiritual agency. He uses ideas about this agency to link disease to causes in the world of visible, tangible events.

The situation here is not very different from that in which a puzzled American layman, seeing a large mushroom cloud on the horizon, consults a friend who happens to be a physicist. On the one hand, the physicist may refer him to theoretical entities. 'Why this cloud?' 'Well, a massive fusion of hydrogen nuclei has just taken place.' Pushed further, however, the physicist is likely to refer to the assemblage and dropping of a bomb containing certain special substances. Substitute 'disease' for 'mushroom cloud', 'spirit anger' for 'massive fusion of hydrogen nuclei', and 'breach of kinship morality' for 'assemblage and dropping of a bomb', and we are back again with the diviner. In both cases reference to theoretical entities is used to link events in the visible, tangible world (natural effects) to their antecedents in the same world (natural causes).

To say of the traditional African thinker that he is interested in supernatural rather than natural causes makes little more sense, therefore, than to say of the physicist that he is interested in nuclear rather than natural causes. In fact, both are making the same use of theory to transcend the limited vision of natural causes provided by common sense.

Granted this common preoccupation with natural causes, the fact remains that the causal link between disturbed social relations and disease or misfortune, so frequently postulated by traditional religious thought, is one which seems somewhat strange and alien to many Western medical scientists. Following the normal practice of historians of Western ideas, we can approach the problem of trying to understand this strange causal notion from two angles. First of all, we can enquire what influence a particular theoretical idiom has in moulding this and similar traditional notions. Secondly, we can enquire whether the range of experience available to members of traditional societies has influenced causal notions by throwing particular conjunctions of events into special prominence.

Theory, as I have said, places events in a wider causal context than that provided by common sense. But once a particular theoretical idiom has been adopted, it tends to direct people's attention towards certain kinds of causal linkage and away from others. Now most traditional African cultures have adopted a personal idiom as the basis of their attempt to understand the world. And once one has adopted such an idiom, it is a natural step to suppose that personal beings underpin, amongst other things, the life and strength of social groups. Now it is in the nature of a personal being who has his designs thwarted to visit retribution on those who thwart him. Where the designs involve maintaining the strength and unity of a social group, members of the group who disturb this unity are thwarters, and hence are ripe for punishment. Disease and misfortune are the punishment. Once a personal idiom has been adopted, then, those who use it become heavily predisposed towards seeing a nexus between social disturbance and individual affliction.

Are these traditional notions of cause merely artefacts of the prevailing theoretical idiom, fantasies with no basis in reality? Or are they responses to features of people's experience which in some sense are 'really there'? My own feeling is that, although these notions are ones to which people are predisposed by the prevailing theoretical idiom, they also register certain important features of the objective situation.

Let us remind ourselves at this point that modern medical men, though long blinded to such things by the fantastic success of the germ theory of disease, are once more beginning to toy with the idea that disturbances in a person's social life can in fact contribute to a whole series of sicknesses, ranging from those commonly thought of as mental to many more commonly thought of as bodily. In making this rediscovery, however, the medical men have tended to associate it with the so-called 'pressures of modern living'. They have tended to imagine traditional societies as psychological paradises in which disease-producing mental stresses are at a minimum. And although this view has never been put to adequate test, it is one held by many doctors practising in Africa.

In criticism of this view, I would suggest that the social life of the small relatively self-contained and undifferentiated communities typical of much of traditional Africa contains its own peculiar and powerful sources of mental stress. Let me recall a few:

*a*.) When tension arises between people engaged in a particular activity, it tends to colour a large sector of their total social life. For in societies of this kind a person performs a whole series of activities with the same set of partners.

*b*.) Being caught up in hostilities or caught out in a serious breach of social norms is particularly crushing, since in societies of this kind it is often extremely hard to move out of the field in which the trouble arose.

*c*.) There are a limited number of roles to be filled, and little scope for personal choice in the filling of them. Hence there is always a relatively large number of social misfits.

Apart from these sources of stress peculiar to such communities, there are others commonly thought to be absent from them, but which they in fact share with modern industrial societies. I am thinking here of fundamental inconsistencies in the values taught to members of traditional communities. Thus aggressive, thrusting ambition may be inculcated on one hand, and a cautious reluctance to rise above one's neighbour on the other. Ruthless individualism may be inculcated on one hand, and acceptance of one's ascribed place in a lineage-system on the other. Such inconsistencies are often as sharp as those so well known in modern industrial societies. As an anthropological field-worker, one has come close enough to these sources of stress to suspect that the much-advertised 'pressures of modern living' may at times be the milder affliction. One may even suspect that some of the young Africans currently rushing from the country to the towns are in fact escaping from a more oppressive to a less oppressive psychological environment.

The point I am trying to make here is that if life in modern industrial society contains sources of mental stress adequate to causing or exacerbating a wide range of sicknesses, so too does life in traditional village communities. Hence the need to approach traditional religious theories of the social causation of sickness with respect. Such respect and readiness to learn is, I suggest, particularly appropriate with regard to what is commonly known as mental disease. I say this because the grand theories of Western psychiatry have a notoriously insecure empirical base and are probably culture-bound to a high degree.

Then again, there are the traditional social-cause explanations of all those mysterious bodily ailments doctors try in vain to cure in their hospitals, and which finally get cleared up by traditional religious healers. Though we have no statistics on such cases, there is little doubt that they are always cropping up. Judging from a recent symposium on traditional medicine[7] even unromantic, hard-headed social anthropologists are now generally convinced of their reality.

Accounts of cases of this kind suggest that they very often fall into the category which Western medical practitioners themselves have increasingly come to label psychosomatic—i.e. marked by definite bodily changes but touched off or exacerbated by mental stress. This category includes gastric and duodenal ulcer, migraine, chronic limb pains, and certain kinds of paralysis, hypertension, diabetes and dermatitis. It includes many agonizing and several potentially lethal complaints. Forward-looking Western medical men now agree that effective treatment of this kind of illness will eventually have to include some sort of diagnosis of and attempt to combat stress-producing disturbances in the individual's social life. As for trying to find out what the main kinds of stress-producing disturbances are in a particular traditional society, the modern doctor can probably do no better than start by taking note of the diagnoses produced by a traditional religious healer working in such a society.

Finally, there are those diseases in which the key factor is definitely an infecting micro-organism. Even here, I suggest, traditional religious theory has something to say which is worth listening to.

Over much of traditional Africa, let me repeat, we are dealing with small-scale, relatively self-contained communities. These are the sort of social units that, as my friend Dr Oruwariye puts it, 'have achieved equilibrium with their diseases'. A given population and a given set of diseases have been co-existing over many generations. Natural selection has played a considerable part in developing human resistance to diseases such as malaria, typhoid, smallpox, dysentery, etc. In addition, those who survive the very high peri-natal mortality have probably acquired an extra resistance by the very fact of having lived through one of these diseases just after birth. In such circumstances, an adult who catches one of these (for Europeans) killer diseases has good chances both of life and of death. In the absence of antimalarials or antibiotics, what happens to him will depend very largely on other factors that add to or subtract from his considerable natural resistance. In these circumstances the traditional healer's efforts to cope with the situation by ferreting out and attempting to remedy stress-producing disturbances in the patient's social field is probably very relevant. Such efforts may seem to have a ludicrously marginal importance to a hospital doctor wielding a nivaquine bottle and treating a non-resistant European malaria patient. But they may be crucial where there is no nivaquine bottle and a considerable natural resistance to malaria.

After reflecting on these things the modern doctor may well take some of these traditional causal notions seriously enough to put them to the test. If the difficulties of testing can be overcome, and if the notions pass the test, he will end up by taking them over into his own body of beliefs. At the same time, however, he will be likely to reject the theoretical framework that enabled the traditional mind to form these notions in the first place.

This is fair enough; for although, as I have shown, the gods and spirits do perform an important theoretical job in pointing to certain interesting forms of causal connection, they are probably not very useful as the basis of a wider view of the world. Nevertheless, there do seem to be a few cases in which the theoretical framework of which they are the basis may have something to contribute to the theoretical framework of modern medicine. To take an example, there are several points at which Western psychoanalytic theory, with its apparatus of personalized mental entities, resembles traditional West African religious theory. More specifically, as I have suggested elsewhere,[8] there are striking resemblances between psychoanalytic ideas about the individual mind as a congeries of warring entities, and West African ideas about the body as a meeting place of multiple souls. In both systems of belief, one personal entity is identified with the stream of consciousness, whilst the others operate as an 'unconscious', sometimes co-operating with consciousness and sometimes at war with it. Now the more flexible psychoanalysts have long suspected that Freud's allocation of particular desires and fears to particular agencies of the mind may well be appropriate to certain cultures only. Thus his allocation of a great load of sexual desires and fears to the unconscious may well have been appropriate to the Viennese subculture he so largely dealt with; but it may not be appropriate to many other cultures. A study of West African soul theories, and of their allocation of particular desires and emotions to particular agencies of the mind, may well help the psychoanalyst to reformulate his theories in terms more appropriate to the local scene.

Earlier, I said that modern Western medical scientists had long been distracted from noting the causal connection between social disturbance and disease by the success of the germ theory. It would seem, indeed, that a conjunction of the germ theory, of the discovery of potent antibiotics and immunization techniques, and of conditions militating against the build-up of natural resistance to many killer infections, for long made it very difficult for scientists to see the importance of this connection. Conversely, perhaps, a conjunction of no germ theory, no potent antibiotics, no immunization techniques, with conditions favouring the build-up of considerable natural resistance to killer infections, served to throw this same causal connection into relief in the mind of the traditional healer. If one were asked to choose between germ theory innocent of psychosomatic insight and traditional psychosomatic theory innocent of ideas about infection, one would almost certainly choose the germ theory. For in terms of quantitative results it is clearly the more vital to human well-being. But it is salutary to remember that not all the profits are on one side.

From what has been said in this section, it should be clear that one commonly accepted way of contrasting traditional religious thought with scientific thought is misleading. I am thinking here of the contrast between traditional religious thought as 'non-empirical' with scientific thought as 'empirical'. In the first place, the contrast is misleading because traditional religious thought is no more nor less interested in the natural causes of things than is the theoretical thought of the sciences. Indeed, the intellectual function of its supernatural beings (as, too, that of atoms, waves, etc.) *is* the extension of people's vision of natural causes. In the second place, the contrast is misleading because traditional religious theory clearly does more than postulate causal connections that bear no relation to experience. Some of the connections it postulates are, by the standards of modern medical science, almost certainly real ones. To some extent, then, it successfully grasps reality.

At this point, I must hasten to reassure the type of critic I referred to earlier that I am not claiming traditional thought as a variety of scientific thought. I grant that, in certain crucial respects, the two kinds of thought are related to experience in quite different ways, and I shall consider these differences in Part II of this paper. Meanwhile, I want to point out that it is not only where scientific method is in use that we find theories which both aim at grasping causal connections and to some extent succeed in this aim. Scientific method is undoubtedly the surest and most efficient tool for arriving at beliefs that are successful in this respect; but it is not the only way of arriving at such beliefs. Given the basic process of theory-making, and an environmental stability which gives theory plenty of time to adjust to experience, a people's belief system may come, even in the absence of scientific method, to grasp at least some significant causal connections which lie beyond the range of common sense. It is because traditional African religious beliefs demonstrate the truth of this that it seems apt to extend to them the label 'empirical'.

All this does not mean that we can dispense with the term 'non-empirical'. The latter remains a very useful label for certain other kinds of religious thinking which contrast sharply with that of traditional Africa in their lack of interest in explaining the features of the space–time world. Here I am thinking in particular of the kind of modern Western Christianity which coexists, albeit a little uneasily, with scientific thought. I shall be saying more about this kind of religious thinking in Part II.

### 3.) *Common sense and theory have complementary roles in everyday life*

In the history of European thought there has often been opposition to a new theory on the ground that it threatens to break up and destroy the old, familiar world of common sense. Such was the eighteenth-century opposition to Newtonian corpuscular theory, which, so many people thought, was all set to 'reduce' the warm, colourful beautiful world to a lifeless, colourless, wilderness of rapidly-moving little balls. Not surprisingly, this eighteenth-century attack was led by people like Goethe and Blake—poets whose job was precisely to celebrate the glories of the world of common sense. Such, again, is the twentieth-century opposition to behaviour theory, which many people see as a threat to 'reduce' human beings to animals or even to machines. Much of the most recent Western philosophy is a monotonous and poorly reasoned attempt to bludgeon us into believing that behaviour theory cannot possibly work. But just as the commonsense world of things and people remained remarkably unscathed by the Newtonian revolution, so there is reason to think it will not be too seriously touched by the behaviour-theory revolution. Indeed, a lesson of the history of European thought is that, while theories come and theories go the world of common sense remains very little changed.

One reason for this is perhaps that all theories take their departure from the world of things and people, and ultimately return us to it. In this context, to say that a good theory 'reduces' something to something else is misleading. Ideally, a process of deduction from the premises of a theory should lead us back to statements which portray the commonsense world in its full richness. In so far as this richness is not restored, by so much does theory fail. Another reason for the persistence of the world of common sense is probably that, within the limits discussed in the last section, commonsense thinking is handier and more economical than theoretical thinking. It is only when one needs to transcend the limited causal vision of common sense that one resorts to theory.

Take the example of an industrial chemist and his relationships with common salt. When he uses it in the house, his relationships with it are governed entirely by common sense. Involving chemical theory to guide him in its domestic use would be like bringing up a pile-driver to hammer in a nail. Such theory may well lend no more colour to the chemist's domestic view of salt than it lends to the chemically uneducated rustic's view of the substance. When he uses it in his chemical factory, however, common sense no longer suffices. The things he wants to do with it force him to place it in a wider causal context than common sense provides; and he can only do this by viewing it in the light of atomic theory. At this point, someone may ask: 'And which does he think is the real salt; the salt of common sense or the salt of theory?' The answer, perhaps, is that both are equally real to him. For whatever the philosophers say, people develop a sense of reality about something to the extent that they use and act on language which implies that this something exists.

This discussion of common sense and theory in Western thought is very relevant to the understanding of traditional African religions. Early accounts of such religions stressed the ever-presence of the spirit world in the minds of men. As Evans-Pritchard has noted, this stress was inevitable where the authors in question were concerned to titillate the imagination of the European reader with the bizarre.[9] Unfortunately, however, such accounts were seized upon by serious sociologists and philosophers like Levy-Bruhl, who used them to build up a picture of primitive man continuously obsessed by things religious. Later on, field-work experience in African societies convinced most reporters that members of such societies attended to the spirit world rather intermittently.[10] And many modern criticisms of Levy-Bruhl and other early theorists hinge on this observation. For the modern generation of social anthropologists, the big question has now become: 'On what kinds of occasion do people ignore the spirit world, and on what kinds of occasion do they attend to it?'

A variety of answers has been given to this question. One is that people think in terms of the spirit world when they are confronted with the unusual or uncanny. Another is that they think this way in the face of anxiety-provoking situations. Another is that they think this way in the face of *any* emotionally charged situation. Yet another is that they think this way in certain types of crisis which threaten the fabric of society. Of all of these answers, the most one can say is: 'sometimes yes, sometimes no'. All of them, furthermore, leave the 'jump' from common sense to religious thinking fundamentally mysterious.

One wants to ask: 'Even if this jump does occur in a certain type of situation, why should the latter require specifically *religious* thinking?' A better answer, I think, is one that relates this jump to the essentially theoretical character of traditional religious thinking. And here is where our discussion of common sense and theory in European thought becomes relevant.

I suggest that in traditional Africa relations between common sense and theory are essentially the same as they are in Europe. That is, common sense is the handier and more economical tool for coping with a wide range of circumstances in everyday life. Nevertheless, there are certain circumstances that can only be coped with in terms of a wider causal vision than common sense provides. And in these circumstances there is a jump to theoretical thinking.

Let me give an example drawn from my own field-work among the Kalabari people of the Niger Delta. Kalabari recognize many different kinds of diseases, and have an array of herbal specifics with which to treat them. Sometimes a sick person will be treated by ordinary members of his family who recognize the disease and know the specifics. Sometimes the treatment will be carried out on the instructions of a native doctor. When sickness and treatment follow these lines the atmosphere is basically commonsensical. Often, there is little or no reference to spiritual agencies.

Sometimes, however, the sickness does not respond to treatment, and it becomes evident that the herbal specific used does not provide the whole answer. The native doctor may rediagnose and try another specific. But if this produces no result the suspicion will arise that 'there is something else in this sickness'. In other words, the perspective provided by common sense is too limited. It is at this stage that a diviner is likely to be called in (it may be the native doctor who started the treatment). Using ideas about various spiritual agencies, he will relate the sickness to a wider range of circumstances—often to disturbances in the sick man's general social life.

Again, a person may have a sickness which, though mild, occurs together with an obvious crisis in his field of social relations. This conjunction suggests at the outset that it may not be appropriate to look at the illness from the limited perspective of common sense. And in such circumstances, the expert called in is likely to refer at once to certain spiritual agencies in terms of which he links the sickness to a wider context of events.

What we are describing here is generally referred to as a jump from common sense to mystical thinking. But, as we have seen, it is also, more significantly, a jump from common sense to theory. And here, as in Europe, the jump occurs at the point where the limited causal vision of common sense curtails its usefulness in dealing with the situation on hand.

## 4.) *Level of theory varies with context*

A person seeking to place some event in a wider causal context often has a choice of theories. Like the initial choice between common sense and theory, this choice too will depend on just how wide a context he wishes to bring into consideration. Where he is content to place the event in a relatively modest context, he will be content to use what is generally called a low-level theory—i.e. one that covers a relatively limited area of experience. Where he is more ambitious about context, he will make use of a higher-level theory—i.e. one that covers a larger area of experience. As the area covered by the lower-level theory is part of the area covered by the higher level scheme, so too the entities postulated by the lower-level theory are seen as special manifestations of those postulated at the higher level. Hence they pose all the old problems of things which are at once themselves and at the same time manifestations of other quite different things.

For an example of how this matter of levels works out in modern Western thought, let us go back to our manufacturing chemist and his salt. Suppose the chemist to be in the employ of a very under-developed country which has extensive deposits of salt and can supply a limited range of other simple chemicals, but which has no electricity. The government asks him to estimate what range of chemical products he can 'get out of' the salt, given the limited resources they can make available to him. Here the limited range of means implies a limited causal context and the appropriateness of a correspondingly low level of theory. In working out what he can do with his salt deposits under these straitened circumstances, the chemist may well be content to use the low-level, 'ball-and-bond' version of atomic theory, whose basic entities are homogeneous spheres linked by girder-like bonds. This level of theory will enable him to say that, with the aid of a few simple auxiliaries like chalk and ammonia, he can derive from his salt such important substances as washing soda and caustic soda.

Now suppose that after some time the chemist is told to assume that an electric power supply will be at his disposal. This additional element in the situation promises a wider range of possibilities. It also implies that salt is to be placed in a wider causal context. Hence a theory of wider coverage and higher level must be brought into play. Our chemist will now almost certainly make his calculations in terms of a more-embracing version of the atomic theory—one which covers electrical as well as strictly chemical phenomena. In this theory the homogeneous atoms of the lower-level schema are replaced by planetary configurations of charged fundamental particles. The atoms of the lower-level theory now become mere manifestations of systems of particles postulated by the higher-level theory. For philosophical puzzle-makers, the old teaser of things that are at once themselves and manifestations of something else is with us again. But the puzzle becomes less acute when we see it as an inevitable by-product of the way theories are used in the process of explanation.

Once again, we find parallels to all this in many traditional African religious systems. It is typical of such systems that they include, on the one hand, ideas about a multiplicity of spirits, and on the other hand, ideas about a single supreme being. Though the spirits are thought of as independent beings, they are also considered as so many manifestations or dependants of the supreme being. This conjunction of the many and the one has given rise to much discussion among students of comparative religion, and has evoked many ingenious theories. Most of these have boggled at the idea that polytheism and monotheism could coexist stably in a single system of thought. They have therefore tried to resolve the problem by supposing that the belief-systems in question are in transition from one type to the other. It is only recently, with the Nilotic studies of Evans-Pritchard and Lienhardt,[11] that the discussion has got anywhere near the point—which is that the many spirits and the one God play complementary roles in people's thinking. As Evans-Pritchard says: 'A theistic religion need be neither monotheistic nor polytheistic. It may be both. It is the question of the level, or situation, of thought, rather than of exclusive types of thought.'[12]

On the basis of material from the Nilotic peoples, and on that of material from such West African societies as Kalabari, Ibo and Tallensi,[13] one can make a tentative suggestion about the respective roles of the many and the one in traditional African thought generally. In such thought, I suggest, the spirits provide the means of setting an event within a relatively limited causal context. They are the basis of a theoretical scheme which typically covers the thinker's own community and immediate environment. The supreme being, on the other hand, provides the means of setting an event within the widest possible context. For it is the basis of a theory of the origin and life course of the world seen as a whole.

In many (though by no means all) traditional African belief-systems, ideas about the spirits and actions based on such ideas are far more richly developed than ideas about the supreme being and actions based on them. In these cases, the idea of God seems more the pointer to a potential theory than the core of a seriously operative one. This perhaps is because social life in the communities involved is so parochial that their members seldom have to place events in the wider context that the idea of the supreme being purports to deal with. Nevertheless, the different levels of thinking are there in all these systems. And from what we have said, it seems clear that they are related to one another in much the same way as are the different levels of theoretical thinking in the sciences. At this point the relation between the many spirits and the one God loses much of its aura of mystery. Indeed there turns out to be nothing peculiarly religious or 'mystical' about it. For it is essentially the same as the relation between homogeneous atoms and planetary systems of fundamental particles in the thinking of our chemist. Like the latter, it is a by-product of certain very general features of the way theories are used in explanation.

5.) *All theory breaks up the unitary objects of common sense into aspects, then places the resulting elements in a wider causal context. That is, it first abstracts and analyses, then reintegrates*

Numerous commentators on scientific method have familiarized us with the way in which the theoretical schemas of the sciences break up the world of commonsense things in order to achieve a causal understanding which surpasses that of common sense. But it is only from the more recent studies of African cosmologies, where religious beliefs are shown in the context of the various everyday contingencies they are invoked to explain, that we have begun to see how traditional religious thought also operates by a similar process of abstraction, analysis and reintegration. A good example is provided by Forte's recent work on West African theories of the individual and his relation to society. Old-fashioned West African ethnographers like Talbot long ago showed the wide distribution of beliefs in what they called 'multiple souls'. They found that many West African belief-systems invested the individual with a multiplicity of spiritual agencies, and they baptized these agencies with fanciful names such as 'spirit double', 'bush soul', 'shadow soul' and 'over soul'. The general impression they gave was one of an unruly fantasy at work. In his recent book,[14] however, Fortes takes the 'multiple soul' beliefs of a single West African people (the Tallensi) and places them in the context of everyday thought and behaviour. His exposition dispels much of the aura of fantasy.

Fortes describes three categories of spiritual agency especially concerned with the Tale individual. First come the *segr*, which presides over the individual as a biological entity—over his sickness and health, his life and death. Then comes the *nuor yin*, a personification of the wishes expressed by the individual before his arrival on earth. The *nuor yin* appears specifically concerned with whether or not the individual has the personality traits necessary if he is to become an adequate member of Tale society. As Fortes puts it, evil *nuor yin* 'serves to identify the fact of irremediable failure in the development of the individual to full social capacity'. Good *nuor yin*, on the other hand, 'identifies the fact of successful individual development along the road to full incorporation in society'. Finally, in this trio of spiritual agencies, we have what Fortes calls the '*yin* ancestors'. These are two or three out of the individual's total heritage of ancestors, who have been delegated to preside over his personal fortunes. *Yin* ancestors only attach themselves to an individual who has a good *nuor yin*. They are concerned with the fortunes of the person who has already proved himself to have the basic equipment for fitting into Tale society. Here we have a theoretical scheme which, in order to produce a deeper understanding of the varying fortunes of individuals in their society, breaks them down into three aspects by a simple but typical operation of abstraction and analysis.

Perhaps the most significant comment on Fortes's work in this field was pronounced, albeit involuntarily, by a reviewer of 'Oedipus and Job'[15] 'If any criticism of the presentation is to be made it is that Professor Fortes sometimes seems to achieve an almost mystical identification with the Tallensi world-view and leaves the unassimilated reader in some doubt about where to draw the line between Tallensi notions and Cambridge concepts!' Now the anthropologist has to find *some* concepts in his own language roughly appropriate to translating the 'notions' of the people he studies. And in the case in question, perhaps only the lofty analytic 'Cambridge' concepts did come anywhere near to congruence with Tallensi notions. This parallel between traditional religious 'notions' and Western sociological 'abstractions' is by no means an isolated phenomenon. Think for instance of individual guardian spirits and group spirits—two very general categories of traditional African religious thought. Then think of those hardy Parsonian abstractions—psychological imperatives and sociological imperatives. It takes no great brilliance to see the resemblance.[16]

One can of course argue that in comparing traditional African thought with modern Western sociological thought, one is comparing it with a branch of Western thought that has attained only a low degree of abstraction. One can go on to argue that traditional African thought does not approach the degree of abstraction shown, say, by modern nuclear physics. Such comparisons of degrees of abstraction are, I think, trickier than they seem at first glance. In any case, they cannot affect the validity of the point already made, which is that abstraction is as essential to the operation of traditional African religious theory as it is to that of modern Western theory, whether sociological or physical.

6.) *In evolving a theoretical scheme, the human mind seems constrained to draw inspiration from analogy between the puzzling observations to be explained and certain already familiar phenomena*

In the genesis of a typical theory, the drawing of an analogy between the unfamiliar and the familiar is followed by the making of a model in which something akin to the familiar is postulated as the reality underlying the unfamiliar. Both modern Western and traditional African thought-products amply demonstrate the truth of this. Whether we look amongst atoms, electrons and waves, or amongst gods, spirits and entelechies, we find that theoretical notions nearly always have their roots in relatively homely everyday experiences, in analogies with the familiar.

What do we mean here by 'familiar phenomena'? Above all, I suggest, we mean phenomena strongly associated in the mind of the observer with order and regularity. That theory should depend on analogy with things familiar in this sense follows from the very nature of explanation. Since the overriding aim of explanation is to disclose order and regularity underlying apparent chaos, the search for explanatory analogies must tend towards those areas of experience most closely associated with such qualities. Here, I think, we have a basis for indicating why explanations in modern Western culture tend to be couched in an impersonal idiom, while explanations in traditional African society tend to be couched in a personal idiom. The reader may see the point most readily if I introduce a little personal reminiscence. The idea that people can be much more difficult to cope with than things is one that has never been far from my own mind. I can recall long periods of my own boyhood when I felt at home and at ease, not with friends, relatives and parents round the fire, but shut up alone for hours with bunsen burners and racks of reagents in a chemistry laboratory. Potassium hydroxide and nitric acid were my friends; sodium phosphate and calcium chloride my brothers and sisters. In later life I have been fortunate enough to break through many times into a feeling of at-homeness with people. But such break-throughs have always been things to wonder at; never things to be taken for granted. My joy in people is all the more intense for being a joy in something precarious. And in the background there is always the world of things beckoning seductively towards the path of escape from people. English colleagues may shrug their shoulders and say I am a freak in this. But if they are honest with themselves, they will admit I am saying things which strike echoes in all their hearts. Nor do I have to depend on their honesty in this; for the image of the man happier with things than with people is common enough in modern Western literature to show that what I am talking about here is the sickness of the times.

Not long ago I was having a discussion with a class of Nigerian students, all of whom, I suppose, still had strong roots in traditional community life. We were discussing some of the characteristic ways in which life in Western industrial cities differed from life in traditional village communities. When I came to touch on some of the things I have just been saying, I felt that I had really 'gone away from them'. What I was saying about a life in which things might seem a welcome haven from people was just so totally foreign to their experience that they could not begin to take it in. They just stared. Rarely have I felt more of an alien than in that discussion.

Now the point I wish to make is this. In complex, rapidly-changing industrial societies the human scene is in flux. Order, regularity, predictability, simplicity, all these seem lamentably absent. It is in the world of inanimate things that such qualities are most readily seen. This is why many people can find themselves less at home with their fellow men than with things. And this too, I suggest, is why the mind in quest of explanatory analogies turns most readily to the inanimate. In the traditional societies of Africa, we find the situation reversed. The human scene is the locus *par excellence* of order, predictability, regularity. In the world of the inanimate, these qualities are far less evident. Here, being less at home with people than with things is unimaginable. And here, the mind in quest of explanatory analogies turns naturally to people and their relations.

7.) *Where theory is founded on analogy between puzzling observations and familiar phenomena, it is generally only a limited aspect of such phenomena that is incorporated into the resulting model*

When a thinker draws an analogy between certain puzzling observations and other more familiar phenomena, the analogy seldom involves more than a limited aspect of such phenomena. And it is only this limited aspect which is taken over and used to build up the theoretical schema. Other aspects are ignored; for, from the point of view of explanatory function, they are irrelevant.

Philosophers of science have often used the molecular (kinetic) theory of gases as an illustration of this feature of model-building. The molecular theory, of course, is based on an analogy with the behaviour of fast-moving, spherical balls in various kinds of space. And the philosophers have pointed out that although many important properties of such balls have been incorporated into the definition of a molecule, other important properties such as colour and temperature have been omitted. They have been omitted because they have no explanatory function in relation to the observations that originally evoked the theory. Here, of course, we have another sense in which physical theory is based upon abstraction and abstract ideas. For concepts such as 'molecule', 'atom', 'electron', 'wave' are the result of a process in which the relevant features of certain prototype phenomena have been abstracted from the irrelevant features.

Many writers have considered this sort of abstraction to be one of the distinctive features of scientific thinking. But this, like so many other such distinctions, is a false one; for just the same process is at work in traditional African thought. Thus when traditional thought draws upon people and their social relations as the raw material of its theoretical models, it makes use of some dimensions of human life and neglects others. The definition of a god may omit any reference to his physical appearance, his diet, his mode of lodging, his children, his relations with his wives, and so on. Asking questions about such attributes is as inappropriate as asking questions about the colour of a molecule or the temperature of an electron. It is this omission of many dimensions of human life from the definition of the gods which give them that rarefied, attenuated aura which we call 'spiritual'. But there is nothing peculiarly religious, mystical or traditional about this 'spirituality'. It is the result of the same process of abstraction as the one we see at work in Western theoretical models: the process whereby features of the prototype phenomena which have explanatory relevance are incorporated into a theoretical schema, while features which lack such relevance are omitted.

8.) *A theoretical model, once built, is developed in ways which sometimes obscure the analogy on which it was founded*

In its raw, initial state, a model may come up quite quickly against data for which it cannot provide any explanatory coverage. Rather than scrap it out of hand, however, its users will tend to give it successive modifications in order to enlarge its coverage. Sometimes, such modifications will involve the drawing of further analogies with phenomena rather different from those which provided the initial inspiration for the model. Sometimes, they will merely involve 'tinkering' with the model until it comes to fit the new observations. By comparison with the phenomena which provided its original inspiration, such a developed model not unnaturally seems to have a bizarre, hybrid air about it.

Examples of the development of theoretical models abound in the history of science. One of the best documented of these is provided by the modern atomic theory of matter. The foundations of this theory were laid by Rutherford, who based his original model upon an analogy between the passage of ray-beams through metal foil and the passage of comets through our planetary system. Rutherford's planetary model of the basic constituents of matter proved extremely useful in explanation. When it came up against recalcitrant data, therefore, the consensus of scientists was in favour of developing it rather than scrapping it. First of the consequent modifications was the introduction of the possibility that the 'planets' might make sudden changes of orbit, and in so doing emit or absorb energy. Then came the substitution, at the centre of the planetary system, of a heterogeneous cluster of bodies for a single 'sun'. Later still came the idea that, at a particular moment, a given 'planet' had a somewhat ambiguous position. Finally, along with this last idea, came a modification inspired by the drawing of a fresh analogy. This was the introduction of the idea that, in some contexts, the 'planets' were to be considered as bundles of waves. Each of these modifications was a response to the demand for increased explanatory coverage. Each, however, removed the theoretical model one step further away from the familiar phenomena which had furnished its original inspiration.

In studying traditional African thought, alas, we scarcely ever have the historical depth available to the student of European thought. So we can make few direct observations on the development of its theoretical models. Nevertheless, these models often show just the same kinds of bizarre hybrid features as the models of the scientists. Since they resemble the latter in so many other ways, it seems reasonable to suppose that these features are the result of a similar process of development in response to demands for further explanatory coverage. The validity of such a supposition is strengthened when we consider detailed instances: for these show how the bizarre features of particular models are indeed closely related to the nature of the observations that demand explanation.

Let me draw one example from my own field-work on Kalabari religious thought which I have outlined in earlier publications. Basic Kalabari religious beliefs involve three main categories of spirits: ancestors, heroes and water-people. On the one hand, all three categories of spirits show many familiar features: emotions of pleasure and anger, friendships, enmities, marriages. Such features betray the fact that, up to a point, the spirits are fashioned in the image of ordinary Kalabari people. Beyond this point, however, they are bizarre in many ways. The ancestors, perhaps, remain closest to the image of ordinary people. But the heroes are decidedly odd. They are defined as having left no descendants, as having disappeared rather than died, and as having come in the first instance from outside the community. The water-spirits are still odder. They are said to be 'like men, and also like pythons'. To make sense of these oddities, let us start by sketching the relations of the various kinds of spirits to the world of everyday experience.

First, the ancestors. These are postulated as the forces underpinning the life and strength of the lineages, bringing misfortune to those who betray lineage values and fortune to those who promote them. Second, the heroes. These are the forces underpinning the life and strength of the community and its various institutions. They are also the forces underpinning human skill and maintaining its efficacy in the struggle against nature. Third, the water-spirits. On the one hand, these are the 'owners' of the creeks and swamps, the guardians of the fish harvest, the forces of nature. On the other hand, they are the patrons of human individualism—in both its creative and its destructive forms. In short, they are the forces underpinning all that lies beyond the confines of the established social order.

We can look on ancestors, heroes and water-spirits as the members of a triangle of forces. In this triangle, the relation of each member to the other two contains elements of separation and opposition as well as of co-operation. Thus by supporting lineages in rivalry against one another, the ancestors can work against the heroes in sapping the strength of the community; but in other contexts, by strengthening their several lineages, they can work with the heroes in contributing to village strength. Again, when they bring up storms, rough water, and sharks, the water-spirits work against the heroes by hampering the exercise of the village's productive skills; but when they produce calm water and an abundance of fish, they work just as powerfully with the heroes. Yet again, by fostering anti-social activity, the water-spirits can work against both heroes and ancestors; or, by supporting creativity and invention, they can enrich village life and so work with them.

In this triangle, then, we have a theoretical scheme in terms of which Kalabari can grasp and comprehend most of the many vicissitudes of their daily lives. Now it is at this point that the bizarre, paradoxical attributes of heroes and water-spirits begin to make sense: for a little inspection shows that such attributes serve to define each category of spirits in a way appropriate to its place in the total scheme. This is true, for example, of such attributes of the heroes as having left no human descendants, having disappeared instead of undergoing death and burial, and having come from outside the community. All these serve effectively to define the heroes as forces quite separate from the ancestors with their kinship involvements. Lack of descendants does this in an obvious way. Disappearance rather than death and burial performs the same function, especially when, as in Kalabari, lack of burial is almost synonymous with lack of kin. And arrival from outside the community again makes it clear that they cannot be placed in any lineage or kinship context. These attributes, in short, are integral to the definition of the heroes as forces contrasted with and potentially opposed to the ancestors. Again, the water-spirits are said to be 'like men, and also like pythons'; and here too the paradoxical characterization is essential to defining their place in the triangle. The python is regarded as the most powerful of all the animals in the creeks, and is often said to be their father. But its power is seen as something very different from that of human beings—something 'fearful' and 'astonishing'. The combination of human and python elements in the characterization of the water-people fits the latter perfectly for their own place in the triangle—as forces of the extra-social contrasted with and potentially opposed to both heroes and ancestors.

Another illuminating example of the theoretical significance of oddity is provided by Middleton's account of traditional Lugbara religious concepts.[17] According to Middleton, Lugbara belief features two main categories of spiritual agency—the ancestors and the *adro* spirits. Like the Kalabari ancestors, those of the Lugbara remain close to the image of ordinary people. The *adro*, however, are very odd indeed. They are cannibalistic and incestuous, and almost every-thing else that Lugbara ordinarily consider repulsive. They are commonly said to walk upside down—a graphic expression of their general perversity. Once again, these oddities fall into place when we look at the relations of the two categories of spirits to the world of experience. The ancestors, on the one hand, account for the settled world of human habitation and with the established social order organized on the basis of small lineages. The *adro*, on the other hand, are concerned with the uncultivated bush, and with all human activities which run counter to the established order of things. Like the Kalabari water-spirits, they are forces of the extra-social, whether in its natural or its human form. The contrast and opposition between ancestors and *adro* thus provides Lugbara with a theoretical schema in terms of which they can comprehend a whole series of oppositions and conflicts manifest in the world of their everyday experiences. Like the oddities of the Kalabari gods, those of the *adro* begin to make sense at this point. For it is the bizarre, perverse features of these spirits that serve to define their position in the theory—as forces contrasted with and opposed to the ancestors.

In both of these cases the demands of explanation result in a model whose structure is hybrid between that of the human social phenomena which provided its original inspiration, and that of the field of experience to which it is applied. In both cases, oddity is essential to explanatory function. Even in the absence of more direct historical evidence, these examples suggest that the theoretical models of traditional African thought are the products of developmental processes comparable to those affecting the models of the sciences.

Some philosophers have objected to the statement that explanatory models are founded on analogy between the puzzling and the familiar, saying that the features of typical models in the sciences rather suggest that in them the relatively familiar is explained in terms of the relatively unfamiliar. They point to the abstract character of theoretical entities, contrasting this with the familiar concreteness of the world of everyday things. They point to the bizarre features of such entities, so far removed from anything found in the everyday world. These very objections, however, merely confirm the validity of the view they aim to criticize. For what makes theoretical entities seem abstract to us is precisely that they have taken over some key features from particular areas of everyday experience, while rejecting other features as irrelevant to their purposes. Again, what makes theoretical entities seem bizarre to us is precisely these features drawn from areas of familiar experience. The presence of some such features leads us to expect others. But the processes of abstraction and development produce results that clear these expectations: hence our sense of the odd.

In treating traditional African religious systems as theoretical models akin to those of the sciences, I have really done little more than take them at their face value. Although this approach may seem naïve and platitudinous compared to the sophisticated 'things-are-never-what-they-seem' attitude more characteristic of the social anthropologist, it has certainly produced some surprising results. Above all, it has cast doubt on most of the well-worn dichotomies used to conceptualize the difference between scientific and traditional religious thought. Intellectual versus emotional; rational versus mystical; reality-oriented versus fantasy-oriented; causally oriented versus supernaturally oriented; empirical versus non-empirical; abstract versus concrete; analytical versus non-analytical: all of these are shown to be more or less inappropriate. If the reader is disturbed by this casting away of established distinctions, he will, I hope, accept it when he sees how far it can pave the way towards making sense of so much that previously appeared senseless.

One thing that may well continue to bother the reader is my playing down of the difference between non-personal and personal theory. For while I have provided what seems to me an adequate explanation of this difference, I have treated it as a surface difference concealing an underlying similarity of intellectual process. I must confess that I have used brevity of treatment here as a device to play down the gulf between the two kinds of theory. But I think this is amply justifiable in reaction to the more usual state of affairs, in which the difference is allowed to dominate all other features of the situation. Even familiarity with theoretical thinking in their own culture cannot help anthropologists who are dominated by this difference. For once so blinded, they can only see traditional religious thought as wholly other. With the bridge from their own thought-patterns to those of traditional Africa blocked, it is little wonder they can make no further headway.[18]

The aim of my exposition has been to reopen this bridge. The point I have sought to make is that the difference between non-personal and personalized theories is more than anything else a difference in the idiom of the explanatory quest. Grasping this point is an essential preliminary to realizing how far the various established dichotomies used in this field are simply obstacles to understanding. Once it is grasped, a whole series of seemingly bizarre and senseless features of traditional thinking becomes immediately comprehensible. Until it is grasped, they remain essentially mysterious. Making the business of personal versus impersonal entities the crux of the difference between tradition and science not only blocks the understanding of tradition. It also draws a red herring across the path to an understanding of science. This becomes obvious from a look at history. So far as we know, an extensive depersonalization of theory has happened spontaneously only twice in the history of human thought. Once in Europe and once in China. In Europe this depersonalization was accompanied by a growth of science, in China it was not.[19] Again, where depersonalization *has* been accompanied by the growth of science, the two have often parted company very readily. Thus in Western lay culture we have a largely depersonalized view of the world which is at the same time totally unscientific.[20] And in many of the developing countries, for which science appears as a panacea, it seems likely that the depersonalized world of the West may get through without the scientific spirit.[21] Yet again, in the recent history of Western psychology, we find both personalized (psychoanalytic) and non-personalized (behaviouristic) theories. And for each category there are those who handle the theories scientifically and those who do not.

All this is not to deny that science has progressed greatly through working in a non-personal theoretical idiom. Indeed, as one who has hankerings after behaviourism, I am inclined to believe that it is this idiom, and this idiom only, which will eventually lead to the triumph of science in the sphere of human affairs. What I am saying, however, is that this is more a reflection of the nature of reality than a clue to the essence of scientific method. For the progressive acquisition of knowledge, man needs both the right kind of theories *and* the right attitude to them. But it is only the latter which we call science. Indeed, as we shall see, any attempt to define science in terms of a particular kind of theory runs contrary to its very essence. Now, at last, I hope it will be evident why, in comparing African traditional thought with Western scientific thought, I have chosen to start with a review of continuities rather than with a statement of crucial differences. For although this order of procedure carries the risk of one's being understood to mean that traditional thought is a kind of science, it also carries the advantage of having the path clear of red herrings when one comes to tackle the question of differences.

## II. THE 'CLOSED' AND 'OPEN' PREDICAMENTS

In Part I of this paper, I pushed as far as it would go the thesis that important continuities link the religious thinking of traditional Africa and the theoretical thinking of the modern West. I showed how this view helps us to make sense of many otherwise puzzling features of traditional religious thinking. I also showed how it helps us to avoid certain rather troublesome red herrings which lie across the path towards understanding the crucial differences between the traditional and the scientific outlook.

In Part II, I shall concentrate on these differences. I shall start by isolating one which strikes me as the key to all the others, and will then go on to suggest how the latter flow from it.

What I take to be the key difference is a very simple one. It is that in traditional cultures there is no developed awareness of alternatives to the established body of theoretical tenets; whereas in scientifically oriented cultures, such an awareness is highly developed. It is this difference we refer to when we say that traditional cultures are 'closed' and scientifically oriented cultures 'open'.[22]

One important consequence of the lack of alternatives is very clearly spelled out by Evans-Pritchard in his pioneering work on Azande witchcraft beliefs. Thus he says:

I have attempted to show how rhythm, mode of utterance, content of prophecies, and so forth, assist in creating faith in witch-doctors, but these are only some of the ways in which faith is supported, and do not entirely explain belief. Weight of tradition alone can do that. . . . There is no incentive to agnosticism. All their beliefs hang together, and were a Zande to give up faith in witch-doctorhood, he would have to surrender equally his faith in witchcraft and oracles. . . . In this web of belief every strand depends upon every other strand, *and a Zande cannot get out of its meshes because it is the only world he knows. The web is not an external structure in which he is enclosed. It is the texture of his thought and he cannot think that his thought is wrong.*[23]

And again:

And yet Azande do not see that their oracles tell them nothing! Their blindness is not due to stupidity, for they display great ingenuity in explaining away the failures and inequalities of the poison oracle and experimental keenness in testing it. It is due rather to the fact that their intellectual ingenuity and experimental keenness are conditioned by patterns of ritual behaviour and mystical belief. Within the limits set by these patterns, they show great intelligence, but it cannot operate beyond these limits. Or, to put it in another way; *they reason excellently in the idiom of their beliefs, but they cannot reason outside, or against their beliefs because they have no other idiom in which to express their thoughts.*[24]

Yet again, writing more generally of 'closed' societies in a recent book, he says:

Everyone has the same sort of religious beliefs and practices, and their generality, or collectivity, gives them an objectivity which places them over and above the psychological experience of any individual, or indeed of all individuals. . . . *Apart from positive and negative sanctions, the mere fact that religion is general means, again in a closed society, that it is obligatory, for even if there is no coercion, a man has no option but to accept what everybody gives assent to, because he has no choice, any more than of what language he speaks. Even were he to be a sceptic, he could express his doubts only in terms of the beliefs held by all around him.*[25]

In other words, absence of any awareness of alternatives makes for an absolute acceptance of the established theoretical tenets, and removes any possibility of questioning them. In these circumstances, the established tenets invest the believer with a compelling force. It is this force which we refer to when we talk of such tenets as sacred.

A second important consequence of lack of awareness of alternatives is vividly illustrated by the reaction of an Ijo man to a missionary who told him to throw away his old gods. He said: 'Does your God really want us to climb to the top of a tall palm tree, then take off our hands and let ourselves fall?' Where the established tenets have an absolute and exclusive validity for those who hold them, any challenge to them is a threat of chaos, of the cosmic abyss, and therefore evokes intense anxiety.

With developing awareness of alternatives, the established theoretical tenets come to seem less absolute in their validity, and lose something of their sacredness. At the same time, a challenge to these tenets is no longer a horrific threat of chaos. For just as the tenets themselves have lost some of their absolute validity, a challenge to them is no longer a threat of absolute calamity. It can now be seen as nothing more threatening than an intimation that new tenets might profitably be tried. Where these conditions begin to prevail, the stage is set for change from a traditional to a scientific outlook.

Here, then, we have two basic predicaments: the 'closed'—characterized by lack of awareness of alternatives, sacredness of beliefs, and anxiety about threats to them; and the 'open'—characterized by awareness of alternatives, diminished sacredness of beliefs, and diminished anxiety about threats to them.

Now, as I have said, I believe all the major differences between traditional and scientific outlooks can be understood in terms of these two predicaments. In substantiating this, I should like to divide the differences into two groups: A, those directly connected with the presence or absence of a vision of alternatives; and B, those directly connected with the presence or absence of anxiety about threats to the established beliefs.

## A. Differences Connected with the Presence or Absence of a Vision of Alternatives

### 1.) *Magical versus non-magical attitude to words*

A central characteristic of nearly all the traditional African world-views we know of is an assumption about the power of words, uttered under appropriate circumstances, to bring into being the events or states they stand for.

The most striking examples of this assumption are to be found in creation mythologies where the supreme being is said to have formed the world out of chaos by uttering the names of all things in it. Such mythologies occur most notably in Ancient Egypt and among the peoples of the Western Sudan.

In the acts of creation which the supreme being has left to man, the mere uttering of words is seldom thought to have the same unconditional efficacy. Thus, so far as we know, there are no traditional cultures which credit man with the ability to create new things just by uttering new words. In most such cultures, nevertheless, the words of men are granted a certain measure of control over the situations they refer to. Often there is a technical process which has to be carried out in order to achieve a certain result; but for success, this has to be completed by a properly-framed spell or incantation foreshadowing the result. Such a situation is vividly described by the Guinean novelist Camara Laye. His father was a goldsmith, and in describing the old man at work, he says:

Although my father spoke no word aloud, I know very well that he was thinking them from within. I read it from his lips, which were moving while he bent over the vessel. He kept mixing gold and coal with a wooden stick which would blaze up every now and then and constantly had to be replaced. What sort of words were those that my father was silently forming? I don't know—at least I don't know exactly. Nothing was ever confided to me about that. But what could these words be but incantations?

Beside the old man worked a sorcerer:

Throughout the whole process his speech became more and more rapid, his rhythms more urgent, and as the ornament took shape, his panegyrics and flatteries increased in vehemence and raised my father's skill to the heavens. In a peculiar, I would almost say immediate and effective, way the sorcerer did in truth take part in the work. He too was drunk with the joy of creation, and loudly proclaimed his joy: enthusiastically he snatched the strings, became inflamed, as if he himself were the craftsman, as if he himself were my father, as if the ornament were coming from his own hands.[26]

In traditional African cultures, to know the name of a being or thing is to have some degree of control over it. In the invocation of spirits, it is essential to call their names correctly; and the control which such correct calling gives is one reason why the true or 'deep' names of gods are often withheld from strangers, and their utterance forbidden to all but a few whose business it is to use them in ritual. Similar ideas lie behind the very widespread traditional practice of using euphemisms to refer to such things as dangerous diseases and wild animals: for it is thought that use of the real names might secure their presence. Yet again, it is widely believed that harm can be done to a man by various operations performed on his name—for instance, by writing his name on a piece of paper and burning it.

This last example carries me on to an observation that at first sight contradicts what we have said so far: the observation that in a great deal of African magic, it is non-verbal symbols rather than words that are thought to have a direct influence over the situations they represent. Bodily movements, bits of plants, organs of animals, stones, earth, water, spittle, domestic utensils, statuettes —a whole host of actions, objects and artefacts play a vital part in the performances of traditional magic. But as we look deeper the contradiction seems more apparent than real. For several studies of African magic suggest that its instruments become symbols through being verbally designated as such. In his study of Zande magic, for instance, Evans-Pritchard describes how magical medicines made from plants and other natural objects are given direction by the use of verbal spells. Thus:

The tall grass *bingba*, which grows profusely on cultivated ground and has feather-like, branching stems, is known to all as medicine for the oil-bearing plant *kpagu*. A man throws the grass like a dart and transfixes the broad leaves of the plant. Before throwing it, he says something of this sort: 'You are melons, you be very fruitful like *bingba* with much fruit.' Or 'You are *bingba*; may the melons flourish like *bingba*. My melons, you be very fruitful. May you not refuse.'[27]

My own field-work in Kalabari constantly unearthed similar examples of non-verbal symbols being given direction and significance by verbal spells. My favourite example is taken from the preparation of a medicine designed to bring clients to an unsuccessful spirit medium. One of the important ingredients of this medicine was the beak of the voracious, mud-dredging muscovy duck— an item which the doctor put into the medicine with the succinct comment: 'Muscovy Duck; you who are always eating.'

Amongst the most important non-verbal magical symbols in Kalabari culture are the statuettes designed to 'fix' the various spirits at times of ritual. Of these, several Kalabari said: 'They are, as it were, the names of the spirits.' Explaining their use, one old man said: 'It is in their names that the spirits stay and come.' It is by being named that the sculpture comes to represent the spirit and to exert influence over it.[28]

In a recent essay on Malagasy magic,[29] Henri Lavondes discusses similar examples of the direction of magical objects by verbal spells. He shows how the various ingredients of a compound medicine are severally related by these spells to the various aspects of the end desired. And, following Mauss, he goes on to suggest that the function of the spell is to convert material objects into *mots réalisés* or concrete words. In being given verbal labels, the objects themselves become a form of language.

This interpretation, which reduces all forms of African magic to a verbal base, fits the facts rather well. One may still ask, however, why magicians spend so much time choosing objects and actions as surrogate words, when spoken words themselves are believed to have a magical potential. The answer, I would suggest, is that speech is an ephemeral form of words, and one which does not lend itself to a great variety of manipulations. Verbal designation of material objects converts them into a more permanent and more readily manipulable form of words. As Lavondes puts it:

Le message verbal est susceptible de davantage de précision que le message figuré. Mais le second a sur le premier l'avantage de sa permanence et de sa matérialité, qui font qu'il reste toujours disponible et qu'il est possible de s'en pénétrer et de le répandre par d'autres voies que celle du language articulé (par absorption, par onction, par aspersion).[30]

Considered in this light, magical objects are the pre-literate equivalents of the written incantations which are so commonly found as charms and talismans in literate but pre-scientific cultural milieux.

Through a very wide range of traditional African belief and activity, then, it is possible to see an implicit assumption as to the magical power of words.

Now if we take into account what I have called the basic predicament of the traditional thinker, we can begin to see why this assumption should be so deeply entrenched in his daily life and thought. Briefly, no man can make contact with reality save through a screen of words. Hence no man can escape the tendency to see a unique and intimate link between words and things. For the traditional thinker this tendency has an overwhelming power. Since he can imagine no alternatives to his established system of concepts and words, the latter appear bound to reality in an absolute fashion. There is no way at all in which they can be seen as varying independently of the segments of reality they stand for. Hence they appear so integrally involved with their referents that any manipulation of the one self-evidently affects the other.

The scientist's attitude to words is, of course, quite opposite. He dismisses contemptuously any suggestion that words could have an immediate, magical power over the things they stand for. Indeed, he finds magical notions amongst the most absurd and alien trappings of traditional thought. Though he grants an enormous power to words, it is the indirect one of bringing control over things through the functions of explanation and prediction. Words are tools in the service of these functions—tools which like all others are to be cared for as long as they are useful, but which are to be ruthlessly scrapped as soon as they outlive their usefulness.

Why does the scientist reject the magician's view of words? One easy answer is that he has come to know better: magical behaviour has been found not to produce the results it claims to. Perhaps. But what scientist has ever bothered to put magic to the test? The answer is, none; because there are deeper grounds for rejection—grounds which make the idea of testing beside the point.

To see what these grounds are, let us return to the scientist's basic predicament—to his awareness of alternative idea-systems whose ways of classifying and interpreting the world are very different from his own. Now this changed awareness gives him two intellectual possibilities. Both are eminently thinkable; but one is intolerable, the other hopeful.

The first possibility is simply a continuance of the magical world-view. If ideas and words are inextricably bound up with reality, and if indeed they shape it and control it, then a multiplicity of idea-systems means a multiplicity of realities, and a change of ideas means a change of things. But whereas there is nothing particularly absurd or inconsistent about this view, it is clearly intolerable in the extreme. For it means that the world is in the last analysis dependent on human whim, that the search for order is a folly, and that human beings can expect to find no sort of anchor in reality.

The second possibility takes hold as an escape from this horrific prospect. It is based on the faith that while ideas and words change, there must be some anchor, some constant reality. This faith leads to the modern view of words and reality as independent variables. With its advent, words come 'unstuck from' reality and are no longer seen as acting magically upon it. Intellectually, this second possibility is neither more nor less respectable than the first. But it has the great advantage of being tolerable whilst the first is horrific.

That the outlook behind magic still remains an intellectual possibility in the scientifically oriented cultures of the modern West can be seen from its survival as a nagging undercurrent in the last 300 years of Western philosophy. This undercurrent generally goes under the labels of 'Idealism' and 'Solipsism'; and under these labels it is not immediately recognizable. But a deeper scrutiny reveals that the old outlook is there all right—albeit in a strange guise. True, Idealism does not say that words create, sustain and have power over that which they represent. Rather, it says that material things are 'in the mind'. That is, the mind creates, sustains and has power over matter. But the second view is little more than a post-Cartesian transposition of the first. Let me elaborate. Both in traditional African cosmologies and in European cosmologies before Descartes, the modern distinction between 'mind' and 'matter' does not appear. Although everything in the universe is underpinned by spiritual forces, what moderns would call 'mental activities' and 'material things' are both part of a single reality, neither material nor immaterial. Thinking, conceiving, saying, etc. are described in terms of organs like heart and brain and actions like the uttering of words. Now when Descartes wrote his philosophical works, he crystallized a half-way phase in the transition from a personal to an impersonal cosmological idiom. Whilst 'higher' human activities still remained under the aegis of a personalized theory, physical and biological events were brought under the aegis of impersonal theory. Hence thinking, conceiving, saying, etc. became manifestations of 'mind', whilst all other happenings became manifestations of 'matter'. Hence, whereas before Descartes we have 'words over things', after him we have 'mind over matter'—just a new disguise for the old view.

What I have said about this view being intellectually respectable but emotionally intolerable is borne out by the attitude to it of modern Western philosophers. Since they are duty bound to explore all the alternative possibilities of thought that lie within the grasp of their imaginations, these philosophers mention, nay even expound, the doctrines of Idealism and Solipsism. Invariably, too, they follow up their expositions with attempts at refutation. But such attempts are, just as invariably, a farce. Their character is summed up in G. E. Moore's desperate gesture, when challenged to prove the existence of a world outside his mind, of banging his hand with his fist and exclaiming: 'It is there!' A gesture of faith rather than of reason, if ever there was one!

With the change from the 'closed' to the 'open' predicament, then, the outlook behind magic becomes intolerable; and to escape from it people espouse the view that words vary independently of reality. Smug rationalists who congratulate themselves on their freedom from magical thinking would do well to reflect on the nature of this freedom!

## 2.) *Ideas-bound-to-occasions versus ideas-bound-to-ideas*

Many commentators on the idea-systems of traditional African cultures have stressed that, for members of these cultures, their thought does not appear as something distinct from and opposable to the realities that call it into action. Rather, particular passages of thought are bound to the particular occasions that evoke them.

Let us take an example. Someone becomes sick. The sickness proves intractable and the relatives call a diviner. The latter says the sickness is due to an ancestor who has been angered by the patient's bad behaviour towards his kinsmen. The diviner prescribes placatory offerings to the spirit and reconciliation with the kinsmen, and the patient is eventually cured. Now while this emergency is on, both the diviner and the patient's relatives may justify what they are doing by reference to some general statements about the kinds of circumstance which arouse ancestors to cause sickness. And it is when he is lucky to be around on such occasions that the anthropologist picks up most of his hard-earned information about traditional theories of the world and its working. But theoretical statements of this kind are very much matters of occasion, not likely to be heard out of context or as part of a general discussion of 'what we believe'. Indeed, the anthropologist has learned by bitter experience that, in traditional Africa, the generalized, 'what do you chaps believe?' approach gets one exactly nowhere.[31]

If ideas in traditional culture are seen as bound to occasions rather than to other ideas, the reason is one that we have already given in our discussion of magic. Since the member of such a culture can imagine no alternatives to his established system of ideas, the latter appear inexorably bound to the portions of reality they stand for. They cannot be seen as in any way opposable to reality.

In a scientifically oriented culture such as that of the Western anthropologist, things are very different. The very word 'idea' has the connotation of something opposed to reality. Nor is it entirely coincidental that in such a culture the historian of ideas is considered to be the most unrealistic kind of historian. Not only are ideas dissociated in people's minds from the reality that occasions them: they are bound to other ideas, to form wholes and systems perceived as such.

Belief-systems take shape not only as abstractions in the minds of anthropologists, but also as totalities in the minds of believers.

Here again, this change can be readily understood in terms of a change from the 'closed' to the 'open' predicament. A vision of alternative possibilities forces men to the faith that ideas somehow vary whilst reality remains constant. Ideas thus become detached from reality—nay, even in a sense opposed to it. Furthermore, such a vision, by giving the thinker an opportunity to 'get outside' his own system, offers him a possibility of his coming to see it *as a system.*

### 3.) *Unreflective versus reflective thinking*

At this stage of the analysis there is no need for me to insist further on the essential rationality of traditional thought. In Part I, indeed, I have already made it out far too rational for the taste of most social anthropologists. And yet, there is a sense in which this thought includes among its accomplishments neither logic nor philosophy.

Let me explain this, at first sight, rather shocking statement. It is true that most African traditional world-views are logically elaborated to a high degree. It is also true that, because of their eminently rational character, they are appropriately called 'philosophies'. But here I am using 'logic' and 'philosophy' in a more exact sense. By logic, I mean thinking directed to answering the question: 'What are the general rules by which we can distinguish good arguments from bad ones?' And by philosophy, I mean thinking directed to answering the question: 'On what grounds can we ever claim to know anything about the world?' Now logic and philosophy, in these restricted senses, are poorly developed in traditional Africa. Despite its elaborate and often penetrating cosmological, sociological and psychological speculations, traditional thought has tended to get on with the work of explanation, without pausing for reflection upon the nature or rules of this work. Thinking once more of the 'closed' predicament, we can readily see why these second-order intellectual activities should be virtually absent from traditional cultures. Briefly, the traditional thinker, because he is unable to imagine possible alternatives to his established theories and classifications, can never start to formulate generalized norms of reasoning and knowing. For only where there are alternatives can there be choice, and only where there is choice can there be norms governing it. As they are characteristically absent in traditional cultures, so logic and philosophy are characteristically present in all scientifically oriented cultures. Just as the 'closed' predicament makes it impossible for them to appear, so the 'open' predicament makes it inevitable that they must appear. For where the thinker can see the possibility of alternatives to his established idea-system, the question of choice at once arises, and the development of norms governing such choice cannot be far behind.[32]

### 4.) *Mixed versus segregated motives*

This contrast is very closely related to the preceding one. As I stressed in Part I of this essay, the goals of explanation and prediction are as powerfully present in traditional African cultures as they are in cultures where science has become institutionalized. In the absence of explicit norms of thought, however, we find them vigorously pursued but not explicitly reflected upon and defined. In these circumstances, there is little thought about their consistency or inconsistency with other goals and motives. Hence wherever we find a theoretical system with explanatory and predictive functions, we find other motives entering in and contributing to its development.

Despite their cognitive preoccupations, most African religious systems are powerfully influenced by what are commonly called 'emotional needs'—i.e. needs for certain kinds of personal relationship. In Africa, as elsewhere, all social systems stimulate in their members a considerable diversity of such needs; but, having stimulated them, they often prove unwilling or unable to allow them full opportunities for satisfaction. In such situations the spirits function not only as theoretical entities but as surrogate people providing opportunities for the formation of ties forbidden in the purely human social field. The latter function they discharge in two ways. First, by providing non-human partners with whom people can take up relationships forbidden with other human beings. Second, through the mechanism of possession, by allowing people to 'become' spirits and so to play roles *vis-à-vis* their fellow men which they are debarred from playing as ordinary human beings.

Examples of the first kind occur very commonly in association with the need for dependence created in children by the circumstances of their family upbringing. In some African societies male children are required to make an abrupt switch from dependence to independence as soon as they reach puberty. A prominent feature of the rites aimed at achieving this switch is the dramatic induction of the candidates into a relation of dependence with a powerful spiritual agency. The latter can be seen as a surrogate for the parents with whom the candidates are no longer allowed to continue their dependent relationships, and hence as a means of freeing the candidates for the exercise of adult independence and responsibility. This appears to be the basic significance of secret society initiations among the peoples of the Congo and the Western Guinea Coast. In other traditional societies, the early relation of dependence on parents is allowed to continue so long as the parents are still alive; and an abrupt switch to independence and responsibility has to be made on their death. Here, it is the dead parent, translated into ancestorhood, who provides for the continuance of a relationship which has had to be abruptly and traumatically discontinued in the purely human social field. This sequence, with its culmination in a highly devout worship of patrilineal ancestors, has been vividly described by Fortes in some of his writings on the Tallensi of Northern Ghana.[33]

Examples of the second kind occur more commonly in association with the need for dominance. Most societies stimulate this need more widely than they grant it satisfaction. In traditional African societies, women are the most common sufferers from this; and it is no accident that in the numerous spirit-possession cults that flourish up and down the continent women are generally rather more prominent than men. For in the male-authority roles which they tend to assume in possession, they gain access to a whole area of role-playing normally forbidden them.

Aesthetic motives, too, play an important part in moulding and sustaining traditional religious systems. This is especially true of West Africa, where narrative, poetry, song, dance, music, sculpture and even architecture use the spirits and their characters as a framework upon which to develop their various forms. These arts in turn influence the direction in which ideas about the spirits develop. In my own field-work on Kalabari religion, I have found a gradual shading of the cognitive into the aesthetic which can at times be most confusing. In oral tradition, for example, serious myths intended to throw light on the part played by the gods in founding social institutions shade into tales which, although their characters are also gods, are told for sheer entertainment. And although Kalabari do make a distinction between serious myth and light tale, there are many pieces which they themselves hesitate to place on one side or the other. Belief shades through half-belief into suspended belief. In ritual, again, dramatic representations of the gods carried out in order to dispose them favourably and secure the benefits which, as cosmic forces, they control, are usually found highly enjoyable in themselves. And they shade off into representations carried out almost solely for their aesthetic appeal. In the Kalabari water-spirit masquerades, for instance, religion seems to have become the servant of art.[34]

There is little doubt that because the theoretical entities of traditional thought happen to be people, they give particular scope for the working of emotional and aesthetic motives. Here, perhaps, we do have something about the personal idiom in theory that does militate indirectly against the taking up of a scientific attitude; for where there are powerful emotional and aesthetic loadings on a particular theoretical scheme, these must add to the difficulties of abandoning this scheme when cognitive goals press towards doing so. Once again, I should like to stress that the mere fact of switching from a personal to an impersonal idiom does not make anyone a scientist, and that one can be unscientific or scientific in either idiom. In this respect, nevertheless, the personal idiom does seem to present certain difficulties for the scientific attitude which the impersonal idiom does not.

Where the possibility of choice has stimulated the development of logic, philosophy and norms of thought generally, the situation undergoes radical change. One theory is judged better than another with explicit reference to its efficacy in explanation and prediction. And as these ends become more clearly defined, it gets increasingly evident that no other ends are compatible with them. People come to see that if ideas are to be used as efficient tools of explanation and prediction, they must not be allowed to become tools of anything else. (This, of course, is the essence of the ideal of 'objectivity'.) Hence there grows up a great watchfulness against seduction by the emotional or aesthetic appeal of a theory—a watchfulness which in twentieth-century Europe sometimes takes extreme forms such as the suspicion of any research publication not written out in a positively indigestible style. Also there appears an insistence on the importance of 'pure' as opposed to 'applied' science. This does not mean that scientists are against practical application of their findings. What it does mean is that they feel there should always be some disjunction between themselves and the people who apply their discoveries. The reasons for this are basically the same as those which lead the scientist to be on his guard against emotional or aesthetic appeals. For one thing, if a scientist is too closely identified with a given set of practical problems, he may become so committed to solving these as to take up any theory that offers solution without giving it adequate testing. Again, those lines of enquiry most closely related to the practical problems of the day are not neces-sarily those which lead to the most rapid advances in explanation and prediction. Finally, in so far as practical interests involve inter-business and inter-national competition, over-identification with them can lead to a fundamental denial of the scientific ideal by encouraging the observance of rules of secrecy. Since it is a primary canon of the scientific ideal that every new theory be subjected to the widest possible testing and criticism, free circulation of new findings is basic to the code of the scientific community. (See below.) Hence, in so far as com-mercial and international competition leads to the curtailment of such circulation, it is inimical to science. This is why brilliant and dedicated scientists tend to be among the most double-edged weapons in wars either hot or cold.

The traditional theoretical scheme, as we have noted, brings forth and nourishes a rich encrustation of cultural growths whose underlying motives have little to do with explanation and prediction. Notable among these are ela-borate systems of personal relationships with beings beyond the purely human social order, and all manner of artistic embellishments.

As the insistence on segregation of theoretical activity from the influence of all motives but those defined as essential to it gains strength, these various growths are forcibly sloughed off and have to embark on an independent exis-tence. To survive without getting involved in a losing battle with the now-prestigious 'science', they have to eschew loudly all explanatory pretensions, and devote great energy to defining their 'true' ends. In doing this, they have often been accused of making a virtue out of sad necessity—of putting a brazen face on what is simply a headlong retreat before science. But their activities in this direction can, I think, also be seen in a more positive way. That is, they too can be seen as a direct outcome of the 'open' predicament, and thence of the general tendency to reflect on the nature of thought, to define its aims, and to formulate its norms. Now the conclusion such reflective activity arrives at for theory-making also holds for spiritual communion and for art: that is, there are several distinct modes of thought; and a particular mode, if it is to fulfil itself completely, must be protected from the influence of all motives except those defined as essential to it. Hence when we hear a Western theologian proclaim loudly the 'modern discovery' that the essence of religion has nothing to do with explanation and prediction of worldly events, but is simply communion with God for its own sake, we are only partly right when we sneer at him for trying to disguise retreat as advance. For in fact he can claim to be undertaking much the same kind of purifying and refining operation as the scientist. The force of this contention emerges when we come to consider the case of the artist. For when the latter proclaims that his activity is no longer the handmaid of religion, of science, or even of representation, we do in fact grant that this drastic circumscription of aims represents a form of progress akin to that of the scientist purging his subject in the pursuit of objectivity. The rationalist who says that the modern theologian is retreating whilst the modern artist is advancing is thus merely expressing an agnostic prejudice. Both, in fact, are in an important sense caught up in the same currents of thought as those that move the scientist.

It will now be clear that the scientist's quest for 'objectivity' is, among other things, a purifying movement. As has happened in many such movements, however, the purifying zeal tends to wander beyond its self-appointed bounds, and even to run to excess within these bounds. Such tendencies are well exemplified in the impact of the quest for objectivity on metaphor.

In traditional Africa, speech abounds with metaphor to a degree no longer familiar in the scientifically oriented cultures of the modern West. The function of such metaphor is partly, as anthropologists never tire of saying,[35] to allude obliquely to things which cannot be said directly. Much more importantly, perhaps, its function is to underline, emphasize and give greater impact to things which *can* be said literally. 'Proverbs are the palm-oil with which words are eaten', say the Ibo.[36] In this capacity, it is clearly a vital adjunct to rational thought. Often, however, metaphor subtly misleads. The analogy between the things which constitute its literal reference and the things which constitute its oblique reference usually involves only limited aspects of both. But there is always a temptation to extend the analogy unduly, and it can then run its users right off the rails. In sociology, for instance, this has happened with the use of organismic metaphors for thinking about societies and social relations. Organisms and societies do perhaps resemble each other in certain limited ways; but sociologists who have become addicted to organismic metaphor often go beyond these limited resemblances and end up by attributing to societies all sorts of properties possessed only by organisms.

These occasional dangers have led the purists to regard metaphor and analogy as one great snare and delusion. No palm-oil with our words, they have decreed with grim satisfaction. The resulting cult of plain, literal speaking, alas, has spread beyond the bounds of strictly scientific activity right through everyday life, taking much of the poetic quality out of ordinary, humdrum social relations. Not only this. The distrust of metaphor and analogy has in some places gone so far as to threaten intellectual processes which are crucial to the advance of science itself. Thus the positivist philosophers of science have often denigrated the activity of theoretical model-building. At best, some of them have contended, such model-building is a dubious help to serious scientific thought; and at worst, its reliance on the process of analogy may be extremely misleading. According to this purist school, induction and deduction are the only processes of thought permissible to the scientist. His job is not to elaborate models of a supposed reality lying 'behind' the data of experience. It is simply to observe; to make inductive generalizations summarizing the regularities found in observation; to deduce from these generalizations the probable course of further observation; and finally to test this deduction against experience. A then B, A then B, A then B; hence all A's are followed by B's; hence if there is an A in the future, it will be followed by a B; check. The trouble about this purist paradigm, of course, is that it condemns the scientist to an eternity of triteness and circularity. It can never account for any of the great leaps in explanatory power which we associate with the advance of science. Only in relation to some model of underlying reality, for instance, can we come to see that A and X, B and Y, so different in the eye of the casual observer, are actually outward manifestations of the same kinds of events. Only in relation to such a model are we suddenly moved to look for a conjunction between X and Y which we would never have noticed otherwise. And only thus can we come to see AB, XY as two instances of a single underlying process or regularity. Finally, so it seems, the only way yet discovered in which scientists can turn out the new models of underlying reality necessary to set such explanatory advance in motion is through the drawing of bold analogies.

To sum up on this point: one of the essential features of science is that it is a purifying movement. But like other purifying movements, alas, it provides fertile soil for obsessional personalities. If we can compare the traditional thinker to an easy-going housewife who feels she can get along quite nicely despite a considerable accumulation of dirt and dust on the furniture, we can compare the positivist who is so often a fellow traveller of science to an obsessional housewife who scrubs off the dirt, the paintwork, and finally the handles that make the furniture of use!

## B. Differences Connected with the Presence or Absence of Anxiety about Threats to the Established Body of Theory

### 5.) *Protective versus destructive attitude towards established theory*

Both in traditional Africa and in the science-oriented West, theoretical thought is vitally concerned with the prediction of events. But there are marked differences in reaction to predictive failure.

In the theoretical thought of the traditional cultures, there is a notable reluctance to register repeated failures of prediction and to act by attacking the beliefs involved. Instead, other current beliefs are utilized in such a way as to 'excuse' each failure as it occurs, and hence to protect the major theoretical assumptions on which prediction is based. This use of *ad hoc* excuses is a phenomenon which social anthropologists have christened 'secondary elaboration'.[37]

The process of secondary elaboration is most readily seen in association with the work of diviners and oracle-operators, who are concerned with discovering the identity of the spiritual forces responsible for particular happenings in the visible, tangible world, and the reasons for their activation. Typically, a sick man goes to a diviner, and is told that a certain spiritual agency is 'worrying' him. The diviner points to certain of his past actions as having excited the spirit's anger, and indicates certain remedial actions which will appease this anger and restore health. Should the client take the recommended remedial action and yet see no improvement, he will be likely to conclude that the diviner was either fraudulent or just incompetent, and to seek out another expert. The new diviner will generally point to another spiritual agency and another set of arousing circumstances as responsible for the man's condition, and will recommend fresh remedial action. In addition, he will probably provide some explanation of why the previous diviner failed to get at the truth. He may corroborate the client's suspicions of fraud, or he may say that the spirit involved maliciously 'hid itself behind' another in such a way that only the most skilled of diviners would have been able to detect it. If after this the client should still see no improvement in his condition, he will move on to yet another diviner—and so on, perhaps, until his troubles culminate in death.

What is notable in all this is that the client never takes his repeated failures as evidence against the existence of the various spiritual beings named as responsible for his plight, or as evidence against the possibility of making contact with such beings as diviners claim to do. Nor do members of the wider community in which he lives ever try to keep track of the proportion of successes to failures in the remedial actions based on their beliefs, with the aim of questioning these beliefs. At most, they grumble about the dishonesty and wiles of many diviners, whilst maintaining their faith in the existence of some honest, competent practitioners.

In these traditional cultures, questioning of the beliefs on which divining is based and weighing up of successes against failures are just not among the paths that thought can take. They are blocked paths because the thinkers involved are victims of the closed predicament. For them, established beliefs have an absolute validity, and any threat to such beliefs is a horrific threat of chaos. Who is going to jump from the cosmic palm-tree when there is no hope of another perch to swing to?

Where the scientific outlook has become firmly entrenched, attitudes to established beliefs are very different. Much has been made of the scientist's essential scepticism towards established beliefs; and one must, I think, agree that this above all is what distinguishes him from the traditional thinker. But one must be careful here. The picture of the scientist in continuous readiness to scrap or demote established theory contains a dangerous exaggeration as well as an important truth. As an outstanding modern historian of the sciences has recently observed,[38] the typical scientist spends most of his time optimistically seeing how far he can push a new theory to cover an ever-widening horizon of experience. When he has difficulty in making the theory 'fit', he is more likely to develop it in the ways described in Part I of this essay than to scrap it out of hand. And if it does palpably fail the occasional test, he may even put the failure down to dirty apparatus or mistaken meter-reading—rather like the oracle operator! And yet, the spirit behind the scientist's actions is very different. His pushing of a theory and his reluctance to scrap it are not due to any chilling intuition that if his theory fails him, chaos is at hand. Rather, they are due to the very knowledge that the theory is not something timeless and absolute. Precisely because he knows that the present theory came in at a certain epoch to replace a predecessor, and that its explanatory coverage is far better than that of the predecessor, he is reluctant to throw it away before giving it the benefit of every doubt. But this same knowledge makes for an acceptance of the theory which is far more qualified and far more watchful than that of the traditional thinker. The scientist is, as it were, always keeping account, balancing the successes of a theory against its failures. And when the failures start to come thick and fast, defence of the theory switches inexorably to attack on it.

If the record of a theory that has fallen under a cloud is poor in all circumstances, it is ruthlessly scrapped. The collective memory of the European scientific community is littered with the wreckage of the various unsatisfactory theories discarded over the last 500 years—the earth-centred theory of the universe, the circular theory of planetary motion, the phlogiston theory of chemical combination, the aether theory of wave propagation, and perhaps a hundred others. Often, however, it is found that a theoretical model once assumed to have universal validity in fact has a good predictive performance over a limited range of circumstances, but a poor performance outside this range. In such a case, the beliefs in question are still ruthlessly demoted; but instead of being thrown out altogether they are given a lesser status as limiting cases of more embracing generalities—still useful as lower-level models or as guides to experience within restricted areas. This sort of demotion has been the fate of theoretical schemes like Newton's Laws of Motion (still used as a guide in many mundane affairs, including much of the business of modern rocketry) and the 'Ball-and-Bond' theory of chemical combination.

This underlying readiness to scrap or demote established theories on the ground of poor predictive performance is perhaps the most important single feature of the scientific attitude. It is, I suggest, a direct outcome of the 'open' predicament. For only when the thinker is able to see his established idea-system as one among many alternatives can he see his established ideas as things of less than absolute value. And only when he sees them thus can he see the scrapping of them as anything other than a horrific, irretrievable jump into chaos.

### 6.) *Divination versus diagnosis*

Earlier in this essay I drew certain parallels between the work of the traditional African diviner and the work of the Western diagnostician. In particular I showed how both of them make much the same use of theoretical ideas: i.e. as means of linking observed effects to causes that lie beyond the powers of common sense to grasp. I now propose to discuss certain crucial differences between these two kinds of agent.

As I noted in the last section, in traditional cultures anxieties about threats to the established theories effectively block many of the paths thought might otherwise take. One path so blocked is the working out of any body of theory which assigns too distinctive an effect to any particular pattern of antecedents

Why this path should be blocked is not hard to see. Suppose that there is a theory X, which makes the following causal connections:

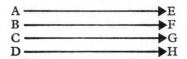

Now if situation E is disagreeable, and is unambiguously ascribable to cause A, action will be taken to get rid of E by manipulating A. If it fails, then the most obvious verdict is that A → E is invalid. A similar argument applies, of course, to B → F, C → G, D → H.

Suppose, on the other hand, that theory X makes the following connections:

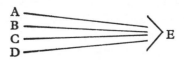

Now things are very different. If E is ascribed to A, action will still be taken to get rid of E by manipulating A. But if it fails, we are no longer compelled to admit that A → E is invalid. We can now say that perhaps B was present as a complicating factor, and that failure to take account of it was responsible for our disappointment. Or we can say that A was not present at all, but only D. So the theory remains protected.

Coming back to concrete terms, we find that traditional African theories of, say, disease approximate to the second of these patterns rather than to the first, and that this is their ultimate protection. In most traditional cultures, diseases are thought to be caused by the anger of several categories of spirits. Each of these categories is aroused by a different kind of situation. Thus in Kalabari thought heroes, ancestors, water-spirits and medicine-spirits are the main unseen bringers of disease. Heroes tend to be activated by offences against 'town laws', ancestors by offences against kinsmen, water-spirits by failure to heed certain tangible signs that they wish to form personal attachments with human partners, medicine-spirits by the machinations of enemies with whom one 'has case'. Hence there is a fairly clear correlation between the kind of activating situation and the kind of spirit brought into play. But although there are the beginnings of a second correlation, between the kind of spirit brought into play and the kind of misfortune inflicted, this has not gone very far. By and large, if a diviner attributes a disease to a certain spirit aroused by certain antecedent circumstances and if the remedy based on this attribution fails, another diviner can always say that the first attribution was a mistake, and that it was really another spirit, aroused by another set of circumstances, who caused the trouble. Studies like those of Evans-Pritchard on the Zande,[39] Nadel on the Nupe[40] and Forde on the Yakö[41] suggest that this particular defensive pattern, based on converging causal sequences, is very widespread.

But a theory which postulates converging causal sequences, though self-protective to a high degree, faces serious problems in its application to everyday life. For the man who visits a diviner with misfortune E does not want to be told that it could be due to any one of four different kinds of spirits, activated by circumstances A, B, C or D. He wants a definite verdict and a definite remedial prescription.

Now given the nature of the theoretical model the diviner operates with, any amount of minute inspection and definition of E will not allow him to give a definite verdict as between A, B, C or D. Sometimes, he can and does find out from the client whether A, B, C or D have occurred in his life-history. But the client may well have forgotten the crucial activating circumstance. Indeed, as it is often a guilt-provoking circumstance, he is likely to have forgotten it. Or, the client may remember that happenings answering to both A B, and C have occurred at various times in his life; and the diviner is still left with the problem of which of these happenings and which category of spirit is actually responsible for the present occurrence of E.

We have, then, an apparently insoluble conflict. For the diviner to give a causal verdict which transcends the limited vision of common sense, he must operate with a theory. But for the theory to survive, it must be of the converging-sequence type which makes the giving of a definite causal verdict very difficult.

As I see it, the essence of divination is that it is a mechanism for resolving this conflict. Faced with a theory postulating several possible causes for a given event, and no means of inferring the actual cause from observable evidence, divination goes, as it were, 'over the head of' such evidence. It elicits a direct sign from the realm of those unobservable entities that govern the casual linkages it deals with—a sign that enables it to say which of the several sequences indicated by the theory is the one actually involved.

Just how it elicits this sign seems immaterial. Indeed, there is a fantastic variety of divination procedures on the African continent. The diviner may enter into a privileged contact with the realm of unobservable entities postulated by his theory, 'seeing' and 'hearing' them in a manner beyond the powers of his client. The diviner may force his client to choose from a collection of twigs, each representing one of the various spirits and causal linkages potentially involved in the situation. He may set spiders to chew leaves, and give his verdict on the basis of a series of correlations between patterns of chewing and kinds of casual sequence. He may cause a dead body to be carried by several men, suggest to the body the various possible causes of its death, and obtain from its consequent movements a reply as to which is the cause actually involved. He may administer poison to a series of fowls, put one of the several potential sequences as a question to each fowl, and infer from the life or death of the animal whether this particular sequence is the one actually involved. One might cite up to a hundred more ingenious procedures.

All of these divination techniques share two basic features. First, as I have said, they are means of selecting one actual causal sequence from several potential sequences. Secondly, they all carry a subtle aura of fallibility which makes it possible to 'explain everything away' when remedial prescriptions based on them turn out not to work. Thus many divination procedures require an esoteric knowledge or faculty which the client does not share with the operator. Hence the client has no direct check on the operator; and in retrospect there is always the possibility of the latter's dishonesty or sheer incompetence. Again, nearly all of these procedures are thought to be very delicate and easily thrown out of kilter. Among other things, they may be affected by pollution, or by the machinations of those who have a grudge against the client.

So, whereas the positive features of the divining process make it possible to arrive at a definite causal verdict despite a converging-sequence theory, the aura of fallibility provides for the self-protecting action of such a theory by making it possible, in the event of a failure, to switch from one potential sequence to another in such a way as to leave the theory as a whole unimpugned. In the last section, we noted that the context of divination provided some of the clearest illustrations of the defence-mechanism known as 'secondary elaboration'. Now I think, we can go further: that is, we can say that divination owes its very existence to the exigencies of this mechanism.

Where the 'open' predicament prevails, anxieties about threats to the established theories decline, and previously blocked thought-paths become clear. We now witness the development of theories that assign distinctive effects to differing causes; and in the face of this development the type of theory that assumes converging sequences tends to disappear. Nowadays, of course, it is more fashionable to talk of covariation than to talk of cause and effect. But the continuous-covariation formula of the type $ds = f.dt$, so prominent in modern scientific theory, is in fact an instance of the tendency I am referring to. For, spelled out, the implication of such a formula is that, to an infinite number of values of a cause-variable, there correspond an infinite number of values of an effect-variable.

Where this type of theory comes into the ascendant, the diviner gives place to the diagnostician. The latter, whether he is concerned with bodily upsets or with aeroplane disasters, goes to work in a way which differs in important respects from that of his traditional counterpart. Dealing as he does with theories that postulate non-converging causal sequences, he has a task altogether more prosaic than that of the diviner. For, given non-convergence, a complete and accurate observation of effect, plus knowledge of the relevant theory, makes it possible for him to give an unambiguous causal verdict. Once these conditions have been fulfilled, there is no need for the additional operations of the diviner. No need for special mechanisms to elicit signs from the realm of unobservable entities. No need for a way of going 'over the head of' observable evidence in order to find out which of several potential causes is the actual one.

Modern Western diagnosis, it is true, has not lost all of the aura of fallibility that surrounds traditional divining. Incomplete and inaccurate observation of effect may sometimes provide a plausible defence for failures of diagnosis based on outmoded theory. But such a defence is a poor thing compared with that provided by converging-sequence theory and a divining mechanism characterized as inherently delicate and subject to breakdown. In the modern West, of course, the diagnosticians and remedialists are usually not the same as the people who are actively concerned with the developing and testing of theory. (Hence the division between 'pure' and 'applied' scientists.) Nevertheless, it is often through reports of failure from these men that the developers and testers get their stimulus for the replacement of an old theory with a new one. Thus in medicine, reports from general practitioners about widespread breakdown of well-tried diagnostic and healing procedures have often provided the stimulus for medical researchers to make drastic revisions in the theory of disease.

Far from being an integral part of any mechanism for defending theory, then, the diagnostician often contributes his share to the circumstances that lead to the abandonment of old ideas and the adoption of new ones.

### 7.) *Absence versus presence of experimental method*

Anyone who has read Part I of this paper should be in little doubt as to how closely adjusted traditional African theoretical systems often are to the prevailing facts of personality, social organization, and ecology. Indeed, although many of the causal connections they posit turn out to be red herrings when subjected to scientific scrutiny, others turn out to be very real and vital. Thus an important part of traditional religious theory posits and attempts to explain the connection between disturbed social relationships and disease—a connection whose reality and importance Western medical scientists are only just beginning to see. Nevertheless, the adjustments of the systems to changing experience are essentially slow, piecemeal and reluctant. Nothing must happen to arouse public suspicion that basic theoretical models are being challenged. If changes are to take place, they must take place like movements in the game of Grandmother's Footsteps: i.e. when Grandma is not looking, and in such a way that whenever she turns round, she sees somebody standing stock-still and in a position not too obviously different from the one he was in when last she looked. The consequence of all this, if the reader will excuse me for mixing my metaphors, is that traditional idea-systems are usually catching up on experience from a position 'one jump behind'.

Scientific thought, by contrast, is characteristically 'one jump ahead' of experience. It is able to be so because of that distinctive feature of the scientist's calling: the experimental method. This method is nothing more nor less than the positive expression of the 'open' attitude to established beliefs and categories which we referred to in Section 5. For the essence of experiment is that the holder of a pet theory does not just wait for events to come along and show whether or not it has a good predictive performance. He bombards it with artificially produced events in such a way that its merits or defects will show up as immediately and as clearly as possible.

Often, the artificially produced events involved in an experiment are ones that would take a long time to observe if left to occur of their own accord. Thus a medical research worker who has a theory about the destructive effect of a certain chemical upon pneumonia germs does not wait for the next severe

English winter to bring its heavy toll of pneumonia victims. He gets a large batch of monkeys (or, in America sometimes, condemned human volunteers), deliberately infects them with pneumonia, gives some the chemical and others an inert substance, and observes the results. In many cases, the artificially produced events are of a kind which would almost certainly never occur were nature left to take her own course; but the experimentalist sets great store by them because they are expressly designed to provide a more unequivocal test of theory than any naturally occurring conditions. Most laboratory experiments in biology, chemistry and especially physics are of this kind.

We can say, then, that whereas in traditional thought there is continual if reluctant adjustments of theories to new experience, in science men spend much of their time deliberately creating new experience in order to evaluate their theories. Whilst in traditional thought it is mostly experience that determines theory, in the world of the experimental scientist there is a sense in which theory usually determines experience.

## 8.) *The confession of ignorance*

The European anthropologist working in a traditional African community often has the experience of soliciting people's theories on a number of (to him) interesting topics, and of getting the reply 'we don't know anything about that' with the implication 'we don't really care'. Thus the anthropologist usually comes to Africa with ideas about the wonderful 'creation myths' to be found there. Very often, however, he finds that the people he has come to live with are not at all curious about the creation of the world; and apart from acknowledging that it was the work of a supreme being, they are apt to say with a shrug of their shoulders 'the old people did not tell us anything about it'. (Often, of course, an equal lack of curiosity on the anthropologist's part leads him to miss an elaborate body of indigenous explanatory theory covering some area of experience his own lack of interest prevented him from enquiring about.)

What the anthropologist almost never finds is a confession of ignorance about the answer to some question which the people themselves consider important. Scarcely ever, for instance, does he come across a common disease or crop failure whose cause and cure people say they just do not know.

Given the basic predicament of the traditional thinker, such an admission would indeed be intolerable. For where there are no conceivable alternatives to the established theoretical system, any hint that this system is failing to cope must be a hint of irreparable chaos, and so must rouse extreme anxiety.

In the case of the scientist, his readiness to test every theory to destruction makes it inevitable that he will have to confess ignorance whenever a theory crumbles under testing and he has no better one immediately available. Indeed, it is only in a culture where the scientific attitude is firmly institutionalized that one can hope to hear the answer 'we don't know' given by an expert questioned on the causes of such a terrible human scourge as cancer. Such willingness to confess ignorance means that the world-view provided by scientists for wider consumption is apt to seem far less comprehensive and embracing than many of the world-views of pre-scientific cultures. In fact, it tends to give the impression of a great expanse of darkness illuminated only at irregular intervals. This impression, of course, is tolerable to scientists precisely because the beliefs they hold at a given time are not things of absolute value to which they can imagine no possible alternatives. If current beliefs let in the dark, this does not rule out the possibility of other beliefs which may eventually shut it out.

### 9.) *Coincidence, chance, probability*

Closely related to the development of a capacity to tolerate ignorance is the development of concepts which formally recognize the existence of various kinds of limitation upon the possible completeness of explanation and prediction. Important among such concepts are those of coincidence, chance and probability.

Let us start with the idea of coincidence. In the traditional cultures of Africa, such a concept is poorly developed. The tendency is to give any untoward happening a definite cause. When a rotten branch falls off a tree and kills a man walking underneath it, there has to be a definite explanation of the calamity. Perhaps the man quarrelled with a half brother over some matter of inheritance, and the latter worked the fall of the branch through a sorcerer. Or perhaps he misappropriated lineage property, and the lineage ancestors brought the branch down on his head. The idea that the whole thing could have come about through the accidental convergence of two independent chains of events is inconceivable because it is psychologically intolerable. To entertain it would be to admit that the episode was inexplicable and unpredictable: a glaring confession of ignorance.

It is characteristic of the scientist that he is willing to face up to the inexplicability and unpredictability of this type of situation, and that he does not shrink from diagnosing an accidental convergence of different chains of events. This is a consequence of his ability to tolerate ignorance.

As with the idea of coincidence, so with that of probability. Where traditional thought is apt to demand definite forecasts of whether something will or will not happen, the scientist is often content to know the probability of its happening—that is, the number of times it will happen in a hypothetical series of, say, a hundred trials.

When it was first developed, the probability forecast was seen as a makeshift tool for use in situations where one's knowledge of the factors operating was incomplete, and where it was assumed that possession of all the relevant data would have made a definite forecast possible. This is still an important context of probability forecasting, and will continue to be so. An example of its use is in prediction of incidence of the mental disease schizophrenia. Psychiatrists have now come to believe that heredity plays a large part in causing the disease; and given a knowledge of the distribution of previous cases in a person's family history, they are able to calculate the probability of his contracting it. Their forecasts only run to probabilities, because they are not yet sure that they know all the other factors which reinforce or inhibit the effect of heredity, and also because they are seldom in a position to observe all those factors they do know to be relevant. Nevertheless, the assumption remains that if all the relevant factors could be known and observed, the probability forecasts could be replaced by unequivocal predictions.

In the twentieth century, a yet more drastic step has been taken in acknowledging the limits of explanation and prediction. For physicists now admit that the entities they postulate as the ultimate constituents of all matter—the so-called elementary particles—have properties such that, even given all obtainable data about their condition at any instant, it is still impossible to give more than a probability forecast of their condition at any instance in the future. Here, the probability forecast is no longer a makeshift for an unequivocal prediction: it is ultimate and irreducible.

From one angle, then, the development of the scientific outlook appears more than anything else as a growth of intellectual humility. Where the pre-scientific thinker is unable to confess ignorance on any question of vital practical import, the good scientist is always ready to do so. Again, where the pre-scientific thinker is reluctant to acknowledge any limitation on his power to explain and predict, the scientist not only faces such limitations with equanimity, but devotes a good deal of energy to exploring and charting their extent.

This humility, I suggest, is the product of an underlying confidence—the confidence which comes from seeing that one's currently held beliefs are not the be-all and end-all of the human search for order. Once one has seen this, the difficulty of facing up to their limitations largely dissolves.[42]

## 10.) *Protective versus destructive attitude to the category-system*

If someone is asked to list typical features of traditional thinking, he is almost certain to mention the phenomenon known as 'taboo'. 'Taboo' is the anthropological jargon for a reaction of horror and aversion to certain actions or happenings which are seen as monstrous and polluting. It is characteristic of the taboo reaction that people are unable to justify it in terms of ulterior reasons: tabooed events are simply bad in themselves. People take every possible step to prevent tabooed events from happening, and to isolate or expel them when they do occur.

Taboo has long been a mystery to anthropologists. Of the many explanations proposed, few have fitted more than a small selection of the instances observed. It is only recently that an anthropologist has placed the phenomenon in a more satisfactory perspective by the observation that in nearly every case of taboo reaction, the events and actions involved are ones which seriously defy the established lines of classification in the culture where they occur.[43]

Perhaps the most important occasion of taboo reaction in traditional African cultures is the commission of incest. Incest is one of the most flagrant defiances of the established category-system: for he who commits it treats a mother, daughter or sister like a wife. Another common occasion for taboo reaction is the birth of twins. Here, the category distinction involved is that of human beings versus animals—multiple births being taken as characteristic of animals as opposed to men. Yet another very generally tabooed object is the human corpse, which occupies, as it were, a classificatory no-man's-land between the living and the inanimate. Equally widely tabooed are such human bodily excreta as faeces and menstrual blood, which occupy the same no-man's-land between the living and the inanimate.

Taboo reactions are often given to occurrences that are radically strange or new; for these too (almost by definition) fail to fit in to the established category-system. A good example is furnished by a Kalabari story of the coming of the Europeans. The first white man, it is said, was seen by a fisherman who had gone down to the mouth of the estuary in his canoe. Panic-stricken, he raced home and told his people what he had seen: whereupon he and the rest of the town set out to purify themselves—that is, to rid themselves of the influence of the strange and monstrous thing that had intruded into their world.

A sort of global taboo reaction is often evoked by foreign lands. As the domains of so much that is strange and unassimilable to one's own categories, such lands are the abode *par excellence* of the monstrous and the abominable. The most vivid description we have of this attitude is that given for the Lugbara by John Middleton.[44] For this East African people, the foreigner is the inverted perpetrator of all imaginable abominations from incest downwards. The more alien he is, the more abominable. Though the Lugbara attitude is extreme, many traditional African cultures would seem to echo it in some degree.[45]

Just as the central tenets of the traditional theoretical system are defended against adverse experience by an elaborate array of excuses for predictive failure, so too the main classificatory distinctions of the system are defended by taboo avoidance reactions against any event that defies them. Since every system of belief implies a system of categories, and vice versa, secondary elaboration and taboo reaction are really opposite sides of the same coin.

From all this it follows that, like secondary elaboration, taboo reaction has no place among the reflexes of the scientist. For him, whatever defies or fails to fit in to the established category-system is not something horrifying, to be isolated or expelled. On the contrary, it is an intriguing 'phenomenon'—a starting point and a challenge for the invention of new classifications and new theories. It is something every young research worker would like to have crop up in his field of observation—perhaps the first rung on the ladder of fame. If a biologist ever came across a child born with the head of a goat, he would be hard put to it to make his compassion cover his elation. And as for social anthropologists, one may guess that their secret dreams are of finding a whole community of men who sleep for preference with their mothers!

## 11.) *The passage of time: bad or good?*

In traditional Africa, methods of time-reckoning vary greatly from culture to culture. Within each culture, again, we find a plurality of time-scales used in different contexts. Thus there may be a major scale which locates events either before, during or after the time of founding of the major institutions of the community: another scale which locates events by correlating them with the lifetimes of deceased ancestors: yet another which locates events by correlating them with the phases of the seasonal cycle: and yet another which uses phases of the daily cycle.

Although these scales are seldom interrelated in any systematic way, they all serve to order events in before–after series. Further, they have the very general characteristic that *vis-à-vis* 'after', 'before' is usually valued positively, sometimes neutrally, and never negatively. Whatever the particular scale involved, then, the passage of time is seen as something deleterious or at best neutral.

Perhaps the most widespread, everyday instance of this attitude is the standard justification of so much thought and action: 'That is what the old-time people told us.' (It is usually this standard justification which is in the forefront of the anthropologist's mind when he applies the label 'traditional culture'.)

On the major time-scale of the typical traditional culture, things are thought of as having been better in the golden age of the founding heroes than they are today. On an important minor time-scale, the annual one, the end of the year is a time when everything in the cosmos is run-down and sluggish, overcome by an accumulation of defilement and pollution.

A corollary of this attitude to time is a rich development of activities designed to negate its passage by a 'return to the beginning'. Such activities characteristically depend on the magical premiss that a symbolic statement of some archetypal event can in a sense recreate that event and temporarily obliterate the passage of time which has elapsed since its original occurrence.[46]

These rites of recreation are to be seen at their most luxuriant in the ancient cultures of the Western Sudan—notably in those of the Bambara and Dogon. In such cultures, indeed, a great part of everyday activity is said to have the ulterior significance of recreating archetypal events and acts. Thus the Dogon labouring in the fields recreates in his pattern of cultivation the emergence of the world from the cosmic egg. The builder of a homestead lays it out in a pattern that symbolically recreates the body of the culture-hero Nommo. Even relations between kin symbolize and recreate relations between the primal beings.[47]

One might well describe the Western Sudanic cultures as obsessed with the annulment of time to a degree unparalleled in Africa as a whole. Yet other, less spectacular, manifestations of the attempt to 'get back to the beginning' are widely distributed over the continent. In the West African forest belt, for instance, the richly developed ritual dramas enacted in honour of departed heroes and ancestors have a strong recreative aspect. For by inducing these beings to possess specially selected media and thus, during festivals, to return temporarily to the company of men, such rituals are restoring things as they were in olden times.[48]

On the minor time-scale provided by the seasonal cycle, we find a similar widespread concern for recreation and renewal. Hence the important rites which mark the end of an old year and the beginning of a new one—rites which attempt to make the year new by a thoroughgoing process of purification of accumulated pollutions and defilements.

This widespread attempt to annul the passage of time seems closely linked to features of traditional thought which I have already reviewed. As I pointed out earlier, the new and the strange, in so far as they fail to fit into the established system of classification and theory, are intimations of chaos to be avoided as far as possible. Advancing time, with its inevitable element of non-repetitive change, is the vehicle *par excellence* of the new and the strange. Hence its effects must be annulled at all costs. Rites of renewal and recreation, then, have much in common with the processes of secondary elaboration and taboo behaviour. Indeed, their kinship with the latter can be seen in the idea that the passage of the year is essentially an accumulation of pollutions, which it is the function of the renewal rites to remove. In short, these rites are the third great defensive reflex of traditional thought.[49]

When we turn from the traditional thinker to the scientist, we find this whole valuation of temporal process turned upside down. Not for the scientist the idea of a golden age at the beginning of time—an age from which things have been steadily falling away. For him, the past is a bad old past, and the best things lie ahead. The passage of time brings inexorable progress. As C. P. Snow has put it aptly, all scientists have 'the future in their bones'.[50] Where the traditional thinker is busily trying to annul the passage of time, the scientist may almost be said to be trying frantically to hurry time up. For in his impassioned pursuit of the experimental method, he is striving after the creation of new situations which nature, if left to herself, would bring about slowly if ever at all.

Once again, the scientist's attitude can be understood in terms of the 'open' predicament. For him, currently held ideas on a given subject are one possibility amongst many. Hence occurrences which threaten them are not the total, horrific threat that they would be for the traditional thinker. Hence time's burden of things new and strange does not hold the terrors that it holds for the traditionalist. Furthermore, the scientist's experience of the way in which successive theories, overthrown after exposure to adverse data, are replaced by ideas of ever greater predictive and explanatory power, leads almost inevitably to a very positive evaluation of time. Finally, we must remember that the 'open' predicament, though it has made people able to tolerate threats to their beliefs, has not been able to supply them with anything comparable to the cosiness of the traditional thinker ensconced amidst his established theories. As an English medical student, newly exposed to the scientific attitude, put it:

You seem to be as if when learning to skate, trying to find a nice hard piece of ice which you can stand upright on instead of learning how to move on it. You continue trying to find something, some foundation piece which will not move, whereas everything will move and you've got to learn to skate on it.[51]

The person who enjoys the moving world of the sciences, then, enjoys the exhilaration of the skater. But for many, this is a nervous, insecure sensation, which they would fain exchange for the womb-like warmth of the traditional theories and their defences. This lingering sense of insecurity gives a powerful attraction to the idea of progress. For by enabling people to cling to some hoped-for future state of perfect knowledge, it helps them live with a realization of the imperfection and transience of present theories.

Once formed, indeed, the idea of progress becomes in itself one of the most powerful supports of the scientific attitude generally. For the faith that, come what may, new experience must lead to better theories, and that better theories must eventually give place to still better ones, provides the strongest possible incentive for a constant readiness to expose oneself to the strange and the disturbing, to scrap current frameworks of ideas, and to cast about for replacements.

Like the quest for purity of motive, however, the faith in progress is a double-edged weapon. For the lingering insecurity which is one of the roots of this faith leads all too often to an excessive fixation of hopes and desires on an imagined utopian future. People cling to such a future in the same way that men in pre-scientific cultures cling to the past. And in doing so, they inevitably lose much of the traditionalist's ability to enjoy and glorify the moment he lives in. Even within the sciences, an excessive faith in progress can be dangerous. In sociology, for instance, it has led to a number of unfruitful theories of social evolution.

At this point, I should like to draw attention to a paradox inherent in the presentation of my subject. As a scientist, it is perhaps inevitable that I should at certain points give the impression that traditional African thought is a poor, shackled thing when compared with the thought of the sciences. Yet as a man, here I am living by choice in a still-heavily-traditional Africa rather than in the scientifically oriented Western subculture I was brought up in. Why? Well, there may be lots of queer, sinister, unacknowledged reasons. But one certain reason is the discovery of things lost at home. An intensely poetic quality in everyday life and thought, and a vivid enjoyment of the passing moment—both driven out of sophisticated Western life by the quest for purity of motive and the faith in progress. How necessary these are for the advance of science; but what a disaster they are when they run wild beyond their appropriate bounds! Though I largely disagree with the way in which the 'Négritude' theorists have characterized the differences between traditional African and modern Western thought, when it gets to this point I see very clearly what they are after.

So much, then, for the salient differences between traditional and scientific thought. There is nothing particularly original about the terms in which I have described the contrast between the two. Indeed, all of my eleven points of difference are to be found mentioned somewhere or other in previous anthropological literature. This literature, however, leaves much to be desired when it comes to interpretation. Thus one author deals with secondary elaboration, another with magic, another with taboo, and so on. A particular explanation covers a particular trait of traditional thought, but seems to have very little relevance to the others. Most social anthropologists would acknowledge that the eleven characteristic traits of traditional thought listed in this essay tend to occur together and vanish together; but so far they have offered no overall interpretation that does justice to this concomitance.

In so far as my paper makes a fresh contribution, I think this lies precisely in its provision of just such an overall interpretation. For the concept of the 'closed' predicament not only provides a key to the understanding of each one of the eleven salient traits of traditional thought, it also helps us to see why these eleven traits flourish and perish as a set. Where formerly we saw them as an assemblage of miscellaneous exotica, we can now see them as the components of a well-defined and comprehensible syndrome.

So far, however, the interpretation, though it breaks new ground, remains largely intellectualist. At this stage, it does not allow us to relate ideational differences to broader socio-cultural differences. It does not as yet allow us to suggest answers to such questions as 'Why did the scientific attitude emerge spontaneously in Europe but not in Africa?' or, 'Why, in Europe, did it emerge at particular times and places?' None the less, I think it does give a valuable clue as to the sort of circumstances we should be looking for: i.e. circumstances tending to promote awareness of alternatives to established theoretical models. Three relevant factors of this kind suggest themselves at once:

(i) *Development of written transmission of beliefs*[52]

Earlier on in this essay, I talked of the paradox of idea-systems whose users see them as static, but which are in fact constantly, albeit slowly, changing. This paradox, as I said, seems to imply something like a game of Grandmother's Footsteps, with Grandson moving a little at a time when Grandma's back is turned, but always taking care to be still when Grandma rounds on him.

Now it is, above all, the oral transmission of beliefs which makes this intellectual Grandmother's Footsteps possible. For in each generation, small innovations, together with the processes of selective recall, make for considerable adjustments of belief to current situation. But where they cannot refer back to the ideas of a former generation 'frozen' in writing, both those responsible for the adjustments and those who accept them remain virtually unaware that innovation has taken place. In a similar manner, a small and seemingly marginal innovation in belief can occur without anyone realizing that it is part of a cumulative trend which, over several generations, will amount to a very striking change.

In these circumstances, everything tends to give the main tenets of theory an absolute and timeless validity. In so doing, it prevents the development of any awareness of alternatives. Oral transmission, then, is clearly one of the basic supports of the 'closed' predicament.

Where literacy begins to spread widely through a community, the situation changes radically. The beliefs of a particular period become 'frozen' in writing. Meanwhile, oral transmission of beliefs goes on, and with it the continuous small adjustments to changing circumstances typical of pre-literate society. As time passes these adjustments produce an idea-system markedly different from that originally set down in writing. Now in an entirely oral culture, as we have seen, no one has the means of becoming aware of this change. But in a literate culture, the possibility of checking current beliefs against the 'frozen' ideas of an earlier era throws the fact of change into sharp relief.

In these circumstances, the main tenets of theory can no longer be seen as having an absolute and timeless validity. In the consciousness that one's own people believed other things at other times, we have the germ of a sense of alternatives. The stage is set for the emergence of the 'open' predicament.

Not only does attention to the question of literacy help us to understand why the 'open' predicament developed in Europe but not in Africa. It also helps us to understand why, in Europe, this predicament developed just when and where it did. Thus in their sketch of the history of writing,[53] Goody and Watt point out that pictographic writing developed in the Middle and Far East from the end of the fourth millennium B.C. But the various pictographic systems were so unwieldy and their assimilation so time-consuming that they tended to be the exclusive possessions of specially trained, conservative ruling elites. The interests of such elites in preserving the *status quo* would naturally counteract the 'opening' tendencies of written transmission. It was in sixth-century-B.C. Greece that a convenient, easily learnable phonetic alphabet became in some communities a majority possession; and it was in this same sixth-century Greece that the 'open' predicament made its first notable appearance. The subsequent fortunes of literacy in the Mediterranean world seem to correspond rather well with the subsequent fortunes of the 'open' predicament. Thus what we term the 'Dark Ages' was at once a period which saw the restriction of literacy to small, conservative ruling elites, and at the same time a period in which the 'closed' predicament reasserted itself in full force. And in the reawakening of the twelfth–seventeenth centuries, a great expansion and democratization of literacy was the precursor of the final, enduring reappearance of the 'open' predicament and the scientific outlook. Notable during the early part of this period was the rediscovery via Arab sources, of the 'lost' writings of the great Greek philosopher-scientists. Since in early medieval times current theoretical tenets were taught very much in the 'this is what the ancients handed down to us' spirit of the closed society, the sudden forced confrontation with the very different reality of what these ancestral heroes actually did believe must have had an effect which powerfully supplemented that due to the growth of literacy generally.

## (ii) *Development of culturally heterogeneous communities*

There is one obvious, almost platitudinous answer to the question: what gives members of a community an awareness of alternative possibilities of interpreting their world? The answer, of course, is: meeting other people who do in fact interpret the world differently. But there are meetings and meetings; and it is clear that whilst some make very little difference to the outlooks of those involved, others are crucial for the rise of the 'open' predicament.

Now neither traditional Africa nor early Europe lacked encounters between bearers of radically different cultures. So our aim must be to show why, in Africa, such encounters did little to promote the 'open' predicament, when in Europe they did so much.

My own very tentative answer goes something like this. Traditional African communities were as a rule fairly homogeneous as regards their internal culture, and their relations with culturally alien neighbours tended to be restricted to the context of trade. Now such restricted relations did not make for mutual encounter of a very searching kind. In extreme cases, indeed, they were carried on without actual face-to-face contact: take, for instance, the notorious 'silent trade' between North African merchants and certain peoples of the Western Sudan—an exercise in which the partners neither met nor spoke. Much trade between bearers of radically different cultures was, of course, carried out under conditions far less extreme than these; and it was even common for members of a given community to speak the languages of the culturally alien peoples they traded with. Yet culturally contrasted trading partners remained basically rooted in different communities, from which they set out before trade, and to which they returned after it. Under these limitations, confrontation with alien world-views remained very partial. The trader encountered the thought of his alien partners at the level of common sense but not usually at the level of theory. Since commonsense worlds, in general, differ very little in comparison with theoretical worlds, such encounters did not suffice to stimulate a strong sense of alternatives.[54]

Even where the member of a traditional community did make contact with his alien neighbours at the level of theory, the content of theory was such that it still presented an obstacle to the development of a real sense of alternatives. As I pointed out in Part I of this paper, the bulk of traditional theory was concerned with its users' own particular community. There was an implicit premise that the world worked one way within one's own community, and another way outside it. Hence if one's neighbours believed some very strange and different things, this was in no way surprising or disturbing in terms of one's own beliefs. In such circumstances, radically contrasting belief-systems could seldom be seen as genuine alternatives.

When we turn from Africa to Europe, it is important to note just when and where the 'open' predicament came to prevail. Its first home, historians seem to agree, was in certain parts of sixth-century-B.C. Greece. Not in such centrally placed, culturally homogeneous states as Sparta, whose self-contained agricultural society remained rigidly 'closed'; but in the small, cosmopolitan trading communities on the frontiers of the Greek world—old-established Ionian cities like Miletus and Ephesus, and more recently established colonies like Abdera and Syracuse.[55]

After declining in this area the fortunes of the 'open' predicament flourished for several centuries in Alexandria. Later, they waxed briefly in the cities of the Arab world. Thence, in late medieval times, the current passed to the cities of the Iberian peninsula and coastal Italy. Finally, it passed to the cities of north-western Europe.

What was it about the communities that lay along this devious path that made them such excellent centres for the development of the 'open' predicament? First and foremost, perhaps, it was the conditions of contact between the bearers of different cultures. Whereas in Africa intercultural boundaries tended to coincide with inter-community boundaries, in these Mediterranean and European cities they cut right through the middle of the community. In these centres, people of diverse origins and cultures were packed together within single urban communities. And although the 'sons of the soil' were frequently the only people who had full citizenship rights, most of the inhabitants had feelings of common community membership and common interests *vis-à-vis* such outsiders as territorial rulers, the lords of the local countryside, other cities, and so on.

Under these conditions, relations between bearers of different cultures were much broader in scope than the purely commercial relations which typically linked such people over much of traditional Africa. And a broader context of social relationship made for a deeper and more searching intellectual encounter. Here, the encounter was not merely at the level of common sense where differences were negligible. It was also at the level of basic theory where differences were striking. Much of the 'open' temper of late and medieval and Renaissance times, for instance, can probably be traced to the confrontation of the basic tenets of the Christian, Islamic and Jewish thought-traditions in the twelfth-century cities of Spain and coastal Italy.[56]

Another factor making for more searching encounter was the actual content of the theories involved. The various traditions of thought making up the intellectual inheritance of these Mediterranean and European cities were the products of peoples who had long been living in communities far more integrally linked to the wider world than was usual in traditional Africa. As such, they were more universalistic in their content. So here, when a confrontation took place, it was no longer possible to rest content with saying: 'My theory works for my little world, and his works for his.' My theory and his theory were now patently about the same world, and awareness of them as alternatives became inescapable.

### (iii) *Development of the trade–travel–exploration complex*

So much for encounter between bearers of different cultures within a single community. A second important kind of encounter arises from voyages of travel and exploration in which members of one community go to live temporarily amongst members of a culturally alien community, with the express aim of intellectual and emotional contact at all levels from the most superficial to the deepest.

Now although individual members of many traditional African cultures must have made such voyages from time to time, these, so far as we know, have never become a dominant theme of life in any of the traditional cultures. But in sixth–third-century-B.C. Greece, in the medieval Arab world, and finally in fifteenth–seventeenth-century western Europe—all crucial centres for the development of the 'open' predicament—these voyages were such important features of social life that they coloured everyone's outlook on the world.

The evidence we have from ancient Greece indicates that many of the great independent thinkers such as Thales, Anaximander, Democritus, Herodotus and Xenophanes probably made extensive exploratory voyages themselves. And in some of their writings, the connection between first-hand experience of a variety of alien ways of looking at the world and an 'open' sceptical tenor of thought becomes explicit.[57] Again in fifteenth–eighteenth-century western Europe, exotic world-views personified in figures like the Noble Savage, the Wise Egyptian and the Chinese Sage haunt the pages of many of the sceptical writings of the times; and here too the link between confrontation with alien world-views and 'open' thinking is often explicit.[58]

It is, of course, possible to argue that these voyages and these confrontations were a consequence and not a cause of the 'open' predicament; that 'open-minded' people embarked on them with the idea of putting parochial views to the deliberate test of wider horizons of experience. This may have been true once the voyages had become a dominant feature of the life of the times. But I believe the beginnings of the eras of exploration can still be best understood in terms of the aims and interests of essentially 'closed-minded' societies.

One's suspicions on this score are aroused in the first instance by the fact that in both of the great eras of exploration, many of the voyages were encouraged if not directed by the pillars of tradition: in early Greece by the Delphic Oracle, and in western Europe by the popes.

Again, it is clear that the motive forces behind the voyages included the aim of reducing population pressure by overseas settlement and that of extending commerce to include new items to be found only in faraway lands. The detailed probings of alien world-views can thus be understood as intelligence operations directed towards solving the problems of human coexistence involved in overseas settlement and commerce. There was probably little 'open-mindedness' in the intentions which originally lay behind them.

Perhaps the most interesting example of the essentially 'closed' motivations behind activities which were to make a great contribution to the development of the 'open' predicament is provided by the operations of Christian missionaries in the fifteenth–eighteenth centuries. The fanaticism with which the missionaries worked to convert distant peoples of alien faith can, I think, be understood as a product of the 'closed' society's determination to protect itself from the possibility of being disturbed by confrontation with alien world-views—a possibility which loomed large in this era of exploration. But the more intelligent missionaries saw that effective evangelization required a prior understanding of the faiths of those to be converted; and they set themselves, however reluctantly, to acquire such an understanding. The result was a body of records of alien world-views that came to colour much of the thought of the times, and that was undoubtedly one of the important contributions to the genesis of the open thinking of the seventeenth century.

The eras of exploration encouraged the growth of the 'open' predicament in a second way. This was through the rich material fruits of the voyages. In traditional cultures, as we have seen, distant lands tend to epitomize all that is new and strange, all that fails to fit into the established system of categories, all that is tabooed, fearful and abominable. Hence, whether among the Lugbara of East Africa or among Dark Age Europeans, we find them peopled with abominations and monsters. In the eras of exploration, however, reports came back not of monsters but of delights and riches. Slowly, these pleasant associations of the Great Beyond extended themselves to new and strange experience generally. The quest for such experience came to be seen not as something dangerous and foolhardy, but as something richly rewarding and pleasantly exciting. This relation between the fruits of exploration and the new attitudes to the strange and category-defying is portrayed very clearly in some of the metaphors of these eras. Take, for instance, Joseph Glanvill's notion of 'An America of Secrets and an Unknown Peru of Nature', waiting to overthrow old scholastic ideas and force men to replace them with something better.[59]

Not only, then, did the events of these eras undermine the feeling that one's established beliefs were the only defence against chaos and the void. They gave a less horrifying, nay benign, face to chaos itself.

In naming these three factors as crucial for the development of the 'open' predicament, I am not implying that wherever they occur, there is a sort of painless, automatic and complete transition from 'closed' to 'open' thinking. On the contrary, the transition seems inevitably to be painful, violent and partial.

Even in ancient Greece, the independent thinking of the great pre-socratic philosophers evoked strong and anxious reactions.[60] In late medieval times, a few decades of confrontation with alien world-views and 'open' sceptical thinking tended to be succeeded by decades of persecution of those responsible for disturbing established orthodoxy and by a general 'closing-up' of thought.[61] In present-day Nigeria, we seem to be seeing yet another example of the atrocious birth-pangs of the 'open' society.

Why should the transition be so painful? Well, a theme of this paper has been the way in which a developing awareness of alternative world-views erodes attitudes which attach an absolute validity to the established outlook. But this is a process that works over time—indeed over generations. Throughout the process there are bound to be many people on whom the confrontation has not yet worked its magic. These people still retain the old sense of the absolute validity of their belief-systems, with all the attendant anxieties about threats to them. For these people, the confrontation is still a threat of chaos of the most horrific kind—a threat which demands the most drastic measures. They respond in one of two ways: either by trying to blot out those responsible for the confrontation, often down to the last unborn child; or by trying to convert them to their own beliefs through fanatical missionary activity.

Again, as I said earlier, the moving, shifting thought-world produced by the 'open' predicament creates its own sense of insecurity. Many people find this shifting world intolerable. Some adjust to their fears by developing an inordinate faith in progress towards a future in which 'the Truth' will be finally known. But others long nostalgically for the fixed, unquestionable beliefs of the 'closed' culture. They call for authoritarian establishment and control of dogma, and for persecution of those who have managed to be at ease in a world of ever-shifting ideas. Clearly, the 'open' predicament is a precarious, fragile thing.

L

In modern western Europe and America, it is true, the 'open' predicament seems to have escaped from this precariousness through public acknowledgement of the practical utility of the sciences. It has achieved a secure foothold in the culture because its results maximize values shared by 'closed-' and 'open-' minded alike. Even here, however, the 'open' predicament has nothing like a universal sway. On the contrary, it is almost a minority phenomenon. Outside the various academic disciplines in which it has been institutionalized, its hold is pitifully less than those who describe Western culture as 'science-oriented' often like to think.

It is true that in modern Western culture, the theoretical models propounded by the professional scientists do, to some extent, become the intellectual furnishings of a very large sector of the population. The moderately educated layman typically shares with the scientist a general predilection for impersonal 'it-' theory and a proper contempt for 'thou-' theory. Garbled and watered-down though it may be, the atomic theory of matter is one of his standard possessions. But the layman's ground for accepting the models propounded by the scientist is often no different from the young African villager's ground for accepting the models propounded by one of his elders. In both cases the propounders are deferred to as the accredited agents of tradition. As for the rules which guide scientists themselves in the acceptance or rejection of models, these seldom become part of the intellectual equipment of members of the wider population. For all the apparent up-to-dateness of the content of his world-view, the modern Western layman is rarely more 'open' or scientific in his outlook than is the traditional African villager.

This takes me back to a general point about the layout of this paper. If I spent the whole of Part I labouring the thesis that differences in the content of theories do more to hide continuities than reveal genuine contrasts, this was not, as some readers may have imagined, through a determination to ignore the contrasts. Rather, it was precisely to warn them away from the trap which the Western layman characteristically falls into—the trap which makes him feel he is keeping up with the scientists when in fact he is no nearer to them than the African peasant.

## NOTES

1] I am grateful to the Institute of African Studies, University of Ibadan, for a grant towards the publication of this paper. The Institute is, however, in no way responsible for the opinions expressed.

[2] 'Destiny and the Unconscious in West Africa', *Africa*, April 1961; 'The Kalabari World-View: on Outline and Interpretation', *Africa*, July 1962; 'Ritual Man in Africa', *Africa*, April 1964.

[3] See, for instance, Beattie, 1966.

[4] See Beattie, *op. cit.*

[5] Turner, 1961 and 1964.

[6] Gluckman, 1965. See especially Chapter VI: 'Mystical Disturbance and Ritual Adjustment'.

[7] Kiev (ed.), 1964, *passim.*

[8] Horton, 1961.

[9] Evans-Pritchard, 1965, p. 8.

[10] See, for instance, Evans-Pritchard, *op. cit.*, p. 88.

[11] Evans-Pritchard, 1956; Lienhardt, 1961.

[12] Evans-Pritchard, *op. cit.*, p. 316.

[13] Horton, 1962, 1964b; Fortes, 1949, especially pp. 21-2 and p. 219.

[14] Fortes, 1959.

[15] R. E. Bradbury in *Man*, September 1959.

[16] Such parallels arouse the more uncomfortable thought that in all the theorizing we sociologists have done about the working of traditional African societies, we may often have done little more than translate indigenous African theories about such workings.

[17] Middleton, 1960.

[18] Just how little headway British social anthropologists appear to be making with traditional religious thought is betrayed by their tendency to confine themselves to the study of its political manipulation, and to leave to psychologists the job of accounting for its substantive features. In this context, I should like to draw attention to the curiously menial role in which the modern British anthropologist has cast the psychologist—the role of the well-disciplined scavenger. On the one hand, the psychologist is expected to keep well away from any intellectual morsel currently considered digestible by the anthropologist. On the other hand, he is tossed all indigestible morsels, and is expected to relieve the anthropologist of the embarrassing smell they would create if left in his house uneaten.

[19] See, for instance, *Scientific Change* (Symposium on the History of Science, University of Oxford, 9–15 July 1961), ed. A. C. Crombie, London, 1963; especially the chapter on 'Chinese Science' and the subsequent interventions by Willy Hartner and Stephen Toulmin.

[20] 'Western society today may be said to harbour science like a foreign god, powerful and mysterious. Our lives are changed by its handiwork but the population of the West is as far from understanding the nature of this strange power as a remote peasant of the Middle Ages may have been from understanding the theology of Thomas Aquinas' (Barzun, 1961).

[21] Coming from Africa, this is something of a *cri de cœur*. In the authoritarian political climate of emergent African nations, there are particular dangers that this may be the outcome of 'westernization'. For since the spirit of science, as I shall emphasize in Part II, is essentially anti-authoritarian, there is a great temptation to take the preoccupation with impersonal models as the essence of science, and to reject the real essence as inconvenient. Hence the need to insist so strongly on disentangling the two.

[22] Philosophically minded readers will notice here some affinities with Karl Popper, who also makes the transition from a 'closed' to an 'open' predicament crucial for the take-off from tradition to science. For me, however, Popper obscures the issue by packing too many contrasts into his definitions of 'closed' and 'open'. Thus, for him, the transition from one predicament to the other implies not just a growth in the awareness of alternatives but also a transition from communalism to individualism, and from ascribed status to achieved status. But as I hope to show in this essay it is the awareness of alternatives which is crucial for the take-off into science. Not individualism or achieved status: for there are lots of societies where both of the latter are well developed, but which show no signs whatever of take-off. In the present context, therefore, my own narrower definition of 'closed' and 'open' seems more appropriate.

[23] Evans-Pritchard, 1936, p. 194.

[24] *Ibid.*, p. 338.

[25] Evans-Pritchard, 1965, p. 55.

[26] Laye, 1955. Quoted in Jahn, 1961 (p. 125). As an attempt to make an inventory of distinctive and universal features of African culture, Jahn's book seems to be highly tendentious. But its imaginative sketch of the assumptions underlying magical beliefs and practices is one of the most suggestive treatments of the subject I have seen.

[27] Evans-Pritchard, 1936, p. 449.

[28] Horton, 1965.

[29] Lavondes, 1963.

[30] *Ibid.*, p. 115.

[31] From the piecemeal, situation-bound character of traditional idea-systems, some have been led to infer that the anthropologist must analyse them in an equally piecemeal situational manner, and not as systems. Thus in her recent *Purity and Danger* (1966),

Mary Douglas talks about the error of pinning out entire traditional idea-systems like Lepidoptera, in abstraction from the real-life situations in which their various fragments actually occur. But abstraction is as abstraction does. Provided that comparison of total idea-systems leads to interesting results, it is surely as justifiable as any other kind of comparison. After all, what about the abstraction and comparison of social structures?

[32] See Gellner, 1964, for a similar point exemplified in the philosophy of Descartes (p. 105).

[33] See, for instance, Fortes, 1961.

[34] See Horton, 1963.

[35] See Beattie, 1966.

[36] Achebe, 1957.

[37] The idea of secondary elaboration as a key feature of pre-scientific thought-systems was put forward with great brilliance and insight by Evans-Pritchard in his *Witchcraft, Oracles and Magic*. All subsequent discussions, including the present one, are heavily indebted to his lead.

[38] Kuhn, 1962.

[39] 1936, *passim*.

[40] Nadel, 1956, especially Chap VI.

[41] Forde, 1958.

[42] Some similar comments on the themes of ignorance and uncertainty in relation to the scientific outlook are made by R. G. Armstrong in a brief but trenchant critique of 'The Notion of Magic' by M. and R. Wax (1963).

[43] This observation may well prove to be a milestone in our understanding of traditional thought. It was first made some years ago by Mary Douglas, who has developed many of its implications in her recent book *Purity and Danger*. Though we clearly disagree on certain wider implications, the present discussion is deeply indebted to her insights.

[44] Middleton, 1960.

[45] This association of foreign lands with chaos and pollution seems to be a universal of pre-scientific thought-systems. For this, see Eliade, 1961, especially Chap. I.

[46] In these rites of recreation, traditional African thought shows its striking affinities with pre-scientific thought in many other parts of the world. The worldwide occurrence and meaning of such rites was first dealt with by Mircea Eliade in his *Myth of the Eternal Return*. A more recent treatment from which the present analysis has profited greatly is to be found in the chapter entitled 'Le Temps Retrouvé', Lévi-Strauss, 1962.

[47] See Griaule and Dieterlen, 1954, and Griaule, 1965.

[48] For some interesting remarks on this aspect of West African ritual dramas, see Tardits, 1962.

[49] Lévi-Strauss, I think, is making much the same point about rites of renewal when he talks of the continuous battle between pre-scientific classificatory systems and the non-repetitive changes involved in the passage of time. See Lévi-Strauss, 1962.

[50] Snow, 1959, p. 10.

[51] Johnson Abercrombie, 1960; quoted on p. 131.

[52] The discussion that follows leans heavily upon Goody and Watt, 1963. Goody and Watt are, I believe, among the first to have spelled out the probable importance of the transition from oral to written transmission of beliefs for the take-off from tradition into science. I have drawn heavily here upon their characterization of the contrasting predicaments of thinkers in oral and literate cultures; though my argument diverges somewhat from theirs in its later stages.

[53] *Ibid.*, pp. 311–19.

[54] This point, I think, is relevant to an argument advanced against my analysis of magic. (John Beattie, personal communication.) The argument is that once a person learns another language, he becomes aware of alternative possibilities of dividing up the world by words and, on my premises, must inevitably adopt a non-magical outlook.

In rebuttal, I would say that where a person learns another people's language and thought only at the commonsense level, he is not exposed to a radically different way of dividing up the world by words. Indeed, he is liable to see most of the commonsense words and concepts of the alien language as having equivalents in his own. They are 'the same words' and 'the same thoughts'. It is only when he learns the alien language and thought at the theoretical level that he becomes aware of a radically different way of dividing the world.

[55] For a brilliant sketch of the beginnings of the 'open' predicament in the Greek city-states, see Popper, 1945. Although, as I said earlier, Popper's definition of 'closed' and 'open' differs somewhat from my own, much of what he says is relevant to my argument and has indeed provided inspiration for it.

[56] For the importance of the confrontation between these three thought traditions, see Heer, 1962.

[57] Take, for instance, the following passage from Xenophanes, quoted in Toulmin, 1961:

'Mortals consider that the gods are begotten as they are, and have clothes and voices and figures like theirs. The Ethiopians make their gods black and snub-nosed; the Thracians say theirs have blue eyes and red hair. Yes, and if oxen and horses or lions had hands, and could paint with their hands, and produce works of art as men do, horses would paint the gods with shapes like horses, and oxen like oxen, and make their bodies in the image of their several kinds.'

[58] For this see Hazard, 1964. (Especially Chap. 4.)

[59] Quoted from *The Vanity of Dogmatizing*, in Willey, 1962, p. 168.

[60] See Popper, 1945, for some of these reactions to pre-socratic 'open' thinking.

[61] See Heer, 1962, for a vivid picture of the way in which the medieval world oscillated crazily between 'open' and 'closed' attitudes.

## *BIBLIOGRAPHY*

ABERCROMBIE, J. M. L. (1960). *The Anatomy of Judgement*. London: Hutchinson.

ACHEBE, C. (1957). *Things Fall Apart*. London: Heinemann.

BARZUN, J. (1961). 'Introduction' to TOULMIN, S. *Foresight and Understanding*. London: Hutchinson.

BEATTIE, J. (1966). 'Ritual and Social Change'. *Man (Journal of the Royal Anthropological Institute)* (n.s), (I(1).

CROMBIE, A. C. (ed.) (1963). *Scientific Change*. London: Heinemann. (Symposium on the History of Science, Oxford, 1961.)

DOUGLAS, M. (1966). *Purity and Danger*. London: Routledge & Kegan Paul.

ELIADE, M. (1954). *Myth of the Eternal Return*. Princeton (N.J.): Princeton University Press.

—— (1961). *Sacred and the Profane*. New York: Harvest Books.

EVANS-PRITCHARD, E. E. (1936). *Witchcraft, Oracles and Magic among the Azande*. London: Oxford University Press.

—— (1956). *Nuer Religion*. London: Oxford University Press.

—— (1965). *Theories of Primitive Religion*. London: Oxford University Press.

FORDE, D. (1958). 'Spirits, Witches and Sorcerers in the Supernatural Economy of the Yakö'. *Journal of the Royal Anthropological Institute*, lxxxviii(2).

FORTES, M. (1949). *The Web of Kinship among the Tallensi*. London: Oxford University Press.

—— (1959). *Oedipus and Job in West African Religion*. Cambridge: University Press.

—— (1961). 'Pietas in Ancestor Worship'. *Journal of the Royal Anthropological Institute*, xci, part 2.

GELLNER, E. (1964). *Thought and Change*. London: Weidenfeld & Nicolson.

GLUCKMAN, M. (1965). *Politics, Law and Ritual in Tribal Society*. Oxford: Basil Blackwell.

GOODY, J., and WATT, I. (1963). 'The Consequences of Literacy'. *Comparative Studies in Society and History*, v(3).

GRIAULE, M. (1965). *Conversations with Ogotemmêli*. London: Oxford University Press.

—— and DIETERLING, G. (1954). 'The Dogon', in FORDE, D. (ed.), *African Worlds*. London: Oxford University Press.

HAZARD, P. (1964). *The European Mind 1680–1715*. Harmondsworth: Penguin.

HEER, F. (1962). *The Mediaeval World*. London: Weidenfeld & Nicolson.

HORTON, R. (1956). 'God, Man and the Land in a Northern Ibo Village Group'. *Africa*, xxvi(1).

—— (1961). 'Destiny and the Unconscious in West Africa'. *Africa*, xxxxi(2).

—— (1962). 'The Kalabari World-View; an Outline and Interpretation'. *Africa*, xxxii(3).

—— (1963). 'The Kalabari *Ekine* Society: a Borderland of Religion and Art'. *Africa*, xxxiiii(2).

—— (1964a). 'Ritual Man in Africa'. *Africa*, xxx(2).

—— (1964b). 'A Hundred Years of Change in Kalabari Religion'. Unpublished.

—— (1965). *Kalabari Sculpture*. Lagos.

JAHN, J. (1961). *Muntu: An Outline of Neo-African Culture*. London: Faber & Faber.

KIEV, A. (ed.) (1964). *Magic, Faith and Healing*. London: Collier-Macmillan.

KUHN, T. (1962). *The Structure of Scientific Revolutions*. Chicago: University of Chicago Press.

LAVONDES, H. (1963). 'Magie et Langage'. *L'Homme*, iii(3).

LAYE, C. (1955). *The Dark Child*. London: Collins.

LEINHARDT, G. (1961). *Divinity and Experience; the Religion of the Dinka*. London: Oxford University Press.

LÉVI-STRAUSS, C. (1962). *La Pensée Sauvage*. Paris: Plon.

MIDDLETON, J. (1960). *Lugbara Religion*. London: Oxford University Press.

NADEL, S. F. (1956). *Nupe Religion*. London: Routledge & Kegan Paul.

POPPER, K. (1945). *The Open Society and its Enemies*. London: G. Routledge & Sons.

SNOW, C. P. (1959). *The Two Cultures and the Scientific Revolution*. Cambridge: Cambridge University Press.

TARDITS, C. (1962). 'Religion, Epic, History: Notes on the Underlying Functions of Cults in Benin Civilisations'. *Diogenes*, 37.

TOULMIN, S., and GOODFIELD, G. J. (1961). *The Fabric of the Heavens*. London: Hutchinson.

TURNER, V. W. (1961). *Ndembu Divination*. Rhodes–Livingstone Paper No. 31. Manchester: Manchester University Press.

—— (1964). 'A Ndembu Doctor in Practice' in Kiev, *op cit*.

WAX, M., and WAX, R. (1963). 'The Notion of Magic'. *Current Anthropology*, 4(5), December.

WILLEY, B. (1962). *The Seventeenth Century Background*. Harmondsworth: Penguin in association with Chatto & Windus.

# 9. IOAN DAVIES

*The Management of Knowledge:*
*a Critique of the Use of Typologies*
*in the Sociology of*
*Education\**

*I*

One of the curiosities of work in the social sciences, as in science, is that the focus of research tends to concentrate on partial areas of immediate concern which in turn come to be defined as the entire field. The study of education is no exception. For many years sociologists have developed research on the relationship between social inequality and educational opportunity (with a few studies on educational institutions included as complements). That there is other research which has a direct bearing on the 'field' is often ignored. The sociology of education *is* the study of educational opportunity while such topics as the development of scientific research and the diffusion of ideas are relegated to other sub-areas of the discipline—the sociology of science or of knowledge. In recent years so widespread has been this practice that when a field of research and theory is developed which is clearly concerned with education, but which seriously challenges the whole framework of sociological research in education, it is immediately 're-written' and absorbed into the conventional wisdom. The reception of Bernstein's work on socio-linguistics is a case in point: so long as he seemed to be talking about stratification everyone assumed that they understood what the research was about. Here was simply a further demonstration of the inequalities in the educational system. The fact that he was using entirely different concepts ('symbolic orders', 'restricted and elaborated codes') to discuss relationships, learning processes and power structures was conveniently ignored.[1]

It is the argument of this paper that the current emphasis is disastrous for the development of a sociology of education which is concerned with both the

* This paper, without the first section, originally appeared in *Sociology*, 4(1), 1970.

societal parameters of education and its system properties. (This procedure is, incidentally, also disastrous for educational sociology which sees stratification as an important indicator of educational competence. Without a theory of knowledge it is difficult to see what the stratification debate is about.) It is also an argument that the sociology of education—like any other branch of the social sciences—cannot begin to develop theory until it is conscious of the importance of comparison in establishing similarities, differences and peculiarities in various systems. For this reason I have chosen to begin the discussion by examining an essay which has both of these concerns, but which demonstrates the distorting effect of assuming that the most important questions in the sociology of education are to do with social stratification and educational opportunity.

## II

In a recent essay[2] Earl Hopper provided a typology for the classification of educational systems. This is a welcome development in the sociology of education which has to date tended to range between unsystematic generalizations, detailed case studies and untheoretical statistical comparisons. But however welcome the attempt, there are difficulties in accepting Hopper's framework as a basis for research. The heuristic value of a typology must be, as he says, 'a preliminary step to more narrowly-focused research'. It must also be capable of providing the basis for effective explanations of differences between systems and of accounting for major processes in particular systems. It can be demonstrated that Hopper's typology poses problems in relation to both of these objectives, but because the exercise is of crucial importance if a viable educational sociology is to develop, I intend to begin with a discussion of the logical properties of the essay and move from there to an alternative formulation.

The first and most striking thing about Hopper's essay is the assumption of what an educational system is for. As he puts it, 'the structure of educational systems, especially those within industrial societies, can be understood primarily in terms of their selection process'.[3] As this selection process is related directly to the demands of the labour market, education is seen by Hopper largely in terms of its economic functions and so might be expected to be treated as an extension of economic sociology. Oddly enough, however, it is not discussed in this context at all. For Hopper the educational system inherits from the economic system certain values which in turn control certain processes of occupational training and selection: the whole point of educational research is how the system does this. ('How does educational selection occur? When are pupils initially selected? Who should be selected? Why should they be selected?') The exercise of analysing selection processes is, of course, extremely important in educational research, and Hopper's method of posing the question allows for more flexible research on this set of problems than more economics-based or stratification-based frameworks. But as he formulates it the typology is open to two major objections.

1.) If education is primarily about the structuring of selection this can surely only be done within a more comprehensive model of economic and stratification systems. Hopper's essay is primarily concerned with industrial societies, yet there is no attempt to adequately distinguish between the different characteristics of those societies in terms of both their relative technology and unit sizes and the selection by industry and commerce of its personnel. Further there is an implicit assumption that there is a one-to-one relationship between the selection process in schools and the requirements of the economy. As the economics literature more than amply demonstrates[4] this is just not true (although politicians in all countries may want to make it come true). It may be conceded that he does classify degrees of standardization of selection procedures but this is only from the point of view of the schools: there is no suspicion of whether economic selection might use educational criteria in non-standard ways. Even within the U.S.S.R. (with remarkable educational standardization) there are a large number of entry points to occupational posts which do not appear to depend on educational selection.[5] Within a more diversified educational system the independence of sectors of the economy from educational selection is even greater.[6] As I shall show later this is not simply a question of using economic and organizational variables to 'explain' educational variations, it is more centrally a question of the actual classifications to be used initially.

A similar objection can be raised against Hopper's assumptions on stratification. The basis of his stratification analysis rests on the 'ideologies of legitimation' and the convergence between stratification and ideology.[7] Although there is some evidence to support convergence, it is doubtful if its assumption helps much in the analysis of education. After all, education is as much about the *creation* of ideologies as it is about anything else. All Hopper is able to say about stratification is in relation to ruling groups who must legitimize their positions, be flexible enough to absorb potentially able leaders from the lower order, and obtain some co-operation from the less powerful groups. This Paretan definition does nothing to provide the basis for analysing different forms of stratification: variations are reduced dramatically to elite competence. It is therefore relatively easy to demonstrate 'convergence' when the only focus of analysis is the ruling culture. Indeed in this sense the definition is tautological: elites have ideologies which are either centralized or diffused according to whether the elites are centralized or diffused. This tells us little about either the nature of the ideologies or the diffusion.

2.) Unfortunately Hopper never discusses whether selection is only a part of the study of education. He seems to confuse systemic goals with extra-systemic ones, and hardly begins to analyse the relationship of goals to culture, organization or the economy.[8] In part this is derived from the initial confusion over the function of education. Hopper plumps for the 'manifest function' of selection, which presumably implies that such issues as research, styles of pedagogy and the different organizational and cultural goals of places of education must be classified as latent or else encapsulated into the manifest function. This is very curious. In the Soviet Union, for example, a manifest function of education must as much be the education of students into the dominant national-ist-communist ideology as to select them according to criteria derived from that ideology or from other social/economic pressures. This is more than amply demonstrated by the literature,[9] which emphasizes the nationalist-communist philosophy all the way from curricula to regular indoctrination through such organizations as the Young Pioneers. In the United States a manifest function of education must surely be the integration of disparate groups into a common value-system. Both of these functions may contribute to the legitimation of the selection process, but they must be kept analytically separate if we are to make any sense of education as part of national culture. But even this overemphasizes the common framework of educational values. The *Gemeinschaft/Gesellschaft* dichotomy is plainly inadequate as a basis for analysing values. The goals of a differentiated system must also be related to stratification discontinuities and to what Etzioni refers to as the 'culture goals' which 'institutionalize conditions needed for the creation and preservation of symbolic objects, their application, and the creation or reinforcement of commitment to such objects'.[10] Hopper's typology ascribes single culture goals to all educational institutions, but surely even within his framework of selection the actual emphasis placed on selection varies enormously within regions and between different schools or institutions: this is as true of the U.S.S.R. as of Britain. In part this may be because of the goals set by the organizations themselves and because of local cultural pressures which operate quite distinctly from the ideologies of the centre. Indeed the centre–periphery framework used by political sociologists[11] would seem to have more relevance to the discussion of national ideologies than a simple framework based on the pattern variables, though in industrial societies the 'periphery' would have to be carefully reformulated in relation to class structures and cultures.[12] In addition to this we have the existence within ruling elites (in all countries) of quite distinct value-systems which are in continual competition for the control of the educational system. This may be for the reasons demonstrated by Gramsci: 'every "essential" social class emerging into history from the preceding economic structure, and as an expression of one of the developments of this structure, has found, at least in all history up to now, intellectual categories which were pre-existing and which, moreover, appeared as representatives of an historical continuity uninterrupted even by the most complicated and radical changes in social and political forms'.[13] Thus if changes take place in ideologies they take place in the context of this struggle, which is at once a cultural and a structural one. Hopper is in danger of identifying ruling ideologies with the residual traditions. The distinction between goals and legitimation is a necessary one. What is more important is to identify the competing sectors (in the U.S.S.R. as in Britain) and assess their relative importance. This can only be a dynamic historical/structural study, whose object is to establish how the particular constellations of ideologies come to hold the influence they do and under what legitimizing symbols changes take place.[14] This is particularly true in societies which are apparently communistic-collectivistic or, as in Britain, where the national attitudes become increasingly collectivistic-meritocratic while competing with residual particularism/individualism. On the first type of society Hopper seems to be reading Marion Levy when he should be reading Franz Schumann, and on the second he reads vintage Shils when Raymond Williams or even Bantock would be more useful.[15] The problem arises partly from discussing only 'various public and official statements'[16] rather than focusing on the conflicts between national policy goals, symbols of legitimation and sectoral goals.

If we take the case of France where Hopper's criteria for selection is pater-nalist-collectivist, it is clear that these values relate more to the domination of a particular kind of social elite (the archtypical bourgeoisie) and the structured nature of its conflict with rural society and the working class than to any abstract concept of polity or culture: why not therefore start with the historical structur-ing of class culture and leave the values to be explained? The problem with the pattern variable approach is that it leaves very little room for the analysis of culture because the cultural variables which form the basis for the classification can in turn only lead to explanations in terms of social stratification. This is why Parsons inexplicably becomes a 'Marxist' when he talks about class[17] but of course it is a class analysis from which culture has already been removed. In certain situations (e.g. in comparing economic and political development) this procedure is capable of producing important insights, but it is doubtful if it helps much in the study of such cultural areas as education. Hence we need to analyse precisely what constitutes a culture. This is bound to involve an analysis of the interrelationships between the organizations themselves, the characteristics of the economy and the political power structure, and communications systems (including language, mass media and folk mores). It is impossible to see a way of including these in any research derived from Hopper's typology without doing serious injustice to the facts and without trivializing the cultural content of education.

But however weak Hopper's conceptual framework, it does have a number of distinct advantages for the comparativist. Too often comparative educational monographs simply list cases side by side or use crude measurements of inputs or outputs. As Hopper demonstrates, there *are* theoretical interconnections between system elements which are capable of being studied *as interconnections*. Further than this he does use the value-system as an important part of this exer-cise. My major complaint is not this—for Hopper comes very close to seeing education as a cultural-political process—but to the methodological confusion that is bound to arise in treating values in the way he does. Having said that it is now necessary to spell out what the alternatives might be.

### III

Sociologists tend to approach education from one of three perspectives: that which stresses educational outputs in terms of wider societal demands (the approach favoured by Hopper); that which sees education as an encapsulated system and therefore most usefully approached from the perspective of organ-izational theory (the work of Turner, Conant, Lambert and others);[18] and the conventional British approach which sees education in terms of inputs. All approaches present great problems. The first masquerades as a general theory though its basic concern is more specific; but at the same time it is incapable of covering the range of problems necessary to answer the specific question because of its overemphasis on education. The second has two major defects. Although educational organizations *may* be studied as enclosed systems for the sake of research convenience, this can provide theoretical importance only if the findings of the research are related to wider societal parameters and if the comparative relevance is established. Of course this is rarely, if ever, done. Either, as with research following from Etzioni (and indeed the whole macro-organizational perspective), educational organizations are studied as case studies within the typology bringing little of wider societal factors to bear on particular situations (except as inputs and outputs) or else, as in the Goffman tradition, they are simply internal interactional situations without the benefit of a comparative or societal context of any description. This latter seems to be the main defect of the work of Royston Lambert in this country.[19] Boarding schools are more or less total institutions with lesser or greater flexibility. If they are to be made less total then they have to be made more flexible. This leaves untouched the relationship of these schools to total cultural milieu, though Lambert's proposals would have a considerable effect on that milieu.

The third (British) perspective is primarily concerned with who gets into the system.[20] It stresses class factors, income factors and other elements of stratification. The system is examined—and conclusions drawn—largely from this perspective: if input suggests an unbalanced selection, then either the selection procedure must be changed (abolish 11+) or else the institutions must be enlarged or made more 'open' (as with comprehensives). Some other questions do follow in the wake of this kind of analysis (such as extra-school socialization,[21] teaching methods[22] and the relationships between different levels of schools) but the emphasis is basically on input. In many respects this type of research has been very important for collecting data, but again one may wonder whether it has done much more than improve our knowledge of social stratification and raise uncomfortable questions about the consequences of political policy.

There is a fourth perspective, more favoured by psychologists than sociologists: the socialization of the child. As most of this is totally psychologistic, it need not concern us here. There are, however, two sociological variations which require comment. The interactional institutional study obviously poses some important questions about socialization, but it is important to stress that this is primarily an exercise in the study of a particular institution on the development of children. It is neither a comparative study of socialization (the data is much too fragmentary for that) nor is it a direct contribution to the sociology of education (the relationship of this particular institutional context to the wider process of education never being made explicit). Secondly, systemic theories which pose questions about compliance structures and multiple goals normally introduce the concept of strain to explain problems in organization. This, too, involves an indirect approach to socialization, but even less satisfactorily, for we are never given the opportunity to assess the nature of the strain except in terms of the organizations: because people break down, mobs go on the rampage, or students revolt this must be because the system is not flexible enough (or tough enough). This may well be true, but it may be equally due to the prior socialization of the people involved in the strain or their concomitant socialization. What a particular institution can do about this may be very minimal indeed, unless it can see itself as part of the total socializing process. Current changes in British secondary education may be based on false premises because they fail to realize this.[23] It is too easy to see changes in access to institutions as a solution to major cultural and social cleavages.

The problem of the sociology of education is thus centrally one of what it is that is being explained. Unfortunately what is often taken to be the sociology of education is not primarily about education at all—but about selection and stratification, socialization and organizations. All of these are obviously contributory factors in the study of education, and it is perhaps useful to indicate how two of them can make their contribution before moving on to the main concern of this paper. (The issue of socialization will be dealt with at greater length in a forthcoming book elaborating on the theme of this paper.)

1.) Stratification and Educational Selection

Let us take the selection issue first. In Hopper's essay the value-orientations are the basic categories for classification. I have suggested that this poses a major problem if it is the value-system that we are actually trying to investigate: but it also poses a problem if we are attempting to account for shifts in social stratification. Hopper argues that most industrial societies are not rapidly changing: but of course in stratification they are changing rapidly enough for the argument to be suspect. And the British and French educational systems are currently in upheaval: pattern-variable classifications provide only marginal use in dealing with these changes. If we were to employ Hopper's strategy in order to explain these changes we would doubtlessly find ourselves in the circular situation of Almond and Verba where 'cultural' differences are 'explained' by reference back to historical factors which are in themselves unexplained.[24] It becomes impossible to analyse processes of change because a time-culture dimension is absent. If the object of investigation is to specify how selection takes place, then we clearly have a number of specific parameters: stratification factors (the actual distribution of populations according to the usual indices), the rates of movement between different levels (including the appearance of new occupations and the disappearance of old ones), the rate of technological/economic development (including size of units, ratios of differential skills), methods of recruitment to jobs (including public education and professional or industrial training and internal promotion) and intervening socio-psychological variables (family size, social communities, income and security differentials of parents, and so on). If we do all this it is important to note that education becomes a secondary factor in the analysis. The basic issue is to analyse the total selection process in a society (or segment of it): educational selection may be of lesser or greater importance. It might be found, for example, that although the educational system is highly centralized and stratified, the selection of people depends also on internal recruitment and in-service training. Conversely, although education may be deliberately selective and related to manpower requirements, many of the trainees may find themselves without jobs or with jobs at variance with their qualifications because of mobility features within industry and commerce. Considerable evidence exists for this in the Soviet, Polish and Hungarian literature.[25] With this in mind, and the very extensive evidence for Britain, Scandinavia, France and the U.S.A., it is inconceivable that educational selection should be studied independently of the total selection process. The most important basis for classification would then be rates of mobility, technological-economic structures and community-ecological features, these being the items most easily derived from cross-national data and in most cases the most reliable. The object of the research should be to find explanations for variations and for this purpose certain intervening variables become important: the educational selection process, patterns of socialization, political structures and so on. Ultimately this means that we are seeking to establish (at a low level) how structures provide personnel for a given set of occupational positions; (at an intermediate level) to analyse discontinuities between selection processes, socialization patterns and systems of stratification; and (at the macro level) to locate mobility as part of a cultural complex which may vary according to the combination of structural features.[26] From the point of view of educational sociology this analysis is important for three reasons (but they are important enough): it establishes part of the wider economic and political parameters within which educational institutions have to operate; it provides a large amount of subsidiary data on the working of particular sectors of the educational system; and it allows us to isolate those attributes which individuals bring into education and distinguish them both from those they acquire during the educational experience, and those they acquire elsewhere during the educational period.

## 2.) Schools and Colleges as Complex and Simple Organizations

A further criticism of Hopper's typology was that it attributed societal goals to the educational system without adequately distinguishing between systemic and extra-systemic goals. A possible alternative would be to use Etzioni's model of complex organizations and distinguish between goals which are derived from power and structural situations extrinsic to the organization itself and those which derive directly from the organization's own norms, traditions and values. It may be one of the outcomes of this research that in collective-communistic societies the educational goals are more directly derived from extra-systemic ones, while in other societies they are not, but this is surely a subject for research, not an *a priori* assumption. In fact one of the major issues in the organizational study of education must be the power structure, and the power structure at all levels. There are two major areas for studying power in education: at the national, policy-making level (involving such organizations in Britain as the Department of Education and Science, the Treasury, the L.E.A.s, the Headmasters' Conference, the U.G.C. and so on) where the focus must be on the resolution of competing interests, and at the lower institutional level where a distilled version of policy (though not necessarily fully resolved) is implemented in schools and colleges against their own culture, order and social goals. The main considerations for this second kind of study have, of course, already been established in the U.S.A.[27] The Harvard Studies on educational decision-making are far superior to anything existing in this country where the emphasis on who gets there has inhibited discussion on how the schools are organized. As Neal Gross[28] has shown, the locus of power in American schools is very much with the parents through the local boards of education. On all existing evidence it is clear in British schools that it is very much with the teachers, but we don't really have the comparative data, in spite of Asher Tropp's pioneering study of the N.U.T.[29] In some respects we need a good old-fashioned study of pressure group politics, but we also need a study of professionalism in relation to the school political situation on lines similar to Eckstein's study of the B.M.A.[30] or an analysis of career structures which has learned something from Michel Crozier.[31] A comparative analysis of decision-making processes, and of professionalism in its organizational context, would immeasurably add to our knowledge of how any one system worked and incidentally improve the quality of sociological theory. These considerations would seem *prima facie* to have validity in all educational systems, though some would be rather more difficult to conduct research into because of political constraints. (A Soviet '*Who Runs the Schools*' is probably further in the future than a British equivalent, though one can never be sure.) But there is no reason to assume complete uniformity in an educational system merely because we are not able to carry out research there.

But the question of the power structure is only part of an organizational study. The issue of goals in education also raises the important issue of the multiplicity of societal-culture goals, even if we were to accept that these derived directly from the value-orientations of the elite. Even for *them* education is not only about occupational selection but also about moral values, research and the transmission of knowledge (of which more anon): it would be rash indeed to argue that all of these can ultimately be reduced to selection. The composite goals of the makers of education policy may be interpreted very differently by the educationalist: and even if they agree in general about what these goals are, they may still differ considerably on the priorities allocated to aspects of them. Thus although the political elites have goals which they try to impose on the educational system these policies have to be transmitted through the educational elites and the teachers and lecturers. The extent to which education is able to counter the political elite's policies will depend in part on its own economic independence, in part on patterns of socialization which are strong enough to resist the norms of the system, and in part on the persistence of centres of local political power which are able to back alternative schemes. This is not simply a question of centralist versus pluralist societies as implied by Hopper. If we examine Eastern

Europe, the centralization of goals has very different consequences for different regions and social groups, producing outputs quite distinct from the objectives of the goals. In part this is because in certain organizational contexts the balance of priorities in implementing the official goals varies because of the exigencies of those contexts. Urban schools in Poland may stress the achievement orientations of the official ideology while rural schools may stress moral and integrative values.[32] This must in part be because of the predominant socialization patterns: urban middle-class and skilled working-class parents want their children to get on (even if they dislike the political context in which they will do this) while rural parents hold back because of resistance as much to the values of the industrial society as to those of communism. In the one case the goals are complemented by the school system (the integrative aspects being either irrelevant or ignored) while in the other the dominant integrative aspects of the social system are used to correct possible deviance while not noticeably increasing the achievement-orientations. This has little to do with official priorities as Hopper suggests, but with the mediation of policies through local structures. On the other hand, as the sad history of the various Academies of Sciences in Eastern Europe suggests, official organizations may consciously be granted relative autonomy from the formal societal goals. Their failure may depend on foreign political pressures (Czechoslovakia, 1968), internal political upheaval (Poland, 1968), and their success on the distance from political centres (Novosibirsk). They are not killed off because their goals are different from societal goals but because they look like challenging them. This is as true in the U.S.A. as in the U.S.S.R.: the main difference is the devolution of power.

For any systematic classification it is therefore necessary to note the degree of compliance in relation to both political and economic policy goals and to subcultural norms and values. Within particular educational systems it is important to be able to categorize the types and variations of schools and colleges on two dimensions—according to both the compliance with policy and the degree of reliance on particular cultural sets.[33] The scale of differentiation within one educational system might be quite wide and the relative degree of goal emphasis may vary not only in relation to different catchment areas but also according to the age levels of education: primary schools may be more 'open' (in goals and in relation to culture sets) than secondary schools, which in turn are more restrictive and dominated by occupational selection of subjects than universities. The 'open' and 'closed' nature of educational institutions is thus related to the two dimensions but the explanations of variations can only be established by comparison.

This poses some problems. For comparative analysis the usual method of classification is to average out the data, so that in this case societies would range from those with centralized control mechanisms and relatively complete domination of pedagogy and research to those with multiple structures and complex control mechanisms.[34] Of course this has to be done, but one of the drawbacks is that averaging out prevents us from investigating what is precisely of greatest theoretical importance: the relationships of particular kinds of institutions to the wider social structure and to their immediate socio-cultural environment. If we produce a typology based on national profiles and on organizational types as Etzioni suggests the problem of interpretation of particular situations is reduced to ringing changes on the intervening variables. Again we have to ask what it is that we are trying to explain. The problem of a general typology which includes developmental stages is that a large number of issues have to be subjected to the same developmental process. For the study of educational institutions this is most unsatisfactory. The typology must be simple enough to be capable of elaboration according to particular situations and features of change. The use of comparison must primarily be to demonstrate both how general particular findings are, and also to check on the reliability of the particular hypothesis generated. For example, in *The Management of Innovation* Burns and Stalker use a simple typology of mechanistic and organic management systems in their attempt to provide a 'description and explanation of what happens when new and unfamiliar tasks are put upon industrial concerns organized for relatively stable conditions'.[35] The typology is expanded by providing a taxonomy of intermediate types and subsequently the adoption of one type or another is discussed in relation to the technological and change process of society and to the 'purposes and commitments of managers'. Why particular institutions accept technological change but do not alter their management system is discussed in the context of this flexible model. The essential point for our concerns here is that the organizational comparisons are made in relation to a specific set of problems: taxonomies are of little use unless they are leading up to something, and they have little purpose unless they can be related to levels of interaction.

In education the problem of organizational *change* is of fundamental importance and comparison can be valuable in indicating how different kinds of institutions respond to changes in public policy and changes in knowledge. Burns's organic and mechanistic types approximate in some measure to the open and closed dichotomies instanced above,[36] but the importance of comparison at this level is that the research method must be clear about its cultural controls. Random cross-cultural-research has little value unless the particular changes being considered have some comparability. The need for concomitant variation studies is suggested in the next section of this paper, but for organizational analysis the cultural 'inputs' must be similar (policy directives and types of knowledge changed) or else (as checks) the organizational system must be similar. This kind of analysis is crucial if anything is to be made of current changes in Britain in comprehensive schools, public schools and grammar schools as well as the universities and technical colleges. Similarly there is little point in indicating that some of these changes have taken place elsewhere unless we are clear what the other social parameters are. The 'success' of comprehensive schools in Sweden is no guarantee of their 'success' in Britain. If we have evidence on the organizational dynamics of Swedish schools and of British, then we have the necessary groundwork for comparison. This task has hardly begun. But even if it were more advanced the problem still remains of the core content of the sociology of education.

## 3.) Culture and the Management of Knowledge

The problem with organizational studies is that, although they are superior to what normally passes for the sociology of education, they tend to over-emphasize the mechanics of the institutions without necessarily contributing to a sociology of knowledge. In particular, studies based on organizational critera tend to stress the power aspects on the one hand and control-communications mechanisms on the other, without having much to say about the sources of the values and knowledge being transmitted. As one of the main exponents of the study of organizations puts it, the only way out of the organization miasma is 'by perceiving behaviour as a medium of the constant interplay and mutual re-definition of individual entities and social institutions.[37] Because the study of education is so much concerted with actually moulding the reality-images of young people, it has remained conscious of this process all along and has never been in danger of completely falling into structural arthritis. But if it is to develop, it is important to stress that the study of education as culture is not peripheral to the subject but central. Selecting people for jobs is one of education's latent functions: its *manifest* function is the management of knowledge. Any comparative study which ignores this is in danger of trivializing the entire subject.

What issues are relevant for this study? Initially they must be concerned with three conceptual distinct entities: values, norms and knowledge, each considered from their internal and external aspects. Although the three aspects have to be kept conceptually separate (because they seem to relate to different things) we cannot conclude that they are not interdependent. One of the major purposes of comparative research is to establish the conditions under which particular degrees of interdependence occur. This is not to assume—as the structural-differentiation thesis often implies—that increased differentiation in structures implies increasing differentiation between norms, values and knowledge. Again this is a matter for research.

Unfortunately there is no major sociological analysis which directs itself to the management of knowledge. Some of the most suggestive literature is found in other fields of sociology,[38] while the most impressive educational literature is often not by sociologists at all.[39] It is one of the curiosities of sociology as a discipline that although early sociologists were concerned with the control and transmission of knowledge, their successors have been primarily interested in the selection process, socialization and organization in ways that tell us little about the business of education. Some suggestive material appears on scientific issues[40] and in some few anthropological studies.[41] But most of this is not concerned with educational processes covering entire systems but with isolated segments.

The problem is best stated by example. The anthropological literature on 'transitional' societies abounds with studies of syncretic religious organizations —millennialism, messianism and so on.[42] The importance of the study is that it focuses on the breakdown of, or dramatic change in, one or all of these. Because of changed information the existing symbols do not make sense and have to be reformulated: what does this mean in terms of values and normative conduct? Alternatively new values arise to legitimize changed interaction regulations; or, dual value systems are held, the one to legitimize order, the other to explain 'facts'. And so on. Crucially most studies stress the importance of changed knowledge and changed patterns of structure on the value-systems. These studies provide us with the nearest thing to closed laboratory tests of theories in the sociology of culture.

A further instance occurs in the wider study of development. In his remarkable study, *The Labyrinth of Solitude*, the Mexican poet Octavio Paz is essentially concerned with the same problem. Mexico has acquired industry, through its revolution has modernized its social institutions, with its increased education has radically enlarged the area of Mexican knowledge. And yet, for all that, the values have not changed. 'The religious feelings of my people are very deep—like their misery and helplessness—but their fervour has done nothing but return again and again to a well that has been empty for centuries ... (I cannot) believe in the fertility of a society based on the imposition of certain modern principles.'[43] If correct, this analysis presents us with a more curious case. The social structure changes, the knowledge changes, but the values remain unchanged. This seems unlikely on the face of it, but at least it offers a challenge to the idea that there is a one-to-many relationship between values and norms as Neil Smelser seems to imply.[44] The central assumption in Smelser's thesis is that the values of a society involve a composite legitimation of *all* normative situations. He thus sees it possible to have campaigns against particular normative structures without challenging values, but that protests against values necessarily involve protests against all norms. This is clearly not true for all millennial or revolutionary movements and still less is it true for education. Education involves both the creation and transmission of values and might be reflected in a variety of normative structures which represent different values. The values of working-class education may be different from middle-class education—note the case of Risinghill Comprehensive School[45] where the Headmaster, Michael Duane, decided to run the school in order to strengthen working-class values rather than middle-class ones: hence the conflict with authority and with middle-class parents and teachers. If he was head of a secondary modern school, there would have been fewer problems. Duane had put his finger on the dilemma of comprehensive education, one which has already been faced in the U.S.A.[46] Education is important both for transmitting values and establishing or reinforcing them. Under what conditions does it act? Is it a mediator or an actor? What part does it play in the creation of social consciousness? This is the crux of the management of education.

Unlike primitive or 'transitional' societies, modern industrial ones involve very complex relationships between values, norms and knowledge. Two examples should make the point. Catholic secondary schools in England tend to be drawn from the children of manual and lower-paid white-collar workers. The normative aspects of education depend in part on the rules adopted by the schools themselves and in part derive from rules operating elsewhere in Britain. Some of these rules may derive from Catholic values (presumably those relating to worship) but most do not. The values of the school are presumably Catholic, and therefore different from those operating in the rest of the country but mediated through the school structure, which is hardly specifically Catholic. The attempt will be made, however, to legitimize the rules by reference to Catholic values. On the other hand much of the knowledge transmitted will again be independent of Catholic values: curricula, exams and even teaching syllabuses are set by central secular bodies. But even if the content is intended to be independent of Catholic values it is again mediated through a Catholic system. What does the value-system do to the knowledge? In some measure this must be related to the social backgrounds of pupils and also to the ways that Catholic teachers resolve their role-conflicts. If the school is drawn from the children of manual workers, the ascriptive communal aspects of Catholicism may be stressed in preference to the individualistic aspects inherent in the examination selection process. On the other hand if the school is predominantly middle-class, one might expect that knowledge might be stressed as a Catholic value. The basic questions for research are therefore the extent to which the Catholic values are adapted to meet particular social exigencies, the extent to which these values intrude in the transmission of knowledge, and the degree to which the normative situation in the school takes precedence over them both. In all of this, the relationship of the school both to the immediate social catchment area and to the dual pressures of Church hierarchies and state educational authorities must be seen as a set of interactive levels influencing the schools 'behaviour'. It is only within this framework that the 'commonsense knowledge of social structures' of both the teachers and the pupils can be studied usefully.[47]

If this example is over-simple (because the Catholic element introduces a simplified form of values), there are many more which illustrate the argument. A challengingly complex one is offered by Jules Henry.[48] 'Rome High School' has two orientations: fun and scholarship, but both are subsumed in the common value-system which demands integration into the adult society. Thus the stress on games and early marriage are partly responses to the competitive nature of the system: games are a form of integration into the school sub-system but also a way of contracting out of the pressing values of the social system. The crucial thing about this school's social milieu is the general upward mobility of nearly all pupils. Thus if the formal values of the wider social system demand academic achievement, the dominating subcultural ones demand integration in the face of competition (which is manifested in the 'hedonistic mindlessness' of games and sex). But for both boys and girls the overriding values are symbolized by 'scholarship': 'Rome High has emphasized scholarship so successfully, and it has come to have so much meaning in this community that is upwardly mobile that it is possible, veritably in the teeth of fun, to get high grades and not be looked upon with disdain.'[49] The interpersonal relationships of the school are not, however, based on 'scholarship' but on the normative structures of the 'slovenly morality' of gamesmanship and the sexual and group norms which dominate their day-to-day relationships. Thus if the values of the system lead students to compete to enter the adult world, the group norms (or the subculture) make them resist the world, though the conflicts, paradoxically, propel them into getting married and entering it earlier than they would otherwise do. The encouragement of 'knowledge' in this case can only be done by stressing its importance for achievement. What this implies is that the study of schools as organizations and as cultural units requires a distinction between the values attached to education both by the managers of institutions and by the pupils, the structuring of knowledge according to the hierarchical-organizational patterns and the regimentation of curriculum[50] and the relationship of these processes to wider societal demands and the ultimate life-chances of the pupils. Most studies of internal school organization in Britain, where they have been concerned with the structure of relationships at all, have ignored curriculum and the relationship between it and authority-patterns. As Bernstein has tried to show, the relationship between hierarchical school structures and failure to innovate in the curriculum and keep knowledge open may be a direct one.[51] In this sense students who campaign for academic freedom and reforms in the teaching, examination and discipline structure of universities are putting their fingers on the one vital area of knowledge-management, but it is one which immediately leads to the wider question of the institutionalization of national culture.

To be effective such an approach must operate on two levels: the development of national intellectual styles, and the transmission of these styles through educational policies. The first is an extremely difficult thing to do but essential if the societal parameters of culture and especially education are to be established. The exercise is partly historical: how do particular styles of learning come to have the importance they do? What relationship have these styles in a particular culture? How are changes in knowledge elsewhere absorbed into the national styles? Attempts to do this for Britain are scarce, though recently a few brief attempts have been made.[52] Elsewhere there is rather more material, though little of it systematic enough to produce adequate comparative theory.[53] What is important is that the intellectual styles are related to particular kinds of social structure and also to the particular choices made because of surviving historical conditions. In a recent study[54] Etzioni has made the important point that choices (and decisions about educational policy can be represented as choices) are determined by three factors: functional prerequisites of situations, historical contingencies and self-conscious choice. This is helpful, but the problem for comparative analysis must surely be to distinguish between varieties of functional prerequisites and varieties of historical factors. Management training may be considered a prerequisite of a certain level of industrial development: but how are we to distinguish between Soviet management and American management? Both countries have managers, but what is central and what is peripheral to their training? Russian managers *may* be given certain kinds of training and be expected to do certain kinds of jobs which are due to cumulative historical features of the Soviet situation but which a western management consultant may consider extraneous to the actual industrial situation. An American imported into Russia may do the same job in a very different way, but be less successful because these extraneous factors are actually vital to good Soviet management.

One of the 'historical' situations is, of course, the educational system itself. The institutionalization of knowledge not only ensures the rapid transmission of intellectual styles, it also inhibits them by making old styles rigid. The study of educational systems must be focused on the ways that the educational power structure and the institutions act as selective filters for different levels of praxis and consciousness. All knowledge is shrouded in ideology: the study of educational systems allows us to see what is ideological, to judge how new information is distorted by the combined historical-structural conditions which determine how it is absorbed or rejected by the ideology of the system. Thus the study of national cultural styles and the study of educational institutions are interrelated. For the development of educational sociology this interrelationship is a crucial and as yet unexplored territory. In Scotland two books have produced something like documentary models of what might be done,[55] though neither with the detailed organizational study that I have called for. Elsewhere, the major comparative attempts are in the study of science, though the models are closer to a natural-history description than concrete theory.[56]

With this kind of research, the qualitative nature of the institutional process attains greater significance. Schools must be studied because they are recipients of this national cultural complex and because praxis for them is at once determined by commonsense knowledge of social structures and by the formal structural contours of the sub-systems themselves. The basic problem is the way that values are transmitted through normative situations and the way that knowledge contributes to the symbolic order of the participants. Returning to organizational studies this involves in part an analysis of types of educational structure (organic-mechanistic with intervening taxonomies), a framework for the study of professionalism (notably the recruitment, training, career structure of teachers and their power-position in relation to the educational structures), and in a large part a consideration of curricula in relation to organizational patterns. But it is difficult to see this being successfully done unless there is also some consideration of the subcultural inputs as emphasized by some British and American research. Even the most flexible, open system is doing something to people against their experience of prior socialization.

On a comparative level for the study of particular institutions, the most important method that should contribute to clarification of basic patterns is the concomitant variation study, in spite of objections advanced by Narroll.[57] This is for two reasons. The actual boundaries of such a study are already set by the general educational and social contours. The problem is of subcultural variations in the context of these contours. The controls are either those of the same or similar educational structures/cultural styles, or of similar institutional/cultural complexes. Secondly with education we are not concerned as Narroll and the anthropologists are with the dilemma of culture-borrowing except in so far as this is demonstrable. (The anthropological functional fallacy[58] has no place in sociological research.) At this level it matters little whether it is indigenous:

282

the crucial thing is how it is mediated through educational structures. Galton's problem[59] is thus of secondary importance at the subcultural level, though it may be very important at the general system level for the reasons advanced above: the problem of how policies are decided and whether they may be effective or accepted/rejected possibly has a lot to do with their origins and the way they have been transmitted. The point, however, is that Galton's problem in one sense (that of being concerned with culture-borrowing in small total systems) is only of marginal importance in our second-order studies, while in our first-order studies it can be confronted directly in the study of cultural styles.

The concomitant variation studies should be conducted on three levels—within societies,[60] between societies which have common neighbourhoods (England, Wales and Scotland for example) or (in the case of former colonies) where there are evident common/historical patterns, and also (though probably with less success) with societies which have widely different cultural styles but where the institutional/subcultural styles can be controlled for. (This latter is effectively done in the study of industrial attitudes in developing countries, and also in some industrial ones.[61] Until this is done, or until existing research is completely reanalysed (and most of it is too inadequate for that) sociological hypotheses derived from individual case studies will remain at an untheoretical level. It is often assumed that sociologists have the same basic data for classification as social anthropologists: they have not. Most of the anthropological data is qualitative and most of the sociological quantitative. In the study of education as a cultural process it is the qualitative that matters.

## IV

The main point of comparative research is to lead to substantive theory. It is used in sociology because it is the nearest substitute for the scientist's laboratory. But if it is used, it is also necessary to have hunches about what is significant and purposeful. I have argued here that there are four major areas affecting sociological research on education: problems affecting the stratification-selection process; problems affecting the dynamics of organizations; the entire question of socialization; and the management of knowledge. It is clear that I accept this last as being the central concern of the sociology of education. Until it is treated as such then such topics (which concern pupils, parents and teachers alike) as the curricula, the values of education and the relationship of education to wider social processes will never be given their proper consideration. Hopper's essay has provided a valuable attempt at reviewing the problems inherent in a comparative approach. But in the last analysis comparative method and theory has little point unless it is directed at specific societal contours. Although there is some advantage in creating comparative models which investigate a number of issues cross-nationally, the ultimate advantage of comparison is that it should generate a dialectic between the particular and the general. Part of the task of

explaining processes in British society is to investigate comparable issues elsewhere. But the comparative exercise is not an end in itself. In this case the
ultimate problem remains: an explanation of British society. Because of the
wealth of research available, education is a useful area with which to begin.
But also for more intrinsically theoretical reasons: it is perhaps the only area
of research in industrial societies where all the major problems in sociological
theory and methodology are focused.

## NOTES

[1] B. Bernstein (1965). (See Introduction, this volume.)

[2] Earl J. Hopper (1968), 'A Typology for the Classification of Educational Systems',
*Sociology* (II), 29–46.

[3] *Ibid.*, p. 30.

[4] For examples, see the essays in Part Four of Blaug, M. (ed.) (1968), *The Economics
of Education*, Harmondsworth: Penguin.

[5] For the best account, Z. Katz, 'Hereditary Elements in Education, Occupations,
Social Structure', unpublished paper.

[6] There are three issues here: (i) the extent to which organizational and technical
changes require categories of workers who are not being produced through the formal
educational system; (ii) the extent to which selection into certain occupations has traditionally been structured in such a way that parts of the educational system are by-passed
(e.g. accountancy, law, as well as many forms of apprenticeship); (iii) the extent to which
particular kinds of education do not enhance entry to certain occupations because the
education is not recognized by the industrial or commercial selection processes as being
relevant.

[7] This argument is further elaborated by Hopper and E. G. Dunning (1966),
'Industrialization and the Problem of Convergence: a critical note', *Sociological Review*
(14) 163–86.

[8] For a simplified analysis see Amitai Etzioni (1961), *A Comparative Analysis of
Complex Organizations*, New York: The Free Press, pp. 71–88.

[9] For surveys see Edmund J. King (ed.) (1963), *Communist Education*, London:
Methuen; Helen B. Redl (ed.) (1964), *Soviet Educators on Soviet Education*, New York:
The Free Press.

[10] Etzioni, *op. cit.*, p. 73.

[11] For a brief outline see Daniel Lerner (1966), 'Some Comments on Centre-
Periphery Relations', in Richard L. Merritt and Stein Rokkan (eds.), *Comparing Nations*,
New Haven: Yale University Press, pp. 259–65.

[12] Preliminary attempts are contained in Josephine Klein (1963), *Samples From
English Cultures*, London: Routledge & Kegan Paul; Perry Anderson (1965), 'Origins of
the Present Crisis', in P. Anderson and Robin Blackburn (eds.), *Towards Socialism*,
London: Collins, pp. 11–52; and Basil Bernstein (1961), 'Social Class and Linguistic
Development: A Theory of Social Learning', in A. H. Halsey, Jean Floud and C. Arnold
Anderson (eds.), *Education, Economy and Society*, New York: The Free Press, pp. 288–
314. But of course most of educational literature *assumes* two levels of centre-periphery
dichotomies: the educational system is itself seen in these terms with public schools/
grammar schools/Oxbridge at the centre and the rest on the periphery, while mobility
studies assume individual progression from the periphery to the centre.

[13] Antonio Gramsci (1957), *The Modern Prince*, London: Lawrence & Wishart, p. 119.

[14] See notes 47 and 48 for some examples.

[15] The most important Levy reference in this context is (1966) *Modernization and
the Structure of Society*, New York: The Free Press, and Schurmann's classic study of
China is (1966) *Ideology and Organization in Communist China*, Berkeley: University of
California Press. Edward Shils has produced several studies on British society, although
the only one in book form is (1956) *The Torment of Secrecy*, London: Heinemann, which

provides exactly the right period flavour. Both Raymond Williams and Bantock owe something to that remarkable British literary critical tradition that reached its apogee in F.R. Leavis and *Scrutiny*. But whereas Williams has absorbed this into a Marxist critique of culture (see in particular (1961) *The Long Revolution*, London: Chatto & Windus), Bantock has retained the high academic *trahison des clercs* tone of the master: witness G. H. Bantock (1952), *Freedom and Authority in Education*, London: Faber & Faber.

[16] Hopper, *op. cit.*, note 23, p. 44.

[17] See essays 14 and 19 in Talcott Parsons (1954), *Essays in Sociological Theory*, New York: The Free Press.

[18] Ralph H. Turner (1964), *The Social Context of Ambition*, San Francisco: Chandler Press; James B. Conant (1959), *The American High School Today*, New York: McGraw-Hill; Royston Lambert, unpublished MSS on English Public and Boarding Schools.

[19] Royston Lambert (1966), 'The Public Schools: a sociological introduction' in Graham Kalton, *The Public Schools*, London: Longmans, pp. xi–xxxii.

[20] The tradition here is too lengthy to cite, but a convenient starting point is D. V. Glass (ed.) (1954), *Social Mobility in Britain*, London: Routledge & Kegan Paul. Representative summaries of sources are cited in Olive Banks (1968), *The Sociology of Education*, London: Batsford, and a sample of the earlier contributions are included in A. H. Halsey, Jean Floud and C. Arnold Anderson (1961), *Education, Economy and Society*, New York: The Free Press.

[21] Recent examples include J. W. B. Douglas (1964), *The Home and the school*, London: MacGibbon & Kee.

[22] There are several non-sociological attempts, but an American book, Vincent Rogers (1968), *The Social Studies in English Education*, London: Heinemann, is one of the more successful attempts at looking at one type of curriculum problem in the schools. Michael Young's (1966), *Innovation and Research in Education*, London: Routledge & Kegan Paul, is an excellent indication of where the reforms might take place.

[23] For an example of research suggesting this see Julienne Ford (1968), 'Comprehensive Schools as Social Dividers', *New Society*, 315, 10 October, and the correspondence in the next two issues.

[24] Gabriel Almond and Sydney Verba (1963), *The Civic Culture*, Princeton: Princeton University Press.

[25] See Katz, *op. cit.*, and (1967), *Social Stratification in Hungary*, Budapest: Hungarian Central Statistical Office, especially section V, 'Social Mobility and the Open and Closed Character of the Strata', pp. 111–28.

[26] Some of the most coherent explorations of such a framework are found in Neil J. Smelser and Seymour Martin Lipset (1966), *Social Structure and Mobility in Economic Development*, London: Routledge & Kegan Paul. See especially, essays by Wilensky, Duncan, Romsøy and Germani.

[27] Representative samples include Neal Gross and others (1958), *Explorations in Role Analysis*, New York: Wiley; Neal Gross and R. E. Herriott (1965), *Staff Leadership in Public Schools*, New York: Wiley; Lavern L. Cunningham and Roderick F. McPhee (1963), *The Organization and Control of American Schools*, Ohio: Charles E. Merrill Books; and Neal Gross (1958), *Who Runs Our Schools?*, New York: Wiley. A summary of some of the literature is included in Cole S. Brembeck (1966), *Social Foundations of Education*, New York: Wiley, Chapters 17 and 18.

[28] Neal Gross, *Who Runs Our Schools?*, *op. cit.*

[29] Asher Tropp (1957), *The School Teachers*, London: Heinemann.

[30] Harry H. Eckstein (1963), *Pressure Group Politics: A Study of the B.M.A.*, London: MacGibbon & Kee.

[31] Michel Crozier (1965), *The Bureaucratic Phenomenon*, London: Tavistock.

[32] Maria Paschalaska (1962), *Education in Poland*, Warsaw: Polonia Publishing House; S. M. Rosen (1964), *Higher Education in Poland*, Washington: U.S. Department of Health, Education and Welfare; and private communication from Z. Baumann.

[33] 'Cultural set' is used in the sense that Bernstein talks about the 'mode of established relationships' in his theory of social learning. Bernstein, *op. cit.*, pp. 295–6.

[34] The literature based on this form of comparison is becoming extremely influential, though most of it refers to political comparisons. For examples and debates on the various forms of comparison see Richard L. Merritt and Stein Rokkan, *op. cit.*, Stein Rokkan (ed.) (1967), *Comparative Research across Cultures and Nations*, Paris: Mouton; and for an

attempt at 'averaging out' see Bruce M. Russell and others (1964), *World Handbook of Social and Political Indicators*, New Haven: Yale University Press.

[35] Tom Burns and G. M. Stalker (1966), *The Management of Innovation*, London: Tavistock Publications, edition vii. The typology is, of course, derived from Durkheim's mechanistic and organic solidarities, developed in *The Division of Labour in Society* (1947), New York: The Free Press.

[36] See essay by Basil Bernstein (1967), 'Open Schools, Open Society?', *New Society*, 259, 14 September, pp. 351–3. This very important statement which argues on lines similar to that developed here poses a number of specific problems of theory which comparative research should be directed towards clearing up. In particular these relate to the congruence between wider societal 'openness' and educational openness. Bernstein's basic concern is with the curriculum—which any study of the management of knowledge would have to examine centrally. What he is not clear about is whether structural openness necessarily leads to curriculum flexibility: the Swedish example would suggest not, and this may have to do with a continuing professionalism carrying through from earlier days. An 'open' entrance system may still be compatible with an educational order controlled by the teachers (contrasted with the U.S.A., where 'citizens' have more control). There are thus a number of variations on the open–closed theme which could only be demonstrated by a comparative analysis. But what Bernstein does do is to place educational sociology firmly as a study of culture. As he rightly stresses, Durkheim is still the most important starting point for this, and *Moral Education* (1961), New York: The Free Press, the most neglected classic. The clearest concise statement of Durkheim's general theories (with a persuasive critique) has been recently published by Percy S. Cohen (1968), *Modern Social Theory*, London: Heinemann, especially pp. 224–34.

[37] Burns and Stalker, *op. cit.*, p. xvi.

[38] For example: the literature on innovations of which Burns and Stalker (*op. cit.*); G. M. Rodgers (1962), *The Diffusion of Innovations*, New York: The Free Press, are fair examples; the literature on economic institutions, e.g. P. M. Blau (1964), *Exchange and Power in Social Life*, New York: Wiley; Georges Freidman (1955), *Industrial Society*, New York: The Free Press; Alvin W. Gouldner (1954), *Patterns of Industrial Bureaucracy*, New York: The Free Press; and the vast amount of anthropological literature, e.g. Claude Lévi-Strauss (1965), *The Savage Mind*, London: Weidenfeld & Nicolson; Mary Douglas (1966), *Purity and Danger*, London: Routledge; John Middleton (ed.) (1967), *Myth and Cosmos*, Garden City, N.Y.: Natural History Press, and Clifford Geertz (1961) 'Ideology as a Cultural System', in David Apter (ed.) (1961), *Ideology and Discontent*, New York: The Free Press.

[39] There are two distinct traditions: that stemming from the literary critical tradition noted in note 15, and the philosophical *belles lettres* tradition of which Jacques Barzun (1959), *The House of Intellect*, London: Secker & Warburg; C. P. Snow (1964), *The Two Cultures and the Scientific Revolution*, Cambridge: Cambridge University Press, are among the best known. Richard Hoggart's (1959), *The Uses of Literacy*, London: Chatto & Windus, has not generated the research on the management of knowledge that it might have. It has merely provided an occasion for further studies of selection and some on public responses to the mass media. There is also the seminal literary-anthropological effort on communications: Jack Goody and Ian Watt, 'The Consequences of Literacy', in J. Goody (ed.) (1969), *Literacy in Traditional Societies*, Cambridge: Cambridge University Press.

[40] For example: A. de Grazia (1965), *The Velikovsky Affair*, London: Chapman & Hall; F. A. von Háyek (1964), *The Counter-Revolution of Science*, New York: The Free Press; H. Kaplan (ed.) (1966), *Science and Society*, Chicago: Rand McNally. Oddly enough however, there is no sociological literature on the teaching of science.

[41] See especially, Jules Henry (1966), *Culture Against Man*, London: Tavistock; and Theodore Brameld (1959), *The Remaking of a Culture: Life and Education in Puerto Rico*, New York: Wiley; George T. Spindler (ed.) (1963), *Education and Culture: Anthropological Approaches*, New York: Holt, Rinehart & Winston.

[42] For representative introductions and summaries see Y. Talmon (1963), 'The Pursuit of the Millennium', *European Journal of Sociology;* Peter Worsley (1968), introduction to *The Trumpet Shall Sound*, London: MacGibbon & Kee; Anthony F. Wallace (1961), 'Revitalization Movements' in S. M. Lipset and Neil J. Smelser, *Sociology—The Progress of a Decade*, Englewood Cliffs (N.J.): Prentice-Hall, pp. 206-19.

[43] Octavio Paz (1967), *The Labyrinth of Solitude*, London: Allen Lane, p. 16.

[44] See Neil J. Smelser (1962), *The Theory of Collective Behaviour*, London: Routledge & Kegan Paul, Chaps. 5 and 10. For suggestions for a counter formulation see Alasdair MacIntyre (1967), *Secularization and Moral Change*, London: Oxford University Press. But my formulation of the problem owes much to an unpublished critique of Smelser by Herminio Martins, Essex University.

[45] For an impressionistic account see: Leila Berg (1968), *Risinghill: Death of a Comprehensive School*, Harmondsworth: Penguin.

[46] See: G. T. Keach, R. Fulton and W. E. Gardner (1967), *Education and Social Crises: Perspectives on Teaching Disadvantaged Youth*, New York: Wiley. But for Britain see also R. S. Peters (ed.) (1969), *Perspectives on Plowden*, London: Routledge & Kegan Paul.

[47] The reference is, of course, to the work of Alfred Schutz, in particular, Volume I of the *Collected Papers* (1967), *The Problem of Social Reality*, The Hague: Martinus Nijhoff. But see also Harold Garfinkel (1967), *Studies in Ethnomethodology*, Englewood Cliffs (N.J.): Prentice-Hall, and Peter L. Berger and Thomas Luckman (1967), *The Social Construction of Reality*, London: Allen Lane. The most convincing sociological research based on this approach is probably Alfred Willener (1967), *Interpretation de L'Organization dans l'Industrie*, Paris: Mouton.

[48] *Op. cit.*, note 40, pp. 182–282.

[49] *Ibid.*, p. 282.

[50] For French examples see Jean-Claude Passeron and M. de Saint Martin (1965), *Rapport Pédagogique et Communication*, Paris: Mouton; Pierre Bourdieu, 'Système d'Enseignement et Système de Pensée'. [See Chap. 7, this volume.] Proceedings of 6th World Congress of Sociology; Pierre Bourdieu and Jean-Claude Passeron (1968), 'L'Examen d'une Illusion', *Revue Française Sociologique*, IX, Special Number, pp. 227–53.

[51] Private communication. But see also Basil Bernstein, 'Open Schools, Open Society?' *op. cit.*, for an early formulation.

[52] Perry Anderson (1968), 'Components of the National Culture', *New Left Review*, 50, July–August, 3–57; earlier, Alasdair MacIntyre (1960), 'Breaking the Chains of Reason' in E. P. Thompson, (ed.), *Out of Apathy*, London: Stevens & Son, pp. 195–240. The first essay is challenging about constituent parts of British national intellectual styles, but does not really answer the following questions: (a) why these particular styles? (b) what relation do they have to the institutions? (c) how profound and deep-rooted are alternative (sub-elite) styles? (d) how does one compare with other national cultural styles? It does, however, make some interesting suggestions about the conditions under which culture is transmitted and how a dying culture is kept alive by transfusion. MacIntyre's essay, though very suggestive about the relationship between intellectual styles and social action, is not really specific enough about the British situation.

[53] Of a wide spectrum two samples are offered: the work of Richard Hofstadter in the U.S.A. and Michael Crozier's (1964), 'The Cultural Revolution: Notes on the Changes in the Intellectual Climate of France', *Daedalus*, 3, i, Winter, pp. 514–42.

[54] Amitai Etzioni (1968), *The Active Society*, New York: The Free Press, especially Part One.

[55] G. S. Osborne (1968), *Change in Scottish Education*, London: Longmans, provides a general account of the current situation, while George Elder Davie (1961), *The Democratic Intellect*, Edinburgh: Edinburgh University Press, is perhaps the finest example of intellectual history that exists in these islands.

[56] This is particularly true of Thomas S. Kuhn (1962), *The Structure of Scientific Revolutions*, Chicago: University of Chicago Press, which, although it offers a stimulating general perspective, says little about *national* developments.

[57] Raoul Narroll (1968), 'Some Thoughts on Comparative Methods in Anthropology', in H. M. and A. B. Blalock, *Methodology in Social Research*, New York: McGraw-Hill, pp. 236–77.

[58] Brought up to date and discussed with some brilliance in Walter Goldschmidt (1966), *Comparative Functionalism*, Berkeley and Los Angeles: University of California Press, but for sociologists a fallacy for all that. Anthropologists (particularly American ones) are basically concerned with function as explaining origins: sociologists with explaining interrelationships.

[59] Narroll, *op. cit.*

[60] See Narroll, *op. cit.*, and Merritt and Rokkan, op. cit., Part III.

[61] For summaries of this kind of research see Arnold S. Feldman and Wilbert E. Moore (1960), *Labor Commitment and Social Change*, New York: Social Science Research Council; Alain Touraine (ed.) (1965), *Workers' Attitudes to Technical Change*, Paris: Organization for Economic Cooperation and Development; and A. C. Ross (ed.) (1966), *Industrial Relations and Economic Development*, London: Macmillan.

# *NOTES ON CONTRIBUTORS*

BASIL BERNSTEIN is Professor of Sociology of Education in the University of London and head of the sociological research unit, University of London Institute of Education. He has published widely in the fields of socio-linguistics and sociology of education, and his collected papers are being published by Routledge & Kegan Paul (1971 in press).

ALAN F. BLUM is on the faculty of the department of sociology at New York University. He has published papers on sociological theory and the sociology of mental illness and is currently preparing a monograph on 'The Process of Socialization'.

PIERRE BOURDIEU is Director of Studies at the École Pratique des Hautes Études in Paris, and Deputy Director of its Centre de Sociologie Européenne, where he is at present responsible for a research project on education and culture. He has published widely in the sociology of culture, art and education and related fields.

IOAN DAVIES is on the faculty of the department of sociology of Queens University, Kingston, Ontario. He has published books and papers on the sociology of education and political sociology and is currently preparing a book on 'The Social Reality of Politics'.

GEOFFREY M. ESLAND teaches sociology in the Faculty of Educational Studies, the Open University, Milton Keynes, England. He is currently working on innovations in educational knowledge.

ROBIN HORTON is Director of the Institute of African Studies at the University of Ife, Nigeria. He has done field-work in West Africa and has published widely on African belief-systems.

NELL KEDDIE teaches sociology at Goldsmiths College, University of London. Her current research interests are on the organization of educational knowledge in schools.

MICHAEL F. D. YOUNG teaches sociology in the department of Sociology of Education, University of London Institute of Education. His current research interests are the control of educational knowledge, and the sociology of science education.